DUNS SCOTUS

Oxford University Press

London   Edinburgh   Glasgow   Copenhagen
New York   Toronto   Melbourne   Capetown
Bombay   Calcutta   Madras   Shanghai
Humphrey Milford Publisher to the UNIVERSITY

DUNS SCOTUS

BY

C. R. S. HARRIS

M.A., D.Phil. (Oxon.), Ph.D. (Princeton), Fellow of All Souls
College, Oxford ; Jane Eliza Procter Visiting Fellow
Princeton University, U.S.A., 1922–3

VOL. I
THE PLACE OF DUNS SCOTUS IN
MEDIEVAL THOUGHT

OXFORD
AT THE CLARENDON PRESS M CM XXVII

TO
FATHER JOSEPH RICKABY S. J.
WHOSE GENEROUS INSTRUCTION AND KINDLY
WISDOM FIRST INSPIRED ME WITH
AN INTEREST IN THESE
MATTERS

PREFACE

THERE is perhaps no celebrated philosopher whose fame has suffered more vicissitudes than that of Duns Scotus. The founder of one of the two great schools of scholasticism, he became during his lifetime an international celebrity and for nearly two centuries after his death was revered as the Subtle Doctor, only to be ' sette in Bocardo ' at the Reformation and finally to lend his name to the ignominious appellation of fools. For, as the Oxford Dictionary informs us, the word Duns is derived from none other than the Scottish doctor, and it was held in the seventeenth century to be actionable—at least when applied to a barrister—and one unfortunate defendant, notwithstanding the plea that Duns Scotus was ' a great learned man ', lost his case and was compelled to pay damages to the tune of 100 marks.[1] But the whirligig of time brings strange revenges; the eponymous Dunce was declared venerable by a decree of the Bishop of Nola, and the existence of a ' cult ' verified in 1710 in accordance with the decree of Pope Urban VIII. This process was confirmed in 1906. Bertoni's book, *Le Bienheureux Jean Duns Scot*, mentions the attestation of diverse miracles wrought by the ' subtle and Marian doctor ', one of which was said to have taken place in Glasgow in the year of grace 1906.

---

[1] Cf. B. Odgers on *Libel and Slander* (5th ed., 1911), p. 60, the case of *Peard* v. *Jones* (1635), Cro. Car. 382. I am indebted for this reference to the late Sir Henry Erle Richards, sometime Chichele Professor of International Law at Oxford and Fellow of All Souls College.

Ever since the coming of Protestantism and the gradual development of the more modern ways of scientific thinking, the scholastics have been somewhat undeservedly neglected in non-Catholic countries, and it is only recently that the interest taken by Englishmen in this important period of the history of Philosophy has shown signs of revival. The works of St. Thomas Aquinas have already been made known to English readers both by means of translations and interpretative literature, but on Duns Scotus no book has, so far as I am aware, been written in 'the vulgar tongue', nor has any translation of his writings been published. It is in order to fill in some measure this lamentable hiatus in our national scholarship that I venture to offer to the public these two volumes, the compilation of which was undertaken to satisfy a statutory obligation to produce a piece of research work entailed by the tenure of a Fellowship at All Souls College.

To be caught stealing were a lugubrious and disgraceful thing, and it is fortunate for a young scholar that the laws of property in the Republic of Letters are based on communistic principles, so that an acknowledgement constitutes a title to use and the plea of guilty is a defence. Lest, therefore, I should seem to presume to lay claim to much of the information contained in this work, I must confess instantly that I have not scrupled to incorporate on a large scale the results of the researches of others ; on so large a scale, indeed, that detailed acknowledgement in the text and footnotes could not but be tedious. To Karl Werner's work on Duns Scotus and his numerous studies in the

Sitzungsberichte of the Viennese Academy I am
indebted for the foundations of this work, and I have
embodied many of his conclusions. Chapter six of the
first volume has been practically taken wholesale from
his book. I am also under a deep debt of gratitude
to the numerous studies of the learned Dr. P. Minges,
with whose views I have found myself mostly in complete agreement and whose works I have used and
incorporated freely. For more general works on
scholasticism I am indebted *imprimis* to Prantl's great
History of Logic, M̤ Grabmann's *Geschichte der
scholastischen Methode*, ᴐ fessor E. Gilson's admirable
Études de Philosophie ᴎ liévale, and Dr. Baumgartner's edition of Ueber g's *Geschichte der Philosophie*. The researches of th̤ wo first-named scholars
I have ventured to embody in ndensed form in the
second chapter of my first volum̤ For the chapter on
the Oxford School I am indebted ꞌefly to the studies
on Roger Bacon of Höver and Pöhl, d also to the late
Dean Rashdall's *History of the Univers̤ es in the Middle
Ages* ; and for my account of St. Anseln̤ theory of the
will to Lohmeyer's essay.

After this necessarily inadequate list ꞌ literary
indebtedness I should like to acknowledg̤ pecially
obligations of a more personal nature to my achers
both at Oxford and at Princeton. To the atter
university this work owes a great debt. The ꞌne
Eliza Procter Foundation enabled me to devote a ꞌar
wholly to research, and the kindness of Dean West, of
the Graduate School, and of Dr. Richardson, the
Director of the Library, in placing at my disposal most
valuable facilities for work, did much to ease the task

of writing. To Dr. Richardson I am especially indebted for the invaluable assistance he gave me, at the cost of much time and trouble, in obtaining materials and preparing the bibliographical side of the work. I would like also to acknowledge the kindness of Professor A. A. Bowman, formerly of Princeton and now of Glasgow, Mr. P. E. More of Princeton, and Professor C. C. J. Webb of Oxford, who read through the manuscript and made many valuable suggestions and corrections.

I also wish to thank the authorities of the three Oxford Colleges, membership of whose foundation I have been privileged to enjoy, for their generous help in subscribing to the publication of these volumes, namely the Charles Oldham Trustees of Corpus Christi College, the President and Fellows of Magdalen College, and the Warden and Fellows of All Souls College, but for whose munificence this work would never have seen the light.

Chapters one, three, five, and eight of the first volume were submitted as a thesis for the degree of Ph.D. at Princeton University, and the second volume as a thesis for the Doctorate of Philosophy at Oxford. To the end of the latter are appended two texts of genuine but hitherto unpublished writings of Duns Scotus, consisting of a fragment, to which my attention was drawn by Fr. Pelster, S. J., of the unfinished treatise *De Cognitione Dei* (Merton Coll. MS. 90), which is not found in Wadding's edition, and several *Collationes* (Ball. Coll. MS. 209) not hitherto printed. I have to thank the Librarians of Merton and Balliol Colleges for their kindness in allowing me to use these manuscripts, and also Miss Parker for revising the transcript of the former MS.

Finally I wish to thank my uncle and former Tutor, Dr. F. C. S. Schiller, of Corpus Christi College, who originally inspired me with the idea of undertaking this work, for his kindness in assuming the laborious task of correcting the proofs, and also for much helpful criticism.

C. R. S. H.

Oxford.

CONTENTS OF VOLUME I

CONTENTS OF VOLUME II

I

THE LIFE AND WORKS OF

DUNS SCOTUS

THE life of a philosopher is always of interest because of the light it throws on the formation of his character and the development of his thought. For no thinker, however abstract and remote from common feeling, can quite dehumanize his speculations; they must inevitably be influenced in some measure by his likes and dislikes, aspirations, endeavours, and all the manifold experiences which contribute to the building of his character; they are, in fact, the expression of his personality. Personal history is therefore not quite irrelevant to the understanding of a great thinker, and although we cannot, like the palaeontologist, reconstruct Hercules from his great toe, it is no spirit of idle curiosity which impels us to examine the biographical details of our author's history. But unfortunately it must be confessed that of Duns Scotus we know next to nothing: the very date and place of his birth are uncertain. Andreas Thevet, in his *Histoires des plus illustres et savants hommes* (Paris, 1584), tells us that he was forty-three years of age when he died. Accepting the generally received tradition that his death took place in 1308, this would give 1265 as the year of his birth, but the authorities are conflicting. Von Döllinger, in *Wetzer u. Welte's Kirchenlexicon* (ed. 1, vol. ix; ed. 2, vol. x), suggested three possible dates—1265, 1274, and 1245. The last, which he favoured in the first edition, is the date of the death of Alexander of Hales, and is therefore open to some suspicion. It is almost certainly too early; there is no good evidence for it, and it would make him sixty

years of age when, according to the letter of the
Minister-General Gonsalvi, he was presented for his
degree at Paris, a fact which the contents of the letter
render highly improbable.[1] The date 1274, on the
other hand, is too late. It would make him only
thirty-three years old at the time of his death, which
took place, according to the most reliable authorities,
in 1308.[2] If we identify him with the Johannes
Douns mentioned in a list of Friars Minor presented
to the Bishop of Lincoln in 1300 for licence to hear
confessions,[3] we must place the date of his birth not
later than 1270, for according to the rule of the order,
no friar was permitted to exercise this function before
the completion of his thirtieth year.[4] In view of these
facts it is safest to conclude, as Döllinger does in his
later article, that he was born in 1265.

Of his parentage or childhood there is not even the
most meagre record ; we do not even know when or
where he joined the Franciscan order. The lives
which have been written about him are almost
entirely apocryphal, and his biographers have used
him mainly as a peg whereon to hang tales of edifying
piety. Never perhaps was there a writer in his time
so illustrious, of whom we know so little, so elusive is
he, so remotely impersonal. Hardly a trace of human
emotion is perceptible in the thousands of his pages :
scarcely a glimpse of humour peeps through the
myriads of his syllogisms—surely a weighty evidence
against those who would make an Irishman of him.
Nor do his writings, where they reveal any personal
character whatever, show him altogether in an attrac-

---

[1] See below, p. 9.

[2] But cf. Bzovius, *Annales Ecclesiastici*, sub anno 1294 : ' Hoc
anno volens nolens ex humanis abiit Joannes Dunsius, natione Scotus,
ex minorum familia.' But Bzovius is scarcely an authority to be
trusted in such matters.   [3] See below, p. 7.

[4] Cf. Ehrle, *Archiv f. Literatur u. Kirchengeschichte*, Bd. VI,
pp. 128–9.

tive light. His criticisms of other writers are petti-
fogging, and often sophistical. Not for nothing did he
earn the glorious title of the ' subtil doctor ' ; [1] which
perhaps commends itself less to modern minds than to
those of the fourteenth-century schoolmen. He appears also to have been somewhat narrow-minded, for
he indulges in undignified abuse of infidels, Jews, and
heretics,[2] in a way quite foreign to the Angelic doctor.
And though there are some fine devotional passages in
the *De primo principio*, his writings lack the warmth of
the burning mysticism of Bonaventura. He exhibits
too something of the unconscious barbarity of the
fanatic ; thus he would have princes baptize forcibly
the children of their infidel and Jewish subjects,[3] a
procedure which Aquinas considers unjustifiable.[4] On
the other hand he shows himself singularly humane
when he denounces the death penalty for stealing.[5]
For the rest, we can see in him an earnest and devoted
theologian, and above all an industrious friar. The
shadow of time has blurred and all but obliterated the
features of the portrait.

The nationality of Duns has long been a matter for
dispute. The generally accepted view has followed
the tradition of the Irish Franciscans, which would
derive his name from Down ; but the latest evidence
seems to show that this theory is without foundation.[6]

[1] Cf. G. De Ruggiero, *Storia della Filosofia del Cristianesimo*,
vol. iii, p. 187 : ' Noi moderni saremmo tentati a interpretare in senso
peggiorativo quel nome, perchè in nessun altro scrittore medievale
come in Duns troviamo una così accentuata degeneratione sofistica
dei metodi della scuola, e un così minuto spiegamento di virtuosità
formalistica.'

[2] Cf. *Op. Ox.*, prol. q. 7 : ' Quid Saraceni, vilissimi porci, Mahometi
discipuli, . . . quid asini Manichaei fabulantur . . . ? ' etc.

[3] *Op. Ox.*, Lib. IV, q. 9. But cf. Longpré, *La philosophie du B.
Duns Scot*, p. 133.

[4] Cf. *Summa Theologica*, 2a, 2ae, q. 10, artt. 8 et 12 ; q. xi, art. 3.

[5] *Rep. Par.* Lib. IV, hist. xv, q. 4 n. 45.

[6] Fitzmaurice and Little, *Materials for the History of the Franciscan*

The controversy turns on the meaning of the words
' Scotus ' and ' Scotia ' at the end of the thirteenth
century. The balance of probability is clearly in
favour of the opinion that at this time Scotia was used
to denote North Britain and not Ireland. Bartholomew the Englishman in his treatise ' De proprietatibus
rerum ' (*circa* 1250) clearly distinguishes between
Hibernia (Ireland) and Scotia (Scotland), while the
Collegium Scoticum, founded in Paris in the year
1299, was founded by a Scotsman, David Moray,
Bishop of Moray. Moreover, when Scotland was made
into a Province, it was called ' Provincia Scotiae ' ;
and the ' Vicaria Scotiae ' which existed from 1329
to 1359 comprised the Franciscan houses of Berwick-
upon-Tweed, Haddington, Roxborough, Dumfries,
Lanark, and Dundee.[1] Between 1239 and 1329 the
Scottish houses were included in the English province.

There remain then two other possibilities for Duns'
nationality ; he may either have been an Englishman
or a Scotsman. The evidence for either of these
hypotheses is very scanty. Thomas de Eccleston [2]
decides that Scotus was probably a Scotsman, and
that he came from Dunse in Berwickshire, and, as
was customary, took the name Duns from his birthplace on entering the Franciscan order.[3] This seems

Province of Ireland, A.D. 1230–1450 (British Society for Franciscan
Studies, vol. ix, pp. 87 sqq.). See also *Arch. Franc. Hist.*, vol. x,
pp. 3–16 ; vol. xiii, pp. 78–88.

[1] Bonaventura, however, speaks of a ' provincia Hiberniae sive
Scotiae ' ; while in an appeal of the Irish people to Pope John XXII,
allusion is made to the fact that Hibernia was formerly known as
Major Scotia. See Fordoun's *Scotichronicon* (ed. Hearne), p. 926.

[2] 'De adventu minorum ', etc. *Monumenta Franciscana*, Rolls
Series, i. 32.

[3] Duns' earliest disciples, Franciscus de Mayron and Johannes de
Bassolis, say that he was born in Scotland. Cf. Mayron, *In IV Sentt.*
I, dist. xxvii, q. i ; Bassolis, *In IV Sentt.*, prol. q. i ; II, dist. vi, q. i.
See Bertoni, *Le B. Jean Duns Scot, sa vie, sa doctrine, ses disciples*
(Levanto, 1917), p. 5. Cf. A. Callebaut, ' La patrie du B. Jean
Duns Scot ', in *Archiv. Franc. Hist.* x (1917), and L'Écosse, ' Patrie

on the face of it to be the most likely theory, but there is also a strong tradition which would claim him as an Englishman. The testimony of a certain Johannes Major, who lived about the year 1400, seems to suggest that he was a Northumbrian. Johannes says that he himself was born at Warke in Northumberland, and that the ' subtil Doctor ' was a fellow countryman of his, having been a native of Emilden or Embleton, a hamlet about twelve miles to the north.[1] Leland also mentions a manuscript in Merton College library, which expressly states that Duns was born at Dunstance, a certain villa of Emyldon, and that he was a fellow of Merton College.[2] But the last statement is almost certainly false,[3] and as Renan points out, the manuscript is a very late one, dating from the second

du B. Jean Duns Scot ', ibid. xiii (1920). But Cardinal Ehrle refuses to draw any conclusions as to the birthplace of our author from the name Duns, though he concedes that he was a Scotsman, on the ground that the form Johannes de Duns appears only very rarely in older manuscripts, the usual form being Johannes Duns, Dons, or Douns, whereas in cases where a name has been taken from a locality, the form ' de ' is the most common. Cf. Fr. Pelster, S. J., ' Handschriftliches zu Skotus mit neuen Angaben über sein Leben ', in *Franziskanische Studien*, 1923, pp. 1 f.

[1] Cf. *Certamen Seraphicum provinciae Angliae pro sancta Dei ecclesia . . . opere et labore R. P. F. Angeli a S. Francisco* (Quaracchi, 1885), p. 253 : ' Hic (Johannes Major) vixit circa an. 1400, asseritque se natum apud Warke, doctorem autem subtilem conterraneum suum—sic enim ipsum vocat—duodecim millaria ultra septentrionem versus, hoc est in Emilden.'

[2] *Comm. de Scriptt. Brit.* I, cccxv. The manuscript in question ends as follows : ' Explicit lectura doctoris subtilis in universitate Oxoniensi super libros Sententiarum, sc. doctoris Joannis Duns, nati in quadam villa de Emylden vocata Dunstance (contracte Duns) in comitatu Northumbriae, pertinente ad dominium scholasticorum de Merton halle in Oxonia, et quondam dictae domus socii.' This MS. is one written by John Reynbold between 1451 and 1455 and is Merton Coll. no. 59. In another MS. by the same hand we get almost the identical words, where his birthplace is given as Dunstañ, which is called ' quaedam villicula parochiae de Emylden '.

[3] See below, p. 9.

half of the fifteenth century.[1]   Antony Wood, in his
Historia et Antiquitates Universitatis Oxoniensis, follow-
ing no doubt the same authority, makes Scotus,
Walter Burleigh, and William of Ockham all fellows
of Merton College, and asserts that Duns joined the
Franciscan Order after leaving the college.[2]

The name ' Scotus ' appears quite early.   Thomas
Jorn, O.P. (*d.* 1310), Provincial Prior of the English
Dominicans from 1297 to 1304, speaks of Duns as
' Magister Johannes Scotus '.   In a letter of the
Minister-General of the Franciscan Order, Gonsalvi,
of the year 1304, he is called ' Frater Johannes Scotus ' ;
while a manuscript belonging to the abbey of Saint
Victor in Paris, written in 1311, ends with the words
' Explicit quodlibet magistri Johannis Scoti, O.F.M. ',
and Ubertinus de Casale, writing about the same time,
cites him as ' Frater Johannes Scotus '.   Antonius
Andreas, O.F.M., of Aragon (*floruit circa an.* 1320), in
his commentary on the *Metaphysics* of Aristotle
claims to have followed ' doctrinam . . . Magistri
Johannis Duns qui fuit natione Scotus, religione
Minor '.   A fourteenth-century manuscript at Cesena
contains some verses on his death, which begin with
the line, ' Scotia plange quia periit tua gloria rara '.
Another manuscript of the same period at Todi in
Umbria reads, ' Explicit summa Joannis Duns, provinciae Anglicae super primum librum sententiarum
secundum lecturam Parisiensem '.   Bartholomew of
Pisa in his *Liber Conformitatum* writes as follows :
' De hac siquidem provincia (sc. Angliae) fuit magister
Johannis Duns Scotus Doctor subtilis : cujus memoria
quoad sufficientiam erat perpetua : qui multa opera
fecit.' [3]   There is, however, one piece of evidence

[1] *Histoire littéraire de la France*, tom. xxv, p. 424.
[2] *Historia et Antiquitates Universitatis Oxoniensis*, ii, p. 87 :
' Relicto collegio habitum Sancti Francisci Oxoniae assumpsit.'
[3] *Liber aureus inscriptus Liber conformitatum vitae beati ac seraphici
Patris Francisci*, Lib. I, Fructus xi, 2 a, f. 161 v.

which would tend to support the view that he was an Irishman. The catalogue of the library at Assisi drawn up by Frate Giovanni de Collo Soldani in 1381, contains the following entry : ' § XCV.—Opus super quatuor libros Sententiarum magistri fratris Johannis Scoti qui et doctor subtilis nuncupatur de provincia Yberniae ordinis minorum cum postibus et cathena, cujus principium est : Quaeritur utrum homini pro statu isto. Finis vero : Utrum beatitudo corporum erit equalis ?—ut est ibi in fine tabula titulorum. In quo libro omnes quaterni sunt xxv f.' This manuscript is still in existence at Assisi, and is no. 137 in the communal library ; the explicit concludes thus : ' Expliciunt questiones super librum quartum sententiarum edite a fratre Johanne Dunz.' The codex itself contains no reference to Ireland, and the words ' de provincia Yberniae ' rest solely on the authority of the compiler of the catalogue, who is, to say the least of it, not always meticulously accurate.[1]

The earliest mention of Duns Scotus is in a letter written in the year 1300 by the Provincial of the friars minor, Hugh of Hartlepool, which contains a list of twenty-two Oxford Franciscans, for whom he claims from the Bishop of Lincoln a licence to hear confessions.[2] Here he appears simply as Johannes Douns. The bishop granted a licence to eight of the candidates, but John Douns does not seem to have been one of them. Duns is said to have been a pupil of William of Ware (Gulielmus Varro), a Franciscan who taught at Oxford and went to Paris in 1304,[3] an author

[1] For instance, he describes Peter of Tarantaise (Petrus Hispanus), afterwards Pope Innocent V, quite wrongly as ' provinciae Burgundiae ordinis minorum '.

[2] See Twine MS., fol. 23, from the register of d'Alderby, Bishop of Lincoln ; printed in Wood, *Hist. et Antiquit. Univ. Oxon.* (Latin ed., p. 734), and in Clark, *Wood's Survey of the Antiquities of the City of Oxford*, ii, p. 386.

[3] Bartholomew of Pisa, *Liber Conformitatum*, f. 61 v : ' Locum Vuare

whom he cites twice.[1] There is also a tradition that
Scotus succeeded him in the chair of divinity at
Oxford ; but this appears to be unlikely. Duns'
name does not occur in the list of readers in theology
given in the *Monumenta Franciscana*. Of the details
of Scotus' life at Oxford we know next to nothing.
Shortly after 1300 he lectured as Bachelor of Divinity
on the Sentences of Peter Lombard,[2] and to this period
we may presumably assign the longer commentary,
which is more familiarly known as the *Opus Oxoniense*.
How far back this work can be dated is quite uncertain.
The manuscripts in Merton College library (nos. 60,
61, and 62) date back only as far as the middle of the
fifteenth century. The tradition which states that
he was a fellow of Merton College rests on the statement of Johannes Major and the manuscripts of
Reynbold just quoted in the notes to p. 5, and seems
highly improbable ; it might almost be denied
a priori on the grounds that Duns being a minorite
could not be a scholar of the college.[3] It is no doubt
this fact which makes Wood state that he took the
Franciscan habit after leaving the college. If the
statement by Johannes Major, however, that he came
from Embleton is true, it would easily account for
his association with Merton College, which owned
estates in that district and still presents to the living
of Embleton, which was at one time held by Bishop
Creighton. It is more probable, however, that

de quo fuit magister Joannes, qui . . . fuit, ut dicitur, magister doctoris
subtilis Scoti.' Cf. also a MS. in the library of St. Antony at Padua,
' In pluteo xxii in calce Varro professionis minoritae doctorum jubar
et praeceptor divi Scoti famosus '. Cf. also Petrus Aureolus, *Tractatus de Conceptione Mariae Virginis*, cap. v : ' Guillelmus Scotus dictus
de Garrone, alias dictus Varro, qui fuit magister Scoti.'

[1] Cf. Wadding's edition of Scotus, tom. vi, p. 45.

[2] For the question of the date, see Wadding, loc. cit., p. 48.

[3] See Dr. Henderson's *History of Merton College*, in the series of the
histories of Oxford Colleges published by F. E. Robinson & Co.
(London, 1899), Appendix C, p. 289.

Johannes has confused Scotus with one John Doune who was a fellow of the college in the reign of Edward II and whose name has been altered by a later hand to Douns in the manuscript of the ' Old Catalogue ', a hand which has added the note ' hic doctor subtilis vulgariter tamen duns '.[1] A. G. Little dismisses the story of his connexion with Merton as a baseless fiction,[2] and Dr. Henderson also comes to the same conclusion.[3]

At the end of the year 1304, according to the commonly accepted tradition, Duns was called to Paris to incept as Master or Doctor of Theology. The letter of the Master-General of the Order, Gonsalvi, recommending the presentation is printed in Wadding's edition (tom. i, p. 9) and is worth quoting in full. It runs as follows :

' From Brother Gundisalvus rejoicing in the Lord, to his most dear Fathers, William the warden at Paris, or his vicar, and to the Masters.

' With respect to the advancement of our beloved Father in Christ, Giles of Legnago, concerning whom I have been informed by your letter, it is desirable, in accordance with custom, to provide for the presentation of another brother on the same occasion. And since according to the statutes both of our order and of your convent, the Bachelor to be presented at this present time should belong to a province other than that of France, I commend to your loving care our beloved brother in Christ, John the Scot, of whose laudable life, admirable knowledge, and most subtle genius, in addition to other qualifications, I have knowledge, partly from personal experience, and partly from his reputation, which has everywhere been noised abroad ; in order that you may present him in due sequence, next after the aforesaid Father Giles. I command you under holy obedience to make this presentation with the proper solemnity, without much expense. If, however,

---

[1] Op. cit., p. 290.

[2] A. G. Little, *The Grey Friars in Oxford* (Proc. Ox. Hist. Soc., vol. xv), p. 219.

[3] Henderson, loc. cit., p. 290.

you have knowledge that the lord Chancellor is willing to licence two of our brothers at once, I wish Brother Albert of Metz, if he is able to return to the convent, to be promoted with the said brother John. In which case I command and ordain that the said Brother Albert, on account of his age, incept before the above-mentioned Brother John, who shall follow immediately after him. Fare well in the Lord, and pray for me.

' Given at Ascoli in the province of the Marches of Ancona, November the 18th, 1304.'

The letter is printed in the *Chartularium* of the University of Paris.[1] To it is appended a note by the editors which is of considerable importance, because it explodes one of the best-known stories of the Scotist legend, namely, the tale that Duns defended the doctrine of the Immaculate Conception at Paris.[2] In discussing this question, Scotus puts forward three possible hypotheses : God could have made His Mother free from all taint of original sin. Or again, He might have permitted her to remain in a state of original sin only for an instant. Finally, He could have allowed her to remain in a state of original sin for a certain period, and at the end of that time purged her from its guilt. Which of these three possibilities actually occurred, God alone knows. But for the honour of our lady, it is convenient to hold the most excellent hypothesis, provided that it is not

---

[1] The same letter is also reproduced in Petrus Rodolphus, *Historiarum Seraphicae Religionis libri tres*, Venetiis, 1586, f. 325 v., and Little, *The Grey Friars in Oxford*, p. 220.

[2] Denifle-Chatelain, *Chartularium*, tom. ii, sect. i, p. 117: ' Johannes Scotus qui anno 1308 obiit, in 1304 fuit adhuc Baccalaureus. Inter fabulas omnino rejicienda sententia Scotum Parisiis venisse ut immaculatam Virginis conceptionem tueretur, et quandam disputationem ejusdem in causa ejus fuisse, cum universitas, aut certe theologiae facultas, decreto cavisset ne ad ullos gradus scholasticos admitteretur ullus, quin prius juraverat se defensuram eandem opinionem. . . . In juramento theologicorum . . . nihil simile reperies. Juramentum de tenenda opinione praedicta est an. 1497 Martii 3.'

repugnant to the authority of the Church or of the sacred Scriptures.[1]

According to the more generally accepted tradition Duns taught at Paris till 1308,[2] when he was sent to Cologne. Wadding states that he was sent to Germany in 1305, but this is scarcely possible. He also tells us that he was appointed Regent in the general chapter of the order held at Toulouse in 1307. Unfortunately no record of this chapter is preserved, and the passage in Wadding is ambiguous; it is not clear whether he is referring to the school of Paris or Cologne. It is usually taken to mean Paris, but it is also possible that he was appointed to both in succession. The motive for this transfer is not known. It has been suggested that it was prompted by the jealousy of the first Magister Regens at Paris, who was now Provincial of the French Province. More probably it was the desire of the order to establish a new school at Cologne, to rival the great Dominican school, which had already become famous owing to the teaching of Albertus Magnus and his pupil Thomas Aquinas.[3] But whatever

[1] *Op. Ox.* III, dist. iii, q. i, n. 9: 'Ad quaestionem dico quod Deus potuit facere quod ipsa nunquam fuisset in peccato originali; potuit etiam fecisse ut tantum in uno instanti esset in peccato; potuit etiam facere, ut per tempus aliquod esset in peccato, et in ultimo instanti illius temporis purgaretur . . . (n. 10.) Quod autem horum trium, quae ostensa sunt esse possibilia, factum sit Deus novit; si auctoritati Ecclesiae, vel auctoritati Scripturae non repugnet videtur probabile quod excellentius est Mariae tribuendum.'

[2] Miss Gertrude Leigh, in an interesting article in the *Church Quarterly Review* for July 1923, entitled 'Links between Dante and Duns Scotus', has attempted to identify the unknown saint of the *Paradiso*, canto x. 109, with Duns Scotus, on the ground that a strong tradition indicates that the poet was residing in Paris at the time that Duns was lecturing there, and that the doctrine of this unnamed spirit concerning the knowledge of the departed soul bears a strong resemblance to that enunciated by Scotus in the *Reportata*, Lib. IV, distt. xlv and xlix. But the evidence for such identification is scarcely conclusive, and the theory must be dismissed as highly problematical.

[3] M. Landry, in his book *Duns Scot*, has suggested that the reason

were the reasons for this transfer, Duns did not long
enjoy his new office : he died, apparently quite
suddenly, in November 1308, only a few months after
his arrival. The notice of his death is quoted by
Wadding from a statement which, though not contemporary, was probably based on some authentic
record,[1] and we have no reason to distrust its accuracy.
He was buried in the church of the friars minor,
'ad introductum sacrarii prope altare trium regum',
and his bones were afterwards transferred to their
present resting-place in the choir during the pontificate
of Pope Sixtus IV (1471–84).

But the chronology here given of Scotus' residence
at Oxford and at Paris has been called in question,
and Fr. Pelster, S.J., in a recent article [2] has brought
to light facts which would seem to compel us to
revise the generally accepted account of Duns' career
as a teacher, and the chronological order of the composition of his works. That he was actually in Paris
in the year 1304, and that he died at Cologne in 1308,
seems fairly certain, but there seems good reason to
suppose that it was in 1302 and not in 1304 that he
left Oxford for Paris, and also that he returned to
Oxford for a period before being sent to Cologne. Now
it was the general custom for a candidate for the

for Duns' transfer from Paris to Cologne was the publication of the
treatise 'De perfectione statuum', as a reply to the pamphlet of
Henry of Ghent attacking the privileges of the mendicant orders.
The work certainly contains some startling doctrines which may well
have roused violent opposition, but its authenticity is more than
doubtful and the date of its composition uncertain. Wadding
refuses to include it in his 'canon', though without giving any reasons.
The earliest known MS. is the Codex in the Laurentian Library at
Florence, which dates from the middle of the fourteenth century.

[1] 'D. P. Frater Johannes Scotus, S.T.P., doctor subtilis nominatus,
quondam doctor Coloniae, qui obiit anno MCCCVIII, iv idus
Novembris.'

[2] 'Handschriftliches zu Skotus mit neuen Angaben über sein
Leben' (*Franziskanische Studien*, 1923).

master's degree to lecture on the Sentences before
admission, and often a considerable period elapsed
before the degree was actually conferred. It would not,
therefore, be unusual to suppose that Duns was
resident in Paris for a considerable time before 1304.
And there is a piece of evidence which makes it appear
highly probable that he was already in Paris by 1302.
In a manuscript in the Cathedral library at Worcester
(Cod. F. 69) are written certain *Quaestiones in IV
Libros Sententiarum*. At the end of the third book of
the commentary a list of contents is appended, whose
first and last *quaestiones* correspond exactly with the
printed edition of Duns' *Reportata Parisiensia*. After
the description of the *quaestiones*, we find the following
note : ' Expliciunt questiones in primum sententiarum date a fratre . . . .to (the name is erased [1])
ordinis fratrum minorum Parisiis, anno domini M°
trecentesimo secundo intrante tercio.' After this
follows immediately the contents of the fourth book
(which ends with the second *quaestio* of the fiftieth
distinction, like the *Reportata*), ending with these
words : ' Expliciunt questiones sententiarum date
a fratre Johanne . . . (name again erased [2]) in studio
Parisiensi anno Domini M°ccc°III°.' The codex then
concludes with the actual commentary on the fourth
book. Fr. Pelster concludes on this evidence that Duns
must have arrived in Paris from Oxford by the autumn
of the year 1302 at the very latest, and that he was still
in residence in the autumn of 1304.

It has been usual, on the testimony of Bartholomew
of Pisa,[3] to regard the longer commentary on the
Sentences, the *Opus Oxoniense*, as prior in date to the

---

[1] Over this erasure a contemporary hand has written ' J. Dons
Scoto '.

[2] Over this erasure also a hand of the same date has written the
word ' Dons '.

[3] ' Hic primo in Anglia Oxoniae sententias legit, deinde in studio
Parisiis ' (*Liber Conformitatum*, quoted by Fr. Pelster, op. cit., p. 9).

Reportata Parisiensia, but if the theory of Fr. Pelster
is accepted, this older view will have to be regarded
as obsolete.   With regard to the date of the Oxford
Commentary, internal evidence affords certain important indications.   In the second *quaestio* of the
prologue, Scotus mentions the *Secta Mahumeti* : ' quae
multum debilitata est anno Christi 1300 et ejus
cultores multi mortui et plurimi sunt fugati.'   The
earliest date, therefore, for the first book is the academic
year 1301–2.   But at the end of 1302 Scotus was,
as we have seen already, at Paris.   He would not have
had time, therefore, to complete the other three books
before leaving Oxford.   Moreover, in *quaestio* 1 of the
twenty-fifth distinction of the fourth book, he refers
to a bull of Pope Benedict XI,[1] which he tells us he
himself saw.   Now Benedict sat on the papal throne
from 22 October 1303 till 7 July 1304, during the
whole of which period Duns was lecturing at Paris.
We cannot therefore place the fourth book earlier
than 1304–5.   Now Wadding tells us, and we have no
reason to doubt his statement, that Duns composed the
first book first, and then went on to the fourth book,
and from this to the second and the third.   The
conclusion would therefore seem to be that the whole
of the Oxford Commentary is posterior in date to the
Parisian.   Now the tradition that one commentary
was composed in Oxford and the other in Paris is
a very ancient one,[2] and scarcely open to questioning.

---

[1] The question under discussion is the impediment of illegitimacy
to the reception of Orders, and Duns remarks : ' Unde Benedictus XI
cum quodam tali sine dispensatione ordinato et in ordinibus mini-
strante postea faciliter dispensavit, sicut ego ipse vidi bullam dis-
pensationis.'

[2] Cf. Cod. Vat. lat. 876 (saec. 14), f. 310 v. b : ' Expliciunt addiciones
secundi libri magistri Johannis de Duns subtilis doctoris extracte per
magistrum Willelmum de Alnewick de ordine fratrum minorum de
lectura Parisiensi et Oxoniensi predicti magistri Johannis, cui propicie-
tur Deus.'

We are led, therefore, to suppose that instead of going to Cologne straight from Paris, Duns returned to his own province of England,[1] and wrote the larger commentary at Oxford before being appointed to his German post.[2]

Such is the brief and meagre chronicle of our philosopher, which still leaves much to be elucidated. Of his title of ' Doctor subtilis ' a few words may be added. We find it in the manuscript catalogue of Assisi and in the Liber Conformitatum of Bartholemew of Pisa ; also, according to Ehrle,[3] in certain other manuscripts which he assigns to the last half of the fourteenth century.

The works attributed to the pen of Duns Scotus are exceedingly voluminous and cover a very wide range of subjects. They show him as a man of very diverse intellectual interests. Besides being a theologian and a philosopher, he was well acquainted with the scientific learning of his time, and his writings abound in references to geometry, mechanics, optics, and astronomy. Civil law he seldom mentions, canon law more frequently, a point in which, as Werner remarks, he resembles Roger Bacon.[4] The most complete edition of his works is that published by Wadding at Lyons in 1629, which has been reprinted

[1] Cf. Cod. 12, in the municipal library at Todi : ' Explicit summa Johannis Duns provincie Anglicane super primum librum sentenciarum secundum lecturam Parisiensem.' This MS. is also of the fourteenth century, and indicates that Duns was not transferred to the French province after his Paris lectures.

[2] But we find no record of him in Oxford after 1304, which constitutes a difficulty if we are to accept Fr. Pelster's theory.

[3] *Archiv f. Literatur u. Kirchengeschichte*, i, p. 368, n. 1 : ' Die Ehrentitel der scholastischen Lehrer des Mittelalters ' (*Sitzungsberichte d. Bayrischen Akad.*, 1919).

[4] Karl Werner, *Geschichte der späteren Scholastik*, vol. i, ' Duns Scotus ', p. 9 note. See also the same author's work entitled *Die Kosmologie und allgemeine Naturlehre des Roger Baco*, pp. 39 and 107.

and published in Paris by Vives (1891–5).[1] The
reprint consists of twenty-six quarto volumes, averaging
some 750 pages each, a considerable portion of which
is devoted to commentary by various scholars and
annotators. Besides the writings published by Wadding, several unpublished manuscripts have been
included by bibliographers among his genuine writings,
the more important of which are expositions of Holy
Scripture, as for instance the *Lectura in Genesim*, the
Commentarii in quatuor Evangelia, and so forth.[2]

The genuineness of many of the works attributed to
Scotus is by no means certain : a large part of them
are open to grave suspicion ; others, if they represent
genuine writings of the master, have been extensively
re-edited before assuming their present form. Moreover the difficulties of attribution are augmented by
the fact that we know of another Johannes Scotus,
who was a Master of Arts in the University of Paris
in 1309 ; besides which, Wadding tells us that there
were several others of the same name. It has been
suggested that it is to some other Johannes Scotus
that the commentary on the physics should be ascribed.
That it is not the work of Duns is generally admitted.
So too the treatise ' In libros Meteororum ' is probably
spurious : it cites the *Tractatus de Proportionibus* of
Bradwardine, who did not die till 1350, forty-two
years after the death of Scotus.[3] It therefore must
almost certainly be the work of a later writer. Wadding
attributes it to the Minorite Simon Tunstede, who

[1] The firm of Vives has now disappeared, and the edition is already
out of print. It contains, in addition to the ' canon ' of Wadding,
a treatise ' De Perfectione Statuum ', which is almost certainly
spurious. Cf. E. Longpré, op. cit., p. 20.

[2] For a complete list of the works attributed to Duns, both published and unpublished, see Appendix I.

[3] Cf. P. Duhem, ' Sur les Meteorologicorum libri quatuor
faussement attribués à Jean Duns Scot ' (*Arch. Franc. Hist.*, iii,
pp. 626–32.)

was Regent of the friars at Oxford in 1351, and who is known to have written a commentary, which has not come down to us, on this work of Aristotle.

The question of the commentaries on the *Metaphysics* is more complicated, and the evidence somewhat confused. The two commentaries differ completely as regards their method : the one is a literal exposition of the Aristotelian text, sentence by sentence ; the other is in the form of *quaestiones* which Scotus generally adopts. Important as the part was which the *Metaphysics* played in the philosophical training of schoolmen, it seems somewhat strange that even the most diligent of professors should have found time to compose two commentaries on them, in addition to the two undoubtedly genuine commentaries on the Sentences, not to mention the host of other works. Moreover, the form of literal exposition is not used by Scotus in any other case ; his commentaries on the *Organum* and the *De Anima* are all in the form of *quaestiones*. Nor does the manuscript itself offer any evidence of genuine authorship ; on the contrary, the note appended to the end of the twelfth book expressly states that the author is not Scotus himself, but that the doctrine is that of the great master.[1] That the author was the Scotist

---

[1] 'Volo autem scire omnes litteram istam legentes, quod tam sententiando quam notando secutus sum doctrinam illius subtilissimi et excellentissimi Doctoris, cujus fama et memoria in benedictione est, utpote qui sua sacra et profunda doctrina totum orbem adimplevit et facit resonare, sc. Magistri Joannis Duns, qui fuit natione Scotus, religione Minor ; unde et verba ejus in isto scripto frequenter reperies, sicut ab ipso tradita scripturae reperiuntur. Et idcirco si aliquid bene dictum in isto opere reperies, scias a fonte et profunditate suae doctrinae ac scientiae emanasse. Si quid vero minus bene dictum, aut ejus doctrinae quomodolibet contra dicens, meae imperitiae adscribatur. Nam ego quantum sapio quantumque capio quidquid est hic quod ipse exprimere intendebat, pes meus ejus vestigia secutus est ; et ideo si aliquid aliud repugnans sibi inveniatur, quandoque, nunc pro tunc revoco, paratus libenti animo emendare.'

Antonius Andreas has often been suggested; yet Hugo Cavell, in his *Judicium* printed in the edition of Wadding, stoutly maintains that Andreas was not the author but only the editor.[1] He bases this assertion on the testimony of Mauritius Hibernicus,[1] Archbishop of Tuam, who brought out the first edition of the commentary. The case is complicated by the fact that in the various catalogues which have come down to us no mention is made of a literal commentary on the *Metaphysics* by Andreas, but only a book of *quaestiones*, which have survived and were published in Venice in 1481. And Henry Willot (*d.* 1599), who compiled a catalogue of works by Franciscan authors, while mentioning Andreas' *Quaestiones*, expressly attributes the literal commentary to Scotus.[2] But as we have seen, the note at the end of the *Expositio* makes it quite clear that Duns was not the author;[3] nor, as we shall see, was it Andreas.

This is made clear from a consideration of the *Quaestiones Subtilissimae in XII libros Metaphysicorum*. That these were edited by the same hand as the *Expositio* is abundantly plain, in view of the numerous cross-references from the latter to the former, which are made in the first person.[4] That Andreas should have written his own *Quaestiones* in addition to the

[1] 'His accedit non levi argumento auctoritas Mauritii nostri, Doctoris Subtilis fidelissimi quondam interpretis . . . qui sequenti post Scotum saeculo floruit. Is in titulo, quem praefixit huic . . . commentario . . . ita habet : " Joannis Duns Scoti Doctoris Subtilis . . . in 12. libros Metaphys. Aristotelis, secundum novam translationem scriptum, recollectum, etc. et pluribus additionibus decoratum ab excellentissimo ipsius discipulo Antonio Andrea etc." '

[2] See Cavell's *Judicium*, printed by Wadding at the beginning of the *Expositio*.

[3] Dr. Carreras, however, in his *Ensayo sobre el voluntarismo de J. Duns Scot* (Gerona, 1923), p. 6, seems to regard the work as genuine.

[4] e. g. *Quaest. Metaph.* VII, q. 1 : ' Illud exemplum corrigitur per paragraphum sequentem, sicut exposui textum,' etc., etc.

literal commentary, as well as edited the *Quaestiones*
of Scotus, seems on the first sight of it highly improbable.   Moreover, as we shall see presently, the
author of the *Expositio* was an Irishman, which Andreas
was not.

Let us consider then first the question of the
Quaestiones. That in their present form they are the
work of Duns himself, it would be difficult to maintain
for a variety of reasons. They differ on several important points from the teaching of Scotus as exemplified
in the two commentaries on the Sentences and the
Quaestiones Quodlibetales. For instance, in the first
quaestio of the first book the author rejects the opinion
of Avicenna that the subject of metaphysic is being
qua being (*ens inquantum ens*), a thesis which is accepted in the *Opus Oxoniense* and the *Reportata*.
Again, in the thirteenth *quaestio* of the seventh book
we find a doctrine of individuation propounded which
differs markedly from that found elsewhere in Scotus'
writings ; but it is clear that here the text has been
tampered with.   Furthermore, the last two books,
which were first discovered by Wadding, contain
theories which are quite irreconcilable with the notion
of genuine authorship, as, for instance, the view that
the pure intelligences are of different species, because
they do not contain matter (Lib. XII, q. 20). Finally,
the workmanship of the treatise is uneven, and it
leaves an indefinable impression that it is in part at
least the work of a mind far inferior to that of Duns.
We have only to compare it with the commentaries
on the Sentences to see this quite distinctly.   On
the other hand there can be do doubt that the
Quaestiones are well authenticated. They appear in
very early lists of Duns' works ; there are a number
of early MSS. of the first nine books ; they have
generally been accepted by scholars, and Dr. Minges,
whose deep and critical knowledge of Scotus' works

has contributed so much to our understanding of the subtle doctor, has declared them to be undoubtedly genuine.[1]

A similar view concerning the first nine books is held by Fr. Pelster, who brings to bear on the point some striking evidence in favour of their authenticity.[2] The earliest testimony is afforded by a manuscript in the Vatican library, Cod. Vat. lat. 869 (membr. ff. 245, 25 by 19·5 cm., 2 col., saec. 14 et 13). This contains besides the *De Rerum Principio*, two *Theoremata*, and the *Quaestiones de Anima* of Scotus, a number of anonymous *quaestiones* by William of Alnwick, Richard of Middleton, Nikolas of Lyra, Albertus Magnus, and other authors as yet undetermined. Ff. 48 r. b–101 r. b form a commentary on the *De Anima* which Fr. Pelster assigns to William of Alnwick. This is followed on ff. 102 r. a–103 v. a by a *quaestio*, 'Utrum noticia quam habet anima de se sit abstractiva?' which also belongs to William, and which contains a reference to the second *quaestio* of Scotus on the first book of the *Metaphysics*.[3] So also in the commentary, Alnwick refers to Scotus' *Quaestiones Metaphysicae* concerning a certain topic.[4] Both references have been verified, and the passages referred to are found in the printed edition.[5] Another

---

[1] 'Beitrag zur Lehre des Duns Scotus über die Equivokation des Seinsbegriffes' (*Phil. Jahrb.* 1907).

[2] 'Handschriftliches zu Duns Skotus,' etc. (*Franzisk. Stud.* 1923), pp. 27–31.

[3] Cf. f. 103 r. b : 'Hic videtur dicere Scotus in questionibus metaphysice, in ista questione, utrum omnes homines naturaliter scire desiderant, et est secunda super primo, ubi infra movet unam questionem utrum possumus habere certam et infallibilem cognicionem de actibus nostris et de quibus.'

[4] Cf. f. 60 v. a : 'Sed iste raciones, que sunt reverendi doctoris magistri Johannis Scoti in questionibus metaphysice, questione illa, utrum accidens sit forma simplex, sunt valde difficiles ad solvendum.'

[5] *Quaestiones super XII lib. Metaph.*, I, q. ii ; VIII, q. i.

manuscript of the first half of the fourteenth century, in the Staatsbibliothek at Munich (Clm. 15829),[1] contains the first nine books of the *Quaestiones*, while in the library of St. Antony at Padua there is a manuscript containing a *Quaternus questionum super Metaphysicam Johannis Duns* which contains the *quaestiones* of the printed edition.[2] Finally, the Cod. Vat. lat. 890 contains among other things a tabula or summary of the same *Quaestiones*.[3] But it is doubtful whether all the *quaestiones* in the printed commentary are from Scotus's own hand. The work was certainly never finally revised by Duns, as is proved by the numerous additions and marginal notes.[4] It would seem probable, therefore, that the treatise in its present form (with the exception of the last two books which are certainly spurious) is a recension of a genuine work of Scotus by a later editor, who also either revised or perhaps wrote the literal commentary. Who the author of this latter work was we can only guess, but it seems almost certain that he was an Irishman. We can gather this from a passage in the seventh book where the following words occur : [5] ' In diffinitione albi non ponitur necessario homo ; sed in diffinitione Francisci vel Sancti Patricii necessario ponitur animal.' Already Dempster in his attempt to prove that Duns was a Scotsman [6] had availed himself of this passage to deny the authenticity of this work, and Wadding

[1] This MS. is of French origin and was originally in the Cathedral Library at Salzburg ; it contains on ff. 5 v. and 6 r. a rubric ' Quodlibet Scoti super Metaphysice ', but this is an error, as the writer of the text writes quite plainly ' Questiones Scoti super Metaphysicam '.

[2] Cod. 186 (membr. sine num. 32 by 22·8 cm., 2 col., saec. 14 init.).

[3] The explicit is as follows (f. 30 r. b) : ' Explicit abbreviatio super questiones metaphysice.'

[4] Cf. Pelster, op. cit., p. 20 ff. The textua criticism of the *quaestiones* contains many difficulties which have yet to be worked out.

[5] *Comm. Lit. in XII lib. Metaph.*

[6] ' Asserti Scotiae cives,' etc. (Bononiae, 1621); *Historia Ecclesiastica* (Ban. Club, 1627).

accuses him of declaring it spurious merely in order to avoid the conclusion that Duns was an Irishman.[1] But in view of the fact that more modern research has shown that he was almost certainly not Irish, the passage again becomes significant. It shows clearly that the author was not Scotus, but an Irish Minorite. Moreover, it must be pointed out that in choosing names for his examples in commenting on the text of Aristotle, Scotus invariably uses those of ancient Greeks, like Socrates or Kallias, and not those of saints. Whether the author was using any genuine materials other than writings of Scotus which have come down to us, it is scarcely possible to decide, but there is no reason to suppose that Duns wrote two commentaries on the *Metaphysics*.

The *De Modis Significandi* or *Grammatica Speculativa* has been attributed at different times to various authors. Thus Henry Willot [2] assigns it to Albertus de Saxonia, but it is now generally recognized as a genuine work of Scotus : the numerous references to doctrines contained in Duns' logical works leave us in little doubt as to its authenticity. The case of the *Quaestiones Miscellaneae de Formalitatibus* is less clear. The second *quaestio* : ' Utrum intellectus et voluntas in Deo, qui dicunt perfectiones absolutas, sint idem totaliter, vel distinguantur aliqualiter ? ' contains a solution which is certainly not Scotist in spirit. Instead of applying the notion of the formal distinction, the author proceeds somewhat lamely to show, first, that will and intellect are not totally identical in God ; and secondly, that they are not in any way distinct.[3] Wadding, after calling attention to this departure

---

[1] *Censura to Quaestiones in Metaph.*

[2] *Athenae Orthodoxorum Sodalitii Franciscani* (1589).

[3] *Quaest. Miscell.*, q. 2, n. 4 : ' Circa istam quaestionem brevissime sic procedam : primo jam declarabo quod intellectus et voluntas in Deo non sunt totaliter idem ; secundo probabo quod non distinguuntur aliqualiter.'

from the normal Scotist doctrine, nevertheless accepts the work as genuine.[1] He tells us in his *Censura* to this treatise that it was taken from a manuscript at the Vatican (Cod. Vat. lat., No. 869), where it was found appended to the *Quaestiones de Anima*, the full description of the manuscript being *Scotus in Libros de Anima, et Alia Pulchra.* The name *Quaestiones Miscellaneae de Formalitatibus* was given by Wadding. Its authenticity is, to say the least of it, doubtful, and Prantl rejects it as spurious.[2] The *Quaestiones de Anima* exist also in several early manuscripts, and are accepted by Pelster as genuine.[3] They are to be found in Cod. 173 in the library of Saint Antony at Padua [4] (with the exception of the last *quaestio*), and also in a fifteenth-century manuscript in the Bibliotheca Angelica at Rome,[5] while Cod. 890 in the Vatican contains a *Tabula super Quaestiones de Anima*, which gives all except the ultimate *quaestio*. The question

[1] Cf. scholion to loc. cit. : ' Dubitari forte posset an haec quaestio sit Doctoris, maxime quia non admittit aliqualem distinctionem inter essentialia in divinis, licet concedat non-identitatem formalem inter eadem. Esse tamen Scoti praefert autographum, nec difficulter suaderi potest ex stylo et discursu,' etc. A similar doctrine is also found in the *De Rerum Principio* : it is not impossible, therefore, that there should be an early work. See Appendix III at the end of this volume.

[2] *Geschichte der Logik im Abendlande*, vol. iii, cap. xix, note 85 (p. 203) : ' Der Bericht selbst welchen Wadding dieser unvollendeten Schrift vorausschickt, enthält eigentlich mehr Gründe der Unächtheit als der Aechtheit. Es versteht sich von selbst, dass das Buch der Scotistischen Schule angehört.'

[3] Op. cit., p. 31.

[4] This MS., which belongs to the fourteenth century, contains a large number of works by different authors, including portions of Scotus's *Quaest. in Metaph.* as well as the *Quodlibeta* and the *De Anima*, which follow each other. The explicit reads thus : ' Expliciunt quolibet cum questionibus de anima doctoris subtilis magistri Johannis Scoti de ordine fratrum minorum, Amen.' For a further discussion of this particularly interesting MS. see Appendix I.

[5] Cod. 1034 (chart. ff. 93, 22·2 by 16·2 col., saec. 15). In this MS. also the last *quaestio* is missing.

of the text is somewhat complicated, and there is reason to suppose that they were never revised by Duns, but were edited by a later hand.[1]

But the greatest puzzle of all is furnished by the *Theoremata*. The treatise has from the beginning been accepted as genuine,[2] and its authenticity has never been questioned in ancient times; yet it raises a mass of almost insoluble problems. Theorems xiv to xvi seem to form a little work by themselves, which has been called a *Tractatus de Creditis*. Here the author asserts the impossibility of proving a number of propositions which have generally been taken to form the basis of a natural theology. Thus he declares that it cannot be demonstrated that God is a living, intelligent, or willing being, or that he is capable of any immanent operation whatsoever. Yet in the *De Primo Principio*, as well as in the first book of the *Opus Oxoniense*, Scotus sets out to prove these very theses whose demonstrability is here denied.[3] Wadding has attempted to reconcile this contradiction in his first scholion to Theorem xiv:

' One may wonder ', he says, ' that the Doctor states in the first four propositions of this theorem, that it cannot be proved that God is living, intelligent, volent, or capable of effecting any immanent operation. But it must be noted that he is speaking of rigorous demonstration according to the rules of logic, not of demonstration of a wider kind than that by which God can be proved evidently to exist, or to be one, or to be implied as the effective principle of things. . . . But

[1] Cf. Pelster, op. cit., p. 32.

[2] Cf. Wadding's *Censura*: ' Nulli dubium opusculum hoc Scoti esse, ingenium quippe ejus sapit, at ab Henrico Willoto, ab Antonio Possevino, et Johanne Pitsaeo inter Scotica recensetur.'

[3] Cf. *De Primo Principio*, cap. iv, where the following propositions are proposed: ' Omnis perfectio simpliciter et in summo inest necessario naturae summae.—Primum efficiens est intelligens et volens.—Intellectus primi intelligit actu semper et necessario et distincte quodcumque intelligibile,' etc., etc. See also *Op. Ox.*, Lib. I, dist. i, q. 2.

whatever theory we may hold as to this opinion ... we may note that Scotus does not assert it ; or if he does, he is talking in accordance with the opinion of others, as Maurice (O'Fihely) here notes ; or, what is still more probable, he only lays down these four propositions without giving any solutions ; a fact which I gather from the fifth proposition where he says, " The first four propositions being conceded, though not proved ". ... From which words it may be taken as certain that according to Scotus, the fact that God could not be demonstrated to be living, etc., was not proven. Therefore ... he does not regard these propositions as proved, or as definitely asserted truths, but leaves them unsolved.' [1]

This attempted reconciliation is obviously unsatisfactory. If we accepted the first part of Wadding's explanation, we should destroy the whole basis of the Scotist natural theology as laid down in the *De Primo Principio* and the *Opus Oxoniense*, where he proves the existence of God and deduces the divine attributes. Nor does the fact that the theorems are not proved but only stated give us any comfort. For the whole treatise is only a skeleton outline, and the words ' concessis quatuor conclusionibus proximis licet non probatis ' do not lend themselves easily to the construction which Wadding has so ingeniously forced

---

[1] ' Mirabitur quis quod Doctor dicat quatuor primis propositionibus hujus Theorematis probari non posse Deum esse vivum, intelligentem, volentem, vel ullius operationis immanentis effectivum, vel capacem. Sed advertendum eum loqui de probatione demonstrativa, sumpta in rigore juxta regulas logicas, non autem de probatione alia citra illam demonstrationem, quo sensu ista tenent quotquot dicunt demonstrari non posse evidenter, Deum esse, aut esse unum, vel dari unum omnium principium effectivum. . . .

' Sed quidquid sit de hac sententia. . . . Scotus eam non asserit ; sed vel loquitur secundum sententiam aliorum, ut notat hic Mauritius, vel, quod verius est, tantum ponit istas quatuor propositiones, nihil de eis resolvens, quod colligo ex propositione quinta ibi, " concessis quatuor conclusionibus proximis licet non probatis ". Quibus verbis constat, secundum eum non probari, quod demonstrari nequeat Deum esse vivum, etc. Ergo illas quatuor conclusiones non tenet ut probatas, vel assertas, sed non resolutas reliquit.'

upon them. A far more natural meaning would be the following : ' Given that God is a living, intelligent, willing being, though this cannot be proved, we are still unable to prove that he knows or wills anything outside Himself.' [1]　One course, then, is to conclude that the treatise is spurious,[2] a supposition which gains some plausibility from the fact that so many of the attributions which we have examined are doubtful. But this somewhat radical method is to cut the knot rather than to untie it. If we examine the treatise more closely, we shall see that it is a composite work which has not been put together very adequately. For the order of the theorems has been confused. Thus Theorems i–x and xiii deal with epistemological problems. Theorems xi and xii make a fragment which treats of the nature of the *compositum*, or concrete reality of the external world. Theorems xiv–xvi form a *Tractatus de Creditis*, which is a sceptical criticism of the content of natural theology ; while Theorems xvii–xxiii give a skeleton of a system of cosmology. The form of these theorems, moreover, differs considerably from the rest of Scotus's works, inasmuch as the propositions contained in them are barely stated without the citation of any *rationes in oppositum*.

[1] Cf. Theorem xiv, n. 2 : ' 5. Concessis quatuor conclusionibus proximis, licet non probatis, non potest probari Deum aliquod aliud a se intelligere vel velle.'

[2] This course has actually been taken by Fr Déodat-Marie de Basly, O.F.M., who has impugned the authenticity of the *Theoremata* in an article in the *Arch. Franc. Hist.*, 1918, on grounds of internal evidence, namely, because they contain doctrines which contradict the teaching of Scotus as laid down in his other works. But the problem cannot be solved so simply. The evidence for the *Theoremata* is too strong for such summary treatment. M. Landry on the other hand is inclined, notwithstanding, to regard them as genuine. In fact his whole view of Duns' philosophy is based on a somewhat exaggerated notion of their significance.

For a further discussion of this problem see Appendix III at the end of this volume.

They seem to be little more than notes, a rough outline for some longer work. It might therefore be
possible, if we are to accept them as genuine, to regard
them as material for an academic disputation, in which
case they need not actually represent the opinions of
their author, any more than those of a speaker in
a public debate. They may therefore be regarded as
a series of arguments brought forward by Duns ὡς
θέσιν διαφυλάττων. On the other hand, we might
attempt to bring their doctrine into harmony with
Scotus' other works by supposing that he is here
speaking of a demonstration *a priori* as opposed to the
empirical *demonstratio quia*. This would perhaps be
the most satisfactory solution to this difficult problem.

The most important of Duns Scotus' works are
undoubtedly the two commentaries on the Sentences
of Peter Lombard, Bishop of Paris, who died in the
year 1160. The *Magister Sententiarum* is, after
Abelard and the Victorines, the most significant figure
in medieval theology between Anselm and Aquinas,[1]
and has been regarded by many authorities as the founder
of Scholastic theology.[2] His Sentences became the

---

[1] Cf. Dante, *Paradiso*, x. 106–8 :

> L' altro, ch' appresso adorna il nostro coro,
> Quel Pietro fu, che con la poverella
> Offerse a Santa Chiesa il suo tesoro.

The allusion to the poor widow in this passage is taken from the
Prologue to the Sentences, where the following words are to be found :
' Cupientes aliquid de penuria ac tenuitate nostra cum paupercula
in gazophylacium Domini mittere, ardua scandere, opes ultra vires
nostras agere praesumpsimus.'

[2] Cf. Mabillon, *Tractatus de Studiis Monasticis*, Latin trans. by
Porta, p. 137 : ' Sed tandem Petrus Lombardus Episcopus Parisiensis
omnibus aliis longe ante celluit et theologica Patrum dogmata in
quatuor Sententiarum libros redegit ; haecque est illa methodus,
quae universo fere Scholasticorum coetui, qui post ipsum fuere, magis
arrisit, usquedum Angelicus Doctor qui eadem pariter usus est,
novam in sua Summa concinnavit, quam subinde Scholastici caeteris
quibusque praeposuerunt.' Cf. also Espenberger, *Die Philosophie*

standard text-book of theology at the universities and assumed the position of a second bible.[1] They were commented upon by almost every philosopher and theologian from the end of the twelfth to the beginning of the sixteenth century, and as many as two hundred and forty-six of these commentaries have been counted.[2] The more illustrious of his commentators include not only Bonaventura, Richard of Middleton, Matthew of Aquasparta, and William of Ockham, but also Thomas Aquinas, whose work on the Sentences forms a kind of preliminary study to his *Summa Theologica*. Scotus' commentaries, the *Opus Oxoniense* and the *Opus Parisiense*, contain the bulk of his philosophical and theological doctrine, to which his other works, with the exception of the *Quodlibeta* and the *Collationes*, may be regarded as ancillary. Their form does not vary in any important respect from that of his Aristotelian commentaries. He does not expound the text literally, but while following it distinction by distinction, discusses certain questions which arise out of the subject matter, after the manner of Bonaventure and Thomas. The *Opus Oxoniense*, which is considerably the larger of the two, was first printed at Venice towards the end of the fifteenth century, but in a very faulty text. An edition was also printed at Nuremburg in 1481. A better edition was prepared by the Minorite Antonius de

---

des Petrus Lombardus, Münster, 1901, s. 32 : ' Mit gutem Recht kann man darum Petrus einen Begründer der streng scholastischen Methode nennen, welche im 13. Jahrhundert üblich wurde, da ja er ihr hauptsächlich zum Siege verhalf.'

[1] Cf. Protois, *Pierre Lombard*, p. 150 : ' Cet ouvrage fameux eut un succès inoui, prodigieux, véritablement incomparable et en peu de temps il conquit dans l'estime et dans l'admiration des théologiens une place presque semblable à celle de l'Écriture Sainte.' So also R. Seeberg in *Herzogs Real-Enzyklopädie*, xi. 641.

[2] Cf. Protois, op. cit., pp. 161–80 ; also Grabmann, *Gesch. der Scholast. Meth.* 2, p. 392.

Fantis in 1510, and another was produced shortly
afterwards by the Servite, Romulus Laurentianus,
which was dedicated to the Praefectus Generalis of the
Servite Order, Angelo Morelli.   The text for the
edition of Wadding was prepared by Hugh Cavell,
and printed in 1620.   Meanwhile a large number of
editions had been brought out during the sixteenth
century.[1]

The *Reportata Parisiensia* are the product of Scotus'
lectures at Paris, and according to Wadding's account
form a shortened summary of the Oxford Commentary.
The first book was the first to be composed ; then
followed the fourth, to which were finally added the
second and the third.   When Duns had reached the
eighteenth distinction of the third book he was called
away to Cologne, and at the end of this distinction the
following note appears in the text : ' Et sic fini,
disputacionis in aula.'   The remaining distinctions
(xix–xxxix) were added by a later Scotist from the
Opus Oxoniense, while the last four are not printed in
Wadding's text because they are a mere reproduction
word for word of the longer Oxford work.[2]

Such is the traditional account of the Parisian
Commentary which has generally been accepted.   But
in the light of the new evidence brought forward by
Fr. Pelster, we can no longer regard it as adequate.
According to his theory the *Reportata* are, as we have
already noted, earlier than the *Opus Oxoniense*.   He
agrees with Wadding concerning the order in which
the four books were composed, and admits that the
commentary originally ended with *quaestio* 3 of the
eighteenth distinction of the third book.   But he
interprets the note in the text which we have just
quoted entirely differently.[3]   The disputation referred

[1] For a list of early editions of Duns' works, see Appendix II.
[2] Cf. Wadding's introduction to the *Reportata*.
[3] Pelster, op. cit., pp. 11 ff.

to, as the Worcester manuscript would suggest, took place before, not after, Duns' presentation to the Master's degree; that is between 1302 and 1304, not 1305 and 1308. The evidence for this theory is so interesting, and throws so much light on the academic procedure of the time, that it is worth stating in detail. If we turn to the Worcester manuscript we shall find that the *quaestio* in question (Lib. III, dist. xviii, q. 3) runs as follows : ' Utrum sit necessarium ponere habitum caritatis in anima Christi propter actum fruitionis vere ? ' Two arguments *contra* and one *pro* are now propounded, whereon the answer begins : ' Respondeo exponendo intellectum questionis, quod non querit de potentia absoluta . . . intelligitur ergo de necessitate indigentie . . . et secundum hoc dico, quid anima Christi indiget habitu caritatis respectu fruitionis vere.' Three reasons are now brought forward for the conclusion posited in the response, and one objection is raised and solved. The two *rationes contra* laid down at the beginning are then disposed of. The argument now is continued thus : ' Tunc arguit frater Egidius primo sic ... secundo sic ... Contra arguit idem Egidius sic . . .' ; and the answers to the objections brought up are given ; whereon a second opponent appears on the scenes : ' Tunc arguit magister Alanus primo sic . . . secundo sic . . . tertio sic,' and the objections raised are again solved. Finally, a third opponent is introduced : ' Tunc arguit Goffredus ' ; four more objections are disposed of, and the *quaestio* closes with the note concerning the *disputatio in aula*. This *disputatio* is none other than the second portion of the exercise on the attainment of the Master's degree, and derives its name from the fact that it was held in the *aula domini episcopi* at Paris. For the exact procedure at this period we have no detailed evidence of a direct kind. But in the statutes of the faculty of theology of the University

of Bologna drawn up in 1365 by the Parisian Master of
Theology, Hugolinus de Malabranca, we possess a
document which prescribes the regulation of just such
a disputation as the *quaestio* represents.[1] The number
of disputants was four : the *responsalis*, who was
a *baccalaureus formatus*, i. e. one who had lectured
already on the Sentences ; the *magister novus aulandus* ;
the *magister aulator* ; and the Chancellor. Now from
the names given in the Worcester manuscript, Fr.
Pelster identifies all four. Egidius, the *magister novus
aulandus*, is the Giles of Legnago mentioned in the
letter of the Minister-General Gonsalvi ;[2] Alanus,
the *magister aulator*, is the Franciscan Master of
Theology, Alanus de Tongris ;[3] Goffredus is Godfrey

[1] *De Tempore et Modis in Multiplici actu Aule*, Ehrle, *Statuta
facultatis Theologiae Universitatis Bononiensis*, 42 f. : ' Magister
aulator imponit sibi ipsi birretum et alius imponit magistro novo,
qui cum benedictione incipit suum breve principium de commenda-
tione sacre scripture. Quo celeriter terminato, per unum studentem
proponitur tertia de quatuor questionibus sub reverendo magistro
novo disputanda, quam responsalis praeordinatus, qui debet esse
formatus bachalaurius, si haberi potest, resumit reverenter, et format
responsivam positionem scientificam et penitus theologicam sub
tribus vel quatuor conclusionibus docte probatis. Primo contra
dicta responsalis opponit magister novus per quatuor media et replicat
tribus vicibus vel quatuor conclusionibus pro primo argumento et
bis pro secundo. Secundo contra eundem responsalem opponit
magister aulator tribus mediis bis replicando ad primum medium et
semel pro secundo. Tertio opponit contra eundem responsalem
dominus cancellarius vel vicem gerens, si voluerit duobus mediis cum
bina replicatione.' Cf. also Denifle-Chatelain, *Chartul.*, etc., ii, p. 693,
n. 1188.   [2] See above, p. 9.

[3] In June 1303, at the command of Philip le Bel, the members of
the Dominican, Franciscan, and Augustinian convents registered a
protest against certain actions of Pope Boniface VIII, in which they
appealed to a general council. The list of participants has come
down to us, and among the Franciscans we find the following :
' Religiosi viri fratres Alanus et Johannes de Tongris ordinis fratrum
minorum, magistri in theologia, de conventu ejusdem ordinis Parisius,
item fratres Egidius de Longniaco et Martinus de Abbatisvilla,
baccalarii in theologia eiusdem conventus . . . Johannes de Anglia,
Gulielmus de Anglia ', etc. Cf. Callebaut, ' La patrie du B. Jean

of Fontaines, a very senior Master, who, though as far as we know he was never actually Chancellor, is known to have acted in the Chancellor's place as *vicem gerens* ;[1] while the *responsalis* is none other than Duns himself.

The first printed edition of the *Reportata* was produced by the Augustinian Eremite, Thomas Penketh, who was Professor of Theology at Padua, and was printed at Venice in 1477. A new edition was brought out by the minorite Philippus a Bagnacavallo in the year 1503, also at Venice, and a third by Mauritius Hibernicus in 1522 at the same place. After this date several other editions of this work made their appearance, among which was that of Hugh Cavell, which was printed at Cologne in 1635, and whose text is incorporated in Wadding's edition of Duns' works.

Three other writings have come down to us, which date from the time of Scotus' residence at Paris. The most important of these are the *Quaestiones Quodlibetales* or *Quodlibeta*, which are disputations held by Scotus after he had been admitted to the Master's degree.[2] The exact date is not easy to

Duns Scot' (*Arch. Franc. Hist.* x, pp. 5 f., 1917) ; G. Picot, *Documents relatifs aux États généraux et Assemblées réunis sous Philippe le Bel* (Paris, 1901), pp. 378–83. Pelster tries to identify Johannes de Anglia with Duns, who belonged to the English province.

[1] Cf. A. Pelzer, ' Godefroid de Fontaines ' (*Revue Néo-Scolastique*, xx (1913), p. 367), who quotes a MS. in the Bibliothèque Nationale, Cod. 16574, which relates a gathering in the College of the Sorbonne in 1303 : ' Presentibus magistris in theologia cancellario Parisiensi, Godefrido de Fontibus, Andrea de Monte Eligii, Henrico Amandi,' etc., etc. With regard to this, Pelster, op. cit., p. 14, n. 1, remarks : ' Gottfried von Fontaines ist zwar, nach allem was wir wissen, nicht Kanzler von Paris gewesen. Dies war vielmehr um jene Zeit Simon de Guibervilla. Aber bei seinem Alter und dem hohen Ansehen dass er genoss, ist es leicht möglich dass er, der ja auch Canonicus Parisiensis war, bei feierlichen Gelegenheiten öfter den Kanzler vertrat. So wäre auch am einfachsten die recht alte Ueberlieferung bei Reiner von Pisa erklärt.'

[2] Cf. The manuscript in the Saatsbibliothek in Munich, Clm. 8717 (saec. 14 init.), where the explicit, f. 100 r. a, reads : ' Explicit quodlibet determinatum Parisiis per venerabilem doctorem fratrem

determine, but according to the view of Fr. Pelster, they must have been composed between 1304 and 1306. To the same period belongs an unpublished disputation between Duns Scotus and the Dominican Gulielmus Godinus,[1] ' Utrum Materia sit Principium Individuationis ? ' in which Godinus takes the affirmative and Scotus the negative side. The manuscript is in the municipal library at Erfurt.[2] Finally there are the *Collationes*, called by Antonius Possevinus *Collationes Parisienses*. These collations are disputations on a particular topic, giving arguments *pro* and *contra* without any ' determination ' at the end, a fact which would imply that they were held by Scotus before attaining to the master's licence,[3] and during the period of his baccalaureate. That they are actual disputations, and not merely treatises in the form of disputations, seems clear, though the role played by Duns himself has yet to be determined by critical scholarship.[4]

The exact chronological order of Duns' writings has unfortunately not been worked out with any degree of accuracy. The *logicalia*, which include all the commentaries on the *Organon* of Aristotle, the *Grammatica Speculativa*, the *Quaestiones de Anima*, the

---

Johannem de ordine minorum.' Now ' determination ' was the privilege of the mastership and not permitted to bachelors. Cf. Ehrle, *Statuta, etc.*, 43–5.

[1] Cf. Pelster, ' Thomas von Sutton O.P., ein Oxforder Verteidiger der thomistischen Lehre ' (*Zeitschr. für Kath. Theol.* xlvi, 1922) p. 237.

[2] Codex Amplonianus, fol. No. 369, ff. 71 v.–75 r. For a further description of this manuscript, see Appendix II.

[3] Cf. Dante, *Par.* xxiv. 46 :

> Sì come il baccellier s' arma, e non parla,
> fin che il maestro la question propone,
> per approvarla, e non per terminarla . . .

[4] For a discussion of the origins and manuscript authority for these *collationes*, see Pelster, *Handschriftliches zu Skotus*, &c., pp. 21–7.

De Rerum Principio, the *De Primo Principio*, the *De Cognitione Dei*, the *Theoremata*, and the *Quaestiones in Metaphysicam* all seem to belong to the earlier part of his life, and were probably composed before he came to Paris in 1302, but their exact order has not yet been established. De Ruggiero [1] is of the opinion that the *De Rerum Principio* and the *De Primo Principio* are early works, while Wadding places the *Theoremata* between the last-named treatise and the *quaestiones* on the *Metaphysics*. If we accept the theory of Fr. Pelster, the *Reportata* and the *Collationes* come next, and then the *Quaestiones Quodlibetales*, while the *Opus Oxoniense* would seem to be the last of Scotus' writings.

The works of Duns do not form a completely elaborated whole. Their author did not live long enough to work out what would in German parlance be called 'ein System', but several of his writings show the beginnings of a systematic presentation of his doctrine, and he writes from a fairly definite philosophic standpoint, which even if it is not absolutely coherent, suffices to give a well-marked structure to his thinking. The outline of his teaching is sketched in the *De Rerum Principio* [2] and the *De Primo*

---

[1] *La Storia della Filosofia del Cristianesimo*, vol. iii, p. 187.

[2] The authenticity of the *De Rerum Principio* has been impugned by Dr. Minges on the ground that the doctrine it contains differs markedly from that of the two commentaries on the Sentences. Cf. *Ist Scotus Indeterminist?* p. x; *Der Gottesbegriff des Duns Scotus*, etc., p. ix; *Das Verhältnis zwischen Glauben und Wissen bei Duns Scotus*, p. vi; *Doctrina philosophica et theologica Scoti, quoad res praecipuas exposita*, etc., vol. i, pp. 24 and 66. The question is discussed at length in Carreras, *Ensayo sobre el voluntarismo de J. Duns Scot*, Appendix I. Dr. Carreras summarizes the chief points in which the teaching of the *De Rerum Principio* differs from that of the *Opus Oxoniense*. M. Landry, who here follows Wadding, is inclined to regard this treatise as an early work, and to account for the discrepancies on the ground that it shows strong Augustinian influences, which might be expected in a pupil of the Oxford School. M. Belmond,

Principio. The former yields the nucleus for a larger treatise on rational cosmology, while the latter lays the foundation of a *philosophia prima* and a natural theology. But interesting as these writings undoubtedly are, they do not give us anything like a complete presentation of Scotus' thinking, and they are plainly only monographs preliminary to a greater work. The two commentaries on the Sentences have a far wider range, and are elaborated with great detail, but it may well be that they too were only intended as a preliminary to a greater work on the lines of the *Summa* of Aquinas.

Of Scotus' Commentaries on Aristotle little need here be said. They do not deal directly with the Aristotelian text, but are, as Werner has aptly remarked, rather ' an exposition and elucidation of the problems of the scholastic peripateticism of the period'. There is one more work which calls for attention, the *Quaestiones Quodlibetales*. These are a series of isolated discussions on certain theological and philosophical problems, which though they do not in any sense form a systematic treatise, yet contain important statements of many of the doctrines most characteristic of Scotus' teaching. They belong to the most mature period of his writings and form a very valuable supplement to the exposition of the two commentaries on the Sentences.

Duns Scotus rapidly became the official Doctor of the Franciscan Order in opposition to the Dominican theologian Thomas, and his doctrines were soon made obligatory in the Minorite schools by the express

in his article ' L'Univocité scotiste — ses fondements ' (*Revue de Philosophie*, 1913), is inclined to regard the work in question as the latest of all Scotus' writings, a hypothesis which Dr. Carreras also regards as possible. For a fuller discussion of this most difficult problem, which is too large to be treated adequately in a foot-note, see Appendix III at the end of this volume.

regulations of a general Chapter of the Order. Exactly at what date this occurred it is impossible to say, but according to Wadding it must have taken place shortly after his death, within the first half of the fourteenth century. The early date of this event may be conjectured from the fact that Duns is called Doctor Ordinis by William of Ockham ; and that Antonius Andreas, who died in the year 1321, prepared a compendium of Scotus' metaphysic and theology for use in the Franciscan schools. But as Werner points out, the actual establishment of a fixed and stable Scotist school of philosophy and theology cannot have taken place until a considerably later period. The more prominent teachers of the Order, like Petrus Aureolus and William of Ockham, though they bear marked traces of Scotus' influence, must claim to be regarded rather as fully independent thinkers than as disciples. The uniformity of an orthodox Scotism could only have been instituted within the Franciscan Order at a time when the works of the Subtle Doctor began to be the subject of commentaries, and these only begin to appear in any considerable number during the second half of the fifteenth century. From that time onwards for a period of more than two hundred years a strong Scotist school flourished among the adherents of the older philosophy (if indeed scholasticism can be said to have flourished at all after the Renaissance) and continued to produce works on Scotist principles right down to the middle of the eighteenth century. But the old scholasticism was by that time already long dead, and the scholastic revival of the nineteenth century passed Scotus by, and devoted itself solely to the exposition of the teaching of the Angelic Doctor. Only in very recent years has a marked revival of interest in his teaching become apparent.

Note.—To keep abreast of the literature of a subject is not altogether easy, and there is always a danger of being out of date before publication. This chapter was already irrevocably printed in page proof before several recent foreign publications fell into my hands, chief among which was Father Ephrem Longpré's book *La Philosophie du B. Duns Scot* (Paris, 1924), a volume composed of articles which first appeared in the *Études Franciscaines*, criticizing M. Landry's book *Duns Scot* (Paris 1922). Writing from the standpoint of the severest philosophical and theological orthodoxy, Fr. Longpré exposes the errors in Landry's careless and unscholarly essay with a wealth of erudition and a profound knowledge of Scotist literature of all periods which are truly admirable. He makes short work of Landry's preposterous charges against the Subtle Doctor, and successfully defends him from the exaggerated voluntarism, scepticism, and metaphysical anarchism with which that author has seen fit to accuse him. With many of Fr. Longpré's conclusions I am in substantial agreement, but I cannot follow him when he condemns the *De Rerum Principio* as spurious. To do so would alter considerably our conception of Scotus' position, and bring him more closely into line with the Aristotelianism of the Thomist School, thus missing what seems to me to be the vital interest and significance of his philosophy—namely, his reconstruction of the Augustinian tradition. (For a further discussion of this important question see Appendix III.)

There seems to be a tendency among Catholic writers both in France and in Germany to force Scotus more and more into agreement with the Angelic Doctor and thus to obliterate important differences between the two thinkers. For example Fr. Klug, in his article 'Die Immaterialität der Engel und Menschenseelen nach Duns Scotus' in *Franziskanische Studien*, 1916, attempts to show that Duns did not really teach the doctrine of the hylemorphic composition of souls. It is true that the immateriality of angels is expressly maintained in the XIIth book of the *Quaestiones in Metaphysicam*, but there is good reason to believe that the last two books of these *quaestiones* are spurious. (See Appendix III.) A view such as Fr. Klug's would scarcely seem to be consistent either with the main principles of Scotus' doctrine of form and matter, or the tradition of his Order. If the *De Rerum Principio* is assumed to be genuine Fr. Klug's case, of course, falls to the ground.

The authenticity of the *Grammatica Speculativa* has recently been attacked by Mgr. Grabmann in an article entitled 'Die Entwicklung der mittelalterlichen Sprachlogik' (*Phil. Jahrb.*, 1922) which brings very strong evidence to show that the author was not Scotus but Thomas of Erfurt.

II

FAITH AND REASON IN THE MIDDLE AGES

IT is a commonplace of philosophical criticism, that in order to understand the thought of any period it is necessary first of all to become acquainted with the assumptions and presuppositions which form, as it were, its psychological background. For in spite of its apparent independence, thinking is organic to life, and its form is everywhere determined by the needs, the purposes, and the aspirations of the age. No more striking illustration of this principle could be brought forward than the history of medieval philosophy. Throughout the whole period of the Middle Ages the form of speculation is determined at each stage of its development by its relation to the theological teaching of the Church, which maintains itself as a permanent and changeless background to the thought of Christendom. It is therefore of the utmost importance to form an adequate conception of the mutual inter-relation of theological and philosophical concepts, in order to grasp the significance of scholasticism as the highest and most characteristic expression of the medieval spirit.

Upon this critical question of the relative independence of these two *scientiae* two very divergent views have been taken by the historians of philosophy. Some, like Cousin,[1] would see in scholasticism nothing

---

[1] *Histoire générale de la philosophie* (Paris, 1864), p. 189. 'The Middle Ages mean simply the absolute reign of the Christian religion and the Church. Scholastic philosophy could not be anything else

but the enslavement of philosophic thought to the dominating conception of theological dogma. To them medieval philosophy is little else than a special branch of theology, namely apologetics. In the words of Tyrrell, it is 'the application of Aristotle to theology, or the expression of the facts and realities of revelation in the mind-language of the Peripatetics '.[1] Others agree with Professor De Wulf in maintaining the almost complete independence of philosophy as an untrammelled search after truth.[2] Neither of these views can be taken as adequate representations of the facts in their entirety. On the one hand, it must be conceded

than the product of thought in the service of the reigning credo, and under the supervision of ecclesiastical authority.' Trans. by P. Coffey of M. de Wulf's *Introduction à la philosophie Néo-Scolastique* (Scholasticism old and new), p. 53.

Cf. also Ueberweg-Heinze, *Geschichte der Philosophie*, p. 146 : ' Die Scholastik ist die Philosophie im Dienste der bereits bestehenden Kirchenlehre oder wenigstens in einer solchen Unterordnung unter dieselbe, das auf gemeinsamem Gebiete diese als die absolute Norm gilt.'

See also Freudenthal, ' Zur Beurtheilung der Scholastik ', *Archiv f. Geschichte der Philosophie*, vol. 3, p. 23 : ' Wie heftig der Streit über Wesen und Bedeutung der Scholastik auch geführt wird, eines war von Freund und Feind zugestanden : ihre vollständige Abhängigkeit von der Kirchenlehre.'

So also Windelband, *Geschichte der Philosophie*, p. 209 : ' Der Augustinismus concentrirt sich um den Begriff der Kirche : für ihn ist die Aufgabe der Philosophie in der Hauptsache darauf gerichtet, die Kirchenlehre als wissenschaftliches System darzustellen, zu begründen und auszubilden : insofern als sie diese Aufgabe verfolgt, ist die mittelalterliche Philosophie die kirchliche Schulwissenschaft, die Scholastik.'

So also Dewey, in his article on ' Scholasticism ' in Baldwin's *Dictionary of Philosophy and Psychology* : ' The name of the period of medieval thought, in which philosophy was pursued under the domination of theology, having for its aim the exposition of Christian dogma in its relation to reason.'

[1] ' The Use of Scholasticism ' in *The Faith of the Millions*, pp. 224-5.

[2] Cf. *Introduction à la philosophie Néo-Scolastique*, ch. 1, sect. 7 ; *Philosophy and Civilization in the Middle Ages*, ch. 7. See also Picavet, *La valeur de la scolastique*, pp. 224-6.

that the liberty of thought permitted within the pale of Catholic Christianity was far greater than has generally been supposed. Orthodoxies of course there were, to which rigid adherence was demanded, but it was just because of the immaturity of philosophical development during the earlier medieval period that theological definition was more fluid, for the need for more accurate and minute determinations had not yet arisen. Scholastic philosophy and scholastic theology evolved *pari passu*, and if theological controversies raised philosophical issues and determined philosophical speculation, it is no less true that philosophical methods and philosophical conceptions played an important part in moulding the destinies of scholastic theology. Without the influence of Arabian peripateticism the theology of Aquinas is as unthinkable as his philosophy. It was only long after the Reformation that the meticulous definition of dogma so characteristic of modern Catholic theologians reached its full development. At the height of its maturity medieval thought displayed a latitude which is truly surprising; the speculations of the twelfth and the thirteenth centuries contain a diversity which quite belies the notion of any orthodoxy rigorously imposed from without.

On the other hand it is undeniable that the dogmas of the Church exercised an influence which was paramount. But this influence was psychological rather than authoritative in the sense of external compulsion. Medieval thought was in fact limited in certain directions in spite of all its latitude, but it was almost wholly unaware of its own limitations. Whenever it came to a struggle between the philosopher and the theologian the dice were almost invariably loaded in favour of the latter, but neither of them was aware of the fact, and this was hardly surprising, for the philosopher no less than the theologian was secure in his belief of the doctrine which his philosophy appeared to contradict. Heretics there were, but they were astonishingly few, even before the age of the great persecutions ; infidels there were practically none. Moreover, until the thirteenth century practically the whole of the educated persons in Christendom were clerics ; lay philosophers up to the time of Dante were non-existent. All the great scholastics without exception were theologians as well as philosophers, and theology was socially the most important study of all the universities—arts, which included philosophy, being merely a necessary preliminary to the higher study. Freedom of thought in the modern sense was thus impossible, not so much because of the consequences it entailed in this world, as of those it was believed to entail in the next ; the captive mind was ignorant of its own fetters, and freedom would only have appeared in the guise of error. Thus in the last analysis theology always had the final word. It is the most fundamental of all the principles of human thinking, that reality cannot contradict itself, and that the revelation of the Church could be false was almost beyond the range of the medieval imagination. Even when the conflict became too glaring to be ignored any longer, the abandonment of theological verity was not even mooted.[1] Anything but that—even if we have to resort with John of Jandun to the desperate expedient of falling back on the Divine omnipotence— an expedient which clearly marks the beginning of the end, and which was stigmatized by its opponents as the theory of the double truth. But there is no necessity to doubt the sincerity even of John and the

[1] It is interesting in this connexion to quote a sentence from the constitution ' Dei Filius ' of the Vatican Council : ' Neque solum fides et ratio inter se dissidere nunquam possunt, sed opem sibi mutuum ferunt, cum recta ratio fidei fundamenta demonstret, ejusque lumine illustrata rerum divinarum scientiam excolat,' etc.

Latin Averroists : their solution to the problem is psychologically, if not logically, intelligible.[1]

Finally, it was in and through the Church herself that medieval thought rose to its greatness ; for it was the Church, and the Church alone, that preserved the precious relics of the Graeco-Roman civilization, and it was under her fostering care that the last pitiful remnants of a great inheritance were handed down generation after generation to peoples who, but for this fact, would have remained in a state of complete barbarism. So from the beginning philosophy and theology were inextricably confused, Greek metaphysic, Roman law, and Christian revelation each playing their part in determining the form of Catholic dogma. It was only at the beginning of the twelfth century that the two sciences definitely began to differentiate themselves within their common matrix, and even then it was impossible to keep them apart, until their final separation at the end of the Renaissance.

It is to Anselm of Canterbury (1033–1109), above all others, that we must look for the first definition of the relation between faith and reason. He has rightly been called the father of scholasticism, and may well be placed on a level with Hildebrand[2]

[1] Cf. Gilson, *Études de Philosophie Médiévale*, p. 65 : ' On peut penser ce que l'on veut de la valeur d'un tel expédient, mais il faut avouer que rien ne nous permettrait de mettre en doute la sincérité de Jean de Jandun si nous n'avions d'autre raison de le faire que la médiocrité du procédé de conciliation dont il use entre la philosophie et la théologie. Il n'y a pas de limite assignable *a priori* a la crédulité humaine en matière de sophismes justificatifs.'

M. Gilson is, however, inclined to regard the acknowledgement of the claims of faith made by John as ironical rather than naïve (ibid., p. 68). Yet it is not impossible to suppose that he was not consciously dishonest.

[2] Cf. De Wulf, *History of Mediaeval Philosophy*, sect. 149 : ' He reminds us of Gregory VII, who in the religious and political orders achieved such a wonderful organization of the Church and adjustment

on account of his influence in determining the subsequent course of Christian speculation. Anselm's standpoint may briefly be summarized in his own famous dictum, ' Credo ut intelligam '.[1] This might at first sight appear a curious reversal of the normal procedure of the modern mind, but in fact it marks a great advance on the more rigorously anti-rational attitude which prevailed during the Dark Ages. Philosophy and theology, it is true, are not yet separate sciences, and their union is in many ways an advantage to both of them. For Anselm as for Peter Damian reason is still the handmaid of faith,[2] but the character of theology has itself been transformed by the interpenetration of philosophical conceptions and a more coherent working out of fundamental philosophical ideas.[3] Theology begins for the first time to be

of its relation to the state : he is the Gregory VII of knowledge.' Cf. also Grabmann, *Die Geschichte der Scholastischen Methode*, vol. I, p. 261 : ' Wie Gregor VII die Kirche aus der das kirchliche Leben erstickenden Umarmung des Staates zu befreien und namentlich den Klerus zu sittlicher Freiheit und Reinheit zu erheben strebte, so hat auch Anselm die Wissenschaft aus den beengenden Bänden formalistischer Dialektik und kompilatorischer Väternachbeterei befreit ; Wie Gregor VII auf religiösem und kirchenpolitischem Gebiete die kirchliche Organisation befestigt und die Beziehungen zwischen Staat und Kirche geregelt hat, so hat auch Anselm auf wissenschaftlichem Gebiete organisatorisch gewirkt, die Beziehungen zwischen Glauben und Wissen scharf formuliert und die hierüber von ihm gewonnenen Grundsätze konsequent durchgeführt.'

[1] *Proslogium*, cap. I.

[2] Cf. Peter Damian, *De Divina Omnipotentia*, cap. 5 (Migne, *Patrol. Lat.*, vol. 145, col. 603) : ' Quae tamen artis humanae peritia, si quando tractandis sacris eloquiis adhibetur, non debet jus magisterii sibimet arroganter arripere, sed velut ancilla dominae quodam famulatus obsequio subservire, ne, si praecedit, oberret, et dum exteriorum verborum sequitur consequentias, intimae virtutis lumen et rectum veritatis tramitem perdat.'

[3] Cf. Funke, *Satisfaktionslehre des hl. Anselm*, p. 87 f. : ' Zunächst im Besitze einer auf das genauste fixierten Fragestellung, verfügt er bei seinen tieferen und korrekteren Ideen, über ein ganz anderes Begriffsmaterial zur Aufführung seines Lehrgebäudes, als seine

systematic,[1] and acquires a new spirit, which it
retains, in spite of the efforts of the more reactionary
theologians, throughout the whole medieval period.
A new era of Christian thought has set in.

The starting-point of Anselm is clear. The human
mind must set out from faith in order to arrive at
understanding; it cannot proceed in the reverse
direction.[2] The function of reason is to attempt to
understand, as much as it may, the mysteries revealed
by the teaching of the Church,[3] in the Sacred
Scriptures and the writings of the fathers. Should
a conflict between faith and reason arise, the latter
must give way,[4] for the mysteries of the faith in the

Vorgänger . . . Daher bei ihm die Untersuchungen über die aus-
drücklich aufgeworfenen Fragen, nach den Begriffen der Freiheit,
Notwendigkeit, Sünde, Ehre Gottes, Genugthuung, u.s.w., wie wir
sie in der ganzen Patristik vor ihm nirgendwo finden,' etc.

[1] Cf. Picavet, *Esquisse d'une Histoire comparée des Philosophies
médiévales*, p. 186: ' Ses œuvres, analysées et rapprochées, offrent
un système théologico-métaphysique, d'unité et d'une liaison in-
contestables.'

Cf. also Harnack, *Dogmengeschichte*, 4th ed. 1905, p. 330: 'Systemati-
ker von besonderer Energie, ja als den Begründer der mittelalterlichen
Systematik, trotz der noch bestehenden Dürftigkeit des philosophischen Stoffes,' etc.

[2] Cf. Ep. II. 41 (' Ad Falconem '): ' Christianus per fidem debet
ad intellectum proficere, non per intellectum ad fidem accedere, aut
si intelligere non valet, a fide recedere; sed cum ad intellectum valet
pertingere, delectatur, cum vero nequit, quod capere non valet
veneratur.'

[3] Cf. *Proslogium*, cap. 1: ' Non tento, Domine, penetrare altitu-
dinem tuam; quia nullatenus comparo illi intellectum meum, sed
desidero aliquatenus intelligere veritatem tuam, quam credit et amat
cor meum. Neque enim quaero intelligere ut credam; sed credo
ut intelligam. Nam et hoc credo, quia nisi credidero non intelligam.'

[4] Cf. *Cur Deus Homo*, Lib. I, cap. 18: ' Certus enim sum, si quid
dico quod Sacrae Scripturae sine dubio contradicat, quia falsum est;
nec illud tenere volo, si cognovero.' Cf. also *De Concord.*, q. iii, c. 6:
' Nam, si quid ratione dicamus aliquando, quod in dictis ejus (sc.
Sacrae Scripturae) aperte monstrare aut ex ipsis probare nequimus,
hoc modo per illam cognoscimus utrum sit accipiendum aut respuen-
dum. Si enim aperta ratione colligitur et illa ex nulla parte contradicit;

fullness of their profundity are inaccessible to the
human mind.[1] Faith is thus everywhere presupposed,
and theology lays down the norms and limits of
philosophical speculation. But within its restricted
sphere reason exercises an important threefold function, its business being to attain to a rational understanding of the truths of the faith, to co-ordinate the
various provinces of particular dogmas, and to solve
the problems raised by the difficulties of the revelation
and to defend it against the objections of those outside
the Christian fold.[2]

This conception of Anselm is noteworthy because
it forms a well-marked stage in the development of
the two branches of speculation. Philosophy is still
inextricably bound up with theology,[3] but reason has
begun to assert her independent claims. Not only has
it sought to establish a proof of a strictly philosophical
nature for the existence of God, in the celebrated
ontological argument, but also to explore once more
the hidden mysteries of the faith, the doctrine of the
Trinity, the Incarnation, and so forth. It is true that
these philosophical *rationes necessariae* [4] propounded

. . . nulli favet falsitati : . . . At, si ipsa nostro sensui indubitanter
repugnat ; quamvis ratio nostra videatur inexpugnabilis, nulla tamen
veritati fulciri credenda est. Sic itaque Sacra Scriptura omnis
veritatis, quam collegit, auctoritatem continet, cum illam aut aperte
affirmat aut nullatenus negat.'

[1] Cf. *De Trinitatis et Incarnatione Verbi praefatio* : ' Veritatis ratio
tam ampla tamque profunda est, ut a mortalibus nequeat exhauriri.'

[2] Cf. Grabmann, op. cit., i, p. 272.

[3] Cf. Gilson, *Études de Philosophie Médiévale*, p. 17 : ' La foi
cherchera donc toujours l'intelligence. Mais il est également vrai que
l'intelligence n'a pas d'autre objet à poursuivre que celui de la foi.
Et c'est ce que S. Anselme ne manque pas de nous rappeler au début
de ceux de ses ouvrages qui nous sembleraient contenir le plus de
philosophie, au sens moderne du mot. Dans la mesure où la philosophie
correspond pour nous à une recherche qui part de prémisses rationelles
pour aboutir à des prémisses rationelles, on peut dire que S. Anselm n'a
pas écrit un seul ouvrage de philosophie.'

[4] Cf. *Monolog.*, cap. 64 : ' Quapropter si ea, quae de summa

by Anselm do not amount to logical demonstration [1]—
such a possibility was quite foreign also to the mind of
Thomas—but they do represent an attempt to carry
over into the sphere of the supernatural analogies
from the world of reason.[2]　Moreover, the connexion
between philosophy and theology had become a vital
problem owing to the logical development of the
theory of universals by Roscelinus, whose so-called
'Nominalism' had landed its author into a virtual
denial of the unity of the Holy Trinity, which called
forth Anselm's denunciation of this apparent tritheism.[3]
The attack had come from the side of logic ; it was
therefore essential to the preservation of the unity of
the truth that logic should be met with logic, and
Anselm was not slow to take up the challenge.　He
came forward as the champion of orthodoxy and the

essentia hactenus disputata sunt, necessariis rationibus sunt asserta,
quamvis sic intellectu penetrari non possint, ut et verbis valeant
explicari ; nullatenus tamen certitudinis eorum nutat soliditas.'
Cf. also *Cur Deus Homo*, Lib. I, cap. 25 : ' Ita volo me perducas
illuc, ut rationabili necessitate intelligam esse oportere omnia illa,
quae nobis fides Catholica de Christo credere praecepit, si volumus
salvari.'

[1] Cf. Saenz D'Aguirre, *Theologia S. Anselmi*, ii. 17, Disp. 51,
sect. 5 : ' Supponit fidem Trinitatis in iis, quos erudiendos accipit
in hoc opusculo (sc. Monologio) et deinde accedit ad excogitandum
varias rationes quibus utcumque suadeat seu ostendat non abhorrere
a vero, quidquid de Trinitate credimus, paretque viam seu modum ad
occurrendum argumentis infidelium seu hereticorum contra dis-
putantium.'

[2] Cf. Franzelin, *De Deo Trino*, p. 321, who remarks in connexion
with Anselm's *rationes necessariae* demonstrating the doctrine of the
Trinity : ' At haec non est demonstratio Trinitatis ex solo lumine
rationis, sed est theologica deductio ex veritate revelata ejusdemque
veritatis analogica aliqua paulo distinctior intellectio ex analogia
spiritus creati.'

[3] Cf. Ep. II, 41 (' Ad Falconem ') : ' Audio (quod tamen absque
dubietate credere non possum) quia Roscelinus clericus dicit in Deo
tres personas esse tres res ab invicem separatas, sicut sunt tres angeli,
ita tamen ut una sit voluntas et potestas : aut Patrem et Spiritum
Sanctum esse incarnatum, et tres deos vere posse dici si usus admitteret.'

defender of realism. The controversy is important because it shows the almost insuperable difficulty of keeping philosophical and theological truth separate, a difficulty which, as we shall see, continues throughout the history of medieval thought. The official triumph of realism was of course inevitable. Roscelin was summoned before a council at Soissons in the year 1093, and forced to recant. No dialectic, however persuasive, could be tolerated, which imperilled the doctrine of the Church—though indeed from Anselm's account of the matter the dialectic of Roscelin was as one-sided as that of his opponents—but the point to notice is that whenever a conflict arose between faith and reason, the result was a foregone conclusion ; the freedom of thought was limited not so much by an external authority—official interference being almost wholly confined to purely theological questions —as by the psychological convictions of the unanimous consensus of Christendom, which was impervious to any argument, however cogent, and totally unaware of any inconsistency in its attitude.

The same inability to draw a defining line between philosophy and theology manifests itself in the later controversy in which Abelard (1079–1142) played so prominent a part. Redoubtable defender of the dialectic method as he was, it would be a mistake to regard him as a rationalist in the modern sense of the word.[1] He attempted to steer a middle course between the extreme dialecticians and the ultra-conservative party, of which Bernard of Clairvaux was the leader.[2] But his personal prominence as a teacher, and the uncompromising aggressiveness of his polemic, singled him out as the object for the violent attack of the extremist theologians, by whom he was assailed with the most unbridled invective. His standpoint is still

[1] Cf. Gilson, op. cit., pp. 23–6.
[2] Cf. Grabmann, op. cit., vol. ii, pp. 177 sqq.

in the main essentials that of Anselm, though the emphasis he lays on the dialectic exploration of the mysteries of the faith is far greater, and the range of his interpretation far wider. Moreover, the extreme boldness of his interpretations and the originality of his opinions gave some grounds for the alarm of the orthodox party.[1] Indeed it is difficult to discover in his works any clear conception of the relation between faith and reason, and the charge of rationalism brought forward by Bernard[2] and William of St. Thierry[3] was not altogether without foundation.[4] Finally, his constant attempts to assimilate the pagan philosophy with Catholic theology, and to see in the teachings of the heathen anticipations of doctrines such as that of the Holy Trinity,[5] seemed to derogate

[1] For a list of Abelard's ' errors ', see the ' Capitula Abaelardi a Concilio Senonensi et ab Innocentio II damnata ' in D'Argentré, *Collectio judiciorum de novis erroribus*, etc., i, Paris, 1728, 21–4 ; see also Article ' Abélard ', in the *Dictionnaire de Théologie Catholique*, by E. Portalié, i. 43–8.

[2] Cf. Epp. cxc and cxciv (' Tract. de error. Ab.'), Migne, *P.L.*, vol. 182, col. 1055.

[3] Cf. ' Disputatio adv. Petrum Abaelardum ' (Migne, *P.L.*, vol. 180, cols. 249–82).

[4] Cf. De Regnon, *Études de la Théologie positive sur la Sainte Trinité*, ii. 31 : ' Cette accusation de Guillaume est fausse, si elle vise les dispositions personnelles d'Abélard ; mais elle porte juste, si elle s'applique a son œuvre, où règne une véritable confusion entre la foi et la conviction rationelle.'

[5] Cf. *Theologia Christiana*, Lib. II, 361, where, speaking of the distinction of the three persons in the Godhead, he says : ' Quam quidem divina inspiratio et per prophetas Judaeis et per philosophos gentilibus dignata est revelare.' Cf. also ibid. : '. . . Reperiemus ipsorum (*sc.* philosophorum) tam vitam quam doctrinam maxime evangelicam seu apostolicam perfectionem exprimere, et a religione Christiana eos nihil aut parum recedere, quod nobis tam rationibus morum quam nomine ipso juncti reperiuntur ; . . . quibus, ut diximus, et fides Trinitatis revelata est, et ab ipsis praedicata, et spes immortalis animae, et aeternae retributionis expectata. . . . Hinc quidem facilius evangelica praedicatio a philosophis quam a Judaeis suscepta est, cum sibi eam maxime invenirent adfinem.' An interesting example

from the peculiar and unique salutariness of the
Christian revelation. But in spite of all these rational-
izing tendencies, in spite of an independence of judgement, which renders him unique in medieval thought,
Abelard still remains firmly rooted to the 'Credo ut
intelligam' of Anselm. 'I would not', he writes to
Héloïse, 'so be a philosopher as to rebel against
Paul; nor so be an Aristotle, as to be cut off from
Christ.' [1] Not one whit less than Anselm does he
recognize the insufficiency of reason to penetrate the
mysteries of the Faith, and the analogical or meta-
phorical character of all attempts to explain such
doctrines as the Incarnation and the Trinity, and so
forth. [2]

of the kind of way in which Abelard saw Christian dogma prefigured
in the pagans is his identification of Plato's World Soul with the
Holy Ghost. Cf. op. cit., II, 379 : 'Nunc autem illa Platonis verba
de anima mundi diligentur discutiamus, ut in eis Spiritum Sanctum
integerrime designatum esse agnoscamus.' We can well understand
Bernard's taunt, that in his anxiety to show Plato as a Christian,
Abelard only shows himself a heathen, *Tr. de erroribus Abelardi*, c. iv.
It must be mentioned, however, that Abelard afterwards repudiated
this identification.

[1] Cf. Ep. 17, 'ad Heloissam' : 'Nolo sic esse philosophus, ut
recalcitrem Paulo ; nolo sic esse Aristoteles, ut secludar a Christo,
non enim aliud nomen est sub coelo, in quo oporteat me salvum
fieri . . . super illam petram fundavi conscientiam meam, super quam
Christus aedificavit ecclesiam suam . . . Haec itaque est fides in qua
sedeo, ex qua spei contraho firmitatem.'

[2] Cf. op. cit., where, in speaking of the generation of the Son and
the procession of the Holy Ghost, he says : 'De quo veritatem non
promittimus, ad quam neque nos neque mortalium aliquem sufficere
credimus ; sed saltem aliquid verisimile atque humanae rationi
vicinum nec sacrae fidei contrarium libet proponere adversus eos,
qui humanis rationibus fidem se impugnare gloriantur nec nisi humanas
curant rationes,' etc. Cf. also *Theol. Christ.*, Lib. III : 'Ex his itaque
liquidum est, quantae subtilitatis sit divina substantia atque animae
a natura corporum disjuncta et a vigore nostrorum sensuum penitus
semota. De qua si quid forte philosophi dicere animati sunt, ad
similitudines et exempla se contulerunt' (p. 1242). Cf. ibid., p. 1226 :
Credi itaque salubriter debet quod explicari non valet, praesertim

Yet in certain important respects Abelard marks a great advance. Not only does he display far greater independence and far more critical ability than his predecessors ; his grasp of philosophic principle is much deeper and more penetrating. Although theology and philosophy have not yet become separate sciences, in the thoroughgoing application of dialectics to theological problems we see an extension of the field of reasoning. The character of the dialectic itself is undergoing a transformation, and the logic of the schools gradually expands until it embraces the whole domain of philosophical problems. And if the starting-point of this development is to be sought in Anselm, it is from Abelard that the great movement of expansion which marks twelfth-century thought derives one of its most vital impulses. For not only did the great controversy which culminated in apparent failure at the council of Sens act as a stimulus to intellectual activity, in spite of the official triumph of reaction, but the compendium of the *Sic et non* left a permanent impression on the theological teaching of Christendom, and laid the foundation of the

cum nec pro magno habendum sit, quod humana infirmitas disserere sufficit, nec pro fide reputandum, quod de manifestis recipimus humana compulsi ratione ; nec apud Deum meritum habent, in quo non Deo creditur qui in sanctis loquitur, sed ratiunculis humanis, quae frequenter falluntur et vix deprehendi possunt quando sunt rationes.' It is interesting also to compare his attack on the extremists of the dialectical movement, whom he assails in very much the same terms as those in which Bernard attacked him: e. g. in Ep. 13, he says of them : ' Quidquid non intelligunt, stultitiam dicunt; quidquid non capiunt deliramentum. Quos quidem rationis expertes quia rationibus refellere non valemus ; testimoniis saltem Scripturarum . . . eorum praesumptionem compescamus.' So also in his treatise, *De Unitate et Trinitate Divina*, ed. Stölzle, p. 20 : ' Supra Judaeos sive Gentiles subtilius fidem trinitatis perquirunt et acutius arguendo contendunt professores dialecticae seu importunitas sophistarum, quos verborum agmine . . . beatos esse Plato irridendo judicat. Hi argumentorum exercitio confisi, quid murmurent, scimus . . . hi, inquam, non utentes arte sed abutentes,' etc.

scholastic method. For the contraposition of conflicting authorities so skilfully accomplished, showed
the necessity of a dialectical reconstruction of the
theological tradition by the use of philosophical conceptions, thus contributing materially to the progress
of both sciences. Abelard may therefore be regarded
as the precursor of the method of the Sentences,
which remained for centuries the standard text-book
of medieval theology. And though he taught before
the full influence of the new logic and the Arabian
commentaries had fully enlarged the sphere of dialectic activity and separated finally the domains of
reason and revelation, he may be classed as one of the
great rationalist theologians, inasmuch as he prepared
the way for the freer and more critical spirit of the
thirteenth century.

Meanwhile, Abelard's contemporary Hugo of St. Victor
(1096–1141) was elaborating a conception of knowledge
and of the articulation of its branches which was to
exercise a dominating influence on the scholasticism
of the twelfth and early thirteenth centuries. In his
Didascalion he lays down a scheme demarcating the
various departments of learning with their mutual
connexion, and in the *De Sacramentis Christianae
fidei* propounds a definition of the relationship of
faith to knowledge which was destined to form one
of the characteristic features of scholastic thought.[1]
Hugo's scheme is as follows : he divides knowledge
into two main divisions, sacred and profane, the
sciences comprising the latter being regarded as
ancillary and propaedeutic to the former, an arrangement on which the whole curriculum of the medieval
university was founded. The profane sciences fall
into four main divisions : *Theorica, Practica, Mechanica,*
and *Logica,*[2] each of which in its turn is also sub-

---

[1] Cf. Grabmann, op. cit., ii, pp. 264 sqq.
[2] *Didascalion*, Lib. II, cap. 2. Migne, *P.L.*, vol. 176, col. 745.

divided. *Theorica*, or *speculativa*, has three subdivisions, *Theologia* (in the Aristotelian sense of the term, i. e. what he calls elsewhere *Theologia mundana*, natural theology, as opposed to *Theologia divina* or revealed theology), *Mathematica*, and *Physica*.[1] *Practica* includes *Ethica*, *Economica*, and *Politica* ;[2] *Mechanica*, the seven *Artes Adulterinae*.[3] *Logica* has as its object the *genera* and *species*, its purpose being to inculcate the *scientia recte loquendi et acute disputandi* ;[4] it is divided into *Grammatica* and *Ratio disserendi*, the latter being again subdivided into three divisions, demonstration or strict proof, probable argumentation, and sophistic.[5] This classification is important, not only because it expresses the theory underlying the *trivium* and *quadrivium*, but also because of the influence it exercised on the thought of some of the greatest of the scholastics. We find almost the same scheme, for instance, in so late a writer as Robert Kilwardby[6] (*d.* 1278). Moreover, it contains two features worthy of notice. Logic is no longer the centre of philosophical activity, it is not one of the speculative sciences proper, and is beginning to assume a place of secondary importance, though it is an essential prerequisite to the pursuit of truth. The distinction between metaphysic and theology is also beginning to make its appearance ; we find it still more explicitly

---

[1] *Didascalion*, II, cap. 19. Migne, *P.L.*, vol. 176, col. 759.

[2] Ibid., cap. 20. Migne, loc. cit.

[3] Ibid., capp. 21–8. Migne, loc. cit., cols. 760–3.

[4] Ibid., cap. 29. Migne, loc. cit., col. 763.

[5] Ibid., cap. 31. Migne, loc. cit., col. 764.

[6] Kilwardby's classification follows that of Hugo fairly closely. He divides philosophy into two main divisions : i, *scientia rerum divinarum*, which is subdivided into *Metaphysica*, *Mathematica*, and *Naturalis* ; and ii, *philosophia rerum humanarum*, which consists of (1) *Practica*, and (2) *Logica*, the former being again subdivided into *Ethica* (*solitaria privata, publica*) and the *artes mechanicae*. See Baur, *Dominicus Gundissalinus, de Divisione Philosophiae*, p. 362, n. 2.

stated in the preface to the commentary on the
Hierarchia coelestis, where *Theologia mundana* is contrasted with *Theologia divina*. The former deals only
with the *opera conditionis*, the creatures and their
elements, the latter is of a more exalted character and
is concerned with the *opera restaurationis*, the work of
supernatural redemption.[1]

In the *De Sacramentis* Hugo defines the faith and
its relation to knowledge. Faith is a kind of certainty
concerning things not present, which is more than
opinion but less than knowledge. For when we hear
a statement there are three attitudes which we can
adopt towards it ; we may deny it outright, adopt it
as a possible hypothesis, or believe it. All these three
states are contrasted with the actual knowledge of
a thing really present. Belief, then, is nearer knowledge than opinion because it excludes doubt, but
cognitively speaking it is less than knowledge, though,
Hugo hastens to add, it is more meritorious.[2] Faith,

---

[1] ' Sed mundana . . . theologia opera conditionis assumpsit et
elementa hujus mundi secundum speciem creata, ut demonstrationem
suam faceret illis. Theologia vero divina opera restaurationis eligit
secundum humanitatem Jesu et sacramenta ejus, quae ab initio sunt,
naturalibus quoque pro modo subjunctis, ut in illis eruditionem
conformaret. Major autem . . . declaratio divinitatis in sacramentis
gratiae et carne Verbi et mystica operatione ipsius ostenditur quam
naturali rerum specie praedicetur ' (Migne, *P.L.*, vol. 176, col. 926 f.).

[2] *De Sacramentis Christianae fidei*, Lib. I, pars. x, cap. 2. Migne,
P.L., vol. 176, cols. 330–1 : ' Si quis plenam ac generalem diffini-
tionem fidei signare voluerit, dicere potest fidem esse certitudinem
quandam animi de rebus absentibus supra opinionem et infra scientiam
constitutam. Sunt enim quidam, qui audita statim animo repellunt
. . . et hi sunt negantes. Alii in iis quae audiunt alteram quamcumque
partem eligunt ad aestimationem, sed non approbant ad affirma-
tionem . . . hi sunt opinantes. Alii sic alteram partem approbant, ut
ejus approbationem etiam in assertionem assumant : hi sunt credentes.
Post ista genera cognitionis illud perfectius sequitur, cum res non
ex auditu solo, sed per suam praesentiam notificatur. . . . Ex his ergo
conici potest, quare fidem certitudinem appellamus, quoniam, ubi
adhuc dubitatio est, fides non est. . . . Quia nimirum aliquid credere

then, has two aspects, one cognitive and the other
affective ; the affective is the substance, the cognitive
the matter.　Both are necessary ; for to believe, we
must believe something, i. e. our belief must have
some intellectual content, while the actual believing is
a matter pertaining to the affective side of our nature,
that is, the will.[1]

This definition of Hugo is of the greatest importance
in scholastic thought.　We find it not only in Richard
of St. Victor,[2] John of Salisbury,[3] and Alanus de
Insulis,[4] but also in St. Thomas himself, where it
occurs in three different passages,[5] in one of which
he characteristically gives it an intellectualistic interpretation by placing the superiority of faith over
opinion in the fact that it is *argumentum*.[6]　In fact

sicut minus est quam scire, sic plus est quam opinari. . . . Minus,
dico, non quantum ad meritum, sed quantum ad cognitionem.'

[1] loc. cit., cap. 3: 'Duo sunt in quibus fides constat: cognitio
et affectus. . . . In affectu enim substantia fidei invenitur ; in cognitione materia.　Aliud enim est fides qua creditur ; et aliud quod
fide creditur.　In affectu invenitur fides ; in cognitione id quod
fide creditur.　Propterea fides in affectu habet substantiam, quia
affectus ipse fides est.　Credere igitur in affectu est, quod vero creditur
in cognitione est. . . . Potest autem cognitio . . . sine omni fide esse ;
fides autem sine omni cognitione esse non potest. . . .'　Cf. Dionysius
Carthusianus' interpretation of this doctrine, *In Sentt. III*, dist. xxiii,
q. 2 : 'Tertia opinio magistri Hugonis . . . dicentis, quod fides quodam
modo est in intellectu, quodam modo in affectu.　Duo sunt enim,
in quibus fides consistit, cognitio atque affectatio : in affectu substantia fidei reperitur, in cognitione materia.　Ratio hujus positionis
est, quoniam actus voluntatis essentialis est fidei.　Nunquam enim
virtuosum est credere, nisi sit voluntarium,' etc.

[2] Cf. 'Declarationes nonnullarum difficultatum Scripturae',
Migne, *P.L.*, vol. 196, col. 226.

[3] *Metalogicus*, Lib. IV, cap. 13.　Migne, vol. 199, col. 924.

[4] Cf. Baumgartner, *Die Philosophie des Alanus de Insulis*, p. 34.

[5] Cf. *Summa Theol.*, 2a, 2ae, q. 4, art. 1 ; 1a, 2ae, q. 67, art. 3 ;
De Veritate, q. xiv, art. 2.

[6] *De Veritate*, loc. cit.: 'Dicitur enim infra scientiam, quia non
habet visionem sicut scientia, quamvis ita firmam adhaesionem.
Supra opinionem tamen dicitur propter firmitatem assensus ; et sic

this formula becomes stereotyped in the thirteenth century, and is cited by nearly all the great doctors, for example, Alexander of Hales,[1] Albertus Magnus,[2] Godfrey of Fontaines,[3] and so forth, who interpret it intellectualistically or voluntaristically according to the nature of their own views.[4] But more especially is its influence apparent in the Franciscan ' school ', which clung more closely to the older tradition than the Dominican, and was less affected by the influx of Greek intellectualism which began to make itself felt so strongly at the beginning of the thirteenth century. It is to Hugo and Richard of St. Victor that we must trace the emphasis laid on the affective character of theology by Alexander of Hales and Bonaventura, a tradition which is to appear once more in the Scotist conception of theology as a practical science.

The relation between knowledge and belief, between reason and faith, is worked out more fully at the end of the third part of the first book, where under the title *De Cognitione Divinitatis* Hugo deals with the doctrine of the Holy Trinity. He distinguishes between four kinds of propositions : those which are demonstrable by reason, or necessary, *ex ratione* ; those which are in accordance with reason, or probable, *secundum rationem* ; those which are above reason, or miraculous, *mirabilia* ; and those which are contrary to reason, or incredible. The first and the last class are alike incapable of being the object of faith ; only the two middle classes are possible contents of belief. In the case of probable truths, *secundum rationem,* reason and belief support each other, belief being sustained by rational grounds, and these grounds being

---

infra scientiam dicitur, inquantum est non apparentium ; supra opinionem, inquantum est argumentum.'

[1] *Summa Theol.*, I, q. I, memb. I ad 4.
[2] Ibid., I, tract. I, q. I.   [3] *Quodlibet.*, iv, q. x.
[4] Cf. Grabmann, op. cit., ii, p. 269.

perfected or supplemented by belief. Even if reason cannot comprehend their truth, it at any rate does not contradict it. But in the case of the supra-rational, faith can accept no assistance from reason, for reason is incapable of comprehending the content of faith; yet in a sense reason can bring some aid, for it can admonish us to venerate the faith.[1]

We can see here a very definite attempt to delimit the provinces of faith and reason, and to attain to a harmonious allocation of their respective territories. Theology and philosophy are not yet independent sciences, but their differentiation is beginning. *Theologia mundana*, if it does not correspond exactly to the metaphysic of the later scholastics, contains at least as much metaphysic as it does theology, indeed it is a somewhat strange mixture of the two, for Hugo assigns the doctrine of the Holy Trinity to the domain of the *opera conditionis,* and not that of the *opera restaurationis*, and it would seem that he would almost regard it as belonging to the province of natural theology.[2] But it would be a mistake, as Grabmann

---

[1] Cf. *De Sacramentis*, etc., Lib. I, pars. tertia, cap. 2. Migne, *P.L.*, v. 176, col. 231–2 : ' Alia enim sunt ex ratione, alia secundum rationem, alia supra rationem : et praeter haec quae sunt contra rationem. Ex ratione sunt necessaria, secundum rationem sunt probabilia, supra rationem mirabilia, contra rationem incredibilia. Et duo quidem extrema fidem non capiunt. Quae enim sunt ex ratione, omnino nota sunt et credi non possunt, quia sciuntur. Quae vero contra rationem sunt, nulla similiter ratione credi possunt, quoniam non suscipiunt ullam rationem, nec acquiescit his aliquando ratio. Ergo quae secundum rationem sunt et quae sunt supra rationem, tantummodo suscipiunt fidem. Et in primo quidem genere fides ratione adjuvatur et ratio fide perficitur, quoniam secundum rationem sunt quae creduntur. Quorum veritatem si ratio non comprehendit, fidei tamen illorum non contradicit. In iis quae supra rationem sunt, non adjuvatur fides ratione ulla ; quoniam non capit ea ratio, quae fides credit, et tamen est aliquid, quo ratio admonetur venerari fidem, quam non comprehendit.'

[2] Cf. Th. Heitz, *Essai Historique sur les Rapports entre la Philosophie et la Foi*, 79 ff. : ' La trinité est donc du ressort de la théologie

points out,[1] to interpret this view in a rationalistic sense ; the boundary line between the natural and the supernatural has not yet been drawn with the precision which was given to it by Aquinas. For the main trend of Hugo's teaching is mystical, and his account of the three stages of knowledge, *cogitatio*, *meditatio*, and *contemplatio*, with its strongly marked Augustinianism, makes it impossible to draw a hard and fast line between the rational and the super-rational. The same indefiniteness is characteristic of the older scholasticism throughout, with its ontologistic theory of knowledge, and is met with again in Alexander of Hales, Bonaventura, and Matthew of Aquasparta. But it is important to note the explicit statement of the fundamental principle which determines the relation between scholastic theology and scholastic philosophy, namely, the notion that the truths of revelation and the truths of natural reason cannot contradict one another, a principle asserted no less strongly by Thomas and by Scotus. We have advanced far beyond the *credo quia impossibile*, which was characteristic of an earlier age. It is no longer the fact of the self-contradictoriness of its content which constitutes the merit of faith ; the blind adherence to a form of words unintelligible and therefore holy ; an attitude which was not unknown in the Dark Ages between the Greek Fathers and the Latin scholastics. Theology has been impregnated with philosophical conceptions and reconstructed by dialectical notions ; its mysteries remain inexplicable and unfathomable by the human reason, but the old antagonism, the product of the struggle with Paganism, has almost died. Yet at the same time the whole

naturelle : la Trinité se rapporte à la nature de Dieu, objet de la théologie naturelle, aussi n'en est-il point question dans l'énumeration de l'objet de la Théologie et de l'écriture.'

[1] Cf. op. cit., p. 281.

process of rationalization has been modified. The conviction that an ultimate conflict between faith and reason is impossible constitutes the differentia of scholastic thought and distinguishes it from that of the Renaissance and the succeeding ages, everywhere setting bounds to it beyond which it may not pass. And it is this fact that has made the Middle Ages seem in the eyes of many critics an age of bondage and slavery to the dogmatic authority of the Church. But it must always be remembered that this authority was no external despotism exercised from without, and superimposed upon an already existing philosophical system. Whenever it intruded itself into the controversies of a purely philosophical nature, and the instances of this are far more rare than is generally supposed, it was as the guardian of a truth universally acknowledged and accepted. That there was any limitation of knowledge involved in this process was an idea which scarcely entered the medieval mind. But it was this very fact, that the unity of truth could only accommodate one system, which rendered a divorce between philosophy and theology finally inevitable ; their spheres included so much common ground that neither could in the end recognize the supremacy of the other.

But for the scholasticism of the twelfth and early thirteenth centuries no such problem existed. The proper spheres of theology and philosophy had yet to be delimited. The Augustinian theory of knowledge which characterized the speculation of this period, in spite of the tentative classification introduced by the Victorine school, was unable to distinguish clearly between natural and supernatural knowledge : it was pervaded by a mystical spirit which postulated the assistance of the 'uncreated light' in all and every act of knowing.[1] For it is only by

[1] Cf. the following citation from Bonaventura, which brings out

knowing the created essence in the light of the divine exemplars that the fullness of truth can be attained.[1] A differentiation between the provinces of natural reason and supernatural illumination was only rendered possible by the substitution of the Aristotelian epistemology for the Platonizing theory of Augustine, and it was only first in the Alberto-Thomistic philosophy that this was definitely accomplished. The separation of theology from philosophy was completed by the influence of Arabian peripateticism on the thought of the Latin West. The rediscovery of the greater portion of the Aristotelian canon, the Prior and Posterior Analytics, the *Physics*, *Metaphysics*, and the *De Anima*, broadened the whole field of philosophic speculation to such an extent that it was no longer possible to regard philosophy as merely a preliminary discipline or methodological introduction to theology. For in the completed *corpus* medieval thought for the first time came in contact with a philosophic system, finished and self-contained, a system which

---

the older point of view very clearly : ' Lux ergo intellectus creati sibi non sufficit ad certam comprehensionem rei cujuscumque absque luce Verbi aeterni ' (*Sermo, Anecdota*, p. 77).

[1] Cf. *De Cogn. Hum., Anecd.*, pp. 61 et 69 : ' Item, si quidquid cognoscitur, cognoscitur rationibus aeternis, aut ergo velate, aut sine velamine. Si velate ergo nihil clare cognoscitur. Si sine velamine, ergo omnes vident Deum et exemplar aeternum absque omni aenigmate ; sed hoc est falsum, etc. . . . dicendum quod in statu viae non cognoscitur in rationibus aeternis sine velamine et aenigmate propter divinae imaginis obscurationem. Ex hoc tamen non sequitur, quod nihil certitudinaliter cognoscatur et clare, pro eo quod principia creata, quae aliquo modo sunt media cognoscendi, licet non sine illis rationibus, possunt perspicue et sine velamine a nostra mente videri. Si tamen diceretur, quod nihil in hac vita scitur plenarie, non esset magnum inconveniens.' This passage shows the transition state between the older Augustinian and the newer Peripatetic theory of knowledge. It is plain how difficult it is to draw an exact dividing line between the natural and the supernatural means of knowing. For the theory of Augustine, and its place in scholastic thought, see below, chap. v, p. 188.

left no field of reality unexplored, but which included in its scope an articulated body of solutions to the questions about the nature of things, which had as yet only been discussed piecemeal, as a problem or group of problems had presented itself during the course of theological investigation.   Moreover, the nature of the Aristotelian system and its Arabian commentaries was in many respects so foreign to the general trend of Catholic theology, that a direct and immediate incorporation of both within a larger whole was scarcely possible.   Indeed, the opposition to the new doctrines on the part of the conservative party in the Church was for the moment decisive.   In the provincial council assembled at Paris in 1210 under the presidency of Peter of Corbeil, Archbishop of Sens, the reading of the natural philosophy of Aristotle and commentaries on the same was forbidden, a prohibition which probably included the *Metaphysics* [1] as well as the *Physics*, while at the same time the heresy of Almaric of Benes was condemned.   Five years later the censures were renewed by the Papal legate, Robert de Courcon, who, while allowing the *Ethics*, expressly prohibited the *Physics*, *Metaphysics*, and the *Summae de eisdem*.[2] But after a short while these inhibitions became inoperative, and by the middle of the century we find both the *Metaphysics* and the *Physics* regularly prescribed for courses by the Faculty of Arts at the University of Paris.   There remained, therefore,

---

[1] Cf. De Wulf, *History of Mediaeval Philosophy*, sect. 228. The prohibition reads as follows: 'Nec libri Aristotelis de naturali philosophia nec commenta legantur Parisiis publice vel secreto.' The continuator of the Chronicle of Rigordus, William le Breton, reports that the metaphysical writings of Aristotle, which had been brought from Constantinople and translated from the Greek into Latin, had been burned and their study prohibited, because they had given rise to the Almarican heresy. Cf. also Denifle-Chatelain, *Chartularium Univ. Par.*, p. 70, tom. i.

[2] De Wulf, loc. cit.

only one solution to the problem, the complete separation of philosophy from theology, and the strict delineation of a dividing line between the two disciplines.

But the achievement of such a separation was not to be fulfilled immediately. The newer peripatetic doctrine did not oust, once and for all, the older Augustinian tradition. It was absorbed gradually, and grafted on the already existing stock of Christian philosophy, piece by piece, in a process of continuous transformation. The doctrine of John of Fidanza, Saint Bonaventura, known as the Seraphic Doctor, admirably illustrates a stage in this continuous development. Less radical than his great contemporaries Albert and Thomas, he clings more closely to the Platonist traditions of the twelfth century and the teaching of his master Alexander of Hales; and he attempts to effect a reconciliation of Aristotle and Augustine after the manner of his predecessor. His theory of knowledge is consequently somewhat confused, and it is difficult to find any definite point in his teaching where reason ends and faith begins, where philosophy passes over into theology. For Bonaventura, like Anselm, is a mystic, and his attitude to the whole problem of the relation between faith and knowledge may be summed up in the words of the Prophet Isaiah, ' Nisi credideritis non intelligetis '. All perfect knowledge is dependent upon an illumination, and in the light of faith the mysteries of the Divine revelation become intelligible. Not that he denies outright the distinction between the natural and the supernatural elements in knowledge; for in a sense faith is ousted by reason,[1] and natural knowledge does not depend in its entirety upon an intuition of the divine ideas,

---

[1] Cf. *In Sentt.*, Lib. I, dist. ii, ad 6 m. : ' Quando assentitur propter se rationi, tunc aufertur locus fidei quia in anima hominis dominatur violentia rationis.'

but also upon the data of sense and the activity of
the active intellect.[1] Yet it is only in such an intuition
that perfect knowledge can be acquired, and only in
the Eternal Word which is Christ are things completely
intelligible.[2] In the last resort, that by means of
which we know is the Divine truth, the eternal idea,
God himself ;[3] and in all knowledge, be it of sense or
intellect, God himself is invisibly present.[4] The effect
of this mystical conception of the nature of knowledge
is twofold. While on the one hand the processes of
natural reason are invested with a quasi-supernatural
significance, on the other the psychology of faith is
interpreted in terms of intellect. For to the eye of
faith the mysteries are no longer utterly incompre-
hensible, they become intelligible in the light of
supernatural grace by the gifts of ' Knowledge ' and

[1] Cf. *Sermo, Anecdota*, pp. 80–1, where Bonaventura argues against
the position that our knowledge depends on the Divine ideas as its
complete *ratio intelligendi* : ' Postremo, si esset (Deus) ratio tota, non
indigeremus specie et receptione ad cognoscendas res, quod manifeste
videmus esse falsum, quia amittentes unum sensum, necesse habemus
amittere unam scientiam,' etc. . . . He then goes on to argue that
Plato and Aristotle were both right in their theories of knowledge,
the one in insisting on the reality of the ideas, and the other on the
empirical sense-element in knowing.

[2] Cf. ibid., p. 75–7 : ' Cum igitur res habeant esse in proprio
genere, habeant etiam esse in mente, habeant esse et in aeterna
ratione, nec esse earum sit omnino immutabile primo et secundo
modo, sed tantum tertio, videlicet prout sunt in Verbo aeterno :
restat quod nihil potest facere res perfecte scibiles, nisi Christus,
Dei filius et magister.'

[3] Cf. *De Cogn. Hum., Anecd.* IV, ad 17, *Anecdota*, p. 53 : ' Omne
immutabile est superius mutabili ; sed illud quo certitudinaliter
cognoscitur est immutabile, quia verum necessarium ; sed mens
nostra est mutabilis ; ergo illud quo cognoscimus est supra mentes
nostras. Sed quod est supra mentes nostras non est ·nisi Deus et
veritas aeterna : ergo illud quo est cognitio est divina veritas et ratio
sempiterna.'

[4] Cf. *De Red. Art. ad Theol.*, n. 26 : ' Patet quam ampla sit via
illuminationis et quomodo in omni re quae sentitur, sive quae cognoscitur, interius lateat ipse Deus.'

'Understanding'.[1] And it is just this double process of assimilation that makes a complete separation between philosophy and theology impossible.

That this is the case may be well illustrated by Bonaventura's teaching concerning our knowledge of God. He distinguishes three ways in which such knowledge is possible, simple assent, rational evidence, and simple intuition. The first of these is the virtue of faith, whose function it is to give assent ; the second is the gift of understanding, which enables the mind to comprehend rationally that which it believes ; the third is the grace of purity of heart, which enables us to see God.[2] This classification is of interest because of the light it throws on Bonaventura's conception of the relation of faith to knowledge. Like Anselm,

---

[1] Cf. *In Sentt.*, Lib. I, dist. ii : ' Et quod objicitur quod credibile est super rationem, verum est quantum ad scientiam acquisitam per rationem evidentem ; sed non supra rationem elevatam per fidem et per donum scientiae et intellectus. Fides enim elevat ad assentiendum ; scientia et intellectus elevant ad ea, quae credita sunt, intelligendum.'

[2] Ibid., III, dist. xxxv, art. 1, q. 3 : ' Cognitio Dei sub ratione veri potest haberi secundum triplicem modum : uno modo habetur cognitio Dei per simplicem assensum ; alio modo per artionis adminiculum ; tertio modo per simplicem contuitum. Primum est virtus fidei, cujus est assentire ; secundum est doni intellectus, cujus est credita per artionem intelligere ; tertium est beatitudinis munditiae cordis, cujus est Deum videre.' Cf. with this passage, Hugo of St. Victor, *De Sacramentis*, Lib. I, pars. x, cap. 4 : ' Duo sunt secundum quae fides crescere dicitur : cognitio et affectus. . . . Secundum cognitionem . . . quando eruditur ad scientiam. Secundum affectum crescit, quando ad devotionem excitatur et roboratur ad constantiam. . . . Item secundum incrementum fidei tria genera credentium inveniuntur. Quidam enim fideles sunt, qui sola pietate credere eligunt, quod tamen utrum sit credendum an non credendum sit ratione non comprehendunt. Alii ratione approbant quod fide credunt. Alii puritate cordis et munda conscientia interius jam gustare incipiunt quod fide credunt. In primis sola pietas facit electionem ; in secundis ratio adjungit approbationem ; in tertiis puritas intelligentiae apprehendit certitudinem.' (Migne, *P.L.*, vol. 176, cols. 332–3.)

he presupposes faith even in the second mode of knowing. Faith comes first in the order of knowledge,
and it is from faith that we proceed to knowledge, and
not vice versa.[1] For in the last resort our knowledge
of God is innate, and it is impossible to deny his
existence.[2] Faith and knowledge thus meet together
in the region of immediate intuition, and Bonaventura
compares the inborn knowledge of God with the
immediate knowledge that the soul possesses of itself.[3]
At the same time he does not fail to distinguish
between those attributes of the Divine being which
can be known by the *a posteriori* process of reasoning
from the creature to the creator, from those which
can only be known by faith, such as the unity of
substance in the Trinity of persons. But he does not
confine faith entirely to the Christian revelation ; he
concedes the possibility of a certain measure of it to
the heathen philosophers.[4] And all along he maintains

[1] *Sermo, Anecdota,* p. 79 : ' Ordo enim est ut inchoetur a stabilitate
fidei, et procedatur per serenitatem rationis ut perveniatur ad suavi-
tatem contemplationis. . . . Hunc ordinem ignoraverunt philosophi,
qui, negligentes fidem et totaliter se fundantes in ratione, nullo modo
pervenire potuerunt ad contemplationem.'

[2] *Sentt.* I, dist. viii, art. 1, q. ii : ' Damascenus dicit quod cognitio
essendi Deum nobis naturaliter est impressa ; sed naturales impres-
siones non relinquunt nec assuescunt in contrarium ; ergo veritas
Dei impressa menti humanae est inseparabilis ab ipsa ; ergo non
potest cogitari non esse.' He also quotes Hugo to the same effect
(*De Sacramentis*, I, pars. 3, cap. 1) : ' Deus ab initio sic cognitionem
suam in homine temperavit, ut sicut nunquam quid esset poterat ab
homine comprehendi, ita nunquam quia esset poterat ignorari.'

[3] Cf. *De Myst. Trinit.* IV, 1, 1 : ' Inserta est animae rationali
notitia sui, eo quod anima sibi praesens est et a se ipsa cognoscibilis ;
sed Deus praesentissimus est ipsi animae, et eo ipso cognoscibilis ;
ergo inserta est ipsi animae notitia Dei sui.'

[4] Cf. *Sentt.* I, dist. iii, art. 1, sq. 4 : ' Pluralitas personarum cum
unitate essentiae est proprium divinae naturae solius, cujus simile
nec reperitur in creatura, nec potest reperiri, nec rationaliter
cogitari ; ideo nullo modo trinitas personarum est cognoscibilis per
creaturam, rationabiliter ascendendo a creatura in Deum. Sed licet

that to the mind illuminated by the gift of faith, the necessity of certain of the mysteries of revelation can be demonstrated. Thus we can show by necessary reasons that the number of persons in the Trinity must be three; neither more nor less being possible.[1] In the same way it must be admitted that the existence of the divine ideas is only rendered possible by the eternal generation of the Eternal Word, and the whole of natural philosophy preaches the doctrine of the incarnation.[2]

Thus a clear dividing line between philosophy and theology, faith and reason, is still wanting; and the teaching of Bonaventura is too indeterminate to supply it, a fact which appears more plainly in his definition of theology in the prologue to his commentary on the Sentences. The intellect, he says, is perfected by knowledge. Now there are three ways in which the intellect may be considered. We may regard it either as it is in itself (*in se*), that is, in its strictly cognitive aspect; or we may regard it from the point of view of the emotions, in its affective aspect (*prout extenditur ad affectum*); or from the pragmatic standpoint in as much as it manifests itself in action (*prout extenditur ad opus*). In these three capacities

non habeat omnino simile, habet tamen aliquo modo quod creditur simile in creatura. Unde dico, quod philosophi nunquam per rationem cognoverunt personarum trinitatem nec pluralitatem, nisi haberent aliquem habitum fidei, sicut habent aliqui haeretici; unde quae dixerunt, aut locuti sunt, non intelligentes, aut fidei radio illustrati.'

[1] *Sentt.*, I, dist. ii, art. i, q. iii : ' Dicendum sicut fides catholica dicit, ponere est tantum tres personas, nec plures nec pauciores. Et ad hoc sumitur ratio necessitatis et congruitatis, ratio utique necessitatis, quare non possunt esse pauciores quam tres, est summa beatitudo et summa perfectio ... item ratio necessitatis quare non possunt esse plures, est summa simplicitas.'

[2] Cf. *De Red. Art. ad Theol.*, 12 sqq.; also ibid., 16 et 21 : ' Praedicat igitur tota naturalis philosophia per habitudinem proportionis dei verbum natum et incarnatum, ut idem sit alpha et omega, natum, scilicet, in principio et ante tempora, incarnatum vero in fine saeculorum.' Cf. Gilson, op. cit., pp. 93 sqq.

it has three corresponding conditions (*habitus direc-tivi*). In its purely cognitive aspect it is essentially speculative, and is perfected by a condition of know-ing for its own sake (*contemplationis gratia*), which is called *scientia speculativa*. In so far as it issues in action it is perfected by a condition or state of moral virtue, the purpose of which is to make men good, which is called practical or moral knowledge (*scientia practica sive moralis*). But intermediate between these two aspects there is the third, namely the affective or emotional, and in so far as the intellect is considered from the emotional side, it is perfected by a third condition (*habitus*) midway between the speculative and the practical which embraces both, which state is called Wisdom (*Sapientia*) because it includes both the cognitive and the affective elements ; and this Wisdom is Theology.[1]

It is scarcely necessary to point out how inadequate this definition is to furnish any line of demarcation between philosophy and theology. The standpoint of the differentiation seems to be almost wholly ' sub-

---

[1] *Proem. in IV Libros Sententiarum*, q. iii : ' Notandum est quod perfectibile a scientia est intellectus noster. Hunc autem contingit considerare tripliciter ; sc. in se ; vel prout extenditur ad affectum ; vel prout extenditur ad opus. Extenditur autem intellectus per modum dictantis et regulantis. Secundum hunc triplicem statum, quia errare potest, habet triplicem habitum directivum. Nam si consideremus intellectum in se, sic est proprie speculativus, et per-ficitur ab habitu qui est contemplationis gratia, qui dicitur scientia speculativa. Si autem consideremus ipsum ut natum extendi ad opus, sic perficitur ab habitu qui est ut boni fiamus ; et hic est scientia practica sive moralis. Si autem medio modo consideretur, ut natus extendi ad affectum, sic perficitur ab habitu medio inter pure specula-tivum et practicum, qui complectitur utrumque ; et hic habitus dicitur sapientia, quae simul dicit cognitionem et affectum. Sapientia enim doctrinae est secundum nomen ejus. Unde hic est contem-plationis gratia et ut boni fiamus, principaliter tamen ut boni fiamus.

' Talis est cognitio tradita in hoc libro. Nam cognitio haec juvat fidem, et fides sic est, in intellectu, ut quantum est de sui ratione, nata sit movere affectum,' etc.

jective', and the distinctions set up lie entirely within the field of psychology. Bonaventura is seeking to define theology in terms of the religious consciousness, rather than to differentiate it from other modes of knowing (such as philosophy, for instance), by virtue of its cognitive content. And above all he is concerned with its teleological function ; the study of theology, while it has its speculative side, is principally directed to the end of moral edification (*ut boni fiamus*), a point of view which we shall see later accentuated by Scotus. Philosophy and theology then are still imperfectly distinguished ; the *scientia speculativa* of Bonaventura, in a sense, covers both ; it remained for Albert first definitely to differentiate them as two sciences.

Like Bonaventura, Albertus Magnus, notwithstanding his great philosophical and scientific interests, is primarily a theologian. For him, as for his predecessors, Theology is the queen of the sciences, the mistress to whom they are all subject.[1] But he differentiates it quite clearly from the philosophical sciences, and effects a complete separation between faith and knowledge (*scientia*). Faith and knowledge may be concerned with the same object, but in different ways, ways which are mutually exclusive.[2] For faith proper, whether it be a revelation *ex auditu* or a *charisma* of the Holy Ghost, has its essence in the fact that its truths are incapable of proof.[3] The natural

---

[1] Cf. *Summa Theol.*, Ia pars, tract. vi, *ad sol.*: 'Ad hoc dicendum, quod . . . impossibile est quod haec scientia finem in aliis scientiis habeat, sed ipsa finis aliarum scientiarum est, ad quam omnes aliae referuntur ut ancillae. Et hoc modo libera est ; omnibus enim existentibus et suffragentibus nobis et ad voluptatem et ad necessitatem, ista post omnia habita et in omnibus habitis quaeritur : et ideo libera est et domina est et sapientia, et in omnibus potior.'

[2] Cf. *Sentt.*, Lib. III, dist. xxiv, art. 9: 'Fides et scientia sunt de eodem, non secundum idem : et ideo unum non evacuat aliud,' etc.

[3] Cf. loc. cit., xxiv a, 1 : 'Quaedam fides est ex auditu et quaedam

and supernatural kinds of knowing (*cognitio*) are thus carefully distinguished both in their subjective and their objective aspects. For in the first place the relation between the knower and the thing known is different; because the natural process is subject to reason, while the process of faith transcends reason; while in the second place there is a difference in the principles from which the two kinds of knowing proceed; for the principles of natural knowledge are self-evident, while those of supernatural knowledge are derived from an illumination from on high, which produces conviction rather by acting on the will through love than by furnishing proofs to the reason.[1] Theology and philosophy are thus two entirely separate sciences proceeding by different methods.[2]

est charisma Spiritus Sancti; illa quae est ex auditu, potest habere rationem inductivam, non probativam; non ut quis consentiat, sed ut facilius consentiat ei, cui tamen per affectum est inclinatus et paratus consentire. Charisma autem est lumen infusum tendens in primam veritatem, et haec non habet rationem inducentem.'

[1] Cf. *Sent.* I, dist. iii, art. 4: 'Prima differentia est in comparatione scientiae ad scientem: quia processus naturalis subest rationi, fidei autem processus est super rationem. Secunda differentia est in principiis in quibus accipitur cognitio ipsa: quia illa in naturali cognitione sunt principia per se nota ... sed in fide est lumen infusum quod informando conscientiam, rationem convincit magis ex amore quodam voluntatis quam ex probatione rationis.' For the distinction between self-evidence and illumination cf. *Summa Theol.*, Ia, tract. 1, q. 4: 'Primum (*sc.* lumen naturale) relucet in per se notis, secundum autem (*sc.* lumen infusum) in fidei articulis.' Cf. *Summa Theol.*, I, tract. 19, q. 1: 'Noster intellectus perficitur luminibus et elevatur; sed ex lumine quidem connaturali non elevatur ad scientiam Trinitatis et incarnationis et resurrectionis. Ex lumine autem fluente a superiori natura ad supermundana elevatur, quae potentia sola divina et voluntate sunt. Et his lumine desuper fluente assentit, et certius ea scit quam ea quae ex lumine sibi connaturali accipit. ... Duo modi sunt revelationis. Unus quidem est per modum generale nobis. Et hoc modo revelatum est philosophis: hoc enim lumen non potest esse nisi a primo lumine Dei. ... Aliud lumen est ad supermundana contuenda, et hoc est elevatum super nos. Et hoc lumine est revelata haec scientia (*sc.* theologia).'

[2] Cf. loc. cit.: 'Dicendum, quod haec scientia separatur ab aliis

As to the question of certainty, the guarantee of faith, considered from one point of view, is the most secure, for it is founded on the authority of God himself. But from the strictly cognitive standpoint it is, humanly speaking, less certain than rational knowledge ; *quoad nos*, knowledge by means of natural reasons is the most certain ; next comes knowledge by means of revelation ; least certain in this human life is the knowledge of intuition.[1] In theology the weight of authority, because of its divine sanction, is the greatest ; in the other sciences it is of little consequence.[2] This order of certitude is strongly reminiscent of the passage from Hugo of Saint Victor quoted earlier in this chapter, and is found likewise in Alexander of Hales,[3] the master of Bonaventura, from whom Albert borrowed extensively.[4]

subjecto, passione et principiis confirmantibus ratiocinationem. . . . Principio vero quia quod in ista scientia probatur, per fidem quae est articulus qui creditur, vel antecedens fidem, quod est Scriptura, vel per revelationem probatur ut principium,' etc.

[1] Cf. *Summa Theol.*, Ia pars, tract. iii, q. xv, memb. 2 : ' Certitudo autem quae est quoad nos, ex notioribus est quoad nos (cf. Aristotle, *An. Post.* I. i. 71 b 33), secundum quod animales sumus enutriti sensibus. . . . Et hoc modo nihil prohibet cognitionem per naturales rationes esse certissimam, et post hoc cognitionem fidei, et minime certam eam quae est facie ad faciem.'

[2] Cf. op. cit., Ia pars, tract. i, q. 5, memb. 2 : ' Dicendum quod in theologia locus ab auctoritate est ab inspiratione Spiritus veritatis. Unde Augustinus dicit . . . " major est scripturae auctoritas, quam omnis humani ingenii perspicacitas ". In aliis autem scientiis locus ab auctoritate infirmus est, et infirmior ceteris, quia perspicacitati humani ingenii quae fallibilis est, innititur.'

[3] Cf. *Summa Theol.*, Ia pars, q. i, memb. 4, art. 2 : ' Est certitudo speculationis, et est certitudo experientiae : praeterea est certitudo secundum intellectum, et certitudo secundum affectum : item est certitudo quoad hominem spiritualem, et est certitudo quoad hominem animalem. Dico ergo quod modus theologicus est certior certitudine experientiae, certitudine quoad affectum, quae est per modum gustus . . . quamvis non certior quoad speculationem intellectus.'

[4] Cf. Martigné, *La Scolastique et les Traditions Franciscaines*,

The separation of theology from philosophy thus effected is of the highest importance to scholastic thought. It marks, according to Professor Gilson, the first step in the long journey of philosophy towards her liberation.[1] Its consequences were felt immediately in every department of learning ; men became aware, almost for the first time, of the sharp contrasts of a dualism which hitherto had been but vaguely apprehended. Contact with the philosophical speculation of non-Christian peoples like the Greeks, the Arabians, and the Jews gradually gave rise to the notion of a body of philosophical truths independent of divine revelation, much as the contact of the Roman with the diversity of peoples had given birth to the conception of the *jus gentium*. Moreover, the rediscovery of the lost works of Aristotle had revealed a completed and systematic ' Weltanschauung ' so different from that of the fathers of the Church that some mediation between the two was imperative. Finally, the study of the new logic, especially of the *Posterior Analytics* and their Arabian and Greek commentaries, had directed attention to the morphology of knowledge, and scientific analysis had defined more clearly the limits and validity of the various processes of reasoning, with the result that it was no longer possible to maintain the dual content of revelation and natural reason within the bounds of a single system.

Such in outline had been the consequences of the critical movement which had arisen out of the expansion of learning during the early years of the thirteenth

pp. 59–76, where he quotes in parallel columns large passages from Alexander and Albert, taken from the first part of their respective *Summae*.

[1] Cf. Gilson, op. cit., pp. 98–9 : ' La théologie, nous dit Albert le grand, est donc une science séparée des autres sciences. . . . Cette décision ferme . . . sépare la philosophie en même temps que la théologie, et cette séparation marque le premier pas de la philosophie sur la longue route de sa libération.'

century, and which found its first complete expression in the work of Albert the Great. The separation of the two sciences, vital as it was to the future develop-ment of philosophy, effected no less significant results by its influence on theological speculation. Once the domain of reason had been clearly restricted to the philosophic sphere, a reconstruction of the theological method became necessary. The older thinkers from Anselm to Bonaventura had attempted to use the forms of logical demonstration in their efforts to make intelligible the mysteries of the faith. To the illumin-ated the necessity of certain theological dogmata might be rendered apparent, and their content proven. The object of the theologian, as far as the *opera conditionis* were concerned, was to adduce wherever possible ' necessary reasons ' in support of the divine revelation. He was firm in his conviction that beneath all the mysteries shrouding the divine nature and the relations of the three Persons in the Holy Trinity there lay some necessary grounds, however inaccessible to the feeble powers of the unassisted human reason. That the eternal truths concerning the divine nature, as it exists in and for itself, could be other-wise than as they were was to him unthinkable. It was therefore his duty, so far as in him lay, to discover them, and to lay bare the ground of their necessity. Such, for instance, was the opinion of Richard of St. Victor, one of the most influential of the twelfth-century theologians.[1] But for Albert

---

[1] Cf. Richard of St. Victor, *Libri sex de Trinitate*, Lib. VIII, cap. 2 : ' Erit itaque intentionis nostrae in hoc opere ad ea quae credimus, in quantum dominus dederit, non modo probabiles, sed etiam necessarias rationes adducere et fidei nostrae documenta veritatis enodatione et explanatione condere. Credo namque sine dubio, quoniam ad quorumlibet explanationem, quae necesse est esse, non modo probabilia, immo etiam necessaria argumenta non deesse, quamvis illa interim contingat nostram industriam latere. Omnia quae coeperunt esse ex tempore pro beneplacito Conditoris,

such a conception was no longer possible. The separation between philosophy and theology placed such an ideal solution to the problem out of the question. Thus, while he will not deny that these necessary grounds exist, he is forced to maintain that they are inaccessible to the human reason.[1]

The result of this divorce between faith and reason was decisive. Theology had purchased her independence from the criticism of logic, and for a moment it seemed as if a permanent settlement had been attained. Henceforth theology and philosophy were to divide the world of truth between them, each sovereign and supreme in her own territory. Was not the universe wide enough to contain them both? So at least it appeared to Thomas Aquinas and his school. At last a harmony had been established; what ugly fact could be found to disturb it? That the two departments of truth should contradict one another was unthinkable, save on the assumption of some diabolic influence corrupting the soul of man by the sin of pride. For the whole order of things natural and supernatural was one and indivisible, ruled and guided by one divine providence and permeated by the one reason, of

possibile est esse, possibile est non esse : unde et eo ipso eorum esse non tam ratiocinando colligitur, quam experiendo probatur. Quae vero aeterna sunt, omnino non esse non possunt, sicut nunquam non fuerunt, sic certe nunquam non erunt, immo semper sunt, quod sunt, nec aliud nec aliter esse possunt. Videtur autem omnino impossibile, omne necessarium non esse, necessariaque ratione carere, sed non est cuivis animae hujusmodi rationes de profundo et latebroso naturae sinu elicere, et velut de intimo quodam sapientiae secretario erutas in commune deducere ' (Migne, *P.L.*, vol. 196, col. 892).

[1] Cf. *Summa Theol.*, Ia pars, tract. iii, q. 13, memb. 3 : ' Ad dictum Richardi dicendum, quod licet rationes necessariae sint ad distinctiones personarum, tamen illae sunt supernaturales et divinae ; et ideo solo lumine naturali inveniri non possunt.' Cf. also loc. cit., q. 15, memb. 3 : ' Ad dictum Richardi dicendum est, quod nihil prohibet ad aliquod creditum rationes esse necessarias, sed illae divinae sunt et nobis ignotae, et ideo inquiri non possunt.'

which the whole creation was but the shadow. But the bond which held together these two spheres of thought was a frail ligature, woven only of the beliefs of men. Even from the very start disharmony and disproportion began to make their appearance. It was only the deep psychological conviction of the impossibility of any contradiction between the two orders of truth which kept scholasticism from disruption ; once this was dissolved its days were numbered. And the beginnings of the inevitable diremption were perceptible even in Albert himself. For the cosmology of Aristotle was ill mated to the doctrine of the Christian Church. The eternity of the world seemed to be the necessary consequence of his notion of form and matter ; and here a conflict with the authority of theological dogma became almost unavoidable.[1] There was only one solution to the problem. Creationism, dethroned from its position as a philosophical truth, was compelled to seek refuge in the dominion of theology and to become a postulate of faith. But this was only the beginning. As time went on an increasing number of propositions, which had hitherto been considered demonstrable by reason, were banished from the realm of philosophy, to find a haven of refuge in the impregnable region of dogmatic security. And finally, the psychological conviction of the necessary harmony between philosophy and revelation was no

---

[1] Cf. *Summa Theol.*, Ia pars, tract. xiii, q. 53, art. 1 : ' Illi enim (*sc.* philosophi) non dicunt esse creatum, nisi quod ante se non praesupponit aliud, sicut ens et unum : quod autem ante se supponit aliquid, non dicunt esse creatum, sed factum per informationem ; creationem autem secundum quod fit ex pure nihilo, per rationem cognoscere non potuerunt. Non enim cum sit entis creati, decurrit nisi de ente in ens, de principio, scilicet, in principiatum, et non potest se fundare in non ente. Et ideo, ut dicit Aristoteles in primo Physicorum, omnes philosophi convenerunt in hoc, quod ex nihilo nihil fit. Propter quod etiam non acceptio intellectus humani, sed articulus fidei est quod dicitur in symbolo Nicaeno : Credo in unum Deum, Patrem omnipotentem, factorem coeli et terrae.'

longer able to maintain itself, with the result that the whole scholastic edifice collapsed into scepticism.

But for the moment all was well. The emancipation of philosophy from the control of theology, and the freeing of the latter from the embarrassing task of inventing reasons to explain mysteries, achieved a decisive triumph in the *Summa Theologica* of Saint Thomas Aquinas. Like his master Albert, Thomas takes great care to distinguish natural theology, which is a branch of metaphysics, from *sacra doctrina*, the theology of revelation. Our knowledge of the divine being is of two different kinds. Certain truths concerning God's nature are attainable by the unaided reason, such, for instance, as God's existence, unity, and so forth ; others are inaccessible to the human intelligence, as, for example, the mystery of the Holy Trinity.[1] There are, then, two sciences which deal with the same subject-matter, but from different standpoints, and on different principles,[2] each developing its own independently of the other. But of these two sciences theology is the superior ; both on account of its certitude and of the lofty nature of its content. For the certitude of the other sciences proceeds from the natural light of human reason, which is liable to

[1] Cf. *Summa contra Gent.*, Lib. I, cap. 3 : ‘ Est autem in his, quae de Deo confitemur, duplex veritatis modus. Quaedam namque vera sunt de Deo, quae omnem facultatem humanae rationis excedunt, ut Deum esse trinum et unum. Quaedam vero sunt, ad quae etiam ratio naturalis pertingere potest, sicut Deum esse, Deum esse unum, et alia hujusmodi ; quae etiam philosophi demonstrative de Deo probaverunt, ducti naturalis lumine rationis.

‘ Quod autem sint aliqua intelligibilium divinarum, quae humanae rationis penitus excedant ingenium, evidentissime apparet.’

[2] Cf. *Summa Theol.*, Ia pars, q. 1, art. 1 : ‘ Unde nihil prohibet de eisdem rebus de quibus philosophicae disciplinae tractant secundum quod sunt cognoscibiles lumine naturalis rationis, etiam aliam scientiam tractare, secundum quod cognoscuntur lumine divinae revelationis. Unde theologia, quae ad sacram doctrinam pertinet, differt secundum genus ab illa theologia, quae pars philosophiae ponitur.’

err ; that of theology from the light of the divine
knowledge, which can never be deceptive. So, too,
in its subject-matter it surpasses all other branches of
learning, for it is chiefly concerned with truths which
in their altitude transcend the capacities of the human
reason.[1] Theology is thus the arbiter of all the
sciences, not because it is its function to demonstrate
their principles, but because it must judge them. For
any doctrine which they may teach which is contrary
to theological truth must be condemned as false and
rejected.[2]

Thomas lays great stress on the scientific character
of theology. Not only is it a science, but in addition
to being a ' practical ' science it is also speculative in
the strict sense of the word,[3] a transcendent metaphysic, as it were, whose systematizing principles are
unattainable by man in his state on earth.   For the

[1] Ibid., art. 5 : ' Speculativarum enim scientiarum una altera
dignior dicitur, tum propter certitudinem, tum propter dignitatem
materiae. Et quantum ad utrumque haec scientia alias scientias
speculativas excedit. Secundum certitudinem quidem, quia aliae
scientiae certitudinem habent ex naturali lumine rationis humanae,
quae potest errare ; haec autem certitudinem habet ex lumine
divinae scientiae, quae decipi non potest. Secundum vero dignitatem
materiae, quia ista scientia est principaliter de iis quae altitudine sua
rationem transcendunt.'

[2] Loc. cit., art. 6 : ' Et ideo non pertinet ad eam probare principia
aliarum scientiarum, sed solum judicare de eis. Quidquid enim in
aliis scientiis invenitur veritati hujus scientiae repugnans, totum
condemnatur ut falsum.'

[3] *Summa Theol.*, loc. cit., art. 4 : ' Respondeo dicendum, quod
sacra doctrina . . . una existens se extendit ad ea quae pertinent ad
diversas scientias philosophicas, propter rationem formalem communem quam in diversis attendit, sc. prout sunt divino lumine
cognoscibilia. Unde licet in scientiis philosophicis alia sit speculativa
et alia practica, sacra tamen doctrina comprehendit sub se utramque,
sicut et Deus eadem scientia se cognoscit et ea quae facit. Magis
tamen est speculativa quam practica : quia principalius agit de rebus
divinis quam de actibus humanis, de quibus agit secundum quod per
eos ordinatur homo ad perfectam Dei cognitionem, in qua aeterna
beatitudo consistit.'

sciences are of two kinds. Some proceed from self-evident principles known by the natural light of reason ; such as arithmetic, geometry, and so forth. Others proceed from principles known by the light of a superior science, as, e. g. music, from principles known through arithmetic. Theology belongs to the second kind, for it proceeds from principles known by the light of a superior science or knowledge, the knowledge possessed by God and the saints,[1] which is communicated to man by revelation. Thus furnished with principles, theology develops by argumentative methods, reasoning, like the other sciences, from given premises. And, like these, theology does not attempt to prove its own premises, but proceeds from them to draw conclusions. Now the inferior sciences neither prove their own presuppositions, nor dispute with those who deny them, but leave this task to a superior science. The highest of the natural sciences, metaphysic, however, disputes against those who deny its principles if they make any positive assertion ; and if not, the metaphysician, though he cannot dispute with them on any positive ground, can at least combat the arguments of their scepticism. So, too, the theologian, if his opponents concede any of his premises, can defend his system, but if they deny the truths of revelation *in toto*, he cannot prove the articles of faith, but he can resolve any negative arguments brought against them

---

[1] *Summa Theol.*, loc. cit., art. 2 : 'Respondeo dicendum sacram doctrinam esse scientiam. Sed sciendum est quod duplex est scientiarum genus. Quaedam enim sunt, quae procedunt ex principiis notis lumine naturali intellectus, sicut arithmetica, geometria, et hujusmodi. Quaedam vero sunt, quae procedunt ex principiis notis lumine superioris scientiae, sicut perspectiva procedit ex principiis notis per geometriam, et musica ex principiis per arithmeticam notis. Et hoc modo sacra doctrina est scientia, quia procedit ex principiis notis lumine superioris scientiae, quae sc. est scientia Dei et beatorum. Unde sicut musicus credit principia sibi tradita ab arithmetico, ita doctrina sacra credit principia revelata sibi a Deo'

and show them to be inconclusive. For the Faith rests upon an infallible truth, and it is impossible for truth to be self-contradictory—one truth cannot be demonstrated to be contrary to another ; it is therefore plain that all so-called proofs against the tenets of the faith are not strictly cogent demonstrations, but can be shown to rest upon paralogisms, and are therefore arguments which can be ' resolved '.[1]

Once more we find here stated the fundamental principle of scholastic thought, the impossibility of any ultimate opposition between the two orders of know-ledge, the natural and the supernatural. The task of proving the necessity of the truth of Catholic dogma has been abandoned, but not the notion of that necessity as ultimately existent in the nature of reality ; only the grounds of it have been removed from the domain of human knowledge, and placed, at least implicitly, in the unfathomable profundity of the divine nature. For the scientific character of theology rests on the fact that it is, in the last resort, the

[1] *Summa Theol.*, loc. cit., art. 8 : ' Respondeo dicendum, quod sicut aliae scientiae non argumentantur ad sua principia probanda, sed ex principiis argumentantur ad ostendendum alia in ipsis scientiis : ita haec doctrina non argumentatur ad sua principia probanda, quae sunt articuli fidei, sed ex eis procedit ad aliquid aliud probandum. . . . Sed tamen considerandum est in scientiis philosophicis, quod inferiores scientiae nec probant sua principia, nec contra negantem sua principia disputant, sed hoc relinquunt scientiae superiori : suprema vero inter eas, sc. metaphysica, disputat contra negantem sua principia, si adversarius aliquid concedit ; si autem nihil concedit, non potest cum eo disputare, potest tamen solvere rationes ipsius. Unde sacra doctrina, cum non habeat superiorem, disputat contra negantem sua principia, argumentando quidem si adversariis aliquid concedat eorum quae per divinam revelationem habentur. . . . Si vero adversarius nihil credat eorum quae divinitus revelantur, non remanet amplius via ad probandum articulos fidei per rationes, sed ad solvendum rationes, si quas inducit contra fidem. Cum enim fides infallibili veritati innitatur, impossibile autem sit de vero demon-strari contrarium, manifestum est probationes quae contra fidem inducuntur, non esse demonstrationes, sed solubilia argumenta.'

revelation of the content of the divine knowing, the
ground of which is contained in the divine essence
itself.   The significance of this standpoint will be
revealed more fully when we contrast with it that of
Scotus, who, while he does not differ from the Angelic
doctor on any fundamental principle, yet gives to his
doctrine a very different flavour by accentuating other
aspects of the problem.   For Thomas, as for the older
school of the Victorine theologians, there persists in
the background the ideal of a rational and systematic
construction of the mysteries of the divine Persons in
their triune nature, an ideal which, although *ex pro-
fesso* it is never capable of fulfilment, is yet implicit
in the characterization of theology as a speculative
science.   Duns, on the other hand, while recognizing
no less than Thomas the necessary character of the
truths relating to the divine nature as such, lays his
emphasis rather on the contingent element, in the
content of the theology of the Church, which is
concerned with the *opera restaurationis,* and so gives
to his conception of theology considered as a science an
ethical as opposed to a metaphysical colouring.

But it must be remembered that this speculative
interpretation of theology is for Thomas only an ideal.
Like Albert he restricts severely the possibility of the
demonstration of the truths concerning the divine
nature.   For it is impossible for the human mind to
attain to any quidditative notion of the essence of
God.   Our knowledge is only proportioned to the
things of sense ; its proper and adequate object is
the quiddity of the material thing,[1] and it is utterly
unable to grasp the divine essence as it is in itself.   By

---

[1] *Summa Theol.,* Ia pars, q. lxxxix, art. vii : ' Intellectus autem
humani, qui est conjunctus corpori, proprium objectum est quidditas,
sive natura in materia corporali existens ; et per hujusmodi naturas
visibilium rerum etiam in invisibilium rerum aliqualem cognitionem
ascendit.'

the light of natural reason, therefore, we can only
know of God *quia est*, the fact of His existence, but
not *quid est*, what He actually is in his own intrinsic
nature.[1] All our proofs of his existence are *a posteriori*,
not *a priori*; they argue only from the effect to the
cause, not vice versa, and are therefore demonstrations
quia, not demonstrations *propter quid*.[2] The existence
of God, though it may be self-evident to an ideal
knowledge, is not so to us. The judgement ' God
exists ' is for us not an analytic but a synthetic one.
Considered of and in itself we may regard it as a *per se
notum*, but *quoad nos* it requires demonstration.[3] Hence

[1] *Summa contra Gent.*, Lib. I, cap. 3 : ' Quum enim principium
totius scientiae, quam de aliqua re ratio percipit, sit intellectus
substantiae ipsius, eo quod . . . demonstrationis principium est " quod
quid est ", oportet quod, secundum modum quo substantia rei
intelligitur, sit eorum modus, quae de re illa cognoscuntur. Unde
si intellectus humanus alicujus rei substantiam comprehendit, puta
lapidis . . . nullum intelligibilium illius rei facultatem humanae
rationis excedet. Quod quidem nobis circa Deum non accidit. Nam
ad substantiam ipsius capiendam, intellectus humanus non potest
naturali virtute pertingere, quum intellectus nostri, secundum modum
praesentis vitae, cognitio a sensu incipiat. Et ideo ea quae in sensu
non cadunt, non possunt humano intellectu capi, nisi quatenus ex
sensibus eorum cognitio colligitur. Sensibilia autem ad hoc ducere
intellectum nostrum non possunt, ut in eis divina substantia videatur
" quid sit " quum sint effectus causae virtutem non adequantes.
Ducitur tamen ex sensibilibus intellectus noster in divinam cognitionem, ut cognoscat de Deo " quia est " et alia hujusmodi, quae
oportet attribui primo principio.'

[2] *Summa Theol.*, Ia pars, q. 2, art. 2 : ' Respondeo dicendum, quod
duplex est demonstratio. Una quae est per causam et dicitur propter
quid, et haec est per priora simpliciter ; alia est per effectum, et
dicitur demonstratio quia, et haec est per ea quae sunt priora quoad
nos. Cum enim effectus aliquis nobis est manifestior quam sua causa,
per effectum procedimus ad cognitionem causae. . . . Unde Deum
esse, secundum quod non est per se notum quoad nos, demonstrabile
est per effectus nobis notos.'

[3] Ibid., art. 1 : ' Respondeo dicendum, quod contingit aliquid
esse per se notum dupliciter. Uno modo secundum se, et non quoad
nos, alio modo secundum se et quoad nos. Ex hoc enim aliqua
propositio est per se nota, quod praedicatum includitur in ratione

Thomas emphatically rejects the ontological argument of Anselm,[1] and lays his stress rather on the argument from motion.[2] The content thus furnished by natural theology is very meagre, and tells us little of the divine attributes, save that God is one, a living, intelligent, and willing being, the first cause of the universe. The deeper mysteries, such as the existence of the triune personality and so forth, are completely beyond the attainment of the unaided reason.[3] We may invent arguments to support our belief in them, but they do not constitute a demonstration, and carry little weight, except with a believer.[4] In fact it is

subjecti . . . si igitur notum sit omnibus de praedicato et de subjecto quid sit, propositio illa erit omnibus per se nota. . . . Si autem apud notum non sit de praedicato et subjecto, quid sit, propositio quidem, quantum in se est, erit per se nota, non tamen apud illos qui praedicatum et subjectum propositionis ignorant. . . . Dico ergo quod haec propositio, "Deus est" quantum in se est per se nota est, quia praedicatum est idem cum subjecto : Deus enim est suum esse. . . . Sed quia nos non scimus de Deo quid est, non est nobis per se nota, sed indiget demonstrari per ea quae sunt magis nota quoad nos, et minus nota quoad naturam, sc. per effectus.'

[1] *Summa contra Gent.*, Lib. I, cap. 11 : 'Nec etiam oportet . . . . Deo posse aliquid majus cogitari, si potest cogitari non esse. Nam quod possit cogitari non esse, non ex imperfectione sui esse est vel incertitudine, quum suum esse sit secundum se manifestissimum, sed ex debilitate nostri intellectus, qui eum intueri non potest per se ipsum sed ex effectibus ejus. Et sic, ad cognoscendum ipsum esse ratiocinando perducitur.' [2] Ibid., cap. 13.

[3] *Summa Theol.*, Ia pars, q. 32, art. 1 : 'Respondeo dicendum, quod impossibile est per rationem naturalem ad cognitionem trinitatis divinarum personarum pervenire. Ostensum est enim supra quod homo per rationem naturalem in cognitionem Dei pervenire non potest, nisi ex creaturis. Creaturae autem ducunt in Dei cognitionem sicut effectus in causam : hoc igitur solum ratione naturali de Deo cognosci potest, quod competere ei necesse est secundum quod est omnium entium principium. . . . Virtus autem creativa Dei est communis toti Trinitati : unde pertinet ad unitatem essentiae, non ad distinctionem personarum. Per rationem igitur naturalem cognosci non possunt de Deo ea quae pertinent ad distinctionem personarum.'

[4] *In Boet. de Trin.* I, 4 : 'Et nullo modo potest demonstrative

a highly dangerous practice to attempt to prove the articles of the faith in the presence of infidels by means of reasons which can never be conclusive. It exposes the faith to derision, by suggesting that these reasons form the grounds of our belief. The proper method of apologetics is to show that the tenets of the faith are not impossible; [1] that is a sufficient answer to the unbelieving.

Moreover, like Albert, Thomas carried his rationalism still further. He saw too plainly the implications of the Aristotelian system, which he had adopted, to attempt to reconcile it with the doctrine of creationism which had formed an integral part of the older Augustinian scholasticism. He maintained stoutly against all opposition that the eternity of the world could not be disproved. Not only did he compose a whole treatise on this subject, the *De Aeternitate Mundi contra Murmurantes*; he also devoted a large section of his *Summa contra Gentiles* to the discussion of the problem (Book II, chaps. xxxi–xxxvii). A beginning of the world in time is not demonstrable by reason any more than its eternity.[2] Philosophically speaking, both are possible hypotheses, and reason alone is unable to decide between them. It is, therefore, only by faith that we can assert the truth of a creation in time.[3]

---

probari, quamvis ad hoc aliquales rationes non necessariae, nec multum probabiles nisi credenti, haberi possint.'

[1] *Summa Theol.*, loc. cit. : ' Cum enim aliquis ad probandum fidem inducit rationes, quae non sunt cogentes, cedit in irrisionem infidelium. Credunt enim, quod hujusmodi rationibus innitamur, et propter eas credamus. Quae igitur fidei sunt, non sunt tentanda probare, nisi per auctoritates his qui auctoritates suscipiunt. Apud alios sufficit defendere non esse impossibile, quod praedicat fides.'

[2] *Summa Theol.* Ia pars, q. 46, art. 1.

[3] Ibid., art. 2 : ' Respondeo dicendum, quod mundum non semper fuisse, sola fide tenetur, et demonstrative probari non potest, sicut et supra de mysterio Trinitatis dictum est. Et hujus ratio est : quia novitas mundi, non potest demonstrationem recipere ex parte ipsius mundi. Demonstrationis enim principium est " quod quid est ".

The attempt to prove such a creation must be abandoned, lest it should cause the enemy to blaspheme.[1]

It is not difficult to understand the opposition aroused by this revolutionary teaching. The conservative party at once took alarm. Here was the whole basis of the faith being destroyed before their eyes. And their alarm was not without good cause. Already there had grown up in the university of Paris a school of Averroists, who by a slight extension of the doctrine of Thomas concerning the relations of philosophy to theology, were openly professing philosophical doctrines contrary to the teaching of the Church, while safeguarding their orthodoxy by falling back on what their opponents miscalled the theory of a double truth.[2] That Thomas himself never departed from the strictest orthodoxy is of course unquestioned, but the complete separation which he effected between the two orders of knowledge was too susceptible of a perverse interpretation not to arouse the suspicions of the more concervative minds. Moreover, the rivalry between the Dominican and Franciscan Orders served to intensify the struggle. Beside the teaching of Alexander and Bonaventura, both Franciscans, the doctrines of the Dominican masters seemed dangerous innovations even to members of their own order like

Unumquodque autem secundum rationem suae speciei abstrahit ab "hic" et "nunc", propter quod dicitur quod universalia sunt ubique et semper. Unde demonstrari non potest quod homo, aut coelum, aut lapis non semper fuit.'

[1] *Summa Theol.*, loc. cit. : ' Unde mundum incoepisse est credibile, non autem demonstrabile vel scibile. Et hoc utile est, ut conderetur, ne forte aliquis quod fidei est demonstrare praesumens, rationes non necessarias inducat, quae praebeant materiam irridendi infidelibus existimantibus nos propter hujusmodi rationes credere, quae fidei sunt.'

[2] Cf. the decree of 1277 : ' Dicunt enim ea esse vera secundum philosophiam, sed non secundum fidem catholicam, quasi sint duae contrariae veritates.' Deniflé-Chatelain, *Chartularium*, i, p. 543.

Cf. Gilson, *Études*, etc., ' La doctrine de la double vérité '.

Robert Kilwardby, whose successor in the see of
Canterbury, John Peckham, gave voice to the protesta-
tions of the adherents of the older teaching against
the perils of this new rationalism. The doctrine of
the Dominican Order, so he writes, has rejected the
opinions of the saints, and is based almost entirely on
philosophical considerations, so that the house of God
is filled with idols.[1]   But his protests were in vain.
Already in 1285 Thomas was made the doctor of his
order, and before a generation had passed the innovations of his teaching had been accepted as part of the
scholastic heritage. The Thomist view of the relation
between faith and reason was finally adopted as the
official teaching of the Roman Church, and has continued to hold that position till the present day.

[1] Cf. John Peckham's letter dated January 1285. Ehrle, ' John
Peckham über den Kampf des Augustinismus und Aristotelismus in
der zweiten Hälfte des 13. Jahrhunderts ', in the *Zeitschrift für
Katholische Theologie*, 1889, p. 181 : ' Et ut sacrosancta Romana
ecclesia attendere dignaretur, quod cum doctrina duorum ordinum
in omnibus dubitabilibus sibi pene penitus hodie adversetur ; cumque
doctrina alteriis eorumdem ; abjectis et ex parte vilipensis sanctorum
sententiis, philosophicis dogmatibus quasi totaliter innitatur, ut
plena sit idolis domus Dei et languore . . . '

III

THE RELATION BETWEEN PHILOSOPHY AND THEOLOGY IN DUNS SCOTUS

THE teaching of Duns Scotus on the relation between philosophy and theology does not differ so widely from that of Thomas as has sometimes been supposed. While criticizing the Angelic Doctor on certain points of detail, he agrees with him on the main issues, and his own theory is little more than an extension in their application to particular aspects of the problem of the principles already laid down by his great predecessor.[1] Thus at the beginning of his prologue to the *Opus Oxoniense* he asks the question whether man, in his earthly state, stands in need of a special supernatural form of knowledge to which he could not attain by the natural light of reason.[2] The question is answered in the affirmative. Man is an agent who acts for the sake of an end; he needs therefore a three-fold knowledge. First, he must know how his end may be acquired; secondly, what means are necessary to pursue it; and finally, he must have some guarantee that these means are sufficient for the attainment. But these conditions are not fulfilled by natural reason. Supernatural happiness (*beatitudo*), which is the last end of man, is, as it were, a reward given him by God for his merits and consequently cannot be deduced by

[1] Cf. A. Schmid, *Die Thomistische und Scotistische Gewissheitslehre*, p. 48.

[2] *Op. Ox.*, Prologus, q. 1: 'Utrum homini pro statu isto sit necessarium aliquam doctrinam specialem supernaturaliter inspirari, ad quam non possit attingere lumine naturali intellectus?'

natural necessity, being a contingent act of the free will of God, and therefore not, scientifically speaking, knowable. It follows, then, that man must have some supernatural knowledge if he is to fulfil his destiny.[1]

Now there are many propositions which are inaccessible to us through the medium of our natural cognitive faculties, the active intellect, and the phantasm, which must be communicated to us by the divine revelation, because we should otherwise be unable to discover them.[2] This revelation is called supernatural because it proceeds from an agent which is not the natural source of our knowing, it is derived from God himself, not from the processes of human reasoning.[3] But it is also supernatural in a further sense; its content is supernatural, that is to say, it supplies the place of an ideal supernatural object. For the object from which the knowledge of the proposition ' God is three and one ' naturally would be derived, i. e. its logical ground, is the divine essence itself, as known *sub ratione propria*, in its own intrinsic nature, which is for us a supernatural object, for we can never know God as He

[1] Loc. cit., n. 8 : ' Omni cognoscenti agenti propter finem, necessaria est triplex cognitio. Primo quomodo et qualiter finis acquiratur. Secundo, cognitio omnium quae sunt necessaria ad finem. Tertio est necessarium cognoscere, quod omnia ista sufficiant ad talem finem. . . . Sed haec tria non potest viator ratione naturali cognoscere. . . . Quia beatitudo confertur tanquam praemium pro meritis ejus, quem Deus acceptat tanquam dignum tali praemio, et per consequens nulla naturali necessitate sequitur ad actus nostros qualescunque, sed contingenter a Deo, actus aliquos . . . tanquam meritorios acceptante. Hoc autem non est naturaliter scibile,' etc. ' Ergo,' etc.

[2] Loc. cit., n. 21 : ' Posita tota actione intellectus agentis et phantasmatum, multae complexiones remanebunt ignotae . . . quarum cognitio est nobis necessaria. Istarum igitur notitiam est necesse nobis supernaturaliter tradi, quia nullus earum notitiam potuit naturaliter invenire,' etc.

[3] Loc. cit., n. 22 : ' Haec autem prima traditio talis doctrinae dicitur revelatio, quae ideo est supernaturalis, quia est ab agente, quod non est naturaliter motivum intellectus nostri pro statu isto.'

actually is, in and for Himself.[1] The revelation,
therefore, supplies the place of the object and gives
us ' knowledge about ' the divine persons, though not
sub propria ratione, which knowledge is therefore
imperfect and obscure.[2] Theology then is supernatural in both senses, both by reason of its origin and
its content.

The subject-matter of theology is God ; [3] but we
must distinguish between the ideal theology and the
theology that is possible for us. The ideal theology
deals with its object as it would be represented to an
intellect which was adequate to conceive it. Our
theology, on the other hand, only deals with that
object in so far as it can be grasped by our finite minds.
Thus an intellect which was unable to comprehend
the science of geometry might believe in the truth of
certain geometrical propositions, though such knowledge of them would not be scientific. Yet geometry
in se would still be a science to an intellect adequate
to understand it.[4] The first object, then, of our

[1] *Op. Ox.*, Prologus, n. 22 : ' Aliter etiam posset dici supernaturalis,
quia est ab agente supplente vicem objecti supernaturalis. Nam
objectum natum causare notitiam hujus : " Deus est trinus et unus "
vel similium, est essentia sub propria ratione cognita ; ipsa autem
sub tali ratione cognoscibilis est objectum nobis supernaturale. Quodcumque igitur causat notitiam aliquarum veritatum, quae per tale
objectum sic cognitum natae sunt esse evidentes, illud agens in hoc .
supplet vicem illius objecti.'

[2] Ibid. : ' Nam revelans hanc (*sc.* veritatem) " Deus est trinus ",
causat in mente aliqualem notitiam hujus veritatis, licet obscuram,
quia causat de objecto non sub propria ratione cognito. Quod
objectum, si cognitum esset, natum esset causare notitiam perfectam
et claram veritatis illius.'

[3] Op. cit., Prol., q. 3, n. 7 : ' Loquendo de theologia in se quantum
ad veritates necessarias ipsius, dico quod primum objectum theologiae
in se non potest esse nisi Deus ' (*Quaestio* II *lateralis*).

[4] Loc. cit., n. 4 : ' Theologia in se est cognitio talis, qualem natum
est facere objectum theologicum in intellectu sibi proportionato.
Theologia vero in nobis, talis est cognitio, qualem intellectus noster
natus est habere de illo objecto. Exemplum. Si aliquis intellectus

theology, in so far as it is ours, is the *primum notum*, of which the first truths are immediately known. This *primum notum* is infinite being, the most perfect conception which we can have of God, who is in himself the prime subject.[1] Theology thus differs from metaphysic, not only by virtue of its method, but also by reason of its subject-matter. For metaphysic does not deal with God as *subjectum primum* ; its province is being as such, and its properties the *passiones entis*, which are presupposed in the special sciences.[2] Yet there is a natural theology which forms part of metaphysic ; for God, though not the prime subject of this science in so far as He falls under the notion of being, is considered by it, and that in the most lofty way possible for a science which is acquired by purely natural processes.[3]

---

non possit intelligere geometralia, posset autem alicui credere de geometralibus; geometria esset sibi fides, non scientia: esset tamen in se scientia, quia objectum geometriae natum est facere de se scientiam intellectui proportionato.'

[1] Loc. cit., n. 12 : ' Theologiae nostrae, ut nostra est, non oportet dari objectum primum nisi primum notum, de quo noto immediate cognoscantur primae veritates. Illud primum notum est ens infinitum, quia iste est conceptus perfectissimus quem possumus habere de illo, quod est in se primum subjectum.'

[2] Loc. cit., n. 20 : ' Dico quod metaphysica non est de Deo tanquam de primo subjecto . . . quia praeter scientias speciales oportet esse aliquam communem in qua probentur in communi omnia quae sunt communia illis specialibus; ergo praeter scientias speciales oportet esse aliam communem de ente, in qua traditur cognitio passionum de ente, quae supponitur in aliis scientiis specialibus. Si igitur aliqua est naturaliter de Deo praeter istam, est alia de ente naturaliter scita inquantum ens. Cf. also *Quaestiones in Metaph.*, Lib. I, q. 1 : ' Utrum subjectum metaphysicae sit ens inquantum ens . . . sicut posuit Avicenna, vel Deus et intelligentiae, sicut posuit Averroes ? ' Here both views are controverted, but the authorship of the *Quaestiones* is, to say the least of it, doubtful. For Avicenna's view, see his *Metaphysica*, Lib. I, cap. 1. With the view here expressed by Scotus cf. Aristotle, *Metaph.* I, 1003a : Ἔστιν ἐπιστήμη τις, ἣ θεωρεῖ τὸ ὂν ᾗ ὄν, καὶ τὰ τούτῳ ὑπάρχοντα καθ' αὐτό, κ.τ.λ.

[3] *Op. Ox.*, loc. cit. : ' Deus vero etsi non est subjectum primum in

The question then arises whether theology is a
science, and if so whether it has other sciences subordinated to it or whether it is itself subordinate to
other sciences.   Now to be a science a discipline must
satisfy four conditions.   It must be a form of cognition
which affords certainty ; its object must be necessary ;
it must proceed causally ; and from step to step by
a syllogism.   The last of these prerequisites is not
fulfilled by theology ; we cannot therefore call it
a science in the strictest meaning of the term.   Nevertheless it may be called a science in as much as it
satisfies the first three conditions.[1]   Moreover, the
theology of the beatified souls is perfectly scientific,
for it fulfils all the four requirements.[2]   But here
a difficulty arises, for theology includes contingent as
well as necessary truths, and it would seem that the
contingent is not susceptible to scientific treatment.[3]
If we define science in the sense which Aristotle
employs in the first book of the *Posterior Analytics*,
where necessity is postulated as a condition of scientific

metaphysica est tamen consideratum in illa scientia nobilissimo modo,
quo potest in aliqua scientia considerari naturaliter acquisita.'

[1] *Op. Ox.*, loc. cit., n. 26 (q. iii et iv *lateralis*) : ' Juxta hoc quaero,
utrum theologica in se sit scientia, et utrum ad aliquam scientiam
habeat habitudinem aliquam subalternantis vel subalternatae ?   Ad
primum dico, quod quatuor includit scientia stricte sumpta : sc. quod
sit cognitio certa, hoc est absque deceptione et dubitatione, de
cognito necessario, causata a causa evidente intellectui, applicata ad
cognitum per discursum syllogisticum. . . . Ergo theologia in se non
est scientia quantum ad ultimam conditionem scientiae, sed quantum
ad alias tres conditiones est scientia in se, et in intellectu divino.'

[2] Ibid., n. 27 : ' Hoc potest concedi, videlicet quod beatus vere
potest habere scientiam theologicam quantum ad omnes conditiones
scientiae, quia omnes conditiones scientiae concurrunt in cognitione
beatorum.'

[3] Ibid., n. 28 : ' Sed aliud dubium est . . . quia sicut ad theologiam
pertinent necessaria, sic et contingentia . . . de contingentibus autem
non videtur posse esse scientia . . . ergo non videtur quod theologia,
ut extendit se ad omnia illa contenta, posset habere rationem
scientiae . . . '

knowledge,[1] then there can be no science of contingent
truths, for to know the contingent as necessary is not
to know the contingent at all.[2] But if we define
science as it is defined in the *Ethics*, where it is contrasted with opinion and assumption,[3] then we may
well call such knowledge science.[4] It would be better,
therefore, with Bonaventura,[5] to use the term *sapientia*;
for the ideal theology deals with the highest and most
perfect being, and as regards its necessary content
supplies certain necessary evidences. In other words,
however inaccessible to the human mind, truths
concerning the divine nature contain within themselves
the grounds of their own necessity and would be
evident to an intellect adequate to grasp them. Not
so the contingent matter of theology. Its evidence is
the evidence of the immediate rather than the mediated
conclusion. The truth may be perceived, but it
cannot be deduced, because as contingent it can have
no ground in anything except the free will of God.[6]

[1] Cf. Aristotle, *An. Post.* I, cap. 2 : Ἐπίστασθαι δὲ οἰόμεθα ἕκαστον
ἁπλῶς . . . ὅταν τήν τ᾽ αἰτίαν οἰώμεθα γινώσκειν, δι᾽ ἣν τὸ πρᾶγμά
ἐστιν, ὅτι ἐκείνου αἰτία ἐστὶν καὶ μὴ ἐνδέχεσθαι ἄλλως ἔχειν. Ib. c. 4
Ἐπεὶ δ᾽ ἀδύνατον ἄλλως ἔχειν, οὗ ἐστιν ἐπιστήμη ἁπλῶς, κ.τ.λ. Ib. c. 6
Εἰ οὖν ἐστιν ἡ ἀποδεικτικὴ ἐπιστήμη ἐξ ἀναγκαίων ἀρχῶν (ὁ γὰρ ἐπί-
σταται, οὐ δυνατὸν ἄλλως ἔχειν), κ.τ.λ.

[2] *Op. Ox.*, loc. cit. : ‘Sed numquid eorum est scientia ? Dico
quod secundum illam rationem scientiae positam in Iᵒ Post., quae
requirit necessitatem objecti, non potest de eis esse scientia ; quia
cognoscere contingens ut necessarium, non est cognoscere contingens.’

[3] Cf. *Eth. Nic.*, VI, 1139b : Ἔστω δὴ οἷς ἀληθεύει ἡ ψυχὴ τῷ
καταφάναι ἢ ἀποφάναι πέντε τὸν ἀριθμόν· ταῦτα δ᾽ ἐστὶ τέχνη ἐπιστήμη φρόνησις σοφία νοῦς. ὑπολήψει γὰρ καὶ δόξῃ ἐνδέχεται διαψεύ-
δεσθαι. But the passage goes on to affirm the necessity of the objects
of knowledge, after the same manner as those in *Post An.*, quoted in
note I.

[4] *Op. Ox.*, loc. cit. : ‘tamen secundum quod accipit philosophus
scientiam VIᵒ Eth. ut dividitur contra opinionem et suspicionem, bene
potest esse scientia, quia est habitus quo determinate verum dicimus.’

[5] See above, ch. 2, p. 66.

[6] Loc. cit. : ‘Magis tamen proprie potest dici quod theologia

Further, theology is not subordinate to any other science ; for notwithstanding the fact that it shares, in some measure, its subject-matter with metaphysic, it accepts no principle from metaphysic, and no theological property or quality can be demonstrated by means of the principles of being as such. Nor has it any other science subordinate to it, because no other science derives its principles from theology,[1] for all other sciences can be deduced from principles which are knowable in a purely natural manner.

Scotus then goes on to describe theology as a practical science, a classification which we find also in Roger Bacon [2] and Richard of Middleton,[3] both Franciscans and also members of the Oxford school. Practice, or praxis, is defined as an act of a faculty other than the intellect, which is naturally posterior to the act of cognition, and which must be elicited according to right reason in order that the act may be a right act.[4] It is carefully distinguished from the act of

secundum se est sapientia, quia de necessariis contentis in ea ipsa habet evidentiam et necessitatem et certitudinem, et objectum altissimum et perfectissimum. Quantum autem ad contingentia habet evidentiam manifestam de contingentibus in objecto theologico ut in se visis, et non habet evidentiam mendicatam ab aliis prioribus. Unde notitia contingentium (ut habetur in ea) magis assimilatur intellectui principiorum quam scientia conclusionum.'

[1] *Op. Ox.*, loc. cit., n. 29 : ' Dico quod haec scientia nulli subalternatur. Quia licet subjectum ejus possit aliquo modo contineri sub subjecto metaphysicae, nulla tamen principia accipit a metaphysica, quia nulla passio theologica demonstrabilis est in ea per principia entis, vel per rationem sumptam ex ratione entis. Nec ipsa aliam sibi subalternat, quia nulla scientia accipit principia ab ipsa ; nam quaelibet alia in genere cognitionis naturalis habet resolutionem suam ultimo ad aliqua principia immediate naturaliter nota.'

[2] *Compendium Studii Philosophiae*, c. 1, Brewer, *Op. inedit.*, p. 396.
[3] *In IV Libros Sententiarum*, Prologus, q. iv.
[4] *Op. Ox.*, Prol., q. 4, n. 3 : ' Dico igitur primo, quod praxis ad quam cognitio practica extenditur est actus alterius potentiae quam intellectus, naturaliter posterior intellectione, natus elici conformiter rationi rectae, ad hoc ut sit actus rectus.'

understanding as such ; the extension of one act of the intellect to another, that is to say the purely intellectual process, is not to be confused with praxis, else we should have to classify logic among the practical sciences.[1] Nor are the acts of the sensitive faculties which are prior to the act of understanding or the animal appetites included in the notion of praxis.[2] Praxis is an act of volition, following upon an act of the understanding, and signifies the psychic act itself, even when it does not result in external action.[3] The act of intelligence is necessarily prior to the action or praxis. But not all such intellectual acts are called practical, but only those which are determinative of the rightness of an act, either formally or virtually. When the previous apprehension is not so determinative it is not, strictly speaking, ' practical ', because it is not normative.[4]

Theology, then, is a practical science, because the

[1] Ibid. : ' Et si dicas unum actum intellectus extendi ad alium, non propter hoc secundus erit praxis . . . nec primus est cognitio practica, quia tunc logica esset practica, quia dirigit in actibus discurrendi.'

[2] Ibid. : ' Actus non habentes ordinem ad intellectum, cujusmodi sunt actus vegetativi, aut actus naturaliter praecedentes intellectionem, ut actus sensitivi, non dicuntur praxes, nec dicitur ad eos extendi notitia practica, ut sunt priores intellectione. Similiter actus appetitus potentiae sensitivae, quatenus praecedunt actum intellectus, non sunt praxes.'

[3] Ibid., n. 5 : ' Actus imperatus a voluntate non est primo praxis, sed quasi per accidens. . . . Oportet igitur aliquem alium actum esse primo praxim, iste non est nisi volitio, quia per istam habet actus imperatus dictas conditiones. . . . '

[4] Ibid., n. 14 : ' Dico quod praxim necessario naturaliter praecedit aliqua cognitio, . . . et secundum hoc, praxi convenit posterioritas, et cognitioni prioritas. . . . Sed non semper ista intellectio prior est practica, sed tantummodo quando est determinativa rectitudinis respectu ipsius praxis, et hoc vel formaliter, vel virtualiter. Quando autem in apprehensione praevia nulla est determinatio formalis vel virtualis de rectitudine praxis, licet ibi sit prioritas, tamen tunc deficit conformitas, . . . quia nihil determinate ostendit de rectitudine praxis.'

end of man is not only to know God, but to love him. Those who have classed theology as a speculative science have ignored this fact.[1] And to love God is a free act of the will. There is therefore a need of some normative form of knowledge, which shall be regulative of the will, as prudence is the norm of the moral virtues. For even were we to concede that man was incapable of error concerning his end *in universali*, that once God was revealed to his intellect his will was bound to love him, there would still be the possibility of error *in particulari*, and consequently a need of directive knowledge. And this particular directive knowledge is theology.[2] Similarly, action is concerned not only with the motive, but also with the circumstances, and here again the possibility of error arises, proving the necessity of theology as a practical science.[3] The whole of this argument, as Scotus well knows, depends on the distinction made by Aristotle in the sixth book of the Nicomachean *Ethics* between σοφία and φρόνησις; but Aristotle himself makes theology a speculative science, and places Man's highest end in θεωρία.[4] Yet he maintains that the

---

[1] *Op. Ox.*, loc. cit., n. 23 : ' Ponunt theologiam esse speculativam, non obstante quod extendatur ad dilectionem finis.'

[2] Loc. cit., n. 17 : ' Contra hoc arguitur . . . etsi voluntas non potest errare circa finem in universali ostensum, potest tamen . . . errare circa finem in particulari ostensum ; ergo ad hoc, ut recte agat circa finem particulariter ostensum requiritur directiva ostensio. Ostensio autem finis in theologia, est finis non in universali sed in particulari. . . . '

[3] Ibid. : ' Habitus directivus non ponitur propter substantiam actus, sed propter circumstantias . . . ergo licet voluntas esset determinata ad substantiam actus tendentis in finem in particulari, requireretur tamen directio quantum ad circumstantias. . . . Ex istis duabus rationibus arguitur, quia ubicumque contingit in praxi errare et recte agere, ibi est notitia practica necessaria ad dirigendum. In ista autem praxi, quae est dilectio finis, ut pertinet ad theologiam, contingit errare dupliciter . . . ergo,' etc.

[4] Cf. *Eth. Nic.* x, cap. vii ; *Eth. Eud.* vii, cap. xv.

prime mover moves the world as an object of love.[1]
Why then, Duns asks, does he not classify theology as
a practical science? The reason is not far to seek;
his theology is speculative, because he did not conceive
the act of loving as a free act of the will, but as necessitated *necessitate naturali*. Had he conceived the love
of the 'first intelligence' as a free act he would have
agreed with us in making theology a practical science.[2]

Finally, theology is a practical science because it is
ultimately the source of the first principles of rightness
in our will. It determines the intellect to the knowledge of the rightness of the acts which are concerned
with the necessities of salvation.[3] For although the
knowledge of the Trinity of the Divine Persons does
not reveal God as a more desirable end than if He were
only one, it being as God and not as triune that He is
the chief end of man, the will, which is ignorant of
the mystery of the Trinity, may err in desiring its end
by desiring to enjoy only one of the divine persons.[4]

---

[1] Cf. *Metaph.* V, 1072a : ἐστί τι ὃ οὐ κινούμενον κινεῖ, ἀΐδιον, καὶ
οὐσία καὶ ἐνέργεια οὖσα, κινεῖ δὲ ὧδε· τὸ ὀρεκτὸν καὶ τὸ νοητὸν κινεῖ
οὐ κινούμενον. . . . 1072b : κινεῖ δὲ ὡς ἐρώμενον.

[2] *Op. Ox.*, loc. cit., n. 23 : 'Sed quare non tenetur in hoc, cum ratio
scientiae practicae et speculative accipiatur ab ipso, etc. Respondeo,
illud amare quod poneret in intelligentia, poneret necessitate naturali
voluntati inesse, ita quod non contingeret ibi eam errare et recte
agere, ita quod respectu illius notitia esset tantummodo ostensiva, non
directiva, nec quantum ad objectum in particulari, nec quantum
ad aliquam ejus conditionem vel aliquam circumstantiam actus
volendi. . . . Si igitur convenisset nobiscum, ponendo amare respectu
finis libere, recte et non recte elici, nec recte elici nisi conformiter
rationi rectae, non tantum ostendenti objectum, se etiam dictanti sic
esse eliciendum, forte posuisset respectu talis notitiam practicam,' etc.

[3] Ibid., n. 31 : 'Primum subjectum theologiae est virtualiter
conforme volitioni rectae, quia a ratione ejus sumuntur principia
prima rectitudinis in volitione. Ipsum etiam determinat intellectum
creatum ad notitiam rectitudinis determinatae ipsius praxis quoad
omnia theologicalia necessaria,' etc.

[4] Ibid., n. 29 : 'Licet enim Trinitas personarum non ostendat
finem appetibiliorem quam si esset non Trinus, quia est finis inquan-

Similarly, one who is ignorant of the fact of creation may err by not repaying by love and gratitude the debt of such great goodness. Or one who is ignorant of the fact of redemption may err likewise by not repaying with love such transcendent benefits.[1]

Such, then, is Scotus's somewhat confused account of the nature of theology, the exact significance of which is not easy to estimate. Indeed, it has been frequently misunderstood by historians of philosophy and dogmatics. The use of the term *scientia practica* might at first suggest a crudely pragmatic interpretation which would be far indeed from his real meaning. A closer examination will serve to show how nearly Scotus approaches to the Thomistic conception. The resemblance between the teaching of the two schoolmen is far greater than has generally been supposed. Their main difference lies in this : while Thomas lays emphasis chiefly on the ' necessary ' element of the divine revelation, the truths concerning the divine being in its intrinsic nature, Scotus accentuates the contingent aspect of theology, the relationship of God to the world, which depends wholly on the free act of the divine will and is therefore not amenable to speculative treatment. And in the last resort this difference proceeds from a diversity between their psychological conceptions. Thomas is throughout an intellectualist, and for him the intellect is the highest faculty, be it human or divine ; hence his tendency to interpret the phenomena of volition in a deterministic

tum est unus Deus, non inquantum Trinus, tamen voluntatem ignorantem Trinitatem contingit errare in amando vel desiderando finem, desiderando frui una persona sola.'

[1] Loc. cit. Some doubt has been thrown on the genuineness of this passage and the one quoted in the last footnote. Mauritius Hibernicus (Maurice O'Fihely, Archbishop of Tuam, *d.* 1513) regards it as a later addition, but Wadding accepts it as genuine in a very characteristic marginal comment : ' Ponitur ut additio a Mauritio sed juxta antiqua MS. est vere textus.'

manner. Not so Duns; for him the will has the priority both in man and God, and becomes, in the latter case, the ultimate principle of his cosmology.

But profound as this difference may be, it is a difference rather of attitude than of objective import. On the chief issues of the problem in question there is almost complete agreement. Thomas and Scotus concur in separating philosophy from theology, making each sovereign in its own sphere, and also in recognizing a dual source of truth: natural reason and revelation. Both thus distinguish sharply two types of theology, one natural, a branch of metaphysic, and the other supernatural; and whatever differences may exist in their conceptions of the actual content of these two departments, the principles which constitute their structure and determine their mutual relations are essentially the same. The realization of this fact is of the greatest importance in view of the widespread misconception of the nature of the Scotist doctrine. The natural theology of Duns presents a problem to which we have already referred in our discussion on the authenticity of the various works attributed to his pen.[1] It is true that the sceptical conclusions maintained in the *Theoremata* form a striking contrast to the constructive metaphysic of the *Summa contra Gentiles* of Aquinas. But it would be in the highest degree misleading to confine our attention to what is but a fragment of our author's work, if indeed it be his at all. Taken as a whole the doctrines of the two great scholastics, while presenting certain important differences of detail, exhibit nevertheless a fundamental unity of principle. Both set out to establish the existence of the Supreme Being and to deduce his attributes by the same method of *a posteriori* reasoning from the facts of the empirical world of experience,

[1] See above, ch. i, p. 24.

and both reach very similar conclusions concerning the philosophical determination of the concept of God. For even if Scotus is somewhat more critical of the strict validity of the formal processes of logic involved, he yet does not hesitate to employ them both in the *De Primo Principio* and the two commentaries on the Sentences, and to sustain those very theses which the *Theoremata* declare to be, strictly speaking, indemonstrable, theses which Thomas was satisfied that he had adequately established by natural reason. And if the result of the Scotist investigation is to be regarded as a critique of the Thomistic conclusions, it is a critique which of itself introduces no new principle, but only carries out more rigorously the method formulated by the Angelic Doctor and his master Albert. And in the last resort it is a vain task to seek to define too closely the exact limits of the reasoning faculties of the human mind, as conceived by the scholastic thinkers, and to hold apart the two processes of belief and logic in a system which postulated the validity of both. For as to the facts of the ultimate reality, there could be no doubt that the data both of reason and revelation were included in one truth, as the fundamental postulate of scholasticism, and it was inevitable that both should be merged in a psychological unity. Where the facts were not disputed, and the knowledge of them presupposed, the exact contribution of each of the two processes could never be determined with accuracy. The psychology of belief is too complicated and too obscure to permit any such consistent delineation. Both were inextricably intertwined in the one whole of the individual consciousness, within which it was impossible to differentiate them with any degree of completeness.

So, too, on the question of the status of theology as a science, in spite of differences, there is a large measure of agreement. We have seen that it is in a sense true, as Dr. Schmid has pointed out,[1] that Scotus denies to our theology the true character of a science in the strictest meaning of the term, on the ground that it is not formally discursive [2] and does not proceed syllogistically. He thus refuses to admit the parallelism introduced by Thomas between theology and the demonstrative sciences ; namely, the fact that theology argues from premisses provided by revelation in the same way that the demonstrative sciences argue from the self-evident premisses of reason.[3] But the force of this denial is not so significant as might at first sight be supposed, for Scotus goes on to admit that the theology of the beatified is discursive, and so fulfils all the requisite conditions of scientific knowledge.[4] And he concedes, furthermore, the existence of a necessary element in theology : [5] the truths concerning the divine persons, as they exist in and for themselves, do not belong to the world of contingent being, but are necessary in so far as it is impossible for God to be in Himself otherwise than as He is. It is only that portion of theology which is concerned with the facts of the world of created things, man and his redemption, &c., that is contingent, because these

---

[1] Cf. A. Schmid, *Die Thomistische und Scotistische Gewissheitslehre*, pp. 48–9 : ' Mit den Hauptgrundlagen der Thomistischen Glaubenslehre ist Duns Scotus einverstanden. Im einzelnen weicht er vielfach von ihr ab : vor allem dadurch dass er ihr den Charakter einer eigentlichen Wissenschaft abspricht, worin ihm viele Andere gefolgt sind. . . . Die Theologie kann den Charakter einer Wissenschaft für uns unmöglich aus Prinzipien erhalten die unserem diesseitigen Wissen ein-für-allemal entrückt sind : u.s.w.' Cf. also M. Verweyen, *Gesch. d. Philos. des Mittelalters*, pp. 126–7.

[2] Cf. Scotus, *Op. Ox.*, Prol., q. 3, n. 26, quoted in note 1, p. 88. Cf. also De Rada, *Controversiae inter S. Thomam et Scotum*, cont. ii.

[3] Cf. the passage from *Summa Theol.* Ia pars, q. 1, art. 8, quoted in n. 1, p. 77.

[4] Cf. the passage from the prologue of the *Op. Ox.*, q. 3, n. 27, quoted in n. 2, p. 88.

[5] Cf. ibid., n. 28, the passage quoted in n. 3, on the same page.

truths have no inward ground of necessity, but depend
solely on the free action of the divine will.

There is one point, however, where he departs
decidedly from the Thomist position. He refuses to
concede that our theology is subordinate to the theology of the beatified, or that it derives its principles
from it.[1]   Knowledge does not depend essentially
(i. e. as the effect depends upon its cause) on any other
factors except those which constitute its actual cause,
namely, the knowing faculty and its object. The
knowledge which the beatified soul has of the truth
of the Holy Trinity is an immediate vision, and cannot
be the cause of our knowing or the object of it in
such a way that by knowing the content of the beatified
mind I can know that God is both Three and One.
Granted even that I ' know ' his knowledge, I do not
know the object of it, i. e. the triune nature of God.
To say that our theology is a science, dependent on
the knowledge of the beatified, is like saying that
I know the science of geometry, because John knows
geometry, and I believe that he knows it.[2]   Thus our
theology cannot be related to the theology of the
beatified in the same way that one science is related

---

[1] Cf. the passage from Thomas, *Summa Theol.* Ia pars, q. 1, art. 2,
quoted in n. 2, p. 76.

[2] Cf. Scotus, *Op. Ox.*, Lib. III, dist. xxiv, q. unica, n. 4 : ' Scientia
non dependet essentialiter ab aliquo, causatum a causa, . . . nisi ab eo
quod est causa illius essentialiter. Sed notitia Beati, quam habet de
Deo trino et uno evidenter viso ex visione terminorum, non est
essentialiter causa nostrae theologiae, quia scientia non dependet
essentialiter nisi ex potentia et objecto in se ; . . . sed scientia illa
Beati non est objectum scientiae meae ita ut cognita notitia ejus,
cognoscam Deum trinum et unum, nec est potentia animae, nec
species objecti, nec aliquid mei quod possit esse causa scientiae meae
. . . ; igitur habitus in me in nullo dependet sicut a causa essentialiter,
a visione Beatorum, nec sequitur quod si scientia beatorum sit de
creditis a nobis, quod in nobis est scientia cum fide, immo esset
simile, si dicerem in me esse geometriam, quia in Joanne, quia ego
credo Joannem habere scientiam geometriae.'

to another ; the parallelism between harmony and arithmetic does not hold, for theology is not a science in the same sense of the term in which arithmetic and harmony are sciences.

Yet theology is a form of knowledge ; it does teach us facts about the nature of reality. What type of science then can it be ? Scotus answers, a practical science ; but the exact meaning of the phrase is open to misinterpretation. There is no implication in the term ' practical ' of any inferiority to the speculative sciences ; indeed, the implication is quite the reverse.[1] Theology is ' practical ' because it carries with it an imperative, and is essentially related to the will in a way in which the speculative sciences like metaphysics are not. And it is exactly in this fact that the superiority of theology is grounded ; for the will, according to Scotus, is a higher faculty than the intellect, and the last end of man consists in the act of the will, beatitude being the act of loving God, the supreme object of the human will.[1] It is thus assimilated to the moral sciences and becomes a kind of supernatural φρόνησις, a normative discipline regulative of the will, standing to the supernatural virtues in the same relation that prudence stands to the moral or natural virtues. It is not speculative, not because it is ranked below the speculative sciences, but because it is ranked above them, by virtue of the imperative which it implies. That this is the true interpretation of Scotus' use of the term *scientia practica* is shown by his treatment of the divine self-knowledge, the *theologia Dei*.[2] This divine theology may be called practical in so far as concerns those truths which belong to the divine

---

[1] Cf. *Reportata Parisiensia*, Lib. IV, dist. xlix, q. 3.

[2] *Op. Ox.*, Prol., q. 4, n. 33 : ' Ad quartum posset concedi quod theologia Dei de necessariis sit practica, quia in intellectu suo natum est primum objectum theologicum, quasi gignere notitiam conformem volitioni rectae, priorem naturaliter ipsa volitione.'

nature considered in and for itself. For God not only knows himself but also wills his own being; and his act of self-volition is determined by a conception consonant with right reason, namely, his own notion of his own essence, which is naturally prior to the divine self-willing. Thus the divine self-knowledge is not merely speculative but also normative; it is the κανὼν καὶ μέτρον of the self-volition of God, and therefore in a sense *scientia practica*. But Duns refuses to commit himself very definitely on this point, because the divine will, though free, cannot hold itself indifferently to rightness, being self-determined to its own rectitude; the divine self-knowledge is therefore not strictly imperative but only ostensive.[1] He therefore concludes by leaving the question undecided.[2] But in the case of the contingent world the divine theology is merely speculative, because in all matters outside the divine essence itself no *cognitio conformis rationi rectae* is prerequisite to the divine volition, for the rightness of the divine praxis is first determined by the divine volition itself.[3] On the other hand, for the created intellect, though *in se* it is speculative, the *theologia de contingentibus* is practical because it is

[1] Loc. cit., n. 36: ' Quia posita notitia quacumque rectitudinis ipsius praxis quamvis ista ex se possit conformare potentiam conformabilem seu rectificabilem aliunde, non tamen voluntatem divinam respectu sui primi objecti, quae ex se sola rectificatur respectu istius objecti, ita quod vel talis naturaliter tendit in illud, vel si libere, nullo modo est de se quasi indifferens ad rectitudinem, et quasi aliunde aliquo modo habens eam, ita quod notitia determinativa non est necessario prior volitione, quasi volitio eam requirat ut recte eliciatur, sed tantum praeexigit ostensionem objecti. Et istam notitiam ex se directivam non praeexigit ut directivam, sed tantum ut ostensivam,' etc.

[2] Ibid., n. 37 : ' In intellectu igitur divino non potest esse theologia contingentium practica. . . . Nam nulla cognitio conformis volitioni contingenti recte praecedit ipsam volitionem Dei, quia primo volitione determinatur praxi illi talis rectitudo.'

[3] Ibid., n. 39.

prescriptive; for the rightness and wrongness of things is ultimately dependent solely on the will of God, and theology communicates to us the revelation of that will.

The correct understanding of this use of the phrase *scientia practica* is essential to the comprehension of Scotus' conception of the relations between Faith and Knowledge, which has been so frequently misunderstood. Thus many have seen in him the beginning of that scepticism which ultimately proved the downfall of the scholastic system. Paul Haffner, for instance, in his *Grundlinien der Geschichte der Philosophie*, accuses him of attempting to show the incompatibility of theology with philosophy.

'While Thomas,' he says, 'lays great stress on the fact that the same truth is known in different ways, by philosophy and theology, Scotus is at great pains to hold the two sciences apart as far as possible. He accentuates the fact that no other science borrows its principles from theology, and that conversely theology shares no portion of its province with any other science, and more especially that it does not borrow any of its principles from metaphysic. Theology is for him rather a practical than a speculative science, for its purpose is not the extension of our knowledge, but the furthering of our salvation.' [1]

Nothing, as Dr. Minges has shown,[2] could be more misleading than such a conception of Scotus' teaching.

[1] P. Haffner, *Grundlinien*, etc., p. 598 : 'Er beweist auch die Unmöglichkeit des Zusammenwirkens der beiden Erkenntnissweisen. Während Thomas gerade darauf Gewicht legt, dass theilweise dieselbe Wahrheit nur in anderer Weise philosophisch und theologisch erkannt werde, bemüht sich Scotus diese beiden Wissenschaften aufs schärfste auseinander zu halten. Er betont dass keine andere Wissenschaft ihre Prinzipien der Theologie entlehne, und umgekehrt auch diese keines ihrer Gebiete mit einer anderen theile, und insbesondere keine Prinzipien der Metaphysik entlehne. Die Theologie ist ihm mehr eine praktische Wissenschaft denn eine spekulative, da sie nicht Erweiterung unser Erkenntniss, sondern Förderung unseres Heiles bezweckt.'

[2] *Das Verhältnis zwischen Glauben und Wissen, Theologie und Philosophie, bei Duns Scotus* (Paderborn, 1908).

Thomas, as we have seen, insists no less strongly than
Scotus on the separation of the theology of revelation,
sacra doctrina, from the natural theology which is
a part of metaphysic. The principles of theology are
the articles of faith ; [1] those of philosophy the self-
evident principles of natural reason.[2] Theology, it
is true, is argumentative, but it argues from the
authority of the sacred scriptures which is founded
upon the divine revelation, and only such authority
is certain and binding. Philosophical arguments and
reasonings founded on the statements of the doctors
of the Church are only tentative and probable ; [3] all
of which Scotus concedes without reservation. Nor
is it true that Scotus denies that theology shares any
portion of its subject-matter with any of the other
sciences. He expressly states in his prologue to the
Opus Oxoniense that God is also considered by the
science of metaphysic,[4] and repeats a similar statement
in the prologue to the *Reportata Parisiensia*, where

[1] *Summa Theol.* Ia pars, q. 1, art. 8, concl. : ' Haec doctrina
non argumentatur ad sua principia probanda, quae sunt articuli
fidei.'

[2] Ibid., art. 2, concl.

[3] Ibid., art. 8, ad 2 : ' Dicendum quod argumentari ex auctoritate est maxime proprium hujus doctrinae, eo quod principia hujus
doctrinae per revelationem habentur, et sic oportet quod credatur
auctoritati eorum quibus revelatio facta est, nec hoc derogat dignitati
hujus doctrinae ; nam licet locus ab auctoritate quae fundatur super
ratione humana sit infirmissimus, locus tamen ab auctoritate quae
fundatur super revelatione divina est efficacissimus. Ututur tamen
sacra doctrina etiam ratione humana, non quidem ad probandum
fidem . . . sed ad manifestandum aliqua alia, quae traduntur in hac
doctrina. . . . Et inde est quod etiam auctoritatibus philosophorum
sacra doctrina utitur. . . . Sed tamen sacra doctrina hujusmodi auctoritatibus utitur quasi extraneis argumenti et probabilibus ; auctoritatibus autem canonicae scripturae proprie, et ex necessitate arguendi ;
auctoritatibus autem aliorum doctorum ecclesiae, quasi argumentando
ex propriis, sed probabiliter.'

[4] Cf. the passage quoted from *Op. Ox.*, Prol., q. 3, n. 20, quoted
in n. 3, p. 87.

he maintains that the existence of God can be proved by metaphysic.[1] Moreover, the whole of his treatise, *De Primo Principio*, is devoted to the working out of a natural theology. Finally, it is quite inaccurate to contend that by calling theology a practical science Scotus means to deny that it contributes to the extension of our knowledge. He nowhere makes any statement of this sort. As we have already seen, by using the term *scientia practica* he means to imply that theology, as well as furnishing us with knowledge of the divine persons, also carries with it an imperative, giving us, like the principles of ethics, not only truth of fact but also norms for our conduct. For just as the truths of morals, no less than those of metaphysics, furnish us with an expansion of our field of knowledge and in their own sphere are no less certain and necessary than the first principles of speculative thought, so the truths of theology not only teach us facts about the nature of God, but also provide us with norms by which to regulate our actions so as to bring them into conformity with His will. Theology is a practical science because it not only teaches us what God is, but also commands us to love Him and shows us those actions by which He is pleased to be worshipped and served.

A similar misconception underlies M. De Wulf's statement in his *History of Mediaeval Philosophy*. In his section on theology and philosophy in Duns Scotus he remarks : ' Indeed his deep conviction about the inferiority of philosophy makes him avoid even the possibility of a conflict between the two sciences. He is excessive in his misgivings about the unaided natural powers of the understanding, and retrenches perhaps

---

[1] Cf. *Rep. Par.*, Prol., q. 3, art. 1 : ' Unde ex actu et potentia, finitate et infinitate, multitudine et unitate, et ex multis talibus quae sunt proprietates et passiones metaphysicae, potest concludi in Metaphysica Deum esse, sive primum ens esse.'

unduly the scope of its investigations.'[1] The author
is evidently referring to the negative conclusions of the
Theoremata, where it is stated that (to use Wadding's
phrase) *juxta regulas logicae in rigore sumptas* it is
impossible to prove that God is a living, intelligent,
and willing being.[2] But as we have already had
occasion to remark, the theorems here laid down are
not proven, and the whole section is a fragment which
is out of place in the context in which it has been
printed in Wadding's edition ; indeed, the treatise is
scarcely more than a collection of notes. It would,
therefore, be unfair to accept it as conclusive in the
face of the evidence provided by the *De Primo Principio*,
where the following conclusions are demonstrated.
1. That the supreme being necessarily possesses all
perfections.[3] 2. That the first efficient cause is an
intelligent and willing being.[4] So, too, both the
commentaries on the Sentences abound in philosophical
arguments by which the above-mentioned theses are
maintained.[5] Nor is it correct to say that Scotus
belittles the reasoning faculties. In two places he
maintains that, epistemologically speaking, belief has
less certainty than knowledge. Thus, in speaking of
the special illumination of the prophets and other holy
men, he contrasts the certitude of their revelation both
with faith and knowledge. Their certitude was as
great as the certitude of natural knowledge, though

---

[1] De Wulf, *History of Mediaeval Philosophy* (English Translation
by P. Coffey), sect. 328, p. 370.

[2] *Theoremata*, th. xiv, concl. 1–3.

[3] *De Primo Principio*, cap. 4 : ' Omnis perfectio simpliciter et in
summo, inest necessario naturae summae.'

[4] Ibid., n. 5 : ' Primum efficiens est intelligens et volens.'

[5] e. g. *Op. Ox.*, Lib. I, dist. ii, q. 2, n. 20 : ' Primo ostendo quod
primum efficiens est intelligens et volens, ita quod sua intellectio est
infinitorum distincte, et ipsa est sua essentia, et quod sua essentia
est repraesentativa infinitorum distincte : et ex hoc secundo . . .
concludetur sua infinitas.'

differing from it in kind. For the certitude of natural reason is derived from self-evident principles, while this certitude comes from elsewhere. And it was greater than the certitude of mere faith because faith leaves room for doubt.[1] So too in the *Collationes* he rejects the notion that faith as such is more noble than knowledge because it contradicts the statement of Hugo of St. Victor that faith stands midway between knowledge and opinion.[2]

In the same way it is highly misleading to compare Scotus with Kant, as W. Kahl has done, on the ground that he was the first to institute a critique of reason, and forbade its incursion into the realm of the transcendental world, thus removing knowledge to make room for faith.[3] Such a comparison is quite inappropriate. Scotus' teaching differs *toto caelo* from that of the *Critical Philosophy*; he remains always within the system of ideas by which the peripateticism of the thirteenth century is bounded, and should be judged only from the standpoint of the medieval mind.[4] To

---

[1] *Op. Ox.*, Lib. III, dist. xxiv, q. unica, n. 17 : ' Illa tamen certitudo non fuit evidens ex evidentia rei, quia tunc contradictio esset quod hujusmodi notitia et fides simul starent ; fuit tamen certitudo illa firma, sicut est certitudo scientialis, quae causatur ex principiis notis ex evidentia terminorum, sed non causabatur a talibus principiis, sed aliunde, ideo scientia non potuit dici ex evidentia rei ; fuit tamen major certitudo quam certitudo fidei, quia fides non excludit omnem dubitationem,' etc.

[2] *Collatio*, IX, n. 3 : ' Et sic fides esset nobilior quam scientia, quod est contra Hugonem de sacramentis, ubi dicitur quod fides est media inter scientiam et opinionem.' Cf. Hugo de S. Victore, *De Sacramentis*, etc., pars x, cap. 2. Migne, *P.L.*, vol. 176, col. 330.

[3] W. Kahl, *Die Lehre vom Primat des Willens bei Augustinus, Duns Scotus, und Descartes*, p. 79 f. : ' Zum ersten Mal klingt hier in der Geschichte der Philosophie jener Kritizismus in dem die Vernunft vor jedem unberechtigten Uebergreifen in das Transzendente zurückweist, der das Wissen aufhebt um für den Glauben Platz zu bekommen.'

[4] Cf. Minges, *Das Verhältnis zwischen Glauben und Wissen bei Duns Scotus*, p. 103 : ' Es ist wahr dass Scotus die Ansicht, die Theo-

compare it with the Kantian doctrine is to misunderstand totally the significance of the Scotist conception of *scientia practica*.[1] To take only two salient points, whereas Kant rejects all the metaphysical proofs of the existence of God, Scotus expressly asserts the validity of the *a posteriori* proofs of the existence of the Supreme Being from the nature of the creature. So also, whereas Kant insists on the impossibility of knowing things-in-themselves, Scotus is a convinced realist and insists on the objectivity of the *Denkbestimmungen* of the Logic of the Schools.

In fact the position of Duns Scotus hardly differs even in words from that of Thomas on the relations between faith and knowledge. The fundamental thesis

logie sei eine praktische Wissenschaft, wenigstens vorzieht. Indes will er etwas ganz anderes lehren als Kant, von dem er um eine ganze Weltanschauung abweicht. Scotus ist auch in diesem Punkte durch und durch Anhänger der peripatetisch-scholastischen Anschauungen, und nur von diesen aus zu erklären und zu verstehen.' Cf. also : *Ist Duns Scotus Indeterminist?* p. 137 f. : ' Ebenso ist es sehr verkehrt wenn man den Willensprimat des Scotus dem Kants gleichstellt. . . . Scotus nimmt in Bezug auf Erkenntnisslehre, speziell betreffs religiöser Erkenntniss, und Begriff der Religion, einen ganz anderen Standpunkt ein als Kant und die an Kant sich schliessenden Philosophen und Theologen.'

[1] Cf. Troeltsch, *Götting'sche gelehrte Anzeigen*, 1903, Februarheft, pp. 103–5 : ' Die Theologie als *scientia practica* zu bezeichnen heisst nur sie als eine an den freien Willen sich verwendende Technik der Erlangung des Heiles betrachten, wobei dann freilich die Kenntniss des Heiles selbst durch Offenbarung gegeben ist und die Offenbarungsbegriffe.'

A similar misconception underlies the statement of Joseph Bernhart, *Die philosophische Mystik des Mittelalters*, p. 208 : ' Erscheinungen wie die Empiristik des Roger Baco und verwandter Repräsentanten der Hinwendung auf eine metaphysisch ungebundene Wissenschaft, dazu die tiefgehende Erkenntnisskritik des Duns Scotus und seiner Schüler, die das Band zwischen Wissen und Glauben zerschnitten und der Theologie, die ja nicht *ad fugam ignorantiae* berufen sei, nur die praktische Förderung des Seelenheils übrig liessen, hatten bereits die Scheidung zwischen der theologischen und philosophischen Erkenntnissweise angebahnt.' See also below, vol. ii, ch. vi.

of both is the same, namely, that there are certain truths which are accessible to the unaided reason, while others are attainable only through revelation. And indeed this unanimity is not surprising when we consider the fact that their doctrines proceed from a common source. Both accepted, on the one hand, the teaching of the Church, and on the other, the peripatetic theory of knowledge as laid down in the *Posterior Analytics*, together with the systematic account of the nature of reality as expounded in the *Metaphysics*. Under these conditions how could they have come to any other solution ? Minor differences of course there were, for Scotus' cosmology contained in it some elements of the older Augustinian scholasticism, but in the main the two doctors are in agreement. As Tenneman has pointed out, their differences are often more verbal than real ; for Scotus is a lover of fine distinctions and subtle shades of meaning, and often takes away with the left hand what he appears to concede with the right.[1] To accentuate too strongly the divergences from Thomism is to misinterpret the Scotist system.

And more especially is this the case with regard to the present problem. To contend, for instance, with Erdmann that the harmony between philosophy and the dogmas of the church is less perfect in Scotus than in Aquinas is to form a radical misconception of the true significance of both doctrines. Erdmann tries to maintain that Duns is less anxious than Thomas to make his philosophy accord with the Catholic doctrine,

---

[1] Cf. Tennemann, *Geschichte der Philosophie*, p. 737 : 'Man darf sich nicht wundern dass Scotus . . ., wo er selbst zuweilen etwas mit der einen Hand zu geben scheint, was er mit der anderen wieder nimmt, so verschieden verstanden und ausgelegt ist. Einige glauben dass er nur in Worten von Thomas abweiche.' The passage occurs as a matter of fact in a quite different context, namely, in connexion with the Scotist doctrine of the reality of the universal and the individual, but it expresses a truth that is more generally applicable.

and that the union between the two is less intimate.
The divergences between philosophy and theology,
he says, almost amount in Scotus to a complete
rupture.   He even goes so far as to accuse him of
declaring that a proposition which is true in philosophy
may sometimes be false in theology.[1]   Nothing could
be further from the true facts.   Scotus maintains no
less stoutly than Thomas that philosophy and theology
cannot contradict each other.   For example, when
dealing with the all-powerful nature of God, he
maintains that the divine omnipotence is a fact (though
indemonstrable, strictly speaking, if we mean by it,
as the theologians do, that God can do all things
immediately without the intervention of a secondary
cause) and that therefore all reasons adduced to the
contrary are sophistical and can consequently be
resolved by natural reason.[2]   Again, in the *Collationes*,
he states still more plainly that all theologians are
agreed that it can be shown by natural reason that the
articles of faith are not impossible, and that the
arguments brought against them can be shown by
natural reason not to be cogent.   The theologian is

---

[1] I. E. Erdmann, *Grundriss der Geschichte der Philosophie*, 3. Aufl.,
p. 412 ff. : ' Dazu kommt dass die völlige Uebereinstimmung zwischen
Kirchenlehre und Philosophie dem Duns gar nicht mehr so sehr zu
Herzen liegt wie dem Thomas : darum aber auch lange nicht mehr
so innig ist wie bei diesem. . . . Bei ihm selbst führt das Auseinander-
halten beider fast zur Trennung.   Es kommt sogar vor, dass er sagt ein
Satz sei zwar wahr für den Philosophen, aber er sei falsch für den
Theologen.'   Almost the same statement is found in Dorner, *Grundriss
der Dogmengeschichte*, p. 317 : ' Er trennt insbesondere die Philosophie
von der Theologie, wenn er sagt ein Satz, der in der Theologie nicht
wahr sei, könne in der Philosophie gelten.'   So also in Guttmann,
*Die Scholastik des 13. Jahrh. in ihren Beziehungen zum Judentum
und zur jüdischen Literatur*, we find the same assertion.

[2] *Op. Ox.*, Lib. I, dist. xlii, q. unica, n. 1 : ' Omnipotentiam esse
in entibus verum est : ergo omnis ratio probans impossibilitatem
omnipotentiae sophistica est.   Omnis autem ratio sophistica potest
per intellectum ex puris naturalibus solvi.'

able, therefore, to demonstrate the possibility of the doctrine of the Holy Trinity.[1] Moreover, in one respect Scotus goes even further than Thomas in advocating the use of arguments which do not amount to demonstrations in support of the articles of faith, even in the presence of the unbeliever. They are useful, he tells us, if they avail to show the possibility of the dogma we believe, because they can show him that we do not believe in impossibilities. It is only sophistical arguments that are dangerous and bring the faith into disrepute.[2] Thomas, on the other hand, is more cautious, and warns us against bringing up any arguments to prove the articles of faith in the presence of the infidel.[3]

The principal passage cited by Erdmann [4] in support of his contention that Scotus holds that a proposition may be philosophically true, though theologically false, is that found in the *Reportata Parisiensia*, Lib. IV,

[1] *Collatio*, X, n. 4 : ' Quilibet theologus fatetur quod potest ostendere naturaliter fidem suam non esse impossibilem, nec illa esse impossibilia, quae credimus, dum potest solvere rationes in contrarium fidem impugnantes ; sed quod non est impossibile est possibile. Ergo theologus potest ostendere per rationem naturalem et probare omnia credibilia esse possibilia, ut Deum esse trinum. . . .' Cf. *Rep. Par.*, Prol., q. 2, n. 6 : ' Sed de omni veritati scibili de Deo possumus scire quod ad ipsam non sequitur impossibile,' etc.

[2] *Op. Ox.*, Lib. II, dist. i, q. 3, n. 10 : ' Nec periculosum quantum ad infideles, si rationes necessariae possunt haberi, et si non possunt haberi rationes necessariae ad probandum esse factum, sc. articulum fidei. Si tamen haberentur ad probandum possibilitatem facti, etiam utile esset eas adducere contra infidelem, quia per hoc aliqualiter persuaderetur ne resisteret talibus creditis sicut impossibilibus. Adducere tamen sophismata pro demonstrationibus periculosum esset contra infideles, quia ex hoc exponeretur fides derisioni,' etc.

[3] Thomas, *Quodl.* III, q. 14, art. 31 : ' Est autem valde cavendum ne ad eas quae fidei sunt, aliquas demonstrationes adducere praesumat, propter duo,' etc.

[4] Op. cit., p. 413. The same passage is also cited by Guttmann, op. cit., p. 156, Dorner, op. cit., p. 317, and Schwane, *Dogmengeschichte der mittleren Zeit*, p. 78.

dist. xliii, q. 3, n. 18. The argument concerns the question whether nature can be the efficient cause of the resurrection. Scotus begins in his usual manner by citing an argument to prove the affirmative, for he is going to conclude with a negative. To every passive potentiality in nature there corresponds an active *potentia*. Now it is evident that there must be a passive potentiality in man for rising again (the resurrection of the dead being a dogma of the Church) ; *ergo* there must be an active potentiality in nature corresponding to this passive potentiality. In note 18 Scotus criticizes this argument and says that the philosophers and the theologians give different answers. *Apud philosophos* the proposition is true that to each natural passive potentiality there corresponds a *potentia activa*, but that *apud theologos* it is false. But he carefully qualifies his statement. He denies that it is *simpliciter verum*, in the first place, because the more perfect creatures in nature have a greater passive potentiality than the corresponding natural *potentia activa*, by which he means that man is capable of a supernatural as well as of a natural destiny ; and he goes on to make it quite clear that the philosophers to which he is referring are the pagan philosophers. According to them, he says, God causes naturally and of natural necessity.[1]   There is no question here,

---

[1] I quote the passage in full ; it reads as follows : ' Et cum probat cuilibet potentiae passivae correspondet propria potentia activa in natura, II° de Anima, dico quod aliter huic respondetur secundum philosophos et aliter secundum Theologos. *Apud philosophos non esset simpliciter verum, quod cuilibet potentiae passivae naturali correspondeat aliqua potentia activa naturalis,* quia entia perfecta in natura ordinantur ad majorem perfectionem passivam habendam quam in eis possit esse per potentiam activam naturalem. Nec propter hoc est potentia passiva frustra in natura, quia etsi per agens naturale non possit principaliter ad actum pervenire, potest tamen per ipsum dispositio ad talem actum induci ; nec hoc vilificat naturam, sed magis dignificat eam. . . . *Tamen apud philosophos est propositio vera, accipiendo potentiam activam naturalem pro potentia activa modo*

as Minges has recognized,[1] of any contradiction
between philosophy and theology. The proposition
holds good as a general principle in the world of nature ;
it is only in the supernatural realm that it is false,
a realm of which those who formulated it were wholly
ignorant. All that Scotus wishes to assert is that man
belongs not only to the natural but also to the supernatural world.

The generally accepted view, then, that Scotus'
philosophy is less concordant with the teaching of the
Church than that of Thomas must be dismissed as
mistaken. Indeed it would be possible to make out
a strong case for the contrary thesis. For the Thomist
philosophy with its orthodox Aristotelian cosmology
and its peripatetic intellectualism was ill fitted to
serve as a philosophical basis for the dogmas of the
Christian Church. And in many ways the older
Augustinian scholasticism with its Platonist tendencies
harmonized more easily with the Catholic faith. Nor
did this fact escape the critical mind of Scotus : in
all the points where he diverges from Thomas and
adheres to the traditions of the older school he does
so with a view to establishing a more vital connexion

---

naturali agente, sive sit creata, sive increata, quia secundum eos, ita
causat Deus naturaliter, et necessitate naturali in suo ordine causandi,
sicut agens creatum. Secundum theologos illa propositio est falsa,
quae dicit quod cuilibet potentiae passivae naturali correspondet
potentia activa naturalis, quia majoris perfectionis est capax natura
in superioribus entibus, quam sit illa, ad quam solam extenditur
virtus potentiae activae naturalis. Nec tamen illa potentia passiva
est frustra, quia aeque potest illa potentia passiva reduci ad actum
per agens liberum, quam per agens naturale, quia in comparatione
ad extra, agens liberum est majoris efficaciae et virtutis quam agens
naturale, quia est infinitum, non sic agens naturale. Debet igitur
sic illa propositio intelligi, quod cuilibet potentiae passivae naturali,
correspondet aliqua potentia naturalis, vel libera reducens ipsam
ad actum ; et hoc concedo ' (*Op. Ox.* IV, dist. xliii, q. 3, n. 18).

[1] *Das Verhältnis zwischen Glauben und Wissen, u. s. w., bei Duns*
Scotus, cap. 1.

between his philosophy and his theology. To take only a few instances. His doctrine of the positive entity of matter was more suitable to form a foundation for a Christian creationist cosmology than the Aristotelian theory of ὕλη as pure δύναμις, whereas the problem of creation forms one of the main cruces of the Thomist system and affords a foothold for the scepticism of the fifteenth century. Again, in his teaching of the relative independence of the body and the soul, and his insistence on the preservation of the older notions of the *forma corporeitatis*, and the hylemorphic composition of the spiritual principle, he avoids another of the pitfalls of Thomism. For the theory of Thomas, as we shall see later, bristles with difficulties. Not only did the Angelic Doctor attempt to interpret the Christian doctrine of the soul, with all its profound sense of personality and all its supernatural associations, in the terms of the Aristotelian ψυχή, a task incongruous enough; he also added complications of his own. His doctrine of individuation, which he placed in *materia quantitate signata*, made it impossible to give a consistent account of the soul in its state of separation from the body and exposed him to accusations of Averroism. Finally, the voluntarism of Scotus was also more nearly in accordance with the ethics of Christianity and their emphasis on personal responsibility, sin, and the necessity of redemption than the cold intellectualism of Thomas, which so narrowly avoids determinism. In all these cases we see a far juster appreciation of the philosophic needs of Christendom than that afforded by the more perfectly systematized teaching of Aquinas. It is in Scotus rather than in Thomas that scholasticism reaches its maturest development.

IV

THE OXFORD SCHOOL AND ITS INFLUENCE ON DUNS SCOTUS

TO estimate the significance of Duns Scotus for medieval philosophy there are three cardinal factors which must be taken into account; three co-ordinates, as it were, which determine his position in the history of scholastic thought, namely, the time at which he lived, the order to which he belonged, and the university at which he studied. First and foremost of these is his date. Born, according to one tradition, in the year which witnessed the death of Thomas Aquinas, or, according to a more probable account, nine years earlier, he found the great intellectual expansion of the thirteenth century behind him. He thus had at his command the full resources of the completed material of medieval learning. Apart from the whole of the surviving works of the Aristotelian canon, which had by this time been translated both from the Arabic and the Greek,[1] he was acquainted

[1] For the history of the Aristotelian translations see A. Jourdain, *Excurs. Hist.*, etc. (1888); Grabmann, 'Forschungen über die lateinischen Aristoteles-Uebersetzungen des xiii. Jahrh.' (*Beiträge zur Geschichte der Philosophie des Mittelalters*, vol. xvii); Wüstenfeld, 'Die Uebersetzung arabische Werke in das Lateinische' (*Abhandl. der Königl. Gesellsch. d. Wissenschaften zu Göttingen*, vol. lxxii, 1897); Steinschneider, 'Die hebräischen Uebersetzungen des Mittelalters,' etc., 1893; 'Die arabischen Uebersetzungen aus dem Griechischen'; 'Die europäischen Uebersetzungen aus d. Arabischen bis Mitte des 17. Jahrh.' (Vienna, 1904, *Sitzungsberichte der kaiserlich. Akademie d. Wissenschaft.*); Marchesi, *L'Etica Nicomachea nella traduzione latina medievale*; Lucquet, 'Herman l'Allemand' (*R. Hist. Relig.*, tom. 44, 1901); J. W. Brown, *An Inquiry into the Life and Legend*

not only with the writings of the Arabian and Jewish commentators, such as Alf-Arabi, Avicenna (Ibn-Sina), Gazali (Algazel), Averroes, and Avicebron, but also with the doctrines of the Byzantine school. Of the scholastics of the thirteenth century he was familiar with the works of Alexander of Hales, Robertus Capito, or Grosseteste, whom he cites as Lincolnensis, Roger Bacon, Petrus Hispanus, Bonaventura, Albertus Magnus, Thomas Aquinas, Godfrey of Fontaines, Henry of Ghent, William Varro, Richard of Middelton, to mention only the more prominent names. Besides this his reading stretched back into the twelfth and eleventh centuries, and his theology shows marked traces of the influence of Hugo and Richard of St. Victor, and more especially of Anselm. With the sources of the older scholasticism he was well acquainted. Cicero, Augustine, John Damascenus, the Pseudo-Dionysios, Porphyry, Boethius are among the authors whom he cites, not to mention the ancient pagan philosophers such as Democritus, Epicurus, Empedocles, Anaxagoras, etc. In short there is no important contribution to philosophical and theological speculation since the time of Anselm onwards which he leaves unobserved. He sums up more completely than any other thinker all the various currents of scholastic thought and learning.

The second decisive influence on the thought of Duns is his membership of the Franciscan Order. In contrast with the Dominicans, who after considerable opposition finally adopted the newer peripateticism of Albert and Aquinas as the official doctrine of their school only a few years after the death of the Angelic Doctor,[1] the Franciscans showed a marked tendency to adhere to the older Augustinianism of the twelfth and eleventh centuries, which had drawn its inspiration from Platonism and Neo-Platonism rather than from Aristotle. This somewhat rigid conservatism, always a powerful influence in human thinking, especially in religious thought, had also manifested itself within the ranks of the followers of Saint Dominic, especially at Oxford, where even more persistently than at Paris the new doctrines of the Thomist system [2] were censured and condemned by Robert Kilwardby, Archbishop of Canterbury, who was himself a Dominican. Already in the year 1270 Stephen Tempier, Bishop of Paris, had condemned certain Averroistic propositions which savoured of heresy. Among these were included, according to Giles of Lessines, two doctrines maintained also by Thomas, namely, the unity of the substantial form or soul in man and the substantial simplicity of the angels. Three other propositions were also censured which, though not actually advocated by Thomas, might be deduced by his opponents as consequences derivable from certain tendencies in his teaching: (1) 'Quod mundus est aeternus'; (2) 'Quod voluntas hominis ex necessitate

[1] Cf. the decisions of the general Chapters of the Dominican Order held at Milan in the year 1278, and also the following year at Paris, with reference to the Thomistic doctrine, quoted by Ehrle in his article, 'Beiträge zur Geschichte der mittelalterlichen Scholastik', in vol. v of his *Archiv für Litteratur und Kirchengeschichte des Mittelalters*, pp. 603 sqq.

[2] The novel character of much of the Thomist teaching is emphasized very strongly by William of Tocco, the biographer of the Angelic Doctor: 'Erat enim in sua lectione novos movens articulos, novum modum et clarum determinandi inveniens, et novas inducens in determinationibus rationes, ut nemo qui ipsum audiisset nova dicere et novis rationibus dubia definire, dubitaret quin eum Deus novi luminis radiis illustraret.'

vult vel eligit ' ; (3) ' Quod liberum arbitrium est potentia passiva, non activa, et quod necessitate movetur ab appetibili '.[1] Thomas had indeed never affirmed the eternity of the world, but he had stoutly maintained that it was impossible to disprove it. Nor had he actually lapsed into psychological determinism, but he had come very near to it, and a one-sided application of his principles, as we shall see, would lead unequivocally to determinism.

But the condemnations of Kilwardby were aimed far closer to the heart of Thomism.[2] In 1277 he censured a large number of philosophical propositions which included almost all the Thomistic innovations. The Thomist doctrine of matter as pure potentiality was condemned and the older theory of the *rationes seminales* reaffirmed. So also the unity of the substantial form in man was proscribed and the doctrine of the *forma corporis* and the plurality of vital principles in the vegetative and sensitive forms defended. The same condemnations were repeated by Kilwardby's successor in the see of Canterbury, the Franciscan John of Peckham.[3] But in spite of these official blows the Dominican Order decided to champion the

---

[1] Denifle-Chatelain, *Chartularium*, i, pp. 543–60.

[2] Cf. Ehrle, ' Der Kampf um die Lehre des hl. Thomas von Aquino in den ersten fünfzig Jahren nach seinem Tode ' (*Zeitschr. f. kath. Theol.*, Bd. 37).

[3] The doctrines condemned by Kilwardby in 1277 include the following : ' Item quod forma corrumpitur in pure nihil.—Item quod nulla potentia est in materia.—Item quod privatio est pure nihil.—Item quod intellectiva introducta corrumpitur sensitiva et vegetativa. —Item quod vegetativa, sensitiva et intellectiva sunt una forma simplex.—Item quod corpus vivum et mortuum est equivoce corpus, et corpus mortuum secundum quod corpus mortuum est corpus secundum quid.—Item quod intellectiva unitur materiae primae ita quod corrumpitur illud quod praecessit usque ad materiam primam.' *Chartularium*, i, p. 558. See also Kilwardby's letter to Peter of Conflans, Archbishop of Corinth, quoted in Ehrle, ' Beiträge ', etc., *Archiv für Litteratur und Kirchengeschichte*, etc., vol. v, pp. 618 sqq.

cause of its illustrious Doctor, and from 1280 onwards Thomism remained the regular doctrine of its
schools.

The attitude of the Franciscans was different. The
peripatetic doctrine indeed had not left them entirely
untouched; Alexander of Hales, Bonaventura, Matthew
of Aquasparta, Richard of Middleton were all alike
profoundly influenced by the newly discovered Aristotelian writings and the interpretation of the Arabian
and Jewish commentators ; but they preserved, in
contrast to Albert and Aquinas, a body of doctrine
derived through Augustine from Neo-Platonic rather
than peripatetic sources, which had been characteristic
of the scholasticism of the two preceding centuries.
Moreover, the continually increasing rivalry between
the two orders, which reached its height towards the
beginning of the fourteenth century, was accentuated
most sharply in theological and philosophical controversy. The decision of the general Chapters of
the Dominicans to support the newer teaching
naturally served to incline Franciscan opinion to the
other side, and the Minorites became in consequence
the defenders of the older doctrine. The one order
being innovators, the other gravitated naturally
towards conservatism. The result on the thought of
Scotus during the formative years of his thinking of this
constant exposure to an atmosphere hostile to Thomism
is plainly apparent in the querulous and often half-
sophistical captiousness of his polemic.

Finally, the fact that he was a student of the University of Oxford, rather than that of Paris, has left
a plainly discernible trace upon his philosophic outlook. For Oxford, in contrast with Paris, on the model
of which it was founded, devoted a large share of
its attention to the study of the mathematical and
physical sciences. In this connexion there are two
great names which stand out prominently among the

philosophers of the thirteenth century, and both are intimately connected with the history of the Franciscan Order: Robert Grosseteste, Bishop of Lincoln, 1235–53, and Friar Roger Bacon (*d.* 1292). Grosseteste may be regarded almost as the father of Oxford University; he was Master of the Schools, the equivalent at that period of the Chancellor,[1] and also the first lecturer in divinity to the Franciscan convent.[2] After his elevation to the bishopric of Lincoln, in which diocese Oxford was then situated, he continued to show himself the warm friend and patron of the order and also of the whole university, which was then coming into being. Not only was he one of the pioneers of the new Aristotelian learning,[3] but also one of the most original and widely read savants of his day. There is scarcely any department of human learning which did not engage his attention. Theologian and metaphysician,[4] as were all the medieval schoolmen, he was besides a student of philology and well acquainted

[1] The office of Chancellor had not yet been created. See Rashdall, *The Universities of Europe in the Middle Ages*, vol. ii, p. 355.

[2] *Monumenta Franciscana*, p. 37. Cf. Rashdall, op. cit., vol. ii, pp. 377–8; also Little, *History of the Grey Friars in Oxford* (Oxf. Hist. Soc., vol. xv), p. 30.

[3] The first translation of the *Nicomachean Ethics* was made under his direction from the original Greek, though he can hardly himself have been the translator. Cf. Rashdall, op. cit. ii, p. 521. Roger Bacon says of him: 'Graecum et Hebraeum non scivit sufficienter ut per se transferret, sed multos habuit adjutores,' *Compendium Stud. Phil.*, c. viii; Brewer, *Op. Ined.*, p. 472.

[4] We cannot accept the statement of Bacon, loc. cit. (Brewer, p. 469) that he neglected Aristotle: 'Unde Dominus Robertus, quondam Episcopus Lincolniensis sanctae memoriae, neglexit omnino libros Aristotelis et vias eorum.' Cf. Prantl, *Gesch. d. Logik*, III, ch. xvii, p. 85. But we may well believe him when he tells us (loc. cit.): 'Per experientiam propriam et . . . per alias scientias negotiatus est in sapientalibus Aristotelis, et melius centies millies scivit et illa de quibus libri Aristotelis loquuntur, quam in ipsius perversis translationibus capi possunt,' that Robert was well versed in philosophic literature.

with the Greek language, and above all things a man
of science,[1] being versed in mathematics, optics, and
medicine.[2] His connexion with the friars minor is of
great interest. Chosen by Agnellus of Pisa, the first
provincial of the English province, who established the
Order at Oxford, to be their lecturer in theology, he
was the lifelong friend of Adam Marsh (Adam de
Marisco), the master of Roger Bacon, who as a young
man may have attended his lectures,[3] and it is tempting
to trace to his influence the scientific interests of his
illustrious pupil. And indeed several of the discoveries
usually attributed to the friar may be traced back to
the speculations of his predecessor.[4] To him also we
may attribute the great esteem in which mathematical
studies were regarded in the rising university. His
works abound in mathematical allusions and illustra-
tions, and he quotes frequently from the writings of
Euclid and once from Ptolemy.[5] How rare an accom-
plishment such mathematical and physical knowledge
was may be gauged from Bacon's statement that the
science of perspective was not taught in the University
of Paris at all, nor anywhere in the Latin world except
at Oxford.[6] Indeed at this period the Oxford mathematicians were the most famous in Europe.[7]

[1] Cf. Bacon, *Op. Majus*, III (Bridges, i, p. 67), 'Et solus dominus
Robertus dictus Grossum caput novit scientias.' For a description
of his works see L. Baur, 'Die Philosophischen Werke des Robert
Grosseteste, Bischofs von Lincoln' (*Beiträge z. Gesch. der Phil. des
Mittelalt.*, Bd. IX).

[2] For a catalogue of his writings see Pegge, *The Life of Robert
Grosseteste* (London, 1793).

[3] Little, *The Grey Friars in Oxford*, p. 192.

[4] Cf. L. Baur, 'Der Einfluss des Robert Grosseteste auf die wissenschaftliche Richtung des Roger Bacon' (*Roger Bacon Commemoration
Essays*, ed. Little, Oxford, 1914).

[5] Prantl, loc. cit., n. 335.

[6] Cf. *Op. Tert.*, c. xi, Brewer, p. 37 : 'Haec autem scientia non est
adhuc lecta Parisiis nec apud Latinos, nisi bis Oxoniae in Anglia.'

[7] Ibid., pp. 34–5 : 'Non sunt enim nisi duo perfecti (mathematici)

This strongly marked mathematical tradition was not without its influence on the thought of Duns Scotus. His works contain many mathematical examples and demonstrations, and in the *Theoremata*, one of the few writings in which he abandons the stereotyped scholastic form of the *Quaestio*,[1] he adopts a style which he assimilates as nearly as possible to the *demonstratio geometrica*. In this love of the mathematical form of reasoning we may detect a trace of the influence of Roger Bacon, who would reduce all logic to mathematics, where alone strict proof is attainable.[2] It has been suggested that in this view lies the solution to the puzzling paradox of the *Theoremata* and its sceptical criticism of the demonstrability of the truths of natural theology. Might it not be mathematical reasoning that Scotus has in mind when he denies the demonstrability of the fact that God is a living and intelligent being. The hypothesis is not without interest, but can scarcely be accepted as a satisfactory explanation of the problem. Scotus's logic follows too closely the Aristotelian *Posterior Analytics* to make such an interpretation possible. The self-evident principles guaranteed by νοῦς, or, as Scotus would put it, known by the light of natural

scilicet magister Johannes London et magister Petrus de Maharncuria Picardus.' Two other famous Oxford mathematicians of this period were Johannes de Sacro Bosco (Holywood), and Johannes Pisanus, the Franciscan John of Peckham, afterwards Archbishop of Canterbury. Campanus de Novara has also been claimed as an Oxford man. Rashdall, op. cit., vol. ii, pp. 525–6.

[1] Two other treatises in which Scotus departs from this form of *Quaestiones* are the *Grammatica Speculativa* and the *De Primo Principio*.

Cf. Bacon, *Op. Maj.* IV, dist. i, c. i (Bridges, i, p. 102): 'Non solum dependet cognitio logicae a mathematica propter suam finem, sed propter medium et cor ejus, quod est liber Posteriorum . . . Sed nec principia demonstrationis, nec conclusiones, nec ipsa tota potest cognosci, nec manifestari, nisi in mathematicis rebus, quia ibi solum est demonstratio vera et potens. . . . Quapropter necesse est logicam a mathematicis dependere.'

reason, are prior to the mathematical principles and hold universally in all genera of science. There is no way of escape here. The truths of natural theology are either logically demonstrable by the same logic which underlies the mathematical method and is prior to it, or they are not so demonstrable. Scotus does not share Bacon's theory of the priority of mathematics to logic, and he therefore does not confine demonstrations to purely mathematical forms. For him the strictness of mathematical proof lies in its conformity to the requirements of the syllogistic canons and not vice versa. He repudiates the notion that only in mathematics strict proof can be obtained.[1]

The influence of Bacon on Duns Scotus is a very difficult question to determine ; indeed it has been doubted whether this solitary experimenter in any way affected the thought of his successors. As Charles has pointed out, none of the thirteenth- or fourteenth-century doctors quote him, at least by name, or combat his opinions. His whole work seems ignored by a conspiracy of silence.[2] Friar Roger is in truth an isolated figure, *vox clamantis in deserto*, the great forerunner of the experimental method. Moreover, it is hard to form any accurate conception of his achievements, so strange a mixture is his character. Notwithstanding all his acuteness of intellect he is as much mystic and magician as he is scientist or philosopher. And besides the occult nature of his speculation the dark suspicion of heresy has thrown a cloud over his work. Condemned and imprisoned, he took precaution to conceal his thoughts in a cypher, no translation of which has yet been published. And in his own order he was without followers ; his doctrine

[1] Cf. *Quaestiones super lib. I, Post. An.*, q. xiv.
[2] Cf. Émil Charles, *Roger Bacon, sa Vie, ses Ouvrages, ses Doctrines, d'après des Textes inédits*, p. 42.

could gain no support, and his 'errors' were proscribed at synods held at Paris in 1277 and at Oxford
in 1288, and also by the general Chapter of the
Minorites held by the Master-General of the Order,
Jerome of Ascoli, who subsequently became Pope
Nicholas IV. He was incarcerated too, *propter quasdam
novitates*, and probably kept in prison for fourteen
years, being released only shortly before his death,
which took place in the year 1294. Such is the
traditional account. We need not therefore be sur-
prised to find that his influence, such as it was, operated
anonymously and that his doctrines, when they were
borrowed by later writers, were incorporated with
their own works without any acknowledgement of
their original author. Yet, clandestine as this influence
was, a careful examination will reveal the fact that it
was by no means negligible. The hand of Bacon may
be traced in several theories of Duns Scotus. Indeed
Werner tries to draw a parallel between the relationship
of the two Minorites and that of Thomas to his master
Albert. Scotus, he maintains, made use of Bacon's
manuscripts, adopted many of his theories, and
embodied them in his own writings in the same way
that the Angelic Doctor had done with the works
of Albert. Not only was Duns an adherent of the
'Oxford School', he was also in a peculiar sense the
pupil of Bacon.[1]

Such a theory, however, can hardly be substantiated.
It is true that Scotus sometimes borrows from his

[1] Karl Werner, *Duns Scotus*, p. 6: 'Duns Scotus verwertete die
aus denselben (Handschriften) geschöpften Anregungen in ähnlicher
Weise wie Thomas Aquina jene seines Albert, nämlich so, dass er sie
so für den Betrieb der Theologie . . . verwertete und umbildete und
das aus Baco geschöpfte sich in selbstständiger Weise aneignete und
umbildete. In diesem Sinne haben wir also in Duns Scotus nicht
bloss ein Zögling der Oxforder Schule, sondern speziell bis auf einem
gewissen Grad auch ein Schüler Baco's, so wie in diesem ein Weg-
bereiter des Duns Scotus zu erkennen.'

fellow Franciscan and that in many places his influence is plainly discernible, but the general outlook of the two thinkers is widely different. Roger is mostly in violent revolt from the general methods and traditions of the schools, Duns is essentially a schoolman who develops to their fullest extent the scholastic doctrines of his age; the one is by temperament a man of science, the other a metaphysician. Bacon occupies a comparatively unimportant place in the history of philosophic thought. His contributions to philosophy, as distinguished from the sciences, is singularly disappointing, and he inclines, in spite of the originality of some of his theories, to a somewhat inconsistent mixture of Aristotelianism and Augustinianism which is characteristic of the earlier ' precursors '[1] of the thirteenth century, whereas Scotus, notwithstanding the persistence in his teaching of certain elements of the older doctrines, belongs in spirit wholly to the epoch of medieval thought which was inaugurated by the Thomist philosophy.

It is an interesting task to work out in some detail the relation between the systems of these two philosophers, to discover those points which their teaching have in common, and to trace the origins of their divergences. To take first the all-important question of the relation between Theology and Philosophy: Following the general tradition of their order, both uphold the primacy of the will over the intellect,[2] and in consequence place theology, the queen of the

---

[1] I use this term in the sense indicated by M. de Wulf in his *History of Mediaeval Philosophy*, p. 270.

[2] *Op. Maj.* iii (Bridges, i, p. 71) : ' Sed cum voluntas seu intellectus practicus sit nobilior quam speculativus, et virtus cum felicitate excellat in infinitor scientiam nudam et nobis sit magis necessaria sine comparatione, necesse est ut habeamus argumenta ad exercitandum per intellectum practicum,' etc. For the voluntarism of Duns see below, ch. v of this volume, pp. 175 sqq. ; also vol. ii, ch. vii.

sciences,[1] among the 'practical' disciplines,[2] thus maintaining a close relationship between divinity and ethics.[3]   But here the resemblance between their doctrines ceases.   Bacon adopts, with certain modifications, a theory of knowledge of the older Augustinian type, and is unable therefore to draw a definite distinguishing line between natural reason and supernatural revelation.   Philosophy and theology thus tend to interpenetrate each other, with the result that the former is almost completely subordinated to the latter ; philosophy is relegated to the sphere of apologetics and is practically denied any independent value.[4] In a manner strongly reminiscent of the Victorine mystics, he tells us that all knowledge depends in a sense on divine revelation, and describes the seven stages of interior illumination.   Thus not only were the sciences revealed to the Patriarchs and Prophets who first gave them to mankind,[5] but also the pagan philosophers, such as Socrates and Aristotle, received

[1] *Op. Majus*, ii, c. i (Bridges, i, p. 33).

[2] *Compendium Studii Philosophiae*, cap. I (Brewer, *Op. ined.*, p. 369) : ' Studium sapientiae habet duas partes, unam scilicet speculativam et aliam practicam. . . . Grammatica enim, logica, naturalis philosophia, vulgata metaphysica, quinque scientiae mathematicae et plures aliae sunt speculativae veritatum quae non consistunt in operibus. Quatuor vero scientiae mathematicae (quae novem sunt in universo) et alkimia, medicina, moralis philosophia, sub qua comprehendo jus civile, theologica cum jure canonico, et multae aliae a parte philosophiae sunt practicae.'

[3] See Gustav Held, *Roger Bacon's praktische Philosophie* (Jena, 1881), p. 41.

[4] Cf. *Op. Maj.* iii (Bridges, i, p. 66) : ' Una est scientia perfecta, quae sacris literis continetur ' ; ibid., ii, c. xiv (Bridges, i, p. 56) : ' Philosophia secundum se considerata nullius utilitatis est ' ; ibid., c. xviii : ' Philosophia non est nisi sapientiae divinae explicatio per doctrinam et opus ' ; cf. ibid., c. xvii (Bridges, i, p. 64), ' Nam philosophia secundum se ducit ad caecitatem infernalem et ideo oportet quod secundum se sit tenebrae et caligo '.

[5] *Op. Maj.*, pars. vi, c. I (Bridges, ii, p. 169) : Sed duplex est experientia. Una est per sensus exteriores, . . . et haec sapientia est humana et philosophica, quantum homo potest facere secundum ei

special illuminations from on high by which they learned many truths concerning the divine nature.[1] Even the philosophical verities need revelation ; [2] such a small question as the problem of universal cannot be solved without it, to say nothing of the graver issues.[3] If, then, we are to attain to philosophic truth we shall have to make a number of theological assumptions in order that the divine wisdom which manifests itself in both sciences may be revealed.[4] It need scarcely be pointed out how far such a view differs from the theory of Duns Scotus, with its strongly marked separation of the domain of natural reason from that of revelation.

datum.   Sed haec experientia non sufficit homini, quia non plane certificat de corporalibus, propter sui difficultatem, et de spiritualibus nihil attingit.   Ergo oportet quod intellectus humanus aliter juvetur et ideo sanctae patriarchae et prophetae, qui primo dederunt scientias mundo, receperunt illuminationes interiores et non solum stabant in sensu. . . . Et sunt septem gradus hujus scientiae.   Unus per illumina-tiones puras scientiales, alius . . . in virtutibus . . ., tertius in septem donis Spiritus sancti . . ., quartus in beatitudinibus . . ., quintus in sensibus spiritualibus . . ., sextus in fructibus . . ., septimus in captibus.' Cf. ii. c. ix (Bridges, i, p. 45) : ' Soli enim patriarchae et prophetae fuerunt veri philosophi, qui omnia sciverunt, non solum legem sed omnes partes philosophiae.'

[1] Cf. *Op. Tert.*, c. xxiv (Brewer, p. 81) : ' Viri tam boni et tam sapientes sicut Pythagoras, Socrates, Plato, et Aristoteles, et alii zelatores maximi sapientiae receperunt a Deo speciales illuminationes quibus intellexerunt multa de Deo,' etc.

[2] Cf. *Op. Maj.* ii, c. ix (Bridges, i, p. 45) : ' Impossibile fuit homini ad magnalia scientiarum et artium venire per se, sed oportet quod habuerint revelationem.'

[3] Ibid., c. vi (Bridges, i, p. 42) : ' Quapropter veritatem horum est necesse a principio fuisse homini revelatam.   Et cum puerilis revelatio est necessaria, multo fortius in tota sapientia philosophiae.'

[4] *Op. Maj.* ii, c. xiv (Bridges, i, p. 56) : ' Ex his sequitur necessario quod nos Christiani debemus uti philosophia in divinis, et in philo-sophia multa assumere theologica, ut appareat quod una sit sapientia in utroque relucens.'

For a detailed examination of the relation between philosophy and theology in Roger Bacon see Carl Pöhl, *Das Verhältnis der Philosophie zur Theologie bei Roger Bacon* (Neu-Strelitz, 1893).

In their doctrines of form and matter both start out from the conception of Avicebron [1] that all created things, spiritual as well as material, are composed of form and matter, but the resemblance between the two theories apparently soon ceases. While Scotus accepts the proposition of the Jewish philosopher that all things share in one common substrate, which he calls *materia primo prima*, to Bacon the theory of the unity of matter is the most pernicious of errors.[2] Its logical consequence is pantheism, for if we suppose that the same matter can be the substrate of different genera we can set no bounds to its community ; in its indeterminateness it becomes infinite, and as infinite being it is indistinguishable from God and identical with Him,[3] a consequence which had been drawn early in the thirteenth century by the condemned heretic, David of Dinant. We must therefore assume a plurality of matters corresponding to the plurality of forms.[4] The *forma prima*, which is predicated of all the different forms, the most general down to the most particular, and which is common to them, is one not with a numerical but with

[1] Werner, ' Die Kosmologie und allgemeine Naturlehre des Roger Baco ' (*Sitzungsberichte*, etc., Wien, vol. xciv, p. 491) ; cf. P. Höver, *Roger Bacons Hylemorphismus als Grundlage seiner philosophischen Anschauung* (Limburg a. d. Lahn, 1912), p. 101.

[2] *Op. Maj.*, iv, dist. iv, c. viii (Bridges, i, p. 144) : ' Multitudo vero philosophantium, non solum in forma propria philosophiae, sed in usu theologiae dicit quod una est materia numero in omnibus rebus, et quod solum est diversitas a parte formarum ; sed hic est error infinitus.'

[3] Ibid., p. 145.

[4] Cf. Cod. Maz. I, col. 15 b : ' Esse formalia sunt gradus substantiales essentiae formae pleniores usque dum fiat perfecta. Ergo cum materia similiter promoveatur in esse materialia et esse nobiliora et perfectiora, ista esse erunt gradus materiae per quos promoveatur ad specificam completionem.' Quoted by Höver, op. cit., p. 92.

Cf. ibid., col. 24 e : ' Sed decipiuntur propter hoc quod credunt solam formam esse causam distinctionis et divisionis ; nam una

a generic unity. In the same way the matter which is predicated of all the different kinds of matter existing in the world of concrete things and which is common to them is not numerically one, but spiritual matter is different from corporeal matter ; that of the heavenly bodies is different from that of sublunary bodies, while that of one individual differs from that of another.[1]   At first sight this conception of Bacon's would seem to be the exact antithesis of the Scotist doctrine of the community of *materia primo prima* in all created substances,[2] but a closer inspection will serve to show that the difference is not so very great. What Bacon is here arguing against is the numerical unity of matter, which is never asserted by Duns, whose theory postulates just such a unity of kind which is here implied by Bacon.[3] How nearly the doctrines of the two thinkers can be approximated we shall be able to see later when we deal with the views of both on the question of individuation.

Passing to the problem of universals we shall find that here again, under an apparent dissimilarity, a large measure of likeness between the teaching of the two friars may be detected. Bacon insists in violent and almost abusive language on the reality of the individual.

---

materia est alia per essentiam ab alia, sicut forma. . . . Et ideo asinus non differt ab equo per solam formam, sed per materiam aliam specificam.'

[1] *Op. Tert.*, c. xxxviii (Brewer, pp. 120–1) : ' Cum omnes ponunt quod materia sit una numero in omnibus rebus . . . et cum hic sit pessimus error, qui unquam fuit a philosophis positus, ideo aggredior hanc positionem. . . . Sicut forma prima quae praedicatur de omnibus formis *et est communis eis* et dividitur . . . usque ad specialissimam, habet unitatem generis *et non est una numero* . . . ergo similiter cum materia praedicetur de omnibus materiis rerum, *et sit eis communis* et dividitur . . ., materia alia est spiritualis, alia est corporalis et paribus passibus descendit sicut compositum et forma.'

[2] Cf. vol. ii, ch. 3, pp. 83 sqq.

[3] Ibid., p. 118, n. 1.

One individual is worth all the universals in the world, for the universal is nothing more than the ' agreement ' (*convenientia*) of a plurality of individuals, i. e. a sum of properties which different individuals hold in common.[1] But he never denies the reality of this common element, and expressly repudiates the suggestion that the universal is a mere fiction of the mind.[2] For the concrete individual is made up of two moments : the principles which constitute its essence or being, the body and soul which make ' this ' man, and the group of properties which he shares with other individuals of his own kind which constitute his ' universal '.[3] The full significance of this doctrine will be apparent when we consider Bacon's theory of individuation. The whole problem of individuation is nugatory, he tells us, for the universal as such has no real existence. Only the individual exists, and as in the conceptual order the notion of ' man ' is obtained by combining

[1] Cf. *Communia Naturalium* I, par. ii, dist. ii, c. vii (Steele, p. 94) : ' Unum individuum excellit omnia universalia de mundo. Nam universale non est nisi convenientia plurium individuorum.'

[2] Cf. ibid., c. x (Steele, p. 102), where Bacon having put forward three theories on the nature of the universal cites a fourth view which he himself holds (Prantl, *Gesch. d. Logik*, etc., III, cap. xvii, p. 125, n. 571) : ' Quarta est (opinio) quod universale sit solum in singularibus et non dependeat ab anima.' Cf. loc. cit. (Steele, p. 106) : falsa est propositio quidquid est in singulari est singulare. Nam Aristoteles . . . distinguit octo modos essendi, et unus est sicut singulare in universali, et alius sicut universale in singulari ; ergo contradicunt Aristoteli. . . . Item secundum hoc essent sola individua sub genere, et nulla species ; ergo tolleretur unum de universalibus famosis, quod esse non potest.'

[3] Cf. ibid., c. vii : ' Duo enim sunt necessaria individuo : unum absolute quod constituit ipsum et ingreditur ejus essentiam, ut anima et corpus faciunt hunc hominem ; aliud est in quo conveniat cum aliqui homine et non cum asino nec porco, et hoc est suum universale. Sed absolute natura individui longe major et melior est quam relata, quia habet esse fixum per se et absolutum ; et ideo singulare est nobilius quam suum universale, et nos scimus hoc per experientiam rerum. . . . Ergo simpliciter loquendo et absolute, debemus dicere quod

the two notions of ' body ' and ' soul ', so in the real order *this* body and *this* soul make up *this* individual man, Peter or Paul.[1]

Now if we examine this conception carefully we shall see that it bears an extraordinary resemblance to the Scotist notion of *haecceitas*. There are six 'entities', Duns tells us, in the *compositum* (the concrete ' real ' or *res*, which is made up of form and matter); form *in communi* and matter *in communi* which constitute the ' *compositum* ' *in communi*, and *this* form and *this* matter which constitute *this* individual.[2] For, accord-

---

individuum est prius secundum naturam, tam secundum opera-tionem quam secundum intentionem . . . quod individuum est natura absoluta et fixa, habens esse per se, et universale non est nisi convenientia individui respectu alterius.'

[1] Cf. ibid., c. viii : ' Dicunt aliqui quod species est tota essentia individuorum, et habet esse solum diversa in eis ; et alii dicunt quod materia addita formae universali facit individuum ; et alii quod potentiae aliquid significatum additur et sic significatur species significanda in diversis. Sed omnia haec convocantur esse falsa, quia postquam linea singularium vadit de incompleto ad completum, sicut linea universalium, patet quod tum sicut se habet animal ad hominem, sic hoc animal ad hunc hominem ; et ideo sicut rationale additum huic animali faciat hunc hominem, et ita nec homo nec aliquid additum homini faciet hunc hominem, licet hoc ponunt.' Cf. Cod. Maz. I, col. 27 a : ' Sicut se habet animal ad hominem ; sic hoc animal ad hunc hominem ; et ideo sicut rationale additum animali facit hominem ; sic hoc rationale additum huic animali facit hunc hominem.' Quoted by Höver, op. cit., p. 169. With reference to this passage Höver remarks as follows : ' Ebenso wurde bereits gezeigt dass das Individuum, dieser bestimmte Mensch, früher ist als das Universale " Mensch " ; denn das Universale ist ja, ähnlich wie das Akzidenz, ausserhalb der Essenz des Dinges, (cf. passage quoted in n. 3 on p. 128 of this chapter) und drückt jenes aus wodurch ein Individuum mit einem anderen übereinkommt. Also vor Entstehen des Universalen hat das Individuum bereits seine ganz Wesenheit. Mithin konstituiren jene Prinzipien das Individuum, die in seine Essenz eintreten, wie z.B. diese Seele und dieser Körper diesen bestimmten Menschen ausmachen. Das Individuationsprinzip hat also nach Bacon in der physischen Wesenheit des Dinges selbst seine tiefste Begründung.'

[2] Cf. *Op. Ox.* II, dist. iii, q. 6, n. 15 ; *Rep. Par.* II, dist. xii, q. 8,

ing to Scotus no less than Bacon, the individual is the real, the unity of the genus or the species being a *unitas naturae* which is less than the numerical unity of the individual.[1] The difference between the two thinkers lies chiefly in the fact that Duns lays his emphasis more strongly on the metaphysical implications of the universal concept, while Roger's notion of *convenientia* is more pronouncedly conceptualistic in tone.[2]

Passing on to the metaphysical doctrine of the soul and its union with the body we find that Bacon, like Scotus, sets out from the theory of Avicebron that the soul, like the angelic spirit, is composed of form and matter.[3] He is also in consequence an upholder of the theory of the plurality of substantial forms. But instead of holding with Duns that the psychic form is

n. 8. Cf. Minges, *Der angeblich exzessive Realismus des Duns Scotus,* etc., pp. 46 sqq. For a more complete exposition of the Scotist doctrine of *haecceitas* see vol. ii, ch. 3, pp. 94–8.

[1] Cf. *Op. Ox.* II, dist. ii, q. 1, n. 8 ; *Rep. Par.* II, dist. xii, q. 5, n. 12.

[2] Cf. Prantl, op. cit., vol. iii, cap xvii, p. 124.

[3] Cf. *Comm. Nat.* IV, dist. iii, cap. iv (Steele, p. 291) : ' Teneo pro certo quod anima est composita ex materia et forma, sicut angeli,' etc.

Cf. Werner, ' Die Psychologie und Erkenntnis und Wissenschafts-lehre des Roger Baco ' (*Sitzungsberichte*, Wien, vol. xciii) : ' Beide aber haben die ihnen gemeinsame Auffassung der metaphysischen Beschaffenheit des Seelenwesens aus Avicebron geschöpft, und Duns Scotus mag durch seinem Landsmann und Ordensgenossen Baco auf diesen ihnen Beiden gemeinsamen Ausgangspunkt ihrer psycholo-gischen Grundanschauung hingeführt worden sein.' For the connexion of Avicebron's theory of the hylemorphic composition of spiritual beings with the doctrine of Plotinus, see Höver, op. cit., p. 101 : ' Plotin, der wissenschaftliche Begründer des Neuplatonismus, hat als erster eine geistige Materie in der Geisteswelt aufgenommen, um die Einheit in der Vielheit der Ideen im göttlichen νοῦς erklären, und der sichtbaren Welt, in der alles aus Materie und Form zusammengesetzt ist, ein vollgültiges Vorbild vorausstellen zu können.

' Avicebron widerholt ganz die Gedanken Plotins wenn er sagt : inferius est ex superiori et est exemplum ejus ; quia si inferius fuerit

a simple entity, he maintains with Kilwardby that the
human soul is made up of three forms, a vegetative,
a sensitive, and a rational, a doctrine which Scotus
expressly repudiates on the ground that it is contrary
to the principle of parsimony.[1] According to Bacon
the vegetative and sensitive souls are produced by the
parents by the normal process of generation: only
the intellectual soul is created [2] and therefore immortal. On the nature of the intellectual soul itself
the doctrine of Bacon differs profoundly from that
of Duns. The former is much influenced by the
works of Avicenna,[3] and like the Arabian commentator
refuses to regard the *intellectus agens* as a portion of
the human personality, conceding to the individual
only an *intellectus possibilis*. This theory must not be
confused with the monopsychism of Averroes, whom
Bacon opposes with much vigour.[4] It is far more
closely allied to the older Augustinian theory of
knowledge with its notion of divine illumination. For
to Bacon, as we have seen, all knowledge was in the
last resort the product of a revelation,[5] and the
identification of the *intellectus agens* with the uncreated

ex superiori debet ut ordo substantiarum corporalium sit ad instar
ordinis substantiarum spiritualium.'

Höver refers to Plotinus, Enn. II, Lib. 4, n. 4 : Εἰ οὖν πολλὰ τὰ
εἴδη, κοινόν μέν τι ἐν αὐτοῖς ἀνάγκη εἶναι· καὶ δὴ καὶ ἴδιον, ᾧ διαφέρει
ἄλλο ἄλλου. . . . Ἔστιν ἄρα καὶ ὕλη ἡ τὴν μορφὴν δεχομένη, καὶ ἀεί
τι ὑποκείμενον· ἔτι εἰ κόσμος νοητὸς ἔστιν ἐκεῖ, μίμημα δὲ οὗτος
ἐκείνου, οὗτος δὲ σύνθετος καὶ ἐξ ὕλης, κἀκεῖ δεῖ ὕλην εἶναι.

[1] *De Rerum Principio*, q. xi, art. 2, n. 8.

[2] Cf. Cod. Maz., col. 82 a : ' Tota igitur philosophia clamat quod
solus intellectus creatus, et omnes theologi alicujus valoris et philo-
sophantes,' etc. Cf. *Com. Nat.*, loc. cit.

[3] Cf. *Op. Maj.* ii, c. viii (Bridges, i, p. 43) : ' Avicenna dux et
princeps philosophorum,' etc.

[4] Cf. *Com. Nat.* IV, dist. iii, cap. iii (Steele, p. 286).

[5] *Op. Maj.* ii, c. v (Bridges, i, p. 39) : ' Quia istud est necessarium
ad persuasionem propositi, ut ostendatur quod philosophia sit per
influentiam divinae illuminationis, volo istud efficaciter probare

light flowing from the divine intelligence was a very natural one.[1] Nor does Bacon stand alone in this matter ; he expressly attributes his theory to William of Auvergne, Robert Grosseteste, and Adam Marsh.[2] With such a doctrine the teaching of Scotus has little in common. His epistemology belongs wholly to the newer and more naturalistic Aristotelian empiricism and resembles far more closely the views of Thomas, with whom he agrees in claiming for the individual soul both an ' active ' and a ' possible ' intellect.[3]

But Bacon's theory of knowledge, in spite of its great dissimilarity to the peripatetic theory of Thomas, was not without its influence on the doctrine of Scotus. The two main features of the Baconian epistemology are the insistence on the direct knowledge of the individual and a kind of intellectual intuition, or, to use the term invented by Werner, a psychic sensism.[4] Knowledge of the singular or individual is not, as Thomas had postulated, a quasi-reflexive

(*sc.* quod intellectus agens non est pars animae) praecipue cum magnus error invaserit vulgus philosophantium in hac parte.'

[1] Cf. *Op. Maj.*, loc. cit. : ' Intellectus agens secundum majores philosophos non est pars animae ; sed est substantia intellectiva alia et separata per essentiam ab intellectu possibili.' *Op. Tert.*, c. xxii (Brewer, p. 74) : ' Intellectus agens est Deus principaliter et secundario angeli qui illuminant nos.'

[2] Ibid. : ' Sed falsum est quod agens sit pars animae. . . . Et omnes sapientes antiqui . . . dixerunt quod fuit Deus. Unde ego bis audivi venerabilem antistitem Parisiensis ecclesiae, dominum Guillielmum Alvernensem, congregata universitate coram eo, reprobare eos . . . et probavit . . . quod omnes erraverunt.' Cf. loc. cit. (Brewer, p. 75) where he tells the celebrated story of Adam Marsh : ' Unde quando per tentationem et derisionem aliqui minores praesumptuosi quaesiverunt a fratre Adam, " Quid est intellectus agens ? " respondit " Corvus Eliae " ; volens per hoc dicere quod fuit Deus vel angelus.'

[3] For Scotus' treatment of the *intellectus agens* see vol. ii, ch. vii.

[4] Cf. Werner, op. cit., p. 487. For the somewhat similar theory of William of Auvergne see Werner, ' Die Psychologie des Wilhelm von Auvergne ' (*Sitzungsberichte*, etc., vol. lxxiii), p. 305.

cognition gathered from sense data and mediated through the universal concept abstracted from these by the human active intellect ; it is rather the intuition of the object both in its particular and universal aspects, in the light of the divine intelligence, which is none other than the active intellect itself. With the details of Bacon's theory of perception and his notion of *species* we are not here concerned ; [1] but it must be noted that he uses the term *species* to connote not merely a psychic image or 'Vorstellung', but in a wider sense to mean the action of any substance upon another.[2] The external object (*res*) acts upon the intellect through the sensitive faculties. The body animated by a sensitive soul is as it were a mirror in which the image of the object is reflected. Now the object itself, the concrete individual which alone exists in nature, contains in itself not only particular but also universal notes or moments, both of which impress their images or *species* [3] upon the mind, the one yielding the singular, the other the universal *species*,[4] and because of the repeated impression of the universal *species* by different individuals of the same

---

[1] For Bacon's theory of species see E. Longwell, *Bacon's Theory of Mind*; also S. Vogl, 'Roger Bacons Lehre von der sinnlichen Spezies,' etc. (*Essays*, ed. Little, pp. 205–27).

[2] Cf. *Comm. Nat.* I, pars. iv, dist. iv, cap. iii (Steele, p. 118): 'Essentia, et substantia, et natura, et potentia, et potestas, et virtus, et vis, . . . sunt penitus idem secundum rem, licet differunt in comparatione '; *Op. Maj.* iv, dist. ii, c. 1 (Bridges, i. p. 111) : 'Haec virtus vocatur similitudo et imago et species et multis nominibus, et hanc facit tam substantia quam accidens, tam spiritualis quam corporalis . . . et haec species facit omnem operationem hujus mundi, nam operatur in sensum, in intellectum, in totius mundi materiam,' etc.

[3] Cf. De Wulf, *History of Mediaeval Philosophy*, p. 395.

[4] *De Multiplicatione Specierum*, i, c. 2 (Bridges, ii, p. 430) : ' Cum universale non sit nisi in singularibus . . . nec potest singulare carere suo universali ; erit proportio species universalis ad speciem singularem, sicut rei universalis ad rem singularem.' Cf. Cod. Maz., col. 28 b : ' Et ideo species rerum universalium sunt universales, et

kind the universal *species* becomes stronger as it were
than the individual, and therefore we may say that
the universal is more intelligible than the singular.[1]
But it must always be remembered that in nature only
the individual is real, and the universal *species* is always
accompanied by the singular *species* and cannot exist
in isolation from it.[2]

In most respects the epistemology of Scotus differs
profoundly from the Baconian theory. While for
Bacon the mind is passive in the process of cognition,
in as much as he regards the human intellect as consisting solely in the *intellectus possibilis,* Duns emphasizes
most strongly the active nature of the cognitive processes, regarding even sensation as essentially active
rather than passive.[3] Yet in his refusal to regard with
Thomas the quiddity of the material thing as the
adequate object of the human intellect and in his
insistence on the intelligibility of the singular we may
trace an unmistakable sign of the influence of his
Oxonian predecessor. Especially is this noticeable in
the account he gives of the process of knowing in the
De Rerum Principio, where, inasmuch as it is an early
work, we should naturally expect to find the Baconian
influence at its strongest. Here we find it expressly

per has intellectus intelligit res universales, sicut per singulares species
intelligit singularia ' (quoted by Höver, op. cit., p. 182).

[1] Cod. Maz., col. 28 c : ' Universale est magis intelligibile a nobis
quam singulare, eo quid ab uno singulari non venit nisi sua species
singularis. Sed a quolibet singulari venit una species universalis cum
specie singulari, et ideo multiplicatur species universalis in animo, et
ideo fit fortior et potentior ad hoc, ut per eam intelligamus universale,
et ideo universalia vocantur objecta intellectus, sed hoc est per auto-
nomasiam non per exclusionem singularis.'

[2] *De Multiplicatione Specierum,* i, c. ii (Bridges, ii. p. 431) : ' Sive
in medio sive in sensu, sive in intellectu sunt species universales ;
oportet quod ibidem sint species singulares eis respondentes.' Cf.
also Cod. Maz., col. 28 d : ' Nam species universales non possunt esse
sine singularibus speciebus.'

[3] See below, vol. ii. ch. i, pp. 18 sqq. ; ch. vii, p. 278.

stated that the universal and particular moments of
the concrete individual are known together but by
different species,[1] and it is the universal and not the
singular that is known ' reflexively '.[2] Moreover, the
term ' abstraction ' is quietly dropped and in its stead
we find the Baconian ' multiplication ' and the earlier
twelfth-century word *colligere* used in this connexion,[3]
and the inseparability of the two activities of sensation
and thought most clearly emphasized.[4] In the commentary on the *De Anima*, however, Duns comes to
the conclusion that the singular and the universal immanent in it are known *per eandem speciem, aliter
tamen consideratam*.[5] But both here and in his later
works he continues to insist on the intuitive knowledge of the individual. Finally, it is interesting to
note that in his account of sense perception it is to
the Baconian conception of *immutatio* that he has recourse in his explanation of the generation of the *species
sensibilis*.[6]

The interest which Scotus shows in the scientific
study of language as exemplified in his *Grammatica
Speculativa* may also be attributed to the influence
of the Oxford School. Both Grosseteste and Bacon
were much engrossed in the investigation of language
as a vehicle of thought, and the latter especially insists
continually on the necessity of learning foreign
languages in order to understand the real meaning
of the writers of the sacred scriptures and the fathers
of the Church ; [7] hence his emphasis on the close

---

[1] *De Rerum Principio*, q. xiv, n. 37. See vol ii, ch. i, p. 20.
[2] Ibid., q. xiii, art. 2, n. 21.
[3] See below, vol. ii, ch. i.
[4] *De Rerum Principio*, loc. cit.
[5] *Quaestiones de Anima*, q. xxi, n. 10. See below, vol. ii, ch. vii.
[6] Cf. *Quaestiones de Anima*, q. iv ; Bacon, *Op. Maj.* (Bridges),
ii, pp. 431–43, quoted by Vogl, op. cit., pp. 216 ff.
[7] See Cardinal Gasquet, ' Roger Bacon and the Latin Vulgate '
(*Essays*, ed. Little, pp. 89 ff.).

connexion between grammar and logic. Thus he characterizes both as accidental modes of philosophy, and in one passage almost identifies the two under the heading of *scientiae sermocinales*.[1] He was himself acquainted with Greek and Hebrew, and in a less degree with Arabic, and much of his work is devoted to problems of a philological nature.[2] Scotus' treatise on speculative grammar, one of the earliest attempts to give a scientific account of the meaning of linguistic forms, must be regarded as the fulfilment of one of Bacon's projects,[3] and in it Duns has appropriated and incorporated much of his doctrine,[4] but there is no evidence that he possessed the philological learning of his predecessor and he does not appear to have known more than a few words of Greek, while his knowledge of Hebrew was practically nil.

In the sphere of mathematics and physics there are two instances in which the influence of Bacon on Duns' speculation can be clearly demonstrated. The

[1] *Op. Maj.* iv. dist. i, c. ii (Bridges, i, p. 99) : ' Modi autem philosophiae accidentales sunt grammatica et logica.' *Op. Tert.*, cap. xxviii (Brewer, p. 104) : ' Logica cum qua comprehendo grammaticam. Quia communi nomine utraque logica dicitur, id est, sermocinalis scientia, nam λόγος idem est quod sermo, in una significatione.'

[2] e.g. part iii of the *Opus Majus*; *Opus Tertium*, chs. xxvi and xxvii; *Compendium Philosophiae*, I.   There is also a *summa de grammatica*, which probably formed part of the *Compendium Philosophiae* (MS. Cambridge, Peterhouse, 191 ; James, 3).   See also *Compendium Theologiae*, part ii (MS. Brit. Mus. Royal, F. vii, pp. 153–61). Cf. Little, *The Grey Friars in Oxford*, pp. 195 f.   Bacon wrote also a ' Grammatica Graeca ' and a ' Grammatica Hebraica ' (fragmentary), printed in *The Greek Grammar of Roger Bacon and a Fragment of his Hebrew Grammar*, ed. Nolan and Hirsch, Cambridge, 1902.   For a complete account of Bacon's works see *Essays*, ed. Little, Appendix, pp. 375–425.

For an account of Bacon's contribution to philology, see S. A. Hirsch, ' Bacon and Philology ' (*Essays*, ed. Little, pp. 101–52).

[3] Cf. Werner's pamphlet, *Die Sprachlogik des Duns Scotus*.

[4] e. g. the phrase ' Grammatica una et eadem est secundum substantiam, licet accidentaliter varietur ' is taken word for word out of Bacon. Quoted Charles, op. cit., p. 263, from an Oxford MS. of the *Grammatica Graeca*, 2 a pars, c. 1.

first of these is concerned with the nature of the spatial continuum. In the larger commentary on the Sentences (Lib. II, dist. ii, q. ix) Scotus raises the question whether the locomotion of angels is continuous, and the *quaestio* leads to a discussion on the nature of the continuity of space, or rather of the bodies filling space, for to both Bacon and Scotus the idea of a vacuum and therefore also the atomistic hypothesis are untenable. Duns proceeds to demonstrate that the continuum cannot be made up of indivisible units or minima by means of a series of geometrical proofs, the most significant of which turns on the incommensurability of the diagonal with the side of a square. For if we regard the continuum as made up of minima the diagonal and the side will each contain a definite number of these units, and will therefore be commensurable, which is absurd.[1] This proof, as Werner points out, is taken straight out of Bacon and is to be found in the *Opus Tertium*.[2]

Duns now proceeds to discuss and criticize a statement of Bacon (whose words he quotes without stating their authorship) to the effect that the continuum is infinitely divisible in all its parts, but that it cannot be actually so divided, because the infinity must always remain potential, and the actual division *in fieri*, because an actually infinite division of every part cannot exist *in facto esse*, and however far you carry on your division you will never get to a point where you cease to be able to go further. The possibil-

---

[1] *Op. Ox.* II, dist. ii, q. 9, n. 13. For another proof of a similar nature see vol. ii, ch. iv, p. 128, n. 2.

[2] *Op. Tert.*, c. xxxix (Brewer, p. 132). ' Aristoteles multum nititur ad solvendum (*sc.* rationes atomistarum) ; nec habemus aliquam reprobationem certam de hac positione per Aristotelem. Et ideo addidi demonstrationem geometricam, quae destruit hanc positionem finaliter. Nam ex ea sequitur quod diameter sit commensurabilis costae, et non solum commensurabilis sed aequalis, quorum utrumque est impossibile.'

ity of division is thus a possibility *ad dividi*, but not a possibility *ad divisum esse*.[1] Scotus submits this statement to a long, obscure, cavilling, and inconclusive criticism, but in the last resort his own view does not really differ in any essential respects from that of his opponent, for Bacon agrees with Duns in rejecting the notion that the continuum can be resolved into discrete elements, or that the (conceptually) possible division into an infinite number of points without magnitude can ever really be accomplished.[2]

[1] Cf. Scotus, loc. cit., n. 22 : 'Ad primum dicitur quod licet possibile sit continuum posse dividi secundum omne signum, non tamen est possibile divisum esse, quia ista divisio est in potentia et in fieri et nunquam potest esse tota in facto esse ; et tunc ad illas probationes adductas in oppositum conceditur de quacumque una potentia ad unam actionem, non tamen de infinitis actionibus, cum quarum una reducta ad actum, necessario stat alia non reducta ad actum ; ita est in proposito, quod sunt infinitae potentiae ad infinita dividi, cum quarum una reducta ad actum necessario stat alia non reducta ad actum, et ideo licet concedatur possibilitas ad dividi, non tamen ad divisum esse.'

[2] Cf. Werner, 'Die Kosmologie, etc., des Roger Baco' (*Sitzungsberichte*, etc., vol. xciv) : 'Duns Scotus formulirt die Ansicht Baco's als jene welcher zufolge die Theilung *in potentia et in fieri* statthabe, jedoch niemals vollständig *in facto esse* statthaben könne ; es wolle nur eine *Possibilitas ad dividi*, nicht aber *ad divisum esse* zugestanden werden. Wenn aber die *Possibilitas ad dividi* in Bezug auf alle einzelnen Punkte zugestanden ist, was hindert, sie auch als wirklich vollzogen zu denken ? Duns spricht hiemit etwas aus, was im Denken Baco sich wirklich bereits vollzogen hat ; für ihn ist wirklich der Körper ein Complex unendlich vieler raumloser Punkte, und seine Meinung ist nur, dass das menschliche Denken mit dem Vollzuge der actuellen Theilung des Continuum in diese seine unendlich vielen unausgedehnten Componenten niemals zu Ende zu kommen vermag. Darum kann er genau wie Duns Scotus auf dem Wege geometrischer Demonstration die Unauflösbarkeit des Continuum in discrete Punkte erweisen ; ja er ist eigentlich Urheber der von Scotus ins Werk gesetzten geometrischen Demonstrationen. . . . Baco gibt zu erkennen das er die Argumente der Atomisten für sehr gewichtig und schwer widerlegbar halte ; . . . Scotus seinerseits sucht die von ihm als verdeckte Zugeständnisse an die Atomisten aufgefassten Anschauungen Baco's durch die Stärke seiner Logik zu entkräften. Seine Ausführungen gelten dem Bemühen, der subjectiven Denknotwendigkeit

The second instance occurs in the thirty-sixth
quaestio of the commentary on the Universals of
Porphyry and is, if possible, even more obscure than
the one we have just examined. According to Werner
Scotus is here reproducing the Baconian doctrine of
the transmission of light. Bacon, following the theory
of the Arabian physicist, Ibn al Haitan (Alhacen),
maintains that light takes time to travel from one
place to another, in spite of the denial of this fact by
Alkindi and Averroes and Aristotle. Though it is
true, he tells us, that the *species* are transmitted with
incredible speed, and that the whole time taken by
light to travel from the East to the West is so small
as to be imperceptible to our senses, like all natural
processes of change, the transmission of light must
occupy a certain minimum of time.[1] Now the passage
in Scotus runs as follows : ' In answer to the second
argument it may be said that if light exists in a luminous
body, and in the medium in the same sense, and is
a sort of quality belonging to the same kind in both, it
nevertheless has not the same mode of being in both.
Now by a concrete entity we mean a form in so far as
it exists in a subject, and therefore no concrete entity
named after light exists in the same sense in a body
and in the medium. For a luminous body is not said
to be illuminated but to shine, while the medium is not
said to shine but to be illuminated.' [2] The meaning of

auch den Charakter objectiver Wahrheit zu vindiziren, im gegebenen
Falle also in der Unmöglichkeit, mit der im Gedanken ins Unendliche
sich fortsetzenden Theilung des stofflichen Continuum je ans Ende
zu kommen, einen Reflex der objectiven sachlichen Beschaffenheit
des stofflichen Continuum zu erkennen ' (pp. 524–5).

[1] *Op. Maj.* v, dist. ix, c. iii (Bridges, ii, pp. 68 seq., also *De Multiplicatione Specierum* iv, c. iii (Bridges, loc. cit., pp. 525 sqq.).

[2] ' Ad secundum potest dici quod si lux univoce sit in corpore
luminoso et in medio, et sit aliqua qualitas eadem specie, non tamen
eundem modum essendi habet utrobique ; concretum autem significat
formam, secundum quod est in subjecto, et ideo nullum concretum
dictum a luce univocum inest huic et illi ; quia nec corpus luminosum

this passage is anything but clear, but Maritius Hibernicus, one of the most celebrated Scotist commentators,
takes it as referring to the Baconian theory that light
is propagated by motion, and hastens to explain away
this unscholastic notion by remarking that Duns is here
only positing this doctrine for the sake of argument.[1]

We have now indicated in the briefest manner
certain outstanding similarities between the doctrines
of the two great Oxford minorites. The features
they possess in common belong, speaking in a general
way, to the commonly accepted tradition of their
order. A more exact comparison would perhaps serve
to show many more interesting resemblances, but the
doctrines of Bacon have as yet been too little studied
to bring such a research within the scope of this
volume. We must pass on, therefore, and consider
in our next chapter the relation of the system of
Scotus to that of his greatest rival, the Angelic Doctor.

dicitur illuminatum sed lucens; medium vero non lucens sed
illuminatum.'

[1] 'Loquitur hic Doctor famose, forte secundum illam opinionem
quae ponit lucem fluere per motum; vel melius potest dici quod non
loquitur assertive, sed conditionaliter, scilicet gratia disputandi
admittendo.'

V

SCOTUS AND THOMAS AND THE OLDER
SCHOLASTICISM

IN order to understand the complex and intricate nature of Duns Scotus' thinking it will be necessary to bear in mind certain general features of the philosophical environment in which he lived. Of the peculiar characteristics of the Oxford School we have already spoken in connexion with the Baconian influence ; our next task will be to consider as briefly as possible the development of thirteenth-century scholasticism with a view to distinguishing those elements which contributed most to the building up of his system, a labour which is assuredly no light one. For the newer sources of Arabian and Jewish peripateticism, mixing with the older currents of the Augustinianism of the twelfth century, issued in a confusion of ideas and theories so heterogeneously various as almost to defy analysis. Since, then, outside the Thomistic philosophy we cannot look for any systematic coherence in the thinkers of the period, we shall find it more convenient for our present purpose to treat their doctrines rather as a congeries of more or less isolated solutions to a number of questions than as forming any organically connected whole. We shall therefore neglect very largely their strict chronological sequence and deal with them problem by problem ; a method by means of which we may hope to be able to trace more easily the various elements which went to compose the somewhat incongruous structure of the scholastic philosophy. We shall thus find ourselves confronted with a series of questions logical, metaphysical, and psychological, to each of which a number of solutions were propounded which varied almost indefinitely between the two opposite extremes, the pure Aristotelianism to which Aquinas approximates, and the 'Augustinianism' of Anselm, and the Platonism of the school of Chartres. Nor will this somewhat discursive method appear too arbitrary when we remember the discontinuous character of the scholastic disputation, with its artificial articulation of philosophical thinking into the elaborately constructed form of the *Quaestio* with its *rationes pro* and *contra*. In the domain of logic the revolution brought about by the rediscovery of Aristotle and the translation of the Arabian and Jewish commentators was as profound as it was far-reaching. The vast accession to the material of philosophic learning by extending the limits of the field of philosophic discussion gradually diminished the importance of the purely logical problem. Logic, which had once been synonymous with philosophy, gradually lost its architectonic character and became a subordinate and propaedeutic discipline. The great controversy between ' Realism ' and ' Nominalism ',[1] which had absorbed almost in its entirety the philosophic energy of the greater part of the twelfth century, was thrust into the background. The names themselves became

---

[1] It is a matter of great difficulty to give any precise meaning to this much misused term. If by ' Nominalism ' we mean a theory which held that universal concepts such as genera or species are nothing more than words, mere *flatus vocis*, then it may reasonably be doubted whether any nominalists existed in the twelfth century. All the more characteristic anti-realist doctrines of this period are more properly described as ' conceptualist ' : as for instance the theory of Abelard and the ' indifference ' theory, and the ' similitude ' theory attributed to William of Champeaux, etc. Even the ' terminalism ' of Ockham could hardly be described as nominalistic in this sense. Cf. De Wulf, *History of Mediaeval Philosophy*.

obsolete, no less than the logical theories they had been invented to designate.[1] Henceforth it is to the Arabian commentators, Alfarabi, Avicenna, Algazel, and Averroes, as well as to the Philosopher himself, that we must look for the materials of logical discussion. The threefold distinction of the universals, *ante rem*, *in re*, and *post rem*, becomes the starting-point of the new disputes concerning the nature of our universal ideas ; but these are no longer of first-rate importance, inasmuch as on the chief issues there is fundamental agreement. A ' moderate ' or ' philosophic ' realism of the ' Aristotelian ' type, as exemplified for instance in the writings of Avicenna, is the predominating— one might almost say the universal—form of logical theory. Controversy centres chiefly round two questions, which are indeed only two aspects of the same problem, namely, the relation between the *intentiones primae*[2] and the *intentiones secundae* ; and the particularization of the universal essence, the problem of individuation. But while on the main doctrine of ' universals ' the agreement is complete, and no scholastic denies that the universal notions exist as archetypal ideas in the divine mind, as general notions or concepts in the human mind, and as somehow individualized in the particulars of sense,[3] concerning

[1] Cf. Prantl, op. cit., vol. iii, ch. xix, p. 181 : ' Man glaube nur ja nicht dass man mit den zwei Schlagworten Realismus und Nominalismus die logische Parteistellung irgendwie erfassen, geschweige denn geschichtlich entwickeln könne.   Jene beiden Worte existiren in derjenigen Periode, mit welcher wir uns vorerst zunächst beschaffen müssen, gar nicht.'

[2] Cf. Avicenna, *Metaph.* I, 2, f. 70 v. a (ed. Venice, 1508) : ' Subjectum vero logicae . . . sunt intentiones ut intellectae secundo, quae apponuntur intentionibus primo intellectis, secundum quod per eas pervenitur de cognito ad incognitum, inquantum ipsae sunt intellectae et habent esse intelligibile.'

[3] Cf. Prantl, op. cit., p. 182 : ' Jene arabische von Albert und Thomas aczeptirte Theorie, dass die Universalien zugleich *ante rem* und *in re* und *post rem* seien, war doch gar zu bequem, um nicht von

the exact nature of this threefold existence there is
a wide diversity of opinion. The minutiae of the
discussions are endless in their obscure and prolix
verbalisms, and their juggling with the jargon of an
infinitely confusing technical terminology. And from
the outset the reader cannot fail to be haunted by
the essential difficulty of the Aristotelian dualism, the
unmediated transition from the ideal to the real order,
the obstinate spectre of the very same χωρισμός which
Aristotle so falsely attributed to his master Plato.

For the ubiquity of this ' universal ' is amazingly
bewildering. Regardless of the laws of space and time,
it is at once *in rebus* and at the same time *in intellectu*,[1]
and, though it exists as singular *in re extra*,[2] it is only
as existing in the mind that it possesses its proper
character as a ' universal '.[3] Nay, more, it is the
mind itself which invests it with its universality, for
of itself it is ' indifferent ', a mere *natura* which is
neither particular nor universal but indifferent to
both universality and singularity.[4] Finally, it has been

Allen zugegeben zu werden. Keiner verneint, dass die allgemeinen
Ideen der Dinge ursprünglich im göttlichen Schöpfer begründet
sind, keiner verneint dass sie in der erscheinenden Welt in das Einzel-
sein hinaustreten, und keiner verneint dass sie aus diesem Gebiete des
Singulären wieder vom menschlichen Denken erfasst werden.'

[1] Cf. Avicenna, *Logica*, fol. 2 v. b (ed. Venice, 1508) : ' Essentiae
vero rerum aut sunt in ipsis rebus, aut sunt in intellectu, unde habent
tres respectus,' etc.

[2] Cf. the commentary of Albertus Magnus on the *Post. An.* I,
i, 3, p. 518 b (ed. Lugdun., 1651) : ' Universale autem in sensu dicit
Alfarabius eo quod in singulari est mixtum et confusum, quo hic
homo est homo.'

[3] Ibid : ' Universale autem in intellectu dicit id quod in univer-
salitate ex singulis apprehensis agit intellectus, ex hoc quod unam
rationem videt in omnibus singulariter apprehensis, quae sunt unius
generis et speciei. Et hanc opinionem videtur approbare Avicenna et
Algazel et quidam alii.'

[4] Cf. Avicenna, *Logica*, fol. 12 r. a : ' Ponamus autem in hoc
exemplum generis dicentes quod animal est in se quoddam, et idem
est, utrum sit sensibile, aut sit intellectum in anima, in se autem hujus

existing eternally in the divine mind as an exemplar, a παραδεῖγμα, form, or idea, an archetype of the divine knowledge and creative activity.[1] This baffling and stupendous mixture of would-be Platonism, metaphysical realism, and logical conceptualism is characteristic of the great period of scholasticism. We find it still unsifted and unclarified in the writings of Albertus Magnus and Thomas Aquinas, who often do little more than repeat word for word the opinions of the various commentators without displaying any considerable regard for consistency or congruity. The result is a confusion of a nature so complicated that it is almost impossible to arrive at any clear conception of their real meaning.

The logic of Scotus, though scarcely less complicated, is in some ways a more consistent system. His doctrine of universals may be regarded as a critique of the Thomist elaboration of the Arabian theories; it is therefore worth our while to make a brief examination of the teaching of the Angelic Doctor in order to understand the difficulties which the Scotist doctrine

nec est universale nec est singulare. Si enim esset universale, ita quod animalitas ex hoc, quod est animalitas, est universalis, oporteret nullum animal esse singulare,' etc., etc. Fol. 12 v. a : ' Convenientius autem est, ut animalitas in se aliquando vocetur forma generalis et aliquando forma intelligibilis; sed ex hoc quod est animalitas non est genus ullo modo nec in intellectu, nec extra intellectum, quia non fit genus nisi adjungitur ei aliquis respectus, aut in intellectu aut extra. . . . Non fit singularis nisi addiderit intellectus aliquid per quod fit singularis,' etc.

[1] Avicenna, loc. cit. : ' Sed quia omnium quae sunt, comparatio ad Deum et ad angelos est, sicut comparatio artificialium quae sunt apud nos, ad animam artificem, ideo id quod est in sapientia creatoris et angelorum, et de veritate cogniti et comprehensi ex rebus naturalibus, habet esse ante multitudinem ; quidquid autem intelligitur de eis, est aliqua intentio et deinde acquiritur esse eis quod est in multiplicitate, et cum sunt in multiplicitate, non sunt unum ullo modo, in sensibus enim forinsecus non est aliquid commune nisi tantum discretio et dispositio ; deinde iterum habentur intelligentiae apud nos postquam fuerint in multiplicitate.'

was designed to overcome. Thomas accepts in principle
the threefold distinction of the universal essence
formulated by Avicenna, *ante multiplicationem, in
multiplicitate*, and *post multiplicationem.* The universal
may thus be regarded as having three aspects ; we may
consider it first as a *natura* or quiddity existing in the
particular *Einzeldingen*, and as such it is not actually
universalized ; secondly as actually universalized, the
universal concept or idea which exists in the mind
and is abstracted from the particulars of the external
world, the *universale post rem* ; and thirdly as an idea
in the divine mind which is prior to the creation of
the world, an archetype or plan according to which
the creature was created.[1] In his account of the
universal as a nature existing in the particular Thomas
follows along Aristotelian lines ; the common nature
is not something existing apart from the particulars,
a ἓν παρὰ τὰ πολλά, but something common existing
in them, a ἓν ἐπὶ πολλῶν, which is ' abstracted ' by the
intellect and universalized into a concept.[2] This
universalizing operation, which is the activity of knowledge and the process of knowing, consists in the

----

[1] Cf. Thomas, *Comm. in Sentt.*, Lib. II, dist. iii, q. 2, art. 2 : ' Est
triplex universal : quoddam quod est in re, seu natura ipsa, quae
est in particularibus, quamvis in eis non sit secundum rationem
universalitatis in actu ; est etiam quoddam universale quod est a re
acceptum per abstractionem, et hoc posterius est re. . . . Est etiam
quoddam universale ante rem, quod est prius re ipsa, sicut forma
domus, in mente aedificantis.'

[2] Cf. *Summa contra Gent.* I, 26 : ' Quod est commune multis non
est aliquid praeter multa nisi sola ratione, sicut animal non est aliud
praeter Socratem et Platonem, et alia animalia, nisi intellectu, qui
apprehendit formam animalis exspoliatam ab omnibus individuantibus
et specificantibus.' Cf. also *Summa Theol.* Ia pars, q. 85, art. 2 :
' Cum dicitur universale abstractum, duo intelliguntur, sc. ipsa
natura rei, et abstractio sua universalitas. Ipsa igitur natura cui
accidit vel intelligi vel abstrahi, vel intentio universalitatis, non est
nisi in singularibus ; sed hoc ipsum quod est intelligi vel abstrahi, vel
intentio universalitatis, est in re intellecta.'

divesting of the common nature of its individuating conditions, that is of matter, which is the principle of quantitative differentiation and of singularity as such, and abstracting from the external concrete object the *species intelligibilis* or universal.[1] But the actual characteristic of universality belongs only to the *natura* in virtue of its existence in the mind as a concept or notion ; for in the external world, the world as we should now say of ' objective ' reality, it exists not as universalized but as individual.[2] Further, as logical universal or generic or specific concept it is not an *ens reale* at all, but an *ens rationis*, for the genus and species as such have no ' natural ' or objective existence, but are wholly creations of the mind.[3] Finally, the universals exist in the Mind of God as ' ideas ' or forms apart from and beside the world of physical objects (*praeter res ipsas*), where they exercise a double function, as exemplary forms or archetypes of things created and creatable, and also as the intelligible principles of the divine understanding, the forms of

[1] Ibid., q. 86, art. 1 : ' Principium singularitatis in rebus materialibus est materia individualis : intellectus autem noster . . . intelligit abstrahendo speciem intelligibilem ab hujusmodi materia ; quod autem ab materia individuali abstrahitur, est universale.'

[2] *De Anima*, II, 12 : ' Ista autem natura cui advenit ratio universalitatis habet duplex esse ; unum quidem materiale, secundum quod est in materia naturali ; aliud autem immateriale, secundum quod est in intellectu. Secundum igitur quod habet esse in materia naturali, non potest ei advenire intentio universalitatis, quia per materiam individuatur. Advenit ergo ei universalitatis intentio secundum quod abstrahitur a materia individuali. Non autem est possibile quod abstrahatur a materia individuali realiter, sicut Platonici posuerunt ; non enim est homo naturalis, id est, realis, nisi in his carnibus. . . . Relinquitur igitur, quod natura humana non habet esse praeter principia individuantia, nisi tantum in intellectu.'

[3] *Comm. in Metaph.* IV, 4 : ' Ens rationis dicitur proprie de illis intentionibus quas ratio adinvenit in rebus consideratis, sicut intentio generis et speciei et similium, quae quidem non inveniuntur in rerum natura, sed considerationem rationis consequuntur, et hujusmodi ens rationis est proprie subjectum logicae.'

the divine cognition (*intelligibilia*),[1] the plurality of which does not conflict with the simplicity of the divine essence.[2]

One of the corollaries of this doctrine of universals is of special interest. It follows from the Thomistic conception of the principle of individuation that the singular as such can never be known directly; for the *species intelligibilis*, which is the 'form' through which the mind knows, is the universal, being 'abstracted' from the individuating material conditions; but matter is of itself unknowable, and individuality is relegated to the lower faculty of sensation. Hence the famous maxim of the schoolmen, *particulare sentitur; universale intelligitur.* Yet the *cognitio* (dare we translate this as 'awareness'?) of the individual must precede the knowledge of the universal; the particular and individual is *notius quoad nos*,[3] for our knowledge is derived from the particulars of sense, the whole of the intellectual functions being based upon the lower faculty of sense-perception. *Nihil est in intellectu quod non prius fuerit in sensu.*[4] Moreover, it has to be admitted that the individual is the object of our knowledge, for the individual, and not the universal, is the *prima substantia.* We are thus faced with a dilemma, for Thomas refuses to concede that the singular can be known directly. The direct object of knowledge,

---

[1] *Summa Theol.* Ia pars, q. 15, art. 1 : 'Necesse est ponere in mente divina ideas. . . . Per ideas intelliguntur formae aliarum rerum praeter res ipsas existentes. Forma autem alicuius rei praeter ipsam existens ad duo esse potest : vel ut sit exemplae ejus cujus dicitur forma, vel ut sit principium cognitionis ipsius, secundum quod formae cognoscibilium dicuntur esse in cognoscente. Et quantum ad utrumque est necesse ponere ideas.'

[2] Ibid., art. 2.

[3] *Summa Theol.* Ia pars, q. 85, art. 3 : 'Quia sensus est singularium, intellectus autem universalium, necesse est quod cognitio singularium quoad nos prior sit quam universalium cognitio.'

[4] *De Principio Individuationis* : 'In cognitione humana fundamentum et origo est sensus.'

the form by means of which we know, is the *species intelligibilis*, which, as we have just seen, is itself the universal.[1] He therefore attempts to solve the problem in two ways. While he admits that the individual is somehow known, his theory of individuation and the purely potential nature of matter prevent him from conceding that it is known directly as such : it is only *per quandam reflexionem* that we can know it.[2] But his statements on this subject are hardly consistent ; in another passage he maintains that the quiddity or essence, as existing in the particular in material things, is the object of a faculty which he calls *ratio particularis*.[3] So also when dealing with the case of the divine knowledge the divine idea represents the thing not only in its universal or formal aspects, but also in its material or particular relationships.[4]

These difficulties and incongruities in the Thomistic

[1] *Summa Theol.* Ia pars, q. 14, art. 11 : ' Intellectus noster speciem intelligibilem abstrahit a principiis individuantibus ; unde species intelligibilis nostri intellectus non potest esse similitudo principiorum individualium, et propter hoc intellectus noster singularia non cognoscit.'

[2] *Summa Theol.* Ia pars, q. 86, art. 1 : ' Principium singularitatis in rebus materialibus est materia individualis ; intellectus autem noster . . . intelligit abstrahendo speciem intelligibilem ab hujusmodi materia ; quod autem a materia abstrahitur est universale ; unde intellectus noster directe non est cognoscitivus nisi universalium ; indirecte autem et quasi per quandam reflexionem potest cognoscere singulare.'

[3] *De Principio Individuationis* : ' Cum enim in ipso objecto suo figitur acies, rationem universalis apprehendit, quod solum in istis inferioribus ab intellectu determinatur ut proprium objectum, cum omnia singularia apud nos materialia sunt ; materia enim impedit intellectum, singulare vero non. . . . Ideo quidditas rei materialis in ipsa sua particularitate est objectum rationis particularis, cujus est conferre de intentionibus particularibus.'

[4] *Quodlibeta*, VIII, 2 : ' Deus est causa rei, non solum quantum ad formam, sed etiam quantum ad materiam, quae est principium individuationis. Unde idea in mente divina est similitudo rei quantum ad utrumque, scilicet materiam et formam ; et ideo per eam cognoscuntur res non tantum in universali, sed etiam in particulari.'

logic which we have just examined constitute the starting-point of Duns Scotus' critique. With the main contentions of the doctrine of universals he is of course agreed. Thus he recognizes their threefold aspects as *ante rem*, *in re*, and *post rem*, though he conceives these somewhat differently. He too, no less than Thomas, would combine metaphysical realism with logical conceptualism and place the objective ground of our universal notion in some extra-mental independent reality, while at the same time he insists even more strongly on the reality of the individual. Like Thomas, too, he adheres to the generally accepted theory of knowledge with its psychological mechanism, the abstraction of the universal by the mind from the sense-data which represent the external objective reality. But he regards this process more in the light of an activity than of a merely passive impression, and insists more strongly than Aquinas on the subjective activity of the thinking intelligence. Yet on the other hand he accentuates the realistic aspect of the scholastic epistemology. Both the tendencies of the Thomist doctrine, its conceptualism as well as its realism, are strongly emphasized, the subjectivity of the process of universalization and the objective validity of the concept itself.

But it is on the metaphysical plane rather than on the purely logical that the divergence between the two thinkers asserts itself most prominently. Their different metaphysical conceptions form a line of cleavage which, though not indeed always as wide as some writers have been inclined to maintain, is however clearly traceable throughout every portion of their systems. For it is in their basic conceptions of form and matter and their mutual relations that a difference of fundamental importance becomes apparent. Thomas, following more closely the purer peripateticism of Averroes and Avicenna, conceives matter as something endowed with only potential existence, possessing no characteristics in its own intrinsic nature. For him matter is pure δύναμις, merely an unlimited possibility which *is* nothing of itself yet is capable of *becoming* anything, and therefore wholly indeterminate and, as we have already noticed, unknowable as such; ἡ γὰρ ὕλη καθ' αὑτὴν ἄγνωστος. Moreover, its very existence is inseparably conjoined with that of the form which determines it. It is impossible to conceive of it apart from form, and not even the divine omnipotence could have created a purely formless matter.[1] Thus in a sense matter appears to be a term almost equivalent to potency and coextensive with it. But in practice Thomas restricts it to a cosmological use as quantitative determination, and as quantitatively determined, *materia signata*, it forms, according to his view, the principle of individuation;[2] he does not use it generally in its wider connotation as potency pure and simple. The *substantiae separatae*, or pure spirits, as for instance the angels and the souls of the departed, do not contain matter; yet they are not absolutely simple and self-existent beings, for he regards them as compounded of essence and existence, a composition which is essential to his thinking in order to preserve the possibility of creation; for were the angels simply pure forms they would be timeless, eternal, and uncreated. Nor will

[1] Cf. *Summa Theol.* Ia pars, q. 66, art. 1, where it is argued that to postulate a formless matter preceding the imposition of forms implies a contradiction: 'Creationis enim terminus est ens actu. Ipsum autem quod est actus, est forma. Dicere igitur materiam praecedere sine forma, est dicere ens sine actu; quod implicat contradictionem.'

[2] Cf. *De Ente et Essentia*, cap. 2: 'Materia non quomodolibet est principium individuationis, sed solum materia (quantitate) signata. Et dico materiam signatam, quae sub certis dimensionibus continetur.' Cf. also *Summa contra Gent.* II, 49: 'Principium diversitatis individuorum ejusdem speciei est divisio materiae secundum quantitatem.'

he admit the unity or homogeneity of matter in all material beings, a doctrine which had been broached by Avicebron, but he interprets that unity as purely analogical, a view which makes his cosmology peculiarly difficult to grasp. Thus, for instance, he insists with Aristotle that the matter of the celestial bodies is different in kind from that of bodies terrestrial and only resembles it in as far as it is in potency to form.[1]

The teaching of Scotus is different : while he admits with Thomas that matter stands to form as potency to act, or determinand to determinant, and defines form as the actuality of matter,[2] he yet regards matter as having some actuality of its own apart from its mere potential existence ; for, he argues, that which has *no* actual existence is nothing, and therefore cannot be regarded as a cosmological principle at all.[3] Moreover, though he will not assert that as an actual historical fact there ever was a purely formless and wholly indeterminate matter in actual existence, he maintains that such a state of things might have been, as it is not in itself impossible.[4] Nor will he allow matter to be *per se* unknowable ; while insisting that *we* cannot know it as absolutely uninformed he

[1] Cf. *Summa Theol.* Ia pars, q. 66, art. 2 : 'Non est eadem materia corporis coelestis et elementorum, nisi secundum analogiam, secundum quod conveniunt in ratione potentiae.'

[2] Cf. *De Rerum Principio*, q. ix, n. 53 : 'Forma communicat materiae suam actualitatem et suam actum essendi et suam operationem,' etc.

[3] *De Rerum Principio*, q. vii, n. 3 : 'Si materia non esset aliqua res actu, ejus entitas non distingueretur ab entitate et actualitate formae, et sic nullam realem compositionem faceret cum ea.'

[4] *Op. Ox.*, Lib. II, dist. xii, q. 2, n. 3 : 'Quidquid Deus absolute facit in creaturis mediante causa secunda, potest facere sine illa causa secunda, quae non est de essentia causati. Sed forma est causa secunda, quae non est de essentia materiae inquantum materia est, mediante qua Deus dat esse materiae ; ergo sine illa Deus potest facere materiam.'

insists that it is knowable as such and that it has a representative idea of its own in the divine mind.[1] This view, combined with his theory of individuation, saves him from the awkward paradox of the Thomistic system that the individual, in spite of the fact that it is the *prima substantia*, is not directly knowable. Finally, he expressly adopts the theory of Avicebron concerning the unity of matter in all created beings, spiritual as well as corporeal.[2] Thus, while on the one hand he will not allow that matter is merely potential, he yet makes it on the other to be coextensive with potential being, and practically identifies it with creaturehood as such. He thus avoids the difficulties which arise in the Thomist system from the notion of angels as pure forms or *substantiae separatae*. Here, as elsewhere, Scotus is drawing on the earlier sources of the Augustinian scholasticism. His doctrine of *materia primo prima* bears distinct resemblances to the ' chaos ' of Augustine [3] and Hugo of St. Victor,[4] while his teaching of the hylemorphic composition of spiritual beings is to be found in Alexander of Hales,[5] Bacon, and Bonaventure.[6] Alexander, however, differs

---

[1] Loc. cit., q. 1, n. 20 : ' Dico quod materia secundum se in sua essentia est cognoscibilis, sed non a nobis. . . . Habet enim ideam in Deo,' etc.

[2] *De Rerum Principio*, q. viii, n. 2, sqq. It would be a mistake to regard this doctrine as pantheistic, as Hauréau and Stöckl would seem to do. Avicebron was no more a pantheist than Scotus. Cf. Munk's article on Jewish philosophy in the *Dictionnaire des Sciences Philosophiques*, 1st ed., vol. iii, p. 359.

[3] Cf. *In Genes. contra Man.*, Lib. I, cap. vi-ix.

[4] *De Sacramentis*, etc., Lib. I, cap. vi (Migne, vol. 176, col. 190).

[5] *Summa Theol.*, Lib. II, q. lxi, memb. 1 : ' Anima humana dicitur composita ex forma et materia intellectuali. Nullatenus autem sic habet materiam et formam sicut habent corpora, . . . sive . . . celestia, sive inferiora. Materiae enim corporalis terminus est magnitudo, spiritualis autem materiae non est terminus.'

[6] *In IV lib. Sentt.*, Lib. II, dist. iii, pars 1, art. 1, q. i : ' Et ideo illa positio videtur verior esse, scilicet quod in angelo sit compositio ex materia et forma.'

from Scotus on two important points. He denies, like Bacon, the community of matter in all created things, and distinguishes three kinds of matter : one subject to motion and change, corruption and generation, the matter of the sublunary sphere ; one subject to motion but not to change, the matter of the celestial bodies ; and a third kind, subject neither to motion nor substantial change, the matter which exists in spirits, which is called *materia intellectualis* in the passage just cited.[1] He also accepts the theory common to the older scholasticism, which Scotus rejects, of the *rationes seminales*, which attributed to matter a *potentia activa* as well as a *potentia passiva*, a kind of latent appetite for a particular form,[2] a doctrine which survived as late as Robert Kilwardby, the great Dominican opponent of Saint Thomas.[3] He appears also to deny the possibility of a purely formless matter,

---

[1] Op. cit. II, q. xliv, memb. 2 : ' Quaedam est materia subjecta motui et contrareitati, et haec est in elementis. Et est quaedam subjecta motui non contrareitati, et haec est in supercoelestibus corporibus. Et est tertia, quae nec est subjecta motui, nec contrareitati ; sed tamen formae, et haec est in inferioribus ut spiritibus.'

[2] Op. cit. II, q. lxxix, memb. 2 : ' Duplex est potentia materiae, scilicet activa et passiva. Passiva quia nihil cooperatur formae inducendo in materiam ipsam, sed est tantum potentia recipiendi formam ; activa, quia aliquo modo cooperatur ipsi agenti ad inductionem formae ; quia aliquid formae latet in materia, vel quia appetitus materiae habet inclinationem ad illam formam, sicut est in omnibus illis in quibus est ratio seminalis ad alia producenda in esse.'

[3] Cf. the letter of Kilwardby to Peter of Conflans, Archbishop of Corinth, quoted by Cardinal Ehrle in his article, ' Beiträge zur Geschichte der mittelalterlichen Scholastik' in vol. v of the *Archiv für Literatur- und Kirchengeschichte des Mittelalters*, pp. 603 sqq. : ' Intelligenda est igitur materia naturalis prima non sicut quaedam proxima inchoatio nihil formae habens, nec aliquid actualitatis aut compositionis, sed est quid dimensiones habens corporeas, impregnatum originalibus rationibus sive potentiis, ex quibus producendi sunt actus omnium specificorum corporum, sive simplicium, sive mixtorum, per operationem naturae. Quae enim tractu temporis disponuntur ut fiant specifica corpora operatione naturae fiunt. Quae autem subito jussu verbi externi exeunt, creantur, sicut prima elementa.'

but he may only be referring to its actual historical existence.[1]

There is also a corresponding difference between Scotus and Thomas in their doctrine of form. Thomas is the great protagonist of the theory of the unity of the substantial form, while Duns, as in many other cases, stands out as the champion of the older teaching. The nature of this divergence is displayed most clearly in the complicated problems arising out of the relation between the soul and the body. Thomas, following more strictly the Aristotelian doctrine, regards the soul as the only substantial form of the body, the unity of which is bound up with that of its formal principle ; [2] for it is by virtue of the soul as form that the body is what it is, man or animal. Further, it is only as animated by the soul that it really is a body in the strict sense of the word ; at death it ceases to be what it was and becomes a body only by an equivocation, for a corpse is not the same thing as a living body. The *forma corporis organici* is succeeded by a new form, a *forma cadavereitatis,* and a real substantial change has taken place ; for the dead eye, as Aristotle maintains, is not an eye in the same sense as the living one.[3] While the substrate of matter remains the same a new form has been educed, *de potentia materiae.* Soul and body are thus not two separate

---

[1] Alexander of Hales, *Summa Theol.* II, q. x, memb. 1 : 'Non puto primam illarum rerum materiam ita informem esse ut nullam omnino formam habuerit : ita tamen informem appellari posse, quia in confusione et permixtione nondum hanc in qua nunc creditur dispositionem optimam et pulchram recepisset.'

[2] Cf. *Summa Theol.* Ia pars, q. 76, art. 4 : ' Nam esse substantiale cujuslibet rei in indivisibili consistet, et omnis additio et substractio variat speciem,' etc.

[3] *De Anima,* Lib. II, 412 b. Εἰ γὰρ ἦν ὁ ὀφθαλμὸς ζῷον, ψυχὴ ἂν αὐτῷ ἦν αὐτοῦ ἡ ὄψις. αὕτη γὰρ οὐσία ὀφθαλμοῦ ἡ κατὰ τὸν λόγον. ὁ δ' ὀφθαλμὸς ὕλη ὄψεως, ἧς ἀπολιπούσης οὐκ ἔστιν ὀφθαλμός, πλὴν ὁμωνύμως, καθάπερ ὁ λίθινος καὶ γεγραμμένος.

things or substances but two principles, each correlative to the other, which by their union form one substance and stand to one another as form to matter, so constituting one *compositum* or σύνολον, for example a human being.[1]　How bitterly this doctrine was attacked we have already seen [2] in our account of the condemnations of the new teaching by Stephen Tempier and Robert Kilwardby.[3]　Nor was the reason of this opposition far to seek.　Taken in conjunction with Thomas's theory of matter as the principle of individuation, it lay open to the peril of dangerous perversion and misrepresentation ; it seemed to be suspended by too slender a cord over the abyss of heresy.　For the doctrine of personal immortality was all too plainly jeopardized.　If the soul be nothing but the form of the body, and matter be the principle of individuation, what can happen at death but the dissolution of the individual and the merging of all souls into an original specific unity, since after separation from matter and its differentiating quantity there is nothing left to distinguish one individual from another ?　And was not this exactly the heresy of Averroes, who taught a monopsychism of this nature ?　It is true that Aquinas himself never followed out to their logical conclusion the implications of his own theory and that he expressly repudiated and refuted them in his *Summa contra Gentiles*, a large portion of which was directly aimed against the great Arabian commentators.　But his defence is surely

---

[1] Cf. *Summa Theol.* Ia pars, q. 76, art. 4 : ' Unius rei est unum esse substantiale.　Sed forma substantialis dat esse substantiale.　Ergo unius rei est una tantum forma substantialis, anima autem est forma substantialis hominis.　Ergo impossibile est quod in homine sit aliqua alia forma substantialis quam anima intellectiva.'

[2] Vide supra, p. 115.

[3] Cf. the letter just quoted : ' Multo melius dicitur tertio modo, viz. quod differant essentialiter ab invicem vegetativa, sensitiva, et intellectiva potentia ' etc.

a lame one, and the price he paid for it was the sacrifice of his own consistency. He can only answer that the soul retains its individuality after death by virtue of its aptitude to the particular body it was created to inform, a theory which in fact involves the actual abandonment of one of the main pillars of his system, namely, the doctrine of *materia signata* as the *principium individuationis*.[1]

This dilemma with which Thomism is faced is not without interest ; it forms a most instructive example of bilingual ambiguity and the non-equivalence of Latin and Greek terminology. For the Greek word ψυχή, as Aristotle used it, did not and could not represent what the word *anima* meant to the Latin theologian. For to Aristotle ψυχή is a biological term indicating the vital principle, that in virtue of which a body is alive, an organization of functions or ἐνέργειαι which in their entirety constitute a living being rather than the metaphysical notion which we indicate by the word soul. But to the Latin Catholic the term *anima* bore a widely different significance. The scholastic conception of the soul, which with its theological and Christian associations had been handed down through long centuries of religious development, was far more nearly akin to the Platonic ψυχή than that of Aristotle. For to the Platonist the soul is something quite independent of and separable from the body, united to it only as it were ' accidentally '

---

[1] Cf. *Summa contra Gent.* II, lxxxi : ' Multitudo igitur animarum a corporibus separatarum, consequitur quidem diversitatem formarum secundum substantiam, quia alia est substantia hujus animae et illius ; non tamen ista diversitas procedit ex diversitate principiorum essentialium ipsius animae, nec est secundum diversam rationem ipsius animae, sed est secundum diversam commensurationem animarum ad corpora ; haec enim anima est commensurata huic corpori et non illi . . . hujusmodi autem commensurationes remanent in animabus etiam pereuntibus corporibus, sicut et ipsae earum substantiae manent, quasi a corporibus secundum esse non dependentes.'

and not 'substantially', even repugnant to it and at
war with it, a notion which harmonized far more
easily with the ascetic teaching of the Christian
religion as manifested in the Catholicism of the
Middle Ages with its fundamental dualism of flesh
and spirit, body and soul. Hence the Aristotelian
conception was quite unfitted to express the essential
characteristics of the Christian beliefs, which would
have seemed to the Stagirite a very strange perversion
of his original scientific doctrine. The Thomist interpretation cannot fail to strike the critic as an incongruous misfit, a pathetic attempt to fit a square peg into
a round hole.

But the judgement of Scotus was too keen to let
so glaring an inconsistency pass unobserved. His
rational psychology shows an attempt to escape from
this dilemma which, if not wholly successful, has yet
resulted in a doctrine far more coherent and far more
harmonious than that of Thomas. And the difference,
it should be noticed, between the two thinkers is in
its origin metaphysical. Just as his conception of
matter is more positive and not restricted to merely
potential being, so he maintains that the activity of
the σύνολον belongs neither to the formal principle
as such nor the material principle as such, but to both
in conjunction, that is to the concrete whole, the
suppositum or *compositum*.[1] Moreover, he conceives
the unity of the substantial form in a manner which
differs very markedly from that of Thomas. The
substantial form is indeed one, but it is one with a
unity which does not exclude plurality of parts. For
the numerical unity of the concrete individual is
derived from a *forma completiva*, an ultimate unifying

---

[1] *De Rerum Principio*, q. ix, art. 1 : 'Videmus quod compositum
totaliter agit et patitur, ergo potentia activa et passiva in composito
vere componunt unum per essentiam, inquantum totum compositum
est activum tantum per formam, et totum passivum per materiam.'

'formality', which unifies and completes the already existing determinations of matter in the *compositum* which these essences have already communicated to it.[1] The significance of this doctrine in its influence on his logic is of the highest importance, forming as it does the coping-stone of his theory of universals, and bridging the gulf between metaphysical realism and logical conceptualism. For by means of it Scotus is able, without hypostatizing concepts into things, to give the former an objective validity by postulating a *formalitas a parte rei*, a *gradus entitatis* which corresponds to the subjective determinations of our universal ideas or conceptions. His doctrine thus stands half-way between the older teaching of a unified plurality of forms, such as we saw for instance in the letter of Robert Kilwardby, and the doctrine of the unity of form, as taught by Thomas Aquinas and his school. By substituting a formal for a real identity of essence between individuals of the same species Scotus thus mediates between the realism characteristic of the school of Chartres and the 'nominalism' of Ockham and his followers.[2] Moreover, he manages

---

[1] *Op. Ox.*, Lib. IV, dist. xi, q. 3, n. 46 : 'Esse totius compositi includit esse omnium partium, et includit multa esse partialia multarum partium vel formarum, sicut totum ens ex multis formis includit illas actualitates partiales. Si tamen omnino fiat vis in verbo, concedo quod formale esse totius compositi est principaliter per unam formam, et illa forma est qua totum compositum est hoc ens ; ista tamen est ultima adveniens omnibus praecedentibus. Et hoc modo totum compositum dividitur in duas partes essentiales, in actum proprium, sc. ultimam formam, qua est illud quod est, et in propriam potentiam illius actus, quae includit materiam primam cum omnibus formis praecedentibus. Et isto modo concedo quod esse illud totale est completive ab una forma, quae dat toti illud quod est ; sed ex hoc non sequitur quod in toto includatur praecise una forma, vel quia in toto includantur plures formae.'

[2] Cf. Poncius, *Integer philosophiae cursus ad mentem Scoti* (Paris, 1649), p. 84 : 'Quo sensu individua ejusdem speciei sunt idem formaliter ? Propter maximam similitudinem quam habent in suis essentiis, sicut etiam solet dici de duobus aliquibus individuis hominum,

to avoid two of the great difficulties of the Thomist logic, its inability to distinguish satisfactorily between the individualized and the universal essence, and the dilemma of the individualizing principle as *materia signata*, which entailed a denial of all direct knowledge of the individual. For though to Scotus, no less than to Thomas, the individual is the primary reality, while safeguarding the real validity of our universal notions, he yet succeeds, at the same time, in maintaining the primary intelligibility of the particular in a way which did not lie open to the latter. His whole handling of the problem illustrates most admirably the pene-trating, subtle, and comprehensive character of his thought ; and his solution marks a real advance on the Thomist doctrine, presenting itself as the most mature and most perfect development of the logic of the schools.

This peculiar conception of the nature of form and matter as ultimate cosmological principles sets its stamp no less upon his psychology than on his logic. Holding as he does the hylemorphic composition of spiritual as well as material beings, he is enabled by virtue of his doctrine of the plurality of forms to give to the body an existence less closely dependent on that of the soul than Thomas,[1] without at the same time denying the proposition that the rational or intellectual soul is the ' substantial ' form of the body.[2] At the

si valde magnam similitudinem habeant, quod non videantur esse distincta, et quod videantur esse unus et idem homo.' This interpreta-tion is perhaps too broadly conceptualistic, but it suggests an interest-ing parallel from Roger Bacon, whose influence may not be altogether absent. Cf. ' Individuum est natura absoluta et fixa, habens per se esse, et universale non est nisi convenientia individui respectu alterius ' (quoted by E. Charles, op. cit., p. 383).

[1] *Op. Ox.*, Lib. IV, dist. xi, q. 3, n. 54 : ' Sic in proposito, forma animae non manente, corpus manet ; et ideo universaliter in quolibet animato necesse est ponere illam formam qua corpus est corpus, aliam ab illa qua est animatum.'

[2] *De Rerum Principio*, q. ix, art. 2 : ' Quamvis sint diversae formae

same time he escapes from the difficulty which forms so great a stumbling-block in the system of Aquinas which arose with regard to the souls of the departed. Moreover, Thomas's conception of the soul as pure forms and the angels as *substantiae separatae* was obviously inadequate. How could a spiritual being be described in terms of the Platonic concept ? How, further, could an angel or a disembodied spirit be distinguished from the archetype or idea in the divine mind, the εἶδος or ἰδέα ? Moreover, must not the εἶδος as such be eternal ? In fact as pure form must it not be uncreate, necessary, and actually divine ? For Scotus this somewhat bizarre problem is entirely non-existent. The soul for him, as well as the body, is compounded both of matter and form, though the spiritual matter differs from that of the corporeal beings in that it is not yet quantitatively determined, though as ultimate cosmological substratum it underlies the latter. Once again we may see how Scotus has gone back to the doctrines of the older Augustinian scholasticism and combined them in a new synthesis of his own, a synthesis in which the violent contraposition of elements, gathered from Arabian peripateticism and Christian theology, is more successfully avoided. True to the traditions of his order, he has worked out more fully the implications latent in the teaching of Alexander of Hales and Bonaventura, purging their theories of their inconsistencies and combining with them those elements of the Thomistic teaching which served to combine with them in a more closely articulated system.

To understand the historical evolution of the Scotist doctrine it will be as well to compare Duns' teaching with the doctrine of Alexander of Hales,

in homine dantes diversa esse, anima intellectiva non solum dat esse intellectui sed perficit actus aliarum formarum. Quod patet quia ipsa recedente materia incipit corrupi, quoad actus aliarum formarum.'

who may be regarded as the founder of the Franciscan
School. Alexander was the first scholastic who
possessed a knowledge of the complete Aristotelian
canon, which had but recently been introduced into
the Latin world, and his early date (he died in 1264)
placed him more strongly than later writers under the
influence of the older Augustinian scholasticism of
the twelfth century. Hence we may not unnaturally
expect to find that his account of the relation of the
soul to the body is somewhat confused and obscure.
He uses two expressions to designate the nature of
this relation. On the one hand, the soul is related to
the body as *motor* to *mobile*, on the other, as *perfectio*
to *perfectibile*. The former couplet would suggest
Platonic, the latter rather Aristotelian associations.
Body and soul are each in their own way complete.
The union subsisting between them is, in the phrase
of Saint Bernard, a *unio naturae*, and may be regarded
as analogous to the union of form and matter; but we
must distinguish in the human being various *formae
naturales* as well as that of the soul. First there is the
forma mixtionis, which makes each part of a material
substance what it is; i. e. it makes every portion
of a lump of gold gold. Then there is an organic form
which makes each part of a plant plant, or each part
of an animal animal. Besides these we must distinguish in the human being the rational soul which does
not inform the parts but only the whole; for the
parts of a man cannot be called a man but only the
whole man, and in this sense this form may be called
the *actus materiae*, but the relation is a special one
and differs from the ordinary relation between form
and matter.[1] Thus while each is complete after its

---

[1] *Summa Theol.* II, q. lxiii, memb. 4: 'Licet enim quaedam sit
similitudo animae et corporis et formae ad materiam, tamen est
similitudo secundum modum jam dictum. Est enim anima aliquid
praeter suam materiam, quod non est dicere in forma naturali simpli-

own fashion, and while the body merely as a body requires no further corporeal perfection, it is nevertheless capable of a further spiritual perfection which gives it life.[1] The exact nature of Alexander's teaching has been disputed, and it has even been contended that his doctrine is consistent with the theory of the unity of the substantial form,[2] though the plurality of forms is plainly asserted. But, however we interpret it, the essential nature of the unity between the body and the soul remains unimpaired. However perfect and complete each may be apart from the other their union is no mere collocation or contiguity in space, for the human body depends on the soul not only for its motion but also for its substantial *esse* as specifically human, as well as for its vital functions.[3]

The view of Bonaventura is somewhat different and approximates more closely to the Aristotelian doctrine. He rejects the ' platonizing ' theory that the soul is united to the body as the boatman to the boat on the ground that this would make the body the instrument of the soul and not its *proprium*, thus identifying the

---

citer, unde non est ibi proprie actus materiae, sed actus naturalis corporis completi in forma naturali, quae dicitur forma corporalis. Sic ergo habet proprium modum unionis, et ideo vocat beatus Bernardus istam unionem proprio nomine unitatem nativam.

[1] Ibid., memb. 1 : ' Licet utrumque (*sc.* anima et corpus) in suo genere sit completum, nec respiciat ulterius perfectionem sui generis, ut corpus non respiciat ulterius perfectionem corporalem in natura ; nihilominus respicit corpus ulteriorem perfectionem spiritualem, sive animalem, quae est mediante vita.'

[2] See Sauvé, *De l'Union substantielle de l'âme et du corps* (Paris, 1878), p. 114.

[3] Alexander of Hales, loc. cit. : ' Corpus humanum indiget anima non tantum ut moveatur, sed etiam ut in esse, quo est, subsistet et permaneat, et ideo duplicem habet operationem, ut mobilis ad motorem, et perfectibilis ad perfectionem ; unde unum in natura constituunt, scilicet hominem.' Cf. also loc. cit., q. lxxxi, mem. 2 : ' Anima est causa perfectiva et completiva corporis. . . . Anima facta est causa corporis, id est, ut sit perfectio sive causa perfectiva corporis.'

relation with that of the angels to the bodies they sometimes assume, whereas the union of body and soul in the human being is of more intimate a nature. His conception of the relationship of form to matter approaches that of Duns ; *unius perfectibilis una sola est perfectio*, a perfection which is given by a *forma completiva* ; but he does not seem to have regarded this as inconsistent with the doctrine of the plurality of forms both in organic and inorganic bodies, though his doctrine on this point is anything but clear.[1] With regard to the union of the soul and the body he distinguishes two aspects of their unity. Certain operations, he tells us, proceed from the soul in its capacity as *motor corporis*, certain others in its capacity as *perfectio corporis*, both terms being taken from his master, Alexander. In the first class he includes the bodily movements such as walking, sitting, and so forth ; in the second, the sensory operations such as seeing, hearing, etc.[2] In another passage he maintains

---

[1] With regard to the doctrine of the plurality of substantial forms there has been considerable controversy as to whether Bonaventura did or did not subscribe to it. Schneid, in his pamphlet, *Die Körperlehre des Duns Scotus*, decides that he did not. Botalla, on the other hand, takes the opposite view and quotes a passage which appears to suggest something very like a *forma corporeitatis* : ' Corpus organicum ex materia et forma compositum est, et tamen habet appetitum ad suscipiendum animam ' (*La composition des corps d'après les deux principaux systèmes qui divisent les écoles catholiques*, p. 31). De Wulf, in his *History of Mediaeval Philosophy*, p. 255, also supports this latter view.

[2] *In II Sentent.*, dist. viii, pars Ia, art. 3, q. ii : ' Cum anima uniatur corpori ut perfectio et motor, quaedam sunt operationes quae consequuntur ipsam animam in corpore, ut est motor ; quaedam ut perfectio ; quaedam partim sic et sic. Differenti autem modo exercet anima in corpore operationes quae sequuntur ipsam ut motorem, et ut perfectionem. Nam operationes quae consequuntur animam ut motorem, sic exercet per corpus, quod illas easdem exercet in corpus, quia non solum movet alia corpora, sed etiam corpus proprium. Operationes vero quae consequuntur animam in corpore ut est perfectio, sic exercet anima in corpore per corpus quod exerceat

that it is the soul which communicates to the body its *esse* as well as its *vivere* and *intelligere*.[1] But like that of Alexander his teaching is confused and obscure ; his mystical soul cared little for the subtleties of the dialectician, and he shows a tendency to blur over controversial issues and leave them somewhat vague. But the main outcome of his teaching on the problem in question seems to be that the soul, while in one capacity it acts as the form of the body, yet retains in another its independence, and stands above it and opposed to it as something different guiding and controlling it.

There is yet another teacher of the Franciscan Order whose doctrine on the question at issue remains to be discussed, namely Richard of Middleton, who was a teacher in the University of Oxford, whose lectures Scotus may perhaps have attended. While maintaining in principle the theory of the plurality of forms,[2] Richard insists that the intellectual or rational soul is the specific form of the human being. He argues from the fact of man's reasoning powers in the following manner. The most perfect operation of a substance proceeds from its principal or constitutive specific form, not from any accidental or incomplete determination. But man's highest activity is rational thought, which is the activity of the intellectual soul. The intellectual soul is therefore the specific form of

---

eas cum corpore, sicut patet ; nam anima clauso oculo aliquod videre non potest. Et ideo primae competunt animae ut est hic aliquid, et motor differens a mobili ; secundae vero ut est forma juncta materiae. ... Motus progressivus, sive quicumque alius sit membrorum exteriorum, est ab anima in corpore ut est motor vel motrix ; sentire vero per organa corporis, competit animae ut est illorum organorum perfectio. Sicut enim anima perficit totum corpus, ita visus sive potentia visiva perficit oculum.'

[1] Cf. *Breviloquium*, pars II, cap. 9 : ' Ipsa (*sc.* anima) non tantum dat esse verum etiam vivere et sentire et intelligere.'

[2] See De Wulf, op. cit., pp. 259–60.

the human being.[1] But the union between soul and body is not altogether similar to the union between other forms and the matter they determine; for though the soul can only have its fullest and most complete existence when united to a body, it is yet capable of a continued existence when separated from it.[2]

The teaching of Scotus follows that of Richard fairly closely in some respects. But it is a compromise between the doctrine of plurality in its extreme shape and the doctrine of the unity of substantial form as held by Thomas. Like Robert Kilwardby, Richard had maintained that the soul was in itself compound, consisting of three distinct principles, the vegetative, sensitive, and the intellectual, which, united together, form one human soul, the intellectual principle being the highest in this hierarchy and constitutive of the specific form.[3] Scotus expressly repudiates this notion

---

[1] Richard of Middleton, *In lib.* II *Sentt.*, dist. xvii, q. 3 : 'Respondeo quod anima rationalis fuit ipsius Adae forma specifica, et etiam cujuslibet hominis sua anima intellectiva est forma specifica. . . . Homo enim experitur se ratiocinari, non tantum de intentionibus particularibus, sed etiam de intentionibus universalibus ; hanc ergo actionem habet homo per aliquid sui principaliter, non per materiam, nec per aliquam substantialem formam incompletam, nec per accidentalem formam, quia cum ratiocinari sit ultimus actus et nobilissimus quem possit homo naturaliter habere sub ratione qua natus est cognoscere, oportet quod sibi conveniat principaliter per nobilissimam sui partem. Nobilissima autem pars compositi est forma specifica . . . ergo forma hominis specifica est anima rationalis.'

[2] Ibid. : 'Cum dicitur quod omnis forma in essendo innititur suae materiae. . . . Dico quod verum est, si vocas inniti materiae naturaliter inclinari ad ipsam, ad hoc, ut ex ipsa et materia possit constitui unum per essentiam : et si vocas inniti materiae dependere ab ea quantum ad completum essendi modum. Sed si vocas inniti materiae non posse esse sine materia quam perficit, sic dico quod propositio habet instantiam in corporis humani specifica forma, potest enim esse sine corpore, quamvis sine illo non habeat suum completum naturalis existentiae modum.'

[3] The doctrine of Kilwardby is worth quoting as it forms a charac-

and argues for the simplicity of the soul in its formal aspect. The intellectual power contains in itself the sensitive and vegetative functions. Hence a plurality is superfluous. He then goes on to support his view by an appeal to the principle of economy. It is futile to postulate a plurality of principles when a fewer number works equally well—a methodological maxim which has been attributed in a metaphysical form to William of Ockham, in the shape of his famous 'Razor'.[1] On the other hand Scotus still retains the plurality of forms, as we have seen, by maintaining the existence of a *forma corporeitatis* as well as the 'partial' forms of the various organs. In respect of the substantial

teristic example of the plurality theory carried to its furthest lengths. Cf. the letter to Peter of Conflans cited above : ' Multo melius dicitur tertio modo, videlicet quod differant essentialiter ab invicem vegetativa sensitiva et intellectiva potentia, ita quod in omnibus vegetantibus . . . producatur vegetativa anima sive vita a potentiis elementorum mediante materia ad vegetationem ordinata ; sensitiva similiter producitur operatione naturae de potentiis elementorum mediante mixtione vel complexione ad sensationem ordinata. . . . Et ideo creata est potentia intellectiva tanquam hoc aliquid, potens quasi personaliter subsistere post corporis separationem ; aliae autem potentiae non sic. . . . Quod vero praedicto modo vegetativum et sensitivum sunt ab intrinseca operatione, et intellectiva ab extrinseca, videtur velle Philosophus.'

[1] Cf. *Quaestiones de Anima*, q. xi, n. 8 : ' Ergo videtur quod ita sit animalium una, et non est per aliam formam, sive partem formalem, vegetativa sensitiva et intellectiva ; sed intellectiva virtus continet vegetativum et sensitivum.' n. 9 : ' Videmus et hanc authoritatem in ratione fundari ; generale enim principium est, quod si aliquid potest aeque bene fieri per pauciora, sicut per plura, nullo modo talis pluralitas debet poni. . . . Si igitur anima humana absque compositione multiplicis partis formalis per intellectivam formam potest facere quidquid potest illa triplici formalitate, nullo modo debet illa triplix formalitas in ea poni.' That the formula, ' Entia non sunt multi-plicanda praeter necessitatem,' which has been attributed to Ockham, is nowhere to be found in his works has been shown by W. Thorburn in his article on Ockham's razor, in *Mind*, July 1918. It occurs, however, in a form similar to that used by Scotus in Dante, *De Monarchia*, Lib. I : ' Quod potest fieri per unum melius est fieri per unum quam per plura.'

union of the soul with the body Duns Scotus takes up a position very similar to that of Richard. His doctrine of the nature of form and its unity is such as to enable him to maintain the thesis that the soul is united to the body as its substantial form, *secundum se totam* and *ut intellectiva*,[1] without at the same time sacrificing the relative independence granted to the body by the *forma corporeitatis*. He thus effects a compromise between the Aristotelian and the Augustinian teaching which is more nearly in accordance with the teaching of the Church.

We have now traced in broad outline one of the principal differences which distinguish the Scotist from the Thomist cosmology, and examined, somewhat cursorily indeed, a few of the implications contained in their respective cosmological theories. We have yet to consider a second fundamental divergence, more subtle perhaps than the last, but at the same time no less far-reaching. Once again Thomas stands out as the champion of the newer doctrine derived from Aristotelian sources, while Scotus defends the older teaching. The older scholasticism of the eleventh and twelfth centuries had been voluntaristic, while most of the Arabian philosophers had been intellectualists. Augustine, Anselm, Alexander of Hales, Roger Bacon, had all asserted the primacy of the will over the intellect ; the Arabians, Avicenna and Averroes, that of the intellect over the will. The controversy seems at first sight, to say the least of it, a sterile one, and one of purely academic interest. Both sides acknowledge that intellect and will are complementary, that neither can exist without the other, and that both are equally essential functions of the divine and human mind. Indeed, to the unsophisticated intelligence it might appear as if the controversy over the primacy of these faculties were of the same metaphysical importance

[1] *De Rerum Principio*, q. ix, art. 2.

as the ' Order of Precedence '.[1]   Yet, strange though it may seem to us, in the thirteenth and fourteenth centuries it was a living problem.   For not only was it brought into some kind of vital relation with the lives of men, as it reflected itself in the dispute as to the relative merits of the active or the contemplative life, but it was also concerned with the interpretation of certain dogmas of Christian theology dealing with the nature of Grace and the Last End of man.   Moreover, its significance went yet a little deeper ; on the side of pure speculation it affected radically not only the conception of human responsibility and human freedom, but also the fundamental notions of the nature of the divine activity.   Finally, as involving the question of determinism, it abutted on one of those puzzles which have been coeval with the history of mankind.

The genesis of the Thomistic doctrine is not difficult to trace.   It is the lineal descendant of the old intellectualism of Socrates and his famous paradox οὐδεὶς ἑκὼν ἁμαρτάνει, a conception from which the thought of classical Greece was never wholly able to free itself, and which, through the translations of the *Ethics* of Aristotle, made its way into scholasticism. After desperate attempts in the third and seventh books of the Nicomachean *Ethics* to escape from it Aristotle fails at last to account satisfactorily for the occurrence of ἀκρασία or conscious wrong-doing by his doctrine of the practical syllogism,[2] because he has.

[1] Some inkling of this kind seems to have been in the mind of Bonaventura, who, in discussing the question whether the intellect and the will are *essentialiter* different, remarks that the problem contains ' plus . . . curiositatis quam utilitatis, propter hoc, quod sive una pars teneatur sive altera, nullum praejudicium nec fidei, nec moribus generatur ' (*In II Sentt.*, dist. xxiv, art. 2, q. 1).

[2] For Aristotle's account of the practical syllogism see the *Nicomachean Ethics*, VII, cap. 3 ; also the article by Dr. F. C. S. Schiller in the *Journal of Philosophy*, 1919, entitled ' Aristotle and the practical Syllogism '.

been unable to arrive at a full analysis of the conception of the will.[1] The notion of a deliberate choice of a course of action, recognized at the time of choosing as the worse of two alternatives, is to him unthinkable. The same difficulty haunts the moral psychology of Thomas, who, although he is perfectly familiar with the conception of the will and is a believer in its freedom, shows a marked tendency to interpret it deterministically. For moral evil is ultimately *praeter intentionem*. All willing is *sub specie boni*, and concerning the willing of man's last end there is no possibility of error. Every man desires his happiness; when he does wrong he does so by mistaking the means to that end, and consequently is acting against his real intention [2]—surely a strange interpretation of the moral teaching of Christianity with its insistence on the malice of sin. The same intellectualistic bias manifests itself in his account of man's final beatitude. He transforms the Aristotelian ideal of the ἐνέργεια ἀκινησίας into the conception of the beatific vision, the intellectual contemplation of the divine being in which the free activity of the will has almost been eliminated.[3] So, too, in his account of the divine

---

[1] The nearest equivalent Aristotle has to the will is προαίρεσις, which is defined in *Eth. Nic.* III, 3, as βουλευτικὴ ὄρεξις τῶν ἐφ᾽ ἡμῖν. and in *Eth. Nic.* VI, 2, as ὀρεκτικὸς νοῦς and ὄρεξις διανοητική. In both these cases he is trying to interpret the phenomena of voluntary action in terms of the two faculties of intellect and appetite.

[2] *Summa contra Gent.* III, 4: 'In agentibus per intellectum et aestimationem, quamcumque intentio sequitur apprehensionem; in illud enim tendit intentio, quod apprehenditur ut finis. Si ergo perveniatur ad aliquid quod non habet speciem apprehensam, erit praeter intentionem; sicut si quis comedat fel, credens illud esse mel, hoc erit praeter intentionem. Sed omne agens per intellectum intendit aliquid secundum quod illud accipit sub ratione boni . . .; si ergo illud non sit bonum sed malum, erit praeter intentionem.' For a further criticism of the Thomist doctrine see below, vol. ii, ch. vii, p. 297.

[3] Cf. Aristotle, *Eth. Nic.* VII, 14 ad fin. : ἐπεὶ εἴ του ἡ φύσις ἁπλῆ

existence we may detect the influence of the Aristotelian deity with his perfect and eternal self-contemplation, the form of forms which exists for ever wrapped in the meditation of its own perfections, and heedless of a world which he did not create and for which he is not morally responsible.[1] It is true that Thomas accepts the notion of a divine providence and the divine knowledge of created things, but the knowledge of them is secondary and is mediated by the contemplation of the divine essence. The same theory is found no less definitely in Scotus himself, but he lays greater stress on the volitional aspect of the divine activity than Thomas, and his analysis of the divine volition lacks the deterministic trend given to it by Aquinas.[2]

Far different were the origins of the voluntarism of the older scholasticism of the eleventh, twelfth, and thirteenth centuries. It arose, not from a scientific analysis of the psychology of moral action as was undertaken by Aristotle in his works on ethics, but from a deep and earnest personal conviction, the conviction of moral responsibility, and above all of an overwhelming sense of guilt, or, to use the theological term, of sin. The starting-point of Augustine's speculation is the problem of the nature and origin of evil.[3] After much searching of heart he finds its roots in his own self and in his own soul, in the will which alone can account for his sense of wickedness.[4]

εἴη, ἀεὶ ἡ αὐτὴ πρᾶξις ἡδίστη ἔσται· διὸ ὁ θεὸς ἀεὶ μίαν καὶ ἁπλῆν χαίρει ἡδονήν. οὐ γὰρ μόνον κινήσεώς ἐστιν ἐνέργεια, ἀλλὰ καὶ ἀκινησίας. Cf. Thomas, *Summa Theol.* Ia, 2ae, q. 3, art. 5.

[1] Cf. the passage from Aristotle, *E. N.* just quoted, and also *Metaphysics* A, vii.

[2] Cf. *Summa Theol.* Ia pars, q. 19 : ' De voluntate Dei.'

[3] *Confessiones*, VII, 5, 7 : ' Et quaerebam unde malum, et male quaerebam ; et in ipsa inquisitione mea non videbam malum. . . . Quae radix ejus, et quod semen ejus ? An omnino non est ? Cur ergo timemus et cavemus quod non est ? '

[4] Ibid., VII, 3 : ' Audiebam liberum voluntatis arbitrium causam

Of any hesitation between freedom and determinism there is no question, for the very existence of the will already implies its freedom, the power to do or to refrain from doing ; [1] without this the will can be nothing ; [2] and in the last resort a man is nothing but his will.[3]   But we must not confuse our conception of the will by identifying its liberty with the mere power of doing wrong.   The divine will is incapable of sinning, but it is not therefore the less free ; nay, for that very reason it is more free than ours ; [4] indeed our will is not free while it is fettered in the bondage of the flesh ; it is only when released from servitude to sin that it attains its true freedom.[5]

The same line of thought finds its expression also in Anselm.   For him, as for Augustine, human responsibility and its bearing upon man's ultimate destiny is the primary consideration.[6]   He distinguishes three aspects of the will : the instrument, or actual motive power of our actions, the desires or affections by which our actions are affected, and the use of the instrument, the fully conscious and deliberate act of willing.[7]   The will considered as

---

esse ut male faceremus. . . . Cum aliquid vellem aut nollem, non alium quam me velle ac nolle certissimus eram, et ibi esse causam peccati mei jam jamque animadvertabam.'

[1] *De Duabus Animabus*, x, 14 : 'Voluntas est motus animi, cogente nullo, ad aliquid vel non amittendum, vel adipiscendum.'

[2] *De Lib. Arb.* III, iii, 8 : 'Voluntas igitur nostra, nec voluntas, nisi esset in nostra potestate.   Porro quia est in potestate, libera est nobis.'

[3] *Soliloq.* I, 1 : 'Nihil aliud habeo quam voluntatem.'   Cf. also *De Civitate Dei*, XIV, 6 : 'Voluntas est quippe in omnibus, imo omnes nihil aliud quam voluntates sunt.'

[4] *Opus Imperf. contra Julianum*, V, 38 : 'In ipso Deo summum est liberum arbitrium, qui peccare nullo modo potest.'

[5] *De Civitate Dei*, XIV, 11 : 'Arbitrium igitur voluntatis tunc est vere liberum, cum vitiis peccatisque non servit.'

[6] *De Concordia*, I, 6 : 'Pro illo autem arbitrio tantum, et pro illa libertate ista ventilatur quaestio, sine quibus homo salvari nequit, postquam potest illis uti.'   Migne, *P.L.* vol. 158, col. 515.

[7] Ibid., III, 11 : 'Voluntas itaque dici videtur aequivoce tripliciter.

instrument is acted on by two diverse tendencies,
a lower tendency towards the comfortable or agreeable
and a higher tendency towards the just and right.[1]
In another treatise he tells us that the will holds the
balance between these two tendencies, which he here
calls after the scriptural names of the flesh and the
spirit, while he uses the term *voluntas* in the third
of the just mentioned senses, namely that of the
usus instrumenti.[2] For Anselm will have nothing to
do with any psychological determinism which alleges
motives and desires as causes of volition; an act of
the will can have no cause, being in itself both cause
and effect.[3] But this apparent indeterminism is not
so absolute in its nature as might at first sight be
imagined. Though he will not admit desires or
motives as causes of any act of volition, he does not
deny their influence upon the will; [4] indeed reason

Aliud enim est instrumentum volendi, aliud affectio instrumenti,
aliud usus ejusdem instrumenti. Instrumentum volendi est vis illa
animae qua utimur ad volendum. . . . Affectio hujus instrumenti est
qua sic afficitur ipsum instrumentum ad volendum aliquid, etiam
quando illud quod vult non cogitat. . . . Usus vero ejusdem instrumenti est quem non habemus, nisi cum cogitamus rem quam volumus.'

[1] Ibid. : ' Instrumentum volendi duas habet aptitudines quas voco
affectiones, quarum una est ad volendum commoditatem, altera ad
volendum rectitudinem. Nempe nihil vult voluntas quae est instrumentum nisi aut commoditatem aut rectitudinem. Quidquid enim
aliud vult, aut propter commoditatem vult, aut propter rectitudinem
vult.' Migne, loc. cit. col. 535–6.

[2] *Med.* xix, 6: ' Est vero inter has duas naturas ex quibus constat,
voluntas quasi medium habens liberum arbitrium. Quo libero
arbitrio si se junxerit cum anima quae naturaliter tendit ad superiora,
tunc anima et voluntas (opitulante tamen divina gratia) carnem sursum
ad excelsa secum elevant.' Migne, loc. cit. col. 807.

[3] *De Casu Diaboli*, cap. 27 : ' Discip. Cur ergo voluit ? Mag. Non
nisi quia voluit, nam haec voluntas nullam aliam habet causam qua
impelleretur aliquatenus aut attraheretur, et ipsa sibi efficiens causa
fuit, si dici potest, et effectus.' Migne, loc. cit. col. 360.

[4] *De Concordia*, III, 6 : ' Omnis sensus vel intellectus rectitudinis
quem mens humana, sive per auditum sive per lectionem sive per
rationem, sive quolibet alio modo concipit, semen est recte volendi.'

is an essential element in human willing and is the mark
which distinguishes human action from that of the
beasts that perish.[1]   Reason and will go hand in hand,
and both are equally essential to the attainment of
Man's final end, which consists in the loving of the
divine essence, for love entails not only an act of the
will, but also the understanding of the beloved object.[2]
Finally, the criterion of rightness for the human will
is its conformity with the divine will, which alone is
justice and righteousness.[3]   Like Augustine, too,
Anselm refuses to identify liberty with the mere power
of doing or not doing wrong ; the human will is only
free when it identifies itself with the divine law and
while it remains in the state of grace.[4]   Nor does the
inability to depart from the path of righteousness in
any way detract from its freedom, for it is only in this
blissful state that it has truly realized the ideal of
freedom.[5]   In fact we may define the freedom of the
will as the power of maintaining a rightness of will for

[1] *De Conceptu Virginis*, 10 : ' Sicut enim est bestiarum nihil velle
cum ratione, ita hominum esset nihil velle sine ratione.'   Migne,
loc. cit. col. 444.

[2] *Monol.* cap. 68 : ' Nihil igitur apertius quam rationalem creaturam
ad hoc esse factam, ut summam essentiam amet super omnia bona. . . .
Amare autem eam nequit, nisi ejus reminisci et eam studuerit intelligere.   Clarum est ergo rationalem creaturam totum suum posse et
velle ad memorandum et intelligendum et amandum summum
bonum impendere debere, ad quod ipsum esse suum se cognoscit
habere.'   Migne, loc. cit. col. 214.

[3] *Cur Deus Homo*, I, 11 : ' Omnis voluntas rationalis creaturae
subjecta debet esse voluntati Dei. . . . Haec est justitia sive rectitudo
voluntatis . . . hic est solus et totus honor quem debemus Deo et quem
a nobis exigit Deus.'   Migne, loc. cit. col. 376.

[4] *De Lib. Arb.* i : ' Libertatem arbitrii non puto esse potentiam
peccandi et non peccandi.   Quippe si haec esset ejus definitio, nec
Deus, nec angeli . . . liberum haberent arbitrium. . . . Potestas ergo
peccandi quae addita voluntati, minuit ejus libertatem.'

[5] Ibid. : ' Liberior igitur est voluntas quae a rectitudine non
peccandi declinare nequit, quam quae illam potest deserere ; ' also
op. cit. ix : ' Cernis itaque nihil liberius recta voluntate, cui nulla
vis potest suam auferre rectitudinem.'

its own sake,[1] a definition which exactly fits the facts, since it includes neither too much nor too little.[2]

Such in outline is Anselm's doctrine of the will, a doctrine whose influence on the thought of Duns Scotus is of the highest importance. Nor is this the only case in which he has derived his teaching from this source. Anselm is throughout one of Duns' principal authorities in the realm of theology, and in the *De Primo Principio*, where he leaves for a moment his normal literary form of *quaestiones* with their perpetual syllogisms, it is the *Monologium* of Anselm that he adopts as his model. Again, in his statement of the proofs of the existence of God in the *Opus Oxoniense* (dist. 1, q. 2), it is on Anselm's ontological argument that he relies for his proof of the infinity of the divine being. Notwithstanding the fact that between Anselm and Scotus there is a great gulf fixed, that, while the former belongs wholly to the older pre-Aristotelian scholasticism, the latter comes at the end of the great movement of expansion which took place in the thirteenth century, there is yet in both thinkers a fundamental similarity. It is true indeed that Scotus has adopted, with certain significant modifications, almost the whole of the Aristotelian psychological classification with its latinized terminology, but when we have divested it of its peripatetic trappings we shall find that the innermost

---

[1] Ibid. xiii : 'Potestas servandi rectitudinem voluntatis propter ipsam rectitudinem.'

[2] Ibid. : 'Est enim potestas libertatis genus. Quod autem additum est, servandi, separat eam ab omni potestate quae non est servandi, sicut est potestas ridendi aut ambulandi. Addendo vero rectitudinem secrevimus eam a potestate servandi aurum. . . . Quoniam igitur nihil est in hac diffinitione quod non sit necessarium ad concludendam libertatem arbitrii rationalis voluntatis et ad alia excludenda, sufficientur illa concluditur . . . nec abundans utique nec indigens est haec nostra diffinitio.'

kernel of his theory of the will is none other than the doctrine of Anselm.[1]

According to Scotus the fundamental distinction between intellect and will lies in the fact that the former is determined 'naturally' while the other is free and spontaneous. For the intellect is determined by its object, the intelligible, and cannot of itself choose whether it will understand or no; it is forced to assent to truths which are 'self-evident' and to conclusions derived from these by logical deduction. The power of choice, on the other hand, belongs to the will as such.[2] Thus far Scotus finds himself in complete agreement with Thomas, but the latter interprets the nature of this freedom in the light of a strongly intellectualistic bias. Man must of necessity will his own happiness as end; choice of alternatives is restricted to the means.[3] The end in willing

[1] Cf. E. Lohmeyer, *Die Lehre vom Willen bei Anselm von Canterbury*, p. 74: 'Darin liegt zuletzt auch die historische Bedeutung der Anselmischen Willenslehre begründet. Weil sie in Gott begründet war, und doch dem menschlichen Willen sein absolutes Recht nicht verkümmerte sich aus sich zu bestimmen. . . . Es lag in ihr der Anfang des Begreifens dass die Innerlichkeit und Subjektivität im System ebenso notwendig ist wie die objektive Wahrheit. So konnte sie für das Denken eines Bernhard von Clairveaux und Wilhelms von St. Thierry, der älteren Franciskaner, bis hin zu Robert Grosseteste und Duns Scotus den Weg weisen, auf dem das Bewusstsein zu seiner wahren Erfüllung und Wirklichkeit, zu der Erkenntniss seiner unendlichen Freiheit fortgeschritten ist.'

[2] *Quodlibeta*, q. xvi, n. 6: 'Intellectus movetur ab objecto naturali necessitate, voluntas autem libere se movet.' *Quaest. in Metaph.* IX, q. xv, n. 6: 'Intellectus cavit sub natura; est enim ex se determinatus ad intelligendum, et non habet in potestate sua intelligere et non intelligere.' *Op. Ox.* II, dist. vi, q. 2, n. 11: 'Dico per idem quod non est in potestate intellectus moderari assensum suum versus quae apprehendit; nam quantum ostenditur veritas principiorum ex terminis, vel conclusionum ex principiis, tantum potest assentire, propter carentiam libertatis.'

[3] *Summa Theol.* Ia pars, q. 82, art. 1: 'Quinimmo necesse est quod sicut intellectus ex necessitate inhaeret primis principiis, ita voluntas ex necessitate inhaeret ultimo fini, qui est beatitudo. Finis enim se

corresponds to the self-evident principle in knowing; hence man must will those means which he recognizes as necessary to his end.[1] It is true that in the concrete case the choice of means is always, or almost always, a various one, but the implication is too clear to escape notice, namely the root of moral error is ultimately intellectual, a failure to grasp where our true happiness lies. We are thus brought face to face once more with the Socratic paradox; as soon as the intellect perceives the essential and necessary goodness of an act the will must follow.

It is at this point that Scotus and Thomas begin to part company. Without denying the influence of the intellect on the will (for he concedes that the cognitive process must necessarily precede every act of volition),[2] Duns maintains that there is no object, either universal or particular, which can force its assent on the will.[3] Not happiness in general, for it may often happen that the intellect is not thinking about happiness at all, and consequently not willing it, and we cannot will that of which we are not conscious. Nor, when we are considering happiness and when the intellect is

habet in operativis, sicut principium in speculativis.' Also ibid. : 'Dicendum quod sumus domini nostrorum actuum secundum quod possumus hoc vel illud eligere. Electio autem non est de fine, sed de his qui sunt ad finem,' etc.

[1] Ibid., art. 2: 'Respondeo dicendum quod voluntas non ex necessitate vult quaecumque vult ... sunt enim quaedam particularia bona quae non habent necessariam connexionem ad beatitudinem, quia sine his potest aliquis esse beatus; et hujusmodi bonis voluntas non ex necessitate inhaeret. Sunt enim quaedam habentia necessariam connexionem ad beatitudinem, quibus, scilicet homo Deo inhaeret, in quo sola beatitudo consistit. Sed tamen antequam per certitudinem divinae visionis necessitas hujusmodi connexionis demonstratur, voluntas non ex necessitate Deo inhaeret.'

[2] *Op. Ox.* II, dist. xxv : 'Non potest causari a voluntate volitio, nisi prius causatur ab intellectu intellectio.'

[3] Ibid., dist. xxiii, n. 8 : 'Ad aliud dico ... quod voluntas creata non necessario tendit in finem sibi ostensum, nec in universali, nec in particulari.'

A a

presenting a particular good to the will as a means to happiness, need the latter choose to act in accordance with its dictates ; it can in fact act ' irrationally ', because in every case in which the intellect proposes a good to the will the will can turn itself away from it, inasmuch as it is able to draw away the contemplation of the intellect from one object to another.[1] It is this power of control which gives to the will its primacy over the intellect, a primacy which was denied by Thomas and his school on the ground that the object of the intellect is more noble than that of the will.[2]

The dispute thus raised might seem to entail hardly more than a verbal controversy, but it was not without its influence on the conception of the nature of Man's final beatitude entertained by the two thinkers. Thomas places this in the act of the intellect, in the beatific vision, while Scotus conceives it more dynamically as being love rather than knowledge, love being for him an act not of the intellect but of the will. Like many other philosophical controversies of the age, this dispute has been embodied by Dante in his *Divine Comedy*, where the poet sides with Aquinas against Scotus.

> Quinci si può veder come si fonda
>   L' esser beato nell' atto che vede,
>   Non in quel ch' ama, che poscia seconda ;
>
> E del vedere è misura e mercede,
>   Che grazia partorisce e buona voglia,
>   Così di grado in grado si procede.
>
> *Il Paradiso*, Canto xxviii, 109–14.

[1] *Quodl.*, q. xvi, n. 4 : 'Voluntas autem, saltem viatoris, non necessario continuat actum circa finem in universali apprehensam quantum posset continuare ; igitur non necessario agit circa illum . . sed vel convertit intelligentiam ad considerationem alicujus alterius, vel saltem non impedit quin objectum aliud occurrens impediat illam aonsiderationem ; illa autem consideratione non continuata, non continuatur circa illud objectum actio voluntatis.'

[2] *Summa Theol.* Ia pars, q. 85, art. 3.

But even for Scotus the will of the beatified, though free, is in a sense determined, not with a physical necessity or *necessitas coactionis*, nor, as Thomas postulated, with a teleological necessity (*necessitas finis*), but with a necessity of immutability.[1] For the act of loving, though a free act, is yet unchangeable, and the greater the love the greater is the freedom.[2]

Notwithstanding the difference in terminology, the similarity between the Scotist doctrine and that of Anselm is at once apparent. Both are indeterminist in the sense that they refuse to admit any compelling psychological motive, whether it be appetite or desire on the one hand or the intellectual presentation of the ' good ' on the other, as the efficient factor in the determination of a volitional act. Moral error cannot be construed in intellectual terms, and the attempt of Scotus to avoid the intellectualistic implications of the Thomist theory is little more than a reiteration of the thesis of Anselm already cited,[3] that it is impossible to assign any cause to an act of the will. So also in his distinction between desire and volition, between the active and passive *potentiae* of the will, Scotus is reaffirming, almost word for word, the Anselmian differentiation of the *affectiones* from the *usus voluntatis*. He distinguishes two tendencies in the will ; one a passive tendency, or *naturalis voluntas*, by which the will is attracted by its object, and the other the active and free faculty of eliciting the act of volition.[4] The former is not the will properly

---

[1] *Quodl.*, q. xvi, n. 7.

[2] *De Rerum Principio*, q. iv, art. 2 : ' Certum est quia nihil tam liberum quam amare, et quanto amor major tanto liberior, . . . ut patet in beatis, qui certi sunt, quod a beatitudine cadere non possunt et tamen non habent aliam certitudinem nisi Dei amorem, qui quanto major, tanto liberior.'

[3] See note 3, p. 173.

[4] *Op. Ox.* III, dist. xvii, q. unica, n. 5 : ' Naturalis voluntas non tendit, sed est ipsa tendentia qua voluntas absolute tendit, et hoc

speaking, but only an imperfect preliminary stage. This natural tendency is on a lower plane and must not be confused with the free act of willing, or *velle elicitum*.[1] It is twofold in form, a double tendency, one towards the agreeable, the other towards the right or just [2]—words taken almost without alteration from the *De Concordia*. The final decision belongs to the will in its active capacity as eliciting the volitional act, the *quasi medium* of which Anselm speaks in his *Meditationes*.[3] Finally, in placing the final end of man in the loving of the divine essence rather than in the vision of it Duns is once more returning to the older doctrine.

With regard to the divine nature the doctrines of Scotus and Thomas, though diverging in certain important respects, show less obviously apparent dissimilarities, for both were conditioned by the ground conceptions of Catholic Christianity. Both agree in maintaining the fundamental theses of Christian Dogma : God is a living Being, endowed with intelligence and will, which are identical with his essence. Both hold also the substantial distinction between God and His creatures, and insist on the self-sufficiency of the one and the dependence of the other, the creature being the product of the divine free will, which is constrained by no internal necessity to manifest itself in creating anything. Thus for Scotus, as well as for Thomas,[4] there is only one necessary object of the divine

---

passive ad recipiendum ; sed est alia tendentia in eadem potentia, ut libere et active agat et tendat eliciendo actum ; ita quod in una potentia est duplex tendentia, activa et passiva.'

[1] *Op. Ox.* III, dist. xv, n. 37 : 'Nec naturaliter velle est velle, quoniam velle simpliciter est velle elicitum.'

[2] Loc. cit., n. 5 : 'Inclinatio naturalis duplex est ; una ad commodum, alia ad justum.'

[3] Vide supra, p. 173, note 2.

[4] Cf. Thomas, *Summa Theol.* Ia pars, q. 19, art. 3 : 'Voluntas enim divina necessariam habitudinem habet ad bonitatem ejus, quae

volition, namely the divine goodness itself. But just as Duns in the case of the human spirit upholds the primacy of the will over the intellect, so also in his account of the divine nature he adheres to his voluntarism and resists any curtailment of the absolute liberty of the divine freedom, though he conceives this in a sense which is by no means as arbitrary as that which some critics have endeavoured to attribute to him.[1] Thomas, on the other hand, inclines to a pronouncedly intellectualistic view and regards the divine will as determined by the divine intelligence,[2] though he refuses at the same time to admit the applicability of the notion of causation to the volition of God.[3] Scotus, however, goes further and denies that any reason whatsoever can be assigned to the divine choice.[4]

This difference is something more than a mere

est proprium ejus objectum. Unde bonitatem suam Deus ex necessitate vult. . . . Unde cum bonitas Dei sit perfecta, et esse potest sine aliis, cum nihil ei perfectionis ex aliis accrescat, sequitur quod alia a se eum velle non sit necessarium absolute.' So also Scotus, *Quodl.*, q. xvi, n. 8 : 'Voluntas divina necessario vult bonitatem suam.' *Op. Ox.* II, dist. i, q. 1, n. 7 : 'Nihil aliud a se vult voluntas divina necessario.'

[1] e. g. in his discussion of the divine omnipotence Scotus maintains that it is bound by the law of contradiction ; a contradiction is an impossibility, and God cannot do the impossible. Cf. *Op. Ox.* IV, dist. 1, q. 1, n. 26 ; also *Rep. Par.* I, dist. xx, q. 2, n. 6.

[2] *Summa contra Gent.* I, 82 : 'Cum enim bonum apprehensum voluntatem sicut objectum proprium determinat, intellectus autem divinus non sit extraneus ab ejus voluntate, cum utraque sit sua essentia, si voluntas Dei ad aliquid volendum per sui intellectus cognitionem determinatur, non erit determinatio voluntatis divinae per aliquid extraneum facta.'

[3] *Summa Theol.* Ia pars, q. 19, art. 5 : 'Respondeo dicendum quod nullo modo voluntas Dei causam habet,' etc.

[4] *Op. Ox.* I, dist. viii, q. 5, nn. 23–4 : 'Et si quaeras quare igitur voluntas divina magis determinatur ad unum contradictorium quam ad alterum ; respondeo : indisciplinati est quaerere omnium causas et demonstrationes . . . et ideo hujus, quare voluntas voluit hoc nulla est causa, nisi quia voluntas est voluntas.'

difference of terminology, as is shown quite clearly in
the divergence of the two doctors with respect to
the problem of contingence. The doctrine of Thomas
on this point is by no means clear; he seems to have
hesitated between two incompatible opinions. The
Aristotelian theory, which he appears at times to
favour,[1] stated that the source of contingence was
a *defectus materiae*, the incalculable nature of ὕλη, the
source of all change and variability in the universe,
and therefore also the source of unknowableness, for
to Aristotle ὕλη was the principle owing to which things
might be otherwise, the principle of τὰ ἐνδεχόμενα
ἄλλως ἔχειν. But this view refused to harmonize with
the teachings of Christian theology, which postulated
not only a divine omniscience but also a divine providence. Hence we also find in Thomas quite a different
doctrine, which would make contingence due to the
plurality of interacting causes, all of which, however,
are equally known to the mind of God, and so the
distinction of the necessary and the contingent
becomes in the last analysis one which is relative
merely to our human ignorance.[2] Again, as the
proximate cause may be contingent while the first
cause is necessary, so the objects of the divine knowledge
may be contingent as regards their proximate cause,
though their first cause, namely the divine knowledge,

---

[1] e. g. in *Summa contra Gent.* III, 73 : 'In rebus autem inanimatis
causarum contingentia ex imperfectione et defectu est ; secundum
enim suam naturam sunt determinatae ad unum effectum, quem
semper consequuntur, nisi sit impedimentum vel ex debilitate virtutis,
vel ex aliquo exteriori agente, vel ex materiae indispositione, et
propter hoc causae naturaliter agentes non sunt ad utrumque, sed ut
frequentius eodem modo suum effectum producunt, deficiunt autem
raro.'

[2] Op. cit., I, 67 : 'Amplius. Sicut ex causa necessaria sequitur
effectus certitudinaliter, ita ex causa contingenti completa, si non
impediatur. Sed quum Deus cognoscat omnia . . . scit non solum
causas contingentium sed etiam ex quibus possunt impediri. Scit
igitur per certitudinem an contingentia sint vel non sint.'

is necessary.[1] Scotus criticizes the Thomist position by maintaining that no proximate or secondary cause can be contingent unless the first cause is also related to it contingently. Further, the will, or something actuated by a will, is the only possible source of contingence.[2] Now the first cause causes by means of intellect and will, nor can we postulate a third faculty in God to account for contingence. Contingence therefore must issue from one or the other of these two, not from the intellect, in so far as it is *actus primus*, that is, antecedent to any volitional act; the principle of contingence must therefore be sought in the will.[3] And as this has but one necessary object,

---

[1] *Summa Theol.* Ia pars, q. 14, art. 13 ad primum : ' Dicendum quod licet causa suprema sit necessaria, tamen effectus potest esse contingens propter causam proximam contingentem. . . . Et similiter scita a Deo sunt contingentia propter causas proximas, licet scientia Dei, quae est causa prima, sit necessaria.' See also *Summa contra Gent.* I, 67 : ' Adhuc effectum excedere suae causae perfectionem non contingit ; interdum tamen ab ea deficit. Unde quum in nobis causetur cognitio ex rebus, contingit interdum quod necessariae non per modum necessitatis cognoscimus, sed probabilitatis. Sicut autem apud nos res sunt causa cognitionis, ita divina cognitio est causa rerum cognitarum. Nihil igitur prohibet ea in se contingentia esse, de quibus Deus necessariam scientiam habet.'

[2] *Op. Ox.* I, dist. ii, q. 2, n. 20 : ' Item tertio arguitur sic : aliquid causatur contingenter ; ergo prima causa contingenter causat. Probatio primae consequentiae ; quaelibet causa secunda causat inquantum movetur a prima ; ergo si prima necessario movet, quaelibet necessario causat ; ergo si aliqua secunda causa contingenter movet, et prima contingenter movebit, quia non causat secunda causa, nisi in virtute primae causae, inquantum movetur ab ipsa. Probatio secundae consequentiae ; nullum est principium operandi contingenter, nisi voluntas vel aliquid concomitans voluntatem, quia quodlibet aliud agit ex necessitate naturae, et non contingenter. Ergo,' etc.

[3] *Op. Ox.*, dist. xxxix, q. unica, n. 14 : ' Supposito ergo isto tanquam manifesto vero, quod aliquod ens est contingens ; inquirendum est quomodo salvari possit contingentia in rebus. . . . Oportet ergo contingentiam istam quaerere vel in voluntate divina, vel in intellectu divino ; non autem in intellectu, ut habet actum primum ante omnem actum voluntatis, quia quidquid intellectus intelligit hoc modo, intelligit mere naturaliter et necessitate naturali ; et ita nulla con-

the divine essence or the divine goodness (for these two are identical), the whole of the created universe is in a sense contingent, for its existence depends solely on the divine will.[1] Yet the divine omnipotence must not, as we have seen, be extended to the irrational or contradictory, for in the last resort the contradictory means and is nothing.[2]

It is clear, therefore, that Scotus would not carry his indeterminism to the lengths of Descartes and maintain that the laws of geometry were purely arbitrary, or that the radii of a circle might, if God had willed it, have been unequal.[3] The doctrine of these

tingentia potest esse in sciendo aliquid. . . . Primam ergo contingentiam oportet quaerere in voluntate divina.'

[1] *Op. Ox.*, dist. xxxix, q. unica, n. 22 : ' Voluntas divina nihil aliud respicit necessario pro objecto ab essentia sua ; ad quodlibet igitur aliud contingenter se habet, ita quod posset esse oppositi. . . . Voluntas divina, inquantum ipsa est sub volitione, est prior naturaliter tendentia illa, et ita tendit in illud objectum contingenter, quod in eodem instanti possit tendere in oppositum objectum, et hoc tam de potentia logica, quae est non repugnantia terminorum . . . quam de potentia reali.'

[2] *Rep. Par.* I, dist. xliii, q. 1, n. 13 : ' Nihil est simpliciter impossibile, nisi quod contradictionem includit et implicat, quod est ratio omnino in se falsa, sive impossibilis, ut homo est irrationalis.'

[3] Cf. Descartes, letter of 1630 : ' Je dis que Dieu a été aussi libre de faire qu'il ne fût pas vrai que tous les lignes tirées du centre à la circonférence fussent égales, comme de ne pas créer le monde.'

Cf. also *Corresp.*, v, p. 223 (Adam-Tannery), ' Pro Arnualdo ' : ' Mihi autem non videtur de ulla unquam re esse dicendum, ipsam a Deo fieri non posse ; cum enim omnis ratio veri et boni ejus omnipotentia dependeat, nequidem dicere ausim Deum facere non posse ut mons sit sine valle, vel ut unum et duo non sint tria ; sed tantum dico illum talem mentem mihi indidisse, ut a me concipi non possit mons sine valle, vel aggregatum ex uno et duobus quod non sint tria, etc., atque talia implicare contradictionem in meo conceptu.' Quoted by A. Koyre, *Descartes und die Scholastik* (Bonn, 1923), p. 36.

It is true that these quotations need not be taken ' au pied de la lettre ' as Descartes's final and considered doctrine, but they do show a marked difference from the vigorous assertion of Scotus that God cannot act self-contradictorily.

For an account of the influence of Scotus on Descartes see Koyre, op. cit., esp. pp. 80–94.

two thinkers must not be confused. In Descartes the question of Primacy has no place; he teaches the superiority of the will to the intellect neither in Man nor in God. His libertarianism bears a superficial resemblance to the theory of the Franciscan School of the scholastics, but it must be kept in mind that the two doctrines are very different. While for Descartes will and intellect are absolutely identical, for Duns and his followers they are formally distinct,[1] and it is just on this distinction that the so-called indeterminism or voluntarism of the Scotists is based.

Duns' position is nearer to that of Leibnitz : ' L'entendement de Dieu est la source des essences, et sa volonté est l'origine des existences,' though he would not agree with the latter in his conclusion : ' Dieu n'est point l'auteur des essences, en tant qu'elles ne sont que de possibilités,' which represents a theory more like that propounded by Henry of Ghent, which Scotus criticizes and rejects.[2] In a sense, therefore, the divine knowledge of contingent truths may be regarded as determined by the divine will, in so far as the being or not being of these contingent events depends upon it, and it is by knowing his will as eternally absolute and immutable that God knows them to be true.[3]

This same conception of the nature of contingence exercised a considerable influence over Scotus' ethical theory. The same dualism between the necessary and the contingent reappears in the sphere of morals.

---

[1] E. Gilson, *La Liberté chez Descartes et la Théologie* (1913), pp. 135 sqq.

[2] See chapter vi, pp. 215 sqq.

[3] Loc. cit. : ' Restat videre . . . qualiter cum hoc stet certitudo scientiae ejus. Hoc potest poni dupliciter : uno modo per hoc, quod intellectus divinus videt determinationem voluntatis divinae, videlicet, illud fore pro A, quia voluntas illud determinat fore pro eo ; scit enim illam esse immutabilem et non impedibilem. Vel aliter, quia ista via videtur ponere quendam discursum in intellectu divino, quasi

Whereas for Thomas the moral law, the *lex naturalis*, is an integral portion of the *lex aeterna*,[1] one, immutable, and indispensable, for Scotus, in so far as it deals with the purely social rights and duties of mankind, it has no eternal and necessary validity. Hence, when dealing with the precepts of the *Decalogue*, he distinguishes between the commandments of the first and the second tables. He concedes that certain moral ἀρχαί are necessary, and therefore antecedent to the divine will, but he is careful to restrict them to such precepts as have God for their immediate object.[2] The commandments of the second table, then, are not all necessary in the strictest sense of the word because they are not immediately directed to God as last end.[3] The case of the first table is different ; these precepts must be regarded as strictly necessary, for they have the divine being as their immediate object.[4] From those commandments which are not

ex intuitione determinationis et immutabilitatis ejus concludit hoc fore.'

[1] *Summa Theol.* Ia secundae, q. 91, art. 1. Thomas here quotes with approval Augustine's definition of the eternal law : ' Lex quae summa ratio nominatur non potest cuipiam intelligenti non incommutabilis aeternaque videri.'

[2] *Op. Ox.* III, dist. xxxvii, n. 4 : ' Praeterea quae vera sunt ex terminis, sive necessaria sint ex terminis, sive consequentia ex talibus necessariis, praecedunt in veritate omnem actum voluntatis. . . . Igitur si praecepta Decalogi . . . haberent talem necessitatem, puta quod haec essent necessaria : " proximus non est occidendus ", " furtum non est faciendum " . . . intellectus divinus apprehendens talia, necessario ea apprehenderet, tanquam ex se vera, et tunc voluntas divina necessario concordaret ipsis, vel ipsa non esset recta. . . . Esset etiam ponere quod voluntas ejus simpliciter necessario determinaretur circa aliqua volibilia alia a se, cujus oppositum dictum est . . . ubi tactum est quod voluntas divina in nihil aliud a se tendit, nisi contingenter.'

[3] Ibid., n. 5 : ' Talia non sunt quaecumque praecepta secundae tabulae, quia rationes eorum . . . non sunt principia practica simpliciter necessariae. Non enim in his quae proponuntur ibi est bonitas necessaria ad bonitatem ultimi finis, convertens ad finem ultimum.'

[4] Ibid., n. 6 : ' De praeceptis autem primae tabulae secus est, quia illa immediate respiciunt Deum pro objecto.'

strictly necessary a dispensation may be given by God under certain circumstances ; from those which are strictly necessary no dispensation can be given, not even by God himself. Thus the voluntarism of Scotus leads to a moral doctrine less rigid than that of the intellectualistic Thomas, who will admit no possibility of dispensation from any of the commandments of the *Decalogue*, which, like the law of the Medes and the Persians, ' altereth not '.[1] Yet in practice the two theories work out to very similar results. The exceptions admitted theoretically by Scotus are so rare as to be scarcely significant for any general consideration of his ethical theory ; for him, as for Thomas, the precepts of the *Decalogue*, even if certain theoretical reservations have to be made, are for all practical purposes absolute.

We have now considered two of the most important features which differentiate the teaching of Scotus from that of Thomas, his doctrine of form and matter and his voluntarism, both of which mark a return to the Augustinian tradition. But there is yet a third aspect of the older teaching which calls for a brief examination, namely its theory of knowledge. In epistemology, as in logic and psychology, the first half of the thirteenth century was a period of transition. In that amazing confusion of philosophic speculation three distinct theories of knowledge may be distinguished, all of which were current during that period

---

[1] *Summa Theol.* Ia secundae, q. 100, art. 1 : ' Necesse est quod omnia praecepta moralia pertinent ad legem naturae.' Ibid., art. 8 : ' Praecepta autem Decalogi continent ipsam intentionem legislatoris, scilicet Dei . . . et ideo praecepta Decalogi sunt omnino indispensibilia . . . ad secundum, dicendum quod sicut Apostolus dicit " Deus fidelis permanet negare se ipsum non potest ". Negaret autem se ipsum, si ordinem justitiae aufferret, cum ipse sit sua justitia. Et ideo in hoc Deus dispensare non potest, ut homini liceat non ordinate se habere ad Deum, vel non subdi ordini justitiae ejus, etiam in his quae homines ad invicem ordinantur.'

and all of which influenced in various degrees the thought of the great masters of scholasticism.[1] Oldest of these was the traditional Augustinian theory, strongly Platonic in its associations, with its doctrine of divine illumination and the *lux aeterna*. The exact significance of Augustine's teaching has been a matter for much controversy ; certain features of it, however, stand forth with comparative clearness in the light of the profound influence which they exercised upon medieval thought. Originally a Neoplatonist, Augustine had accepted at first the doctrine of ἀνάμνησις,[2] but he was forced to abandon it on account of its involving the heresy of reincarnation. How, then, is it that the ignorant, when questioned on certain subjects of which they know nothing beforehand, often give right and reasonable answers? It can only be, Augustine answers, by the illustration of the light of the eternal reason, by which each man according to his condition is illuminated, that they are able to perceive the immutable truths.[3] These truths have their ground in the divine ideas, which are the archetypes of all created things and are eternal, uncreate, and immutable,[4] the impression of which is planted by God in the human soul.[5] Hence knowledge comes

---

[1] Cf. Dr. E. F. Jacob, ' The Conception of Personality in Medieval Philosophy ' (*Church Quarterly Review*, Jan. 1924).

[2] *Soliloq.* II, 20, 35 ; *De Quant. Anim.* 20, 34.

[3] *Retractionum*, I, 4, 4 : ' Credibilius est enim propterea vera respondere de quibusdam disciplinis, etiam imperitos earum, quando bene interrogantur, quia praesens est eis, quantum id capere possunt, lumen rationis aeternae, ubi haec immortalia conspiciunt.'

[4] *De Ideis*, 2 : ' Sunt namque ideae principales formae quaedam vel rationes rerum stabiles et incommutabiles, quae ipsae formatae non sunt, atque per hoc aeternae ac semper eodem modo se habentes, qui in divina intelligentia continentur, et quum ipsae neque oriuntur neque intereant, secundum eas tamen formari dicitur omne quod interire potest, et omne quod oritur et interit.'

[5] *De Trinitate*, xiv. 15, 21 : ' Ubinam sunt istae regulae scriptae, ubi quid sit justum et injustum cognoscit, ubi cernit habendum esse

rather from within than from without.[1] The master
who teaches his disciple is not impressing upon him
new knowledge from the outside; he is only furnishing
the occasion for the making explicit what was already
implicit; the true teacher is the eternal wisdom which
enlightens the soul from within.[2] The truth which
you and I recognize when we converse together we
do not see it one in the other, but rather in the eternal
and incommutable truth which is above us.[3] For the
soul in knowing is bathed in an atmosphere of incor-
poreal light.[4]

quod ipse non habere ? Ubi ergo scriptae sunt, nisi in libro lucis illius
quae veritas dicitur ? Unde omnis lex justa describitur, et in cor
hominis, qui operatur justitiam, non migrando, sed tanquam impri-
mendo transfertur; sicut imago ex annulo in ceram transit, et
annulum non relinquit.' For a discussion of Augustine's ideogeny
see the article on Augustine by Portalié in Vacant's *Dict. de Theol.
Cath.*, vol. i, col. 2234 sqq.

[1] *De Vera Religione*, 72 : ' Noli foras ire, in te redi, in interiore
homine habitat veritas, et si animam mutabilem inveneris, transcende
te ipsum.'

[2] *De Magistro* 11 : ' De universis autem quae intelligimus, non
loquentem qui personat foris, sed intus ipsi menti praesidentem con-
sulimus veritatem. . . . Ille autem qui consulitur docet, qui in interiore
homine habitare dictus est, Christus, id est incommutabilis Dei
Virtus, atque sempiterna Sapientia, quam quidem omnis rationalis
anima consulit, sed tantum cuique panditur quantum capere propter
bonam sive malam voluntatem potest.'

Cf. with this the passage from Aristotle's *Eudemian Ethics*, VII, 14 :
τὸ δὲ ζητούμενον τοῦτ' ἔστι· τίς ἡ τῆς κινήσεως ἀρχὴ ἐν τῇ ψυχῇ·
δῆλον δὴ ὥσπερ ἐν τῷ ὅλῳ θεός, καὶ πᾶν ἐκείνῳ. κινεῖ γάρ πως πάντα
τὸ ἐν ἡμῖν θεῖον· λόγου δ' ἀρχὴ οὐ λόγος ἀλλά τι κρεῖττον. τί οὖν ἂν
κρεῖττον καὶ ἐπιστήμης εἴποι, πλὴν θεός; ἡ γὰρ ἀρετὴ τοῦ νοῦ ὄργανον.

[3] *Confessiones*, xii. 25 : ' Si ambo videamus verum esse quod dicis,
et ambo videmus verum esse quod dico, ubi, quaeso, id videmus ?
Nec ego utique in te, nec tu in me. Sed ambo in ipsa quae super
mentes nostras est veritate.'

[4] Cf. *De Trinitate*, xii. 15, 24, where, after criticizing the Platonic
doctrine of ἀνάμνησις, he continues : ' Sed potius credendum est
mentis intellectualis ita conditam esse naturam, ut rebus intelligibilibus
naturali ordine disponente creatore subjuncta sic ista videat in
quadam luce sui generis incorporea, quemadmodum oculus carnis
videt quae in hac corporea luce circumjacent.'

This Augustinian doctrine of the *lumen increatum*, with its half-mystical theory of knowledge, exercised a profound influence on the speculation of the Middle Ages. It forms the basis of the early ' realist ' epistemologies, and we can trace its influence not only in the works of Anselm and the school of Chartres but also in Isaac of Stella, Alcher of Clairveaux, and the mystical theologians of St. Victor, as well as in anti-realists like Adelard of Bath and Peter Abelard. Nor does it vanish with the twelfth century. Side by side with the newer Aristotelian theories it continues to hold its ground. William of Auvergne, the father of the new scholastic psychology, Alexander of Hales, Robert Grosseteste, Bonaventura, Matthew of Aquasparta, Albertus Magnus, Henry of Ghent, and the great Thomas himself, all show in varying degrees plain tokens of its influence. But with the rediscovery of Aristotle and the translations of the Arabian and Jewish commentators two new epistemological theories begin to make their appearance. The recovery of the *Posterior Analytics* and the *Metaphysics* effected something which may well be called a revolution in scholastic thought. The older form of realism exemplified by the teaching of men like William of Conches and Bernard of Chartres, whom John of Salisbury mentions as being the most accomplished Platonist of his day,[1] had already been bitterly attacked by Abelard and Gilbert de la Porrée. After the end of the twelfth century it gradually decayed, giving way to a more moderate realism of the Aristotelian type, while the older dualistic psychology was replaced by the peripatetic theory of the substantial union of the soul and the body as form and matter in the *compositum*. At the same time the older ' a priorist ' theory of knowledge, with its doctrine of ' innate ideas ' and

[1] ' Perfectissimus inter Platonicos saeculi nostri ', *Metalogicus*, IV, 3.

divine illumination, began to be dispossessed by the Aristotelian empiricism and the doctrine of the *intellectus agens*.[1] This newer conception took two distinct forms, one of which we may call for the sake of convenience the Averroistic, and the other the scholastic, both being derived from Aristotle's doctrine of *νοῦς* as laid down in the *De Anima*, a doctrine which is still obscure and still a subject of controversy. Both forms agree in maintaining that knowledge is the product of the extraction or 'abstraction' by the active intellect of the quiddity or universal essence of the material thing (*res*) from the phantasm or sensuous presentation.[2] Their difference lies in the fact that the Arabian commentators conceived this active intellect to be impersonal, immortal, and numerically one, a sort of eternal 'Weltgeist', the last and lowest of the Intelligences emanating from the One, while the Latin Christians interpreted it as being the individual personality. According to the

---

[1] Cf. Aristotle, *De Anima*, III, 5 : ἐπεὶ δὲ ὥσπερ ἐν ἁπάσῃ τῇ φύσει ἐστί τι, τὸ μὲν ὕλη ἑκάστῳ γένει· τοῦτο δέ, ὅτι πάντα δυνάμει ἐκεῖνα· ἕτερον δὲ τὸ αἴτιον καὶ ποιητικόν, τῷ ποιεῖν πάντα, . . . ἀνάγκη καὶ ἐν τῇ ψυχῇ ὑπάρχειν ταύτας τὰς διαφοράς· καὶ ἔστιν ὁ μὲν τοιοῦτος νοῦς τῷ πάντα γίγνεσθαι· ὁ δὲ τῷ πάντα ποιεῖν ὡς ἕξις τις, οἷον τὸ φῶς. τρόπον γάρ τινα καὶ τὸ φῶς ποιεῖ τὰ δυνάμει ὄντα χρώματα ἐνεργείᾳ χρώματα· καὶ οὗτος ὁ νοῦς χωριστὸς καὶ ἀμιγὴς καὶ ἀπαθής, τῇ οὐσίᾳ ὢν ἐνεργείᾳ.

[2] Cf. Alexander of Hales, *Summa Theol.* pars IIa, q. lxix, mem. 2 : 'Cognitio illarum formarum intelligibilium, quae veniunt ad intellectum per abstractionem a phantasmate sensibili.' Cf. with this Aristotle, *Metaph.* I, 1, 980 b : τὰ μὲν οὖν ἄλλα ταῖς φαντασίαις ζῇ καὶ ταῖς μνήμαις, ἐμπειρίας δὲ μετέχει μικρόν· τὸ δὲ τῶν ἀνθρώπων γένος καὶ τέχνῃ καὶ λογισμοῖς. γίνεται δ' ἐκ τῆς μνήμης ἐμπειρία τοῖς ἀνθρώποις· . . . ἀποβαίνει δ' ἐπιστήμη καὶ τέχνη διὰ τῆς ἐμπειρίας τοῖς ἀνθρώποις. . . . γίνεται δὲ τέχνη ὅταν ἐκ πολλῶν τῆς ἐμπειρίας ἐννοημάτων, καθόλου μία γένηται περὶ τῶν ὁμοίων ὑπόληψις. Cf. also, *Post. An.* II, 19 : ἐκ μὲν οὖν αἰσθήσεως γίνεται μνήμη, ὥσπερ λέγομεν. ἐκ δὲ μνήμης πολλάκις τοῦ αὐτοῦ γινομένης ἐμπειρία . . . ἐκ δ' ἐμπειρίας ἢ ἐκ παντὸς ἠρεμήσαντος τοῦ καθόλου ἐν τῇ ψυχῇ, τοῦ ἑνὸς παρὰ τὰ πολλά, ὃ ἂν ἐν ἅπασιν ἓν ἐνῇ ἐκείνοις, τὸ αὐτό, τέχνης ἀρχὴ καὶ ἐπιστήμης.

Averroistic view the act of understanding in the individual man is performed by the action of this intelligence on the sensuous or imaginative faculty proper to each individual, the νοῦς παθητικός of Aristotle.[1] The active intellect forms an accidental union with this passive faculty, or *vis cogitativa* as Thomas calls it, and effects the act of knowledge without thereby suffering any detriment to its numerical unity.[2] The scholastic theory, on the other hand, combats this interpretation of Aristotle,[3] and insists that the active intellect is no impersonal pan-psychic principle, but, as Christian theology and right reason plainly demonstrate, the individual soul, personal and immortal. Moreover, this intellectual soul is the substantial form of the body as such—a doctrine enforced by a decree of the council of Vienne[4] in the year 1311.

During the first half of the thirteenth century all these three theories were current ; we find them mixed in various proportions in the scholastic writings, often

[1] Cf. *De Anima*, III, 5 : ὁ δὲ παθητικὸς νοῦς φθαρτός, καὶ ἄνευ τούτου οὐθὲν νοεῖ.

Cf. also Averroes, *Destructio Destructionum*, fol. 17 : ' Scientia autem non est scientia rei universalis, sed est scientia particularium modo universali, quem facit intellectus in particularibus, quum abstrahit ab eis naturam unam communem, quae divisa est in materiis.'

[2] Cf. Averroes, *De Anima*, III (ed. Juntes, Venice, 1550, p. 164) : ' Et, cum declaratum est . . . quod impossibile est ut intellectus copuletur cum unoquoque hominum, et numeretur per numerationem eorum, per partem quae est de eo quasi materia, secundum intellectum materialem (i. e. intellectus possibilis = the δυνάμει νοῦς of Aristotle) remanet ut intellectorum continuatio (ittisâl) cum nobis hominibus sit per continuationem intentionis intellectae cum nobis, et sunt intentiones imaginatae.'

[3] Cf. Thomas, *Summa contra Gent.* II, 77 : ' Quod non fuit sententia Aristotelis quod intellectus agens sit substantia separata, sed magis quod est aliquid animae.'

[4] The decree runs as follows : ' Quod si quisquam deinceps asserere, defendere seu tenere pertinaciter praesumpserit, quod anima rationalis seu intellectiva non sit forma corporis humani per se et essentialiter, tanquam haereticus sit censendus.'

in an almost incredible confusion. Perhaps the most interesting example of this astounding patchwork is afforded by the work of Robert Grosseteste, in whom we are able to detect elements taken from all three. His theory of the genesis of the universal idea is half Aristotelian, half Augustinian. He accepts Aristotle's account of the origin of the καθόλου from memory and sense-experience,[1] and supports the peripatetic view of the universal *in re* as opposed to the ' Platonizing ' realism of the twelfth century.[2] Yet he combines this form of empiricism with the doctrine of the *lux eterna*. Clear knowledge is only to be obtained by the intuition of the divine essence, and the intelligibility of things is assured only by this spiritual illumination.[3] At the same time, if we may trust the authority of Roger Bacon [4] (who, as a member of the Franciscan house at Oxford in which Grosseteste lectured, ought to have been in possession of the facts), he seems to have taught the strange doctrine that the *intellectus*

[1] *Comment. in Post. An.* II, 6 : ' Ex sensu igitur fit memoria, et memoria multiplicata experimentum, et ex experimento universale, quod est praeter particularia, non quasi separatum a particularibus, sed est idem in illis, artis scilicet et scientiae principium.'

[2] Ibid., I, 15 : ' Formae separatae a subjectis, quas posuit Plato, genera et species et praedicabilia, sunt prodigia, quae format error intellectus.'

[3] *De Veritate*, fol. 9 r. a : ' Cum lucidioris essentiae res quam sua similitudo vel exemplar, clarior et apertior oculo mentis sano est rei in se ipsa cognitio, quam in sua similitudine vel exemplari. Ac per hoc, cum divina essentia sit lux lucidissima, omnis cognitio per similitudines est per se ipsam obscurior : in rationibus enim aeternis creaturarum in mente divina lucidissima, quae sunt creaturarum exemplar lucidissimum, omnis creaturarum cognitio certior et purior et manifestior est.'

Comment. in Post. An. I, 17 : ' Est lux spiritualis quae superfunditur rebus intelligibilibus, et oculus mentis se habet ad res intelligibiles sicut se habet sol corporalis ad res visibiles. . . . Res igitur intelligibiles . . . magis receptibiles ab acie mentis, quae similiter est irradiatio spiritualis, perfectius penetrantur.'

[4] Cf. *Op. Tert. c.* xxii (Brewer, p. 74), quoted above, ch. iv, p. 131, note 5.

agens is not a part of the soul, a thesis pointing to an Arabian influence, being a combination of the teaching of Augustine with that of Avicenna.

A similar confusion of terminology at least, if not of thought, is to be found in Bonaventura. He also combines with the peripatetic empiricist theory of knowledge the Augustinian doctrine of the uncreated light [1]—a confusion which his recent editors and commentators have hastened (almost indecently) to explain away.[2] The same mixture of theories is to be seen even more clearly in his pupil, Matthew of Aquasparta, who was Cardinal Bishop of Porto at the end of the thirteenth century. Matthew accepts, as Bonaventura also does, the Arabian-Aristotelian account of the ' abstraction ' of the *species intelligibiles* from the sensuous phantasm. This operation is performed by the intellect through its unaided powers, but it is an active, not a passive, process. The things of sense do not act upon the intellect, but vice versa. By this means he hopes to have reconciled Aristotle and Augustine.[3] But at the same time he postulates the influence of a divine illumination,[4] by means of which

---

[1] *Itinerarium* : ' Conjunctus intellectus noster ipsi aeterni veritati, nisi per illam docentem nihil verum potest certitudinaliter capere ; ' so also *In I Sentt.*, dist. iii, art. 1, q. 2 : ' Quum Deus lux summe spiritualis non potest cognosci in sua spiritualitate ab intellectu ; quasi materiali luce indiget anima ut cognoscat ipsam, scilicet per creaturas.' Cf. also *Sentent.* II, dist. xxiv.

[2] Cf. the scholion of the Quaracchi edition to distinction xxiv of the commentary on the Sentences : ' Manifeste ostenditur Sanctum Doctorem ab aliis principalibus scholasticis in hac doctrina (i. e. de ratione cognitionis humanae) non discrepare nisi in modo loquendi, vel in re exigui momenti.'

[3] Matthew of Aquasparta, *De Fide et Cognitione humana*, Quaracchi ed., p. 291 : ' Sic igitur dico sine praejudicio, quod anima sive intellectus accipit species a rebus extra, non virtute rerum corporalium agentium in animam vel intellectum, sed intellectus sua virtute facit et format. Huic sententiae Augustinus concordat . . . concordat nihilominus Philosophus.'

[4] *Ibid.*, p. 255 : ' Lumen ergo illud, movendo nostrum intellectum,

the human mind grasps the truth in its objective relation to the eternal exemplar in the divine mind,[1] and a special co-operation of God with the human mind in the act of understanding.[2] Thus knowledge comes partly from without and partly from within and partly from above. There are, therefore, three factors whose co-operation is essential to the fulfilment of the cognitive process : the *ratio materialis*, which is derived from the ' external ' world, and the *ratio formalis*, which is constituted partly by the light of interior reason, but in its completeness consummated by the eternal *regulae*, the divine ideas.[3]

Thomas also attempts to combine Aristotle and Augustine, but he will admit no theory of innate ideas.[4] All knowledge is derived from sense-experience : the mind prior to experience is a blank ; without the sensuous phantasm the human intellect could know nothing.[5] The active intellect, by operating on the

influit quoddam lumen menti nostrae, ita quod per lucem divinam videt objective et quasi effective, sed per illud et in illo lumine videt formaliter ; quod quidem lumen continuatur et conservatur in mentibus nostris ad praesentiam divinam. Nec alicui subtrahitur cognoscenti ; immo omnibus, bonis et malis, indifferenter assistit, secundum ordinationem et dispositionem immutabilem suae sapientiae, qua cooperatur in intellectuali operatione.

[1] Ibid., p. 233 : 'Quidditas ipsa concepta ab intellectu nostro, relata tamen ad artem, sive exemplar aeternam.'

[2] Ibid., p. 262 ad primum : 'Operatio intellectualis circa naturalia naturalis est. Deus autem operatur et cooperatur in operationibus creaturarum secundum modum et exigentiam suae naturae, ut visum est. Et quia creatura rationalis imago Dei est, vel ad imaginem, ipsa ratio imaginis exigit ut in ejus operationibus cooperetur secundum modum objecti moventis, eo quod mens nata est moveri et illuminari illa luce.'

[3] Ibid., p. 261 : 'Ratio cognoscendi materialis est ab exterioribus, unde ministrantur species rerum cognoscendarum ; sed ratio formalis partim est ab intra, scilicet a lumine rationis, partim a superiori, sed completive et consummative a regulis et rationibus aeternis.'

[4] *Summa Theol.* Ia pars, q. 84, art. 3 : 'Et ideo dicendum est quod anima non cognoscit corporalia per species naturaliter inditas.'

[5] Ibid., art. 7 : 'Impossibile est intellectum nostrum secundum

phantasm, makes it intelligible by abstracting the
intelligible species,[1] the 'whatness' of the sense
object. In this process it is the active intellect which
is the principal agent, the part played by the phantasm
itself being merely secondary or instrumental.[2] But
the species itself is only an 'idea', the means by
which (*id quo intelligitur*) knowledge is obtained;
the real object of knowledge (*id quod intelligitur*) is
the thing itself, or *res*.[3] With reference to the Augustinian theory of the *lumen increatum* and the *rationes
aeternae* he makes the following distinction. If by
knowledge in the light of the eternal ideas we mean
a direct intuition, as it were in a mirror of the divine
exemplar, then in this mortal life we cannot know
things in this way; such intuitive knowledge of all
things in God is reserved only for the beatified. If,
on the other hand, we mean knowledge in the light
of the ideas as cognitive principles, then we must say
that we know all things after this manner. For it
is by participation in the ideas, that is by thinking
the universals as embodied in material things, that
all knowledge comes to us. And so understood, the
lumen intellectuale is a kind of similitude of the uncreated light in which the eternal notions are contained.
But besides this intellectual light we need the *species
intelligibiles* abstracted from the phantasm produced
by the action of the external reality upon our sense

praesentis vitae statum, quo passibili corpori conjungitur, aliquid
intelligere in actu, nisi convertendo se ad phantasmata.'

[1] *Summa Theol.* Ia pars, q. 79, art. 3: 'Intellectus agens facit phantasmata a sensibus accepta intelligibilia per modum abstractionis
cujusdam,' etc.

[2] *De Veritate*, q. 10, art. 6: 'Intellectus vero agens, ut agens
principale et primum . . . se habent phantasmata ut agens instrumen-
tale et secundarium.'

[3] *Summa Theol.* Ia pars, q. 85, art. 2: 'Dicendum est quod species
intelligibilis se habet ad intellectum, ut id quo intelligit intellectus . . .
species intellecta secundario est id quod intelligitur . . . sed id quod
intelligitur est res, cujus species intelligibilis est similitudo.'

organs in order to know it, the light by itself being
insufficient.[1]

This explanation is, to say the least of it, somewhat
obscure ; the terminology is markedly Augustinian
and might at first sight seem to suggest a theory not
unlike that of Matthew of Aquasparta, but a closer
inspection will show its meaning to be rather as follows.
Thomas denies that we have any direct intuition of
the divine ideas as such. So much is plain. The
concepts of the human mind, the *species intelligibiles*,
participate in the divine ideas because these ideas are
the prototypes, the dies as it were from which the
material things were struck ; so that our ideas of these
things, seeing that they are abstracted from them,
are in a way copies of them. So also the comparison
of the *lumen intellectuale* with the *lumen increatum*
hardly means more than that our mind, in so far as we
are intellectual beings, is fashioned in the image of the

---

[1] *Summa Theol.* Ia pars, q. 84, art. 5 : ' Cum ergo quaeritur utrum
anima humana in rationibus aeternis omnia cognoscat ; dicendum
est quod aliquid in aliquo dicitur cognosci dupliciter. Uno modo,
sicut in objecto cognito, sicut aliquis videt in speculo ea quorum
imagines in speculo resultant ; et hoc modo in statu praesentis vitae
anima non potest videre omnia in rationibus aeternis ; sed sic in rationibus aeternis cognoscunt omnia beati qui Deum vident, et omnia in ipso.
Alio modô dicitur aliquid cognosci in aliquo, sicut in cognitionis
principio ; sicut si dicamus quod in sole videntur ea quae videntur
per solem. Et sic necesse est dicere quod anima humana omnia
cognoscit in rationibus aeternis, per quarum participationem omnia
cognoscimus. Ipsum enim lumen intellectuale, quod est in nobis,
nihil est aliud quam quaedam participata similitudo luminis increati,
in quo continentur rationes aeternae. Unde dicitur " multi dicunt,
quis ostendit nobis bona ? " (Psal. iv. 6). Cui quaestioni Psalmista
respondit, dicens : " signatum est super nos lumen vultus tui, Domine ",
quasi dicat per ipsam sigillationem luminis divini in nobis omnia
demonstrantur. Quia tamen praeter lumen intellectuale in nobis
exiguntur species intelligibiles a rebus acceptae, ad scientiam de rebus
materialibus ; ideo non per solam participationem rationum aeter-
narum de rebus materialibus notitiam habemus, sicut Platonici
posuerunt, quod sola idearum participatio sufficit ad scientiam
habendam.'

mind of God. There is no need to understand Thomas as postulating any supernatural or special illumination co-operating with us in the act of knowing beyond the due concurrence of the divine will which accompanies and sustains all the events of nature.

This modification of the Augustinian theory is carried one step further in the doctrine of Scotus, in which the *lumen intellectuale* is identified simply with the *intellectus agens*.[1] Scotus merely expresses more clearly what Thomas had conveyed in terms of the Augustinian terminology. He expressly rejects the notion that we know eternal truths, as Henry of Ghent had supposed, through the conformity of our ideas with the divine exemplars, for we cannot know these exemplars directly.[2] Nor have we any need of Henry's special illuminations.[3] The active intellect itself is the guarantor of our certitude.[4] Yet, inasmuch as the truths we perceive through the activity of our own intellect operating on our sense experience are dependent on the divine mind and express the divine perfection, we know them more perfectly by recognizing their place in the system of the universe, and thus we may be said to know them in the light of the *rationes*

---

[1] *Op. Ox.* I, dist. iii, q. 4, n. 24 : ' Sed virtute intellectus agentis, qui est participatio lucis increatae, illustrantis super phantasmata, cognoscitur quidditas rei, et ex hoc habetur sinceritas vera.'

[2] Ibid., p. 16 : ' Aut tertio intelligit per veritatem conformitatem ad exemplar ; et si ad creatum, patet propositum : si autem ad exemplar increatum, conformitas ad illud non potest intelligi, nisi illo exemplo cognito, quia relatio non est cognoscibilis, nisi cognito extremo : ergo falsum est quod ponitur, scilicet exemplar aeternum esse rationem cognoscendi non cognitum.' Cf. Henry of Ghent ; *Summa Theol.*, art. 1, q. 2 ; *Quodl.*, II, q. vi ; V, q. xiv.

[3] *Op. Ox.*, loc. cit., n. 20.

[4] Ibid., n. 24 : ' Regulae enim in lumine intellectus agentis intellectum rectificant, et ipsa species intelligibilis terminorum, licet in essendo sit mutabilis, in praesentando tamen in lumine intellectus agentis, immutabiliter repraesentat, et per duas species intelligibiles cognoscuntur termini primi principii, et illa unio est vera et evidenter.'

aeternae ;[1] but it must not be supposed that this knowledge is the result of a special illumination; it is only the fruit of a greater natural endowment or a deeper search.[2]

We have now taken as it were a bird's-eye view of Duns Scotus' philosophical position. We have seen how he combined in his system certain elements of the older doctrines of scholastic thought with the newer peripateticism of Thomas and the Arabians, and how his teaching differentiates itself from that of the Thomist school. And it is time this chapter, already far too long, were drawing to its close. But our survey may not have been without profit, and we have gained a knowledge of a few landmarks which, we may venture to hope, will assist us in the further study of this complicated territory. We must pass on, then, and hasten to complete our historical introduction, for there are as yet several important questions to engage our attention. We have as yet scarcely touched upon the relation of Scotus to Aristotle and the Jewish and Arabian commentators, not to mention his immediate contemporaries and the post-Thomist philosophers. These topics, then, will furnish the subject-matter for our next two chapters.

[1] Ibid., n. 23 : ' Et isto ultimo modo potest concedi quod cognoscuntur veritates sincerae in luce aeterna, sicut in objecto remoto cognito ; quia lux increata est primum principium entium speculabilium, et ultimus finis rerum practicarum, et ideo ab ipsa sumuntur principia tam speculabilia quam practica. Et ideo cognitio omnium, tam speculabilium quam practicabilium per principia sumpta a luce aeterna, ut cognita, est perfectior et purior cognitione sumpta per principia in genere proprio. . . . Cognoscere enim triangulum habere tres, ut est quaedam participatio Dei, et habens talem ordinem in universo quod quasi exprimit perfectionem Dei, hoc est nobiliori modo cognoscere triangulum habere tres, quam per rationem trianguli.'

[2] Ibid., n. 22 : ' Paucorum igitur est pertingere ad rationes aeternas, quia paucorum est habere intellectiones per se, et multorum est habere conceptiones tales per accidens. Sed isti non dicuntur distingui ab aliis per specialem illustrationem, sed per meliora naturalia, quia habent intellectum magis abstrahentem et perspicaciorem, vel per majorem inquisitionem,' etc.

VI

SCOTUS, ARISTOTLE, AND THE COMMENTATORS

AS we have already noted, a very large proportion of the works of Scotus were composed in the form of a commentary on the treatises of Aristotle. These include not only all the books of the *Organon* together with the *Isagoge of Porphyry*, but also the *De Anima* and the *Metaphysics*. The question of the authenticity of the two commentaries on the latter work, which have come down to us under the name of Scotus, we have already discussed in our first chapter, where we concluded that while the *Quaestiones* were probably genuine the *Expositio* was certainly the work of a later writer, though it is possibly based on genuine materials, perhaps in the shape of lecture-notes or other unfinished documents. But the term commentary is in a sense misleading. None of them, with the exception of the *Expositio*, deals directly with the Aristotelian text. The *Quaestiones subtilissimae super libros Metaphysicorum* is written in Scotus' usual form, and its method is much freer than that of the ' exposition '. In fact it can scarcely be said to be a commentary at all in the modern meaning of the term. The range of its discussions is exceedingly wide, embracing nearly the whole field of logic, metaphysic, and psychology, and though the questions discussed arise more or less directly out of the Aristotelian text, they are treated with an independence which renders the book less a commentary than an original work. Nor are the topics by any means confined to Aristotle; a large portion of the treatise is devoted to Avicenna, Averroes, Thomas, Henry of Ghent, and other scholastics.

The same in substance may be said of the commentaries on the *De Anima* and the *Organon*. The former is rather an independent discussion of psychological problems and should be regarded as one of Scotus' original works. In the case of the *Logicalia* Duns prefaces his commentary on the *Isagoge* with a long introduction of his own, dealing mainly with the nature of logic and the character of universal concepts. It is only in the twelfth of the thirty-one *quaestiones* that he arrives at the actual subject-matter of the Porphyrian text. So too in his commentary to the *Liber de Categoriis* he does not reach the Aristotelian subject-matter till the fifth *quaestio*. From this point to the end he follows the text, but he confines his discussions mainly to the first four categories which he treats at great length in *quaestiones* xii to xxxvi. In *quaestiones* xxxvii–xlii he deals in detail with contrareities and opposites, while the rest of the Aristotelian work he dismisses summarily in two *quaestiones*, presumably because the same subjects are discussed in the work on the *Metaphysics*.

There are two commentaries on the *De Interpretatione*, which during the Middle Ages was divided into two books. The first commentary, like the original text, is separated into two parts, the first of which deals only with the first two chapters of Aristotle (*quaestiones* i–iv and v–xiii). At the end of *quaestio* xiii is appended a detailed discussion of the doctrines of *suppositio* and *distributio*. The second book, consisting of ten *quaestiones*, treats the subject-matter of the beginnings of chapters ten and eleven of the Greek. The second commentary is not subdivided into two halves. It is composed of eight *quaestiones* and deals with more of the Aristotelian text, but reaches out beyond it, discussing at some length the truth and falsity of judgements. A corresponding relation to the text is found in the commentary on the *Elenchi*.

The commentaries on the *Prior* and *Posterior Analytics* each fall into two books of unequal length. The first book of the *Prior Analytics* contains thirty-seven *quaestiones*, the second only ten, while in the case of the *Posterior* the first book contains forty-seven and the second thirteen *quaestiones*. Neither of these commentaries deals ostensibly with the text. They may be regarded rather as independent discussions dealing in a general manner with the subject-matter of the original in the light of the traditions of the contemporary exegesis of the formal logical doctrine. They show, as Werner points out, distinct traces of the influence of the logical writings of Robert Grosseteste and Robert Kilwardby. They are in fact a kind of text-book of the contemporary Oxford school-logic.

Scotus's general attitude to Aristotle is, as might be expected, one of profound respect. He is always referred to as The Philosopher in accordance with the general usage of the thirteenth century, and the citations of texts from his various works are extraordinarily numerous throughout Scotus' writings, not only in the commentaries but also in the works on the Sentences and the original treatises. The Aristotelian works most often cited are the *Metaphysics* and the *Physics*, the *Organon*, the *De Anima*, and the *De Generatione et Corruptione*; the *Ethics* are less frequently referred to and the *Politics* are very seldom mentioned. In questions of logic, metaphysics, psychology, and natural sciences, and to a less degree natural theology, he is regarded as the highest authority, far higher indeed than any other single writer. In all these matters he is the weightiest piece in the artillery of controversy; for Scotus, as for Dante, he is 'Il maestro di color che sanno '. But his *ipse dixit* is by no means allowed to pass unquestioned, and Duns is a far less slavish adherent of the Stagirite than Albert or Aquinas. Nor is the reason for this far to seek. He is far less anxious to reconcile Aristotle with the doctrines of the Christian faith, and the temper of his mind is radically different from that of Thomas. He is too acutely critical not to realize the impossibility of such a task, and his tendency is to emphasize rather than to diminish the gulf which separates them. Thus he maintains that on Aristotelian principles the soul must be corrupted with the death of the body, and he insists that this was the opinion of the Master.[1] The passage is interesting for the criticism it implies of the Aristotelian doctrine of form and matter as adopted by Thomas, whose views seem to him to endanger the Christian dogma of the immortality of the soul. With reference to the passage in the *De Generatione Animalium* in which Aristotle speaks of the soul as coming from without he refuses to accept the interpretation in the literal sense, and objects that Aristotle never meant to say that the intellectual soul was an adventitious principle ; he only wished to say that the activity of the intellect is not dependent upon any bodily organ.[2] But in another passage he inclines to attribute to him the theory of Averroes[3]

---

[1] *Rep. Par.* IV, dist. xliii, q. 2, n. 17 : ' Si simpliciter esset ab extrinseco, non poneret Philosophus quod esset forma naturalis ipsius corporis proprie, quia principium apud eum est quod de nihilo nihil fit, et quod cuilibet potentiae passivae correspondet potentia activa in natura. Et ideo quia ponit eam propriam formam ipsius corporis organici ... ponit eam corrumpi ad corruptionem totius.'

[2] Cf. *De Generatione Animalium*, II, 736 b : λείπεται τὸν νοῦν μόνον θύραθεν ἐπεισιέναι, καὶ θεῖον εἶναι μόνον with *Rep. Par.*, loc. cit. : ' nunquam invenitur a Philosopho, quod ipse asserat animam intellectivam esse ab extrinseco, sed si hoc alicubi dicit, hoc dicit propter operationem ejus, respectu cujus non utitur organo, vel dubitando, secundum opinionem aliorum.'

[3] *De Rerum Principio*, q. ix, n. 12 : ' Doctrina Aristoteles ponit,

that the active intellect is one in all men and united
to the body only *sicut motor*. This interpretation is
given in the *De Rerum Principio* and may therefore
be regarded as an earlier view ; in his commentaries
on the Sentences, on the other hand, he concedes that
this is a misunderstanding of the Aristotelian doctrine
on the part of the commentator.[1]   But it is difficult
not to suspect a certain scepticism in his earlier
attitude when, after laying down the Averroist interpretation, he proceeds to give what is in substance the
orthodox Thomistic doctrine of the soul as the substantial form of the body, ' for those who wish to
interpret Aristotle in a Catholic manner '.[2]   In fact
we may hazard the suggestion that he was not above
using Aristotle somewhat unscrupulously to support
any thesis which he found convenient at the moment—
a practice not at all foreign to the methods of the
schools, which were frequently directed not so much
to the attainment of truth as to the scoring of a dialectical victory ; and to show that Aristotle was on
your side practically amounted to winning the game.
And in general Duns is disposed to treat all philo-

---

secundum quod eum exponit Commentator suus . . . quod homo est
homo per animam sensitivam meliorem aliis (viz. νοῦς παθητικός)
eductam de potentia materiae ; et quod intellectiva non unitur nobis
sicut forma, sed sicut motor, inquantum a phantasmatibus accipit
species intelligibiles, per quas ipse format actum intelligendi. Et hoc
necesse habuit dicere, eo quod ponit unum intellectum omnium hominum ; quod verum non esset si nobis ut forma uniretur, eo quod
secundum ipsum propria forma est in propria materia. Sic enim
exponit eum Commentator suus . . . qui sequens ipsum in duplicem
errorem lapsus est, quod, scilicet, non esset nisi unus intellectus
omnium, et quod non uniretur nobis sicut forma, sed sicut motor per
operationem.'

[1] Cf. *Op. Ox.* IV, dist. xliv, q. 2, and the passage just cited from
Rep. Par.

[2] *De Rerum Principio*, q. ix, n. 29 : ' Quamvis autem secundum quod
Commentator exponit, Aristoteles videatur dixisse intellectum non
esse formam, volentibus tamen ipsum exponere catholice, hoc videtur
de intellectu sentire.'

sophical authorities very critically, especially with reference to this question of the immortality of the soul, in which context he remarks that the philosophers have often accepted reasons which were, strictly speaking, not logically cogent so long as their 'systems' appeared consistent with their principles.[1]

There were also other reasons why the authority of Aristotle should weigh less with Duns Scotus than with Thomas Aquinas. The Aristotelian doctrines had, as we have seen, not yet received the full favour of the ecclesiastical authorities in spite of their acceptance by the Dominican Order, and the Franciscans were inclined to adopt a somewhat more conservative attitude to the new teaching. This conservatism, too, was perhaps more powerful in Oxford than elsewhere, and Scotus showed himself in some ways more than usually sensitive to the strictures of ecclesiastical authority. Nor will this appear unnatural when we consider the circumstances in which he was placed. The fate of Roger Bacon, the Oxford Minorite, must have presented itself to him as a terrible example, and he took good care that a Minister-General of his order should have no opportunity of sinning for a second time against philosophy. Moreover, his thinking contained in it many elements which could not be reconciled with the teaching of Aristotle, and Augustine and Anselm are to him authorities little less weighty than the Philosopher himself. For in the last resort Duns, like all the medieval schoolmen,

---

[1] *Op. Ox.* IV, dist. xliii, q. 2, n. 16 : ' Est et alia responsio realius, quia non omnia dicta a philosophis etiam assertive, erant ab eis probata per necessariam rationem naturalem ; sed frequenter non habebant nisi quasdam probabiles persuasiones, vel vulgarem opinionem praecedentium philosophorum. . . . Unde parvae semper sufficientiae suffecerunt philosophis ubi non poterant ad majora pervenire, nec contradicerent principiis philosophiae. . . . Unde quandoque philosophi acquiescunt propter suas persuasiones probabiles, quandoque propter assertiones suorum principiorum praeter rationem necessariam.'

was primarily a theologian, and where a conflict arose between the philosopher and the monk the issue was already prejudged.

And indeed the attempt to reconcile Aristotelianism with Christianity was doomed to failure from the very outset. The pouring of new wine into old bottles is scarcely ever a satisfactory or successful performance—not even in philosophy—and the manifest inconsistencies and confusions of thought everywhere abounding in the writings of Albert and Thomas had not escaped the critical eyes of Duns. In more than one respect Platonism was more fitted to harmonize with the teachings of the Church ; it had inspired the Greek fathers and Augustine, as well as Scotus Erigena, and Anselm, even as in the present day it continues to inspire a certain type of Christian thinking. For Platonism contained within it not a few mystical elements which have appealed to the religious consciousness of all subsequent ages, elements which the Christian thinkers from the third century downwards had not been slow to incorporate with their theology. For Platonism, in spite of the abstract idealism of Plotinus and the Neoplatonists, yet managed to retain its hold on the subjective aspect of the world, and it satisfied the ethical and spiritual needs of mankind in a way which the cold, impersonal, naturalistic Aristotelianism failed to do. Hence it has always had a special attraction for the more intellectual types of the religious consciousness, while Aristotelianism has at best furnished only a precarious foundation for the ' over-beliefs ' of the theologian. And in the last analysis it will be found that the medieval mind employed not Aristotelian but Platonic notions in the interpretation of the mysteries of the Catholic faith. Thus the theology of Thomas, no less than that of Scotus and the older theologians, abandons peripatetic naturalism and has recourse to the symbolism of the pseudo-Dionysius, Augustine, and Plotinus. Plato, not Aristotle, is the philosophic sponsor of the Nicene and Athanasian Creeds.

The philosophy of Aristotle contained not a few doctrines which no amount of interpretation could reconcile with Christian thought. To begin with what is perhaps the most obvious instance, his cosmology is essentially naturalistic. For him the world is eternal and uncreate, having neither beginning nor end,[1] and the problem thus mooted forms an insoluble puzzle for Thomas, who is in the end obliged to take refuge in revelation, a proceeding which in philosophy is the equivalent of going into bankruptcy. For the arguments for and against a creation in time, he tells us, are so evenly balanced that the issue is philosophically indecisive.[2] Again, with respect to God, though Aristotle conceives Him as a mind, his conception of His attributes is quite inconsistent with any form of Christian dogma. For, as Mr. Benn has pointed out,

'The Stagirite agrees with Catholic theism in accepting a personal God, and he agrees with the first article of the English Church, though not with the Pentateuch, in saying that God is without parts or passions. But there his agreement ceases. Excluding such a thing as divine interference with nature, his theology of course excludes the possibility of relation, inspiration, miracles, and grace. Nor is this mere omission :

---

[1] *De Caelo*, II, 1 : ὅτι μὲν οὖν οὔτε γέγονεν ὁ πᾶς οὐρανός, οὔτε ἐνδέχεται φθαρῆναι, καθάπερ φασί τινες αὐτόν, ἀλλ᾽ ἔστιν εἷς καὶ ἀίδιος ἀρχὴν μὲν καὶ τελευτὴν οὐκ ἔχων τοῦ παντὸς αἰῶνος, ἔχων δὲ καὶ περιέχων ἐν ἑαυτῷ τὸν ἄπειρον χρόνον, ἔκ τε τῶν εἰρημένων ἔξεστι λαβεῖν τὴν πίστιν, κτλ.

[2] For a discussion of this problem see *Summa contra Gent.* II, chs. xxxii–xxxviii. In spite of Thomas's conclusion that the arguments are equally balanced, it is difficult not to suspect a balance of probability on the side of naturalism. Thomas has accepted *in toto* the principles of the Aristotelian cosmology, and it is hard to see how he can escape its conclusions without sacrificing the consistency of his whole system.

it is a necessity of the system. If there can be no existence without time, no time without motion, no motion without unrealized desire, no desire without an ideal, no ideal without eternally self-thinking thought, then it must logically follow that God, in the sense of such a thought, must not interest himself in the affairs of men.'

The Deity of Aristotle is not a moral being at all, and is in no wise concerned with the rest of the universe which he has not created and of which he is not and cannot be conscious. 'He is in fact an Egoist of the most transcendent kind, who does nothing but think about himself and his perfections.'[1] Such a being, remote and separate from mankind, was ill-fitted to serve as the model for Christian philosophy, and provided but a slippery foundation for Catholic theology. And in a sense Scotus realized this fact. In his proofs for the existence of God he does not betake himself, like Thomas, to the naturalistic Aristotelian argument from motion,[2] but turns instinctively, as it were, to Augustine and to Anselm.

In the Scotist commentaries on Aristotle, especially those on the *Metaphysics*, much space is devoted to polemical discussions turning on the interpretations of other commentators, especially Aquinas, and much criticism is directed against the chief points of the Thomist system in which it differs from that of Scotus. It will therefore be worth our while to examine a few of the more important instances. Thus in the literal commentary, while expounding the five different meanings of the word *natura*, the author takes the opportunity to criticize Thomas's interpretation of the *natura* as the *forma totius*. The text out of which this dispute arises is taken from book Δ (which was known in medieval times as book 5), and runs as follows : 'Natura autem materia prima, et haec

---

[1] A. W. Benn, *The Greek Philosophers*, pp. 293 and 294.
[2] Cf. *Summa contra Gent.*, I, cap. xiii sqq.

dupliciter; ut quae ad ipsum prima, aut omnino prima, ut operum aereorum, ad ipsum quidem primum aes; totaliter vero forsan aqua si omnia liquibilia aqua. Et species et substantia; haec autem est finis generationis. Metaphora vero jam et omnis omnino substantia natura dicitur, propter hanc, quia et natura substantia quaedam est.'[1]

Thomas tries to identify the *natura* taken in this sense with the *species* as definition,[2] but his opponent will not allow this, and distinguishes between the *species* as a logical essence or quiddity and the form as metaphysical principle of the concrete substance which is the *terminus generationis*. The latter, he maintains, is the sense in which the Philosopher is using the term in the passage in question.[3] So, too, in the *Quaestiones super universalia Porphyrii*, Scotus maintains a similar distinction. The *species* as such is a form of predication and must be separated in thought from the concrete reality which is the subject of predication.[4] The difference here noted might appear at first sight to amount to scarcely more than hair-splitting, but it implies a metaphysic divergence

---

[1] The Greek original reads thus: Φύσις δὲ ἥδε πρώτη ὕλη καὶ αὕτη διχῶς ἢ ἡ πρὸς αὐτὸ πρώτη (ἢ ἡ ὅλως πρώτη), οἷον τῶν χαλκῶν ἔργων, πρὸς αὐτὰ μὲν πρῶτος ὁ χαλκός· ὅλως δ' ἴσως ὕδωρ, εἰ πάντα τὰ τηκτὰ ὕδωρ· καὶ τὸ εἶδος καὶ ἡ οὐσία· τοῦτο δ' ἐστὶ τὸ τέλος τῆς γενεσέως. μεταφορᾷ δ' ἤδη καὶ ὅλως πᾶσα οὐσία φύσις λέγεται, διὰ ταύτην, ὅτι καὶ ἡ φύσις οὐσία τίς ἐστιν.—*Metaph.* Δ. 1015 a.

[2] Thomas, *Comm. in Metaph.* V, lect. 6: 'Ut si diceremus quod hominis natura non solum est anima, sed humanitas et substantia quam significat definitio.'

[3] Scotus, *Comm. Litt. in Metaph.* V, cap. 4: 'Forma de qua hic loquitur Philosophus est terminus generationis, ut patet ex littera; quidditas autem, ut quidditas est, abstrahit ab omni generatione. Nam equinitas est tantum equinitas, secundum Avicennam.' Cf. Avicenna, *Metaph.* V, cap. 1.

[4] *Quaest. super Porph. Univ.*, q. 11: 'Species inest homini secundum quod homo praedicatur de multis, loquendo de praedicatione signata, non de praedicatione exercitata, id est, non secundum quod est idem suppositis.'

of considerable importance, involving, as it does, the
question of the *unitas formae* as is shown by the discussion in the seventh book of the *Quaestiones Sub-
tiliisimae*, where the latent implications of the two
doctrines are brought out more fully. According to
the view accepted by Thomas, who cites Boethius in
support of his theory, it is the specific difference which
completes the substantial determination of the thing
or *species* which is the *ultimus actus in re*, the concept
of the *genus* containing in itself potentially that of the
difference,[1] while the inferior *differentiae* contain in
themselves the *differentiae superiores*.[2] The *species*
therefore as such expresses the complete nature of the
concrete thing, and in it lies the unity of the form.
Scotus, on the other hand, will not have it so. According to his opinion the concept of the *genus* does not
include in itself that of the difference even potentially ;
the two concepts are formally diverse, they correspond
to different grades of being in the same concrete whole.[3]
Nor does the *differentia inferior* contain within itself
the *differentiae superiores*.[4] For every *differentia* is an
actuality perfective of the essence which may in some
cases be derived from an actual form, in which case
we may regard it as determining or perfecting the
matter of the *compositum*, while in other cases it is
taken only from a ' formal perfection ' (as for instance
rationality, which is the *differentia* of man). In such

---

[1] Cf. Thomas, *Tractatus de Natura Generis* ; *Comm. in Metaph.*
VII, lect. 4 et 1.

[2] Op. cit. VII, lect. 12.

[3] *Quaest. in Metaph.* VII, q. xix, n. 3 : ' Alia est opinio, quae ne
ponat conceptus simpliciter diversos generis et differentiae esse
fictitios ; sed cum utroque illorum aliquid in re concipiatur, cum
illorum actuum sint objecta inquantum objecta, ita formaliter
diversa, sicut si essent res omnino diversae ponit quod illis correspon-
dent aliqualiter in re realiter diversa, ita realiter quod circumscripta
omni operatione intellectus agentis vel possibilis . . . est in re illa
differentia.'			[4] Loc. cit., q. xvii, n. 3.

cases the *perfectibile* is not matter as such, but the total compound, in so far as it is perfectible according to a particular *ratio perfectiva*[1] or definite order of perfection. This theory is taken by Scotus from Avicebron, from whom the doctrine of the plurality of forms is also derived. *Genus* and *differentia* are thus formally distinct, though really identical, in the sense that they go to constitute a single concrete reality,[2] the ultimate or individual unity of which is conferred by the *haecceitas*, which does not however annihilate the plurality of forms.[3]

Another important difference between the Scotist and Thomist interpretations of the Aristotelian text is concerned with the principle of individuation. The passage in question is found in the literal commentary, book 5, cap. 6: 'Amplius autem alia secundum numerum sunt unum, alia secundum speciem, alia secundum genus, alia secundum analogiam : numero quidem quorum materia una ; specie quorum ratio una ; genere, quorum eadem figura praedicationis ; secundum proportionem quaecumque se habent ut aliud ad aliud.'[4] Thomas uses this text as the foundation for his theory of matter as the principle of

---

[1] *Op. cit.*, q. xix, n. 12 : 'Aliter potest dici quod differentia sumitur per se ab actualitate essentialiter perfectiva ; quandoque autem talis est realiter forma et perfectibile materia ... sic Avicebron posuit omni differentiae correspondere propriam formam ; quandoque actualitas a qua sumitur differentia non est forma, sed perfectio formalis, et hoc sufficit pro differentia ; et tunc perfectibile non est materia, sed totum ut perfectibile secundum aliquam rationem (in) realem perfectivam.'

[2] *Quaest. de An.*, q. xxi, n. 1 : 'Licet genus et differentiae non sint idem formaliter, quia ratio differentiae non includit rationem formalem generis, tamen sunt idem realiter vel identice.'

[3] Cf. *Op. Ox.* IV, dist. xi, q. 3.

[4] Aristotle, *Metaph.* 1016 b : ἔτι δὲ τὰ μὲν κατ᾽ ἀριθμόν ἐστιν ἕν, τὰ δὲ κατ᾽ εἶδος, τὰ δὲ κατὰ γένος, τὰ δὲ κατ᾽ ἀναλογίαν. ἀριθμῷ μὲν ὧν ἡ ὕλη μία· εἴδει δὲ ὧν ὁ λόγος εἷς· γένει δὲ ὧν τὸ αὐτὸ σχῆμα τῆς κατηγορίας· κατ᾽ ἀναλογίαν δὲ ὅσα ἔχει ὡς ἄλλο πρὸς ἄλλο.

individuation. It is by virtue of matter as quantitatively determined that one individual is differentiated from the other.[1] The Scotists object that this cannot be the case. Matter is of the essence of the *species*, and what is of the essence of the *species* cannot be the cause of individuation, because were this so the *species* would itself be individual, which is absurd.[2] This objection had already occurred to Thomas himself, and he answers it elsewhere by making a distinction between *materia communis* and *materia signata* or *individualis*. The former, not the latter, is the principle of individuation.[3] Another passage which Thomas quotes in favour of his theory of individuation is taken from *Metaph.* 1074 a : ἀλλ' ὅσα ἀριθμῷ πολλά, ὕλην ἔχει. εἷς γὰρ λόγος καὶ ὁ αὐτὸς πολλῶν οἷον ἀνθρώπου. Σωκράτης δὲ εἷς. τὸ δὲ τί ἦν εἶναι οὐκ ἔχει ὕλην τὸ πρῶτον· ἐντελέχεια γάρ, from which self-same passage the writer deduces his theory of the hylemorphic composition of all created things.

Another interpretation of a text from *Metaph.* 1044 a turns on the same point. The Latin translation which he used runs thus : ' Et numerum oportet esse aliquid quo unus, quod nunc non habent dicere,

---

[1] Thomas, *Comm. in Metaph.* V, lect. 8 : ' Numero quidem sunt unum quorum materia est una. Materia autem secundum quod stat sub dimensionibus signatis, est principium individuationis formae. Et propter hoc ex materia habet singulare, quod sit unum numero ab aliis divisum.'

[2] *Comm. Lit. in Metaph.* V, cap. 6, n. 60 : ' Materia est de essentia speciei . . . sed quod est de essentia speciei non est causa individuationis, quia tunc species esset individua et haec ; ergo materia non erit causa individuationis.'

[3] *Summa Theol.* Ia pars, q. 85, art. 1 : ' Dicendum quod quidam putaverunt quod species rei materialis sit forma solum, et quod materia non sit pars speciei. Sed . . . aliter dicendum est, quod materia est duplex, sc. communis et signata vel individualis. Communis igitur ut caro et os ; individualis autem ut hae carnes et haec ossa. Intellectus igitur abstrahit speciem rei naturalis a materia sensibili individuali, non autem a materia sensibili communi,' etc.

quo unus siquidem est unus ; aut enim non est, sed ut acervus, aut est dicendum quid quod est faciens unum ex multis et definitio una est.   Similiter autem hanc habent dicere, et hoc merito accidet; ejusdem enim rationis et substantia est unum ita, sed non ut dicunt quidam, ut unitas quaedam existens, aut punctum, sed entelecheia ; et natura una quaedam ' (*Comm. Lit. in Metaph.* VIII, cap. 3, n. 23).[1]   Thomas in his interpretation draws the analogy between number and the *substantia* of the *compositum* still more closely by maintaining that both are one by virtue of an *ultima unitas* or *specific difference*.[2]   His opponent, however, will not admit the legitimacy of such an interpretation ; he too draws the same comparison but construes it differently, his whole conception of form and substance being, as we have seen, different from that of the Angelic Doctor.   Moreover, as regards number, the Thomistic exposition will not hold ; if we change the units about we should, according to Thomas, change the substance of our number, which is absurd.   His own interpretation of numerical unity follows that of substance, and he construes it on the analogy of the *haecceitas*.[3]

[1] Καὶ τὸν ἀριθμὸν δεῖ εἶναί τι ᾧ εἷς, ὃ νῦν οὐκ ἔχουσι λέγειν τίνι εἷς, εἴπερ ἐστὶν εἷς· ἢ γὰρ οὐκ ἔστιν, ἀλλ' οἷον σωρός, ἢ εἴπερ ἐστί, λεκτέον τι τὸ ποιοῦν ἓν ἐκ πολλῶν, καὶ ὁ ὁρισμὸς εἷς ἐστίν. ὁμοίως δὲ οὐδὲ τοῦτον ἔχουσι λέγειν, καὶ τοῦτο εἰκότως συμβαίνει. τοῦ αὐτοῦ γὰρ λόγου, καὶ ἡ οὐσία ἓν οὕτως, ἀλλ' οὐκ ὡς λέγουσί τινες, οἷον μονάς τις οὖσα ἢ στιγμή, ἀλλ' ἐντελέχεια καὶ φύσις τις ἑκάστη.

[2] Thomas, *Comm. in Metaph.* VIII, lect. 3 : ' Dicit Aristoteles quod numerus est id quo est unum.   Est enim per se unum numerus, inquantum dat numero speciem et unitatem, sicut etiam in rebus compositis ex materia et forma, per formam est aliquid unum, et unitatem et speciem sortitur.'

[3] *Comm. Lit. in Metaph.* VIII, cap. 4, n. 24 : ' Notandum hanc convenientiam stare in hoc ; quod sicut est numerus per se unus, et non est unus sicut acervus, sic et quidditas rei, sive definitio, est per se una, sicut ostensum est . . . scilicet quia differentia comparatur ad genus ut actus proprius ad proprium perfectibile.   Sed occurrit unum dubium. . . . Dicitur a quodam expositore, quod numerus est

We have seen from these examples, which are but a few selected from numerous instances,[1] the way in which both Thomas and Scotus used Aristotle for their own ends by reading into his text their own particular theories. How far these interpretations represent a genuine attempt to arrive at the real meaning which lay in the mind of the Philosopher as he wrote it would be difficult to say. The authority with which he was invested, if we may credit the somewhat exaggerated statements of Roger Bacon, must have been

unus ab ultima unitate, ita quod omnes aliae sunt partes materiales ; sola autem ultima est formalis et completiva omnium aliarum, ut sicut definitio est una ab ultima differentia specifica, sic numerus fit unus ab ultima unitate. Sed contra hoc, dicitur quod in quibuscumque positio non facit differentiam in substantia, vel in figura ; ibi dicitur omnis et non totum, et exemplificat in liquidis et numeris ; ergo si prima unitas fiat ultima, et e converso, nulla fiet differentia in substantia numeri, quod est impossibile secundum te ; quoniam ultima unitate mutata, cum sit per te specifica et formalis, fieret alia forma, et per consequens alius numerus. . . . Dicendum ergo aliter, quod in numeris est considerare unitatem in duplici genere, quia quaedam sunt unitates materiales, ex quibus materialiter integratur, et est unitas a qua numerus, puta quinarius, est unus numerus specie. Haec autem unitas est sua forma specifica, vel passio consequens formam, sicut homo est unus sua forma, vel unitate consequente ut passio suam formam ; haec autem unitas non ponit in numerum, cum quinarii unitatibus quinque materialibus, quia non est materialis ; et haec unitas est totalis a qua dicitur totum denominative unum . . . haec autem unitas est innominata ; similiter est in aliis speciebus numerorum.'

[1] The minor divergences between Thomas' and the 'literal' commentary in their interpretation of the text of the *Metaphysics* are of course exceedingly numerous. The following table compiled by Werner gives the most important :

Metaph.	Thomas, *Comm. Met.*	*Comm. Lit.*
Δ. 1015 a, 7–11.	V, lect. 5.	V, cap. 3, n. 23.
Δ. 1015 a, 34 sq.	V, lect. 6.	V, cap. 4, n. 34.
Δ. 1016 b, 31 sq.	V, lect. 8.	V, cap. 6, n. 60.
Δ. 1019 a, 15 sq.	V, lect. 14.	V, cap. 11, n. 91.
Z. 1032 a, 12 sq.	VII, lect. 6.	VII, Summa 2, cap. 6, n. 46.
Z. 1041 b, 9 sq.	VII, lect. 17.	VII, Summa 2, cap. 17, n. 144.
H. 1044 a, 3 sq.	VIII, lect. 3.	VIII, cap. 5, n. 24.
K. 1068 b, 15 sq.	XI, lect. 12.	XI, Summa 4, cap. 3, n. 105.
Λ. 1074 a, 31 sq.	XII, lect. 10.	XII, Summa 2, cap. 5, n. 67.

overwhelming. There was no escape from it, and the only road to freedom lay through his territory. Hence, to gain acceptance for an original view, the scholastic had to find in Aristotle what he had already placed there. Thomas, it is true, remained as faithful to the text as he was able to do, but we cannot help suspecting that for Scotus Aristotle is in some ways almost as much a convention as an authority, and he shows marked tendencies to use him as a controversial device for defending quite un-Aristotelian opinions.

Scarcely less important than the authority of Aristotle was that of the Arabian and Jewish commentators whose works provided so large a portion of the subject-matter of medieval academic discussions. Our next task, therefore, is to examine the relation of Scotus's teaching to these thinkers, the introduction of whose writings into Western Europe exercised so profound an influence on the thought of the Middle Ages. We have seen how the Arabian logic became the basis of the ' Schul-logik ' of the thirteenth century and how the distinction of the threefold aspect of the universal *ante rem*, *in re*, and *post rem* forms the starting-point of the epistemological theory of Scotus no less than that of Albert or Aquinas. Hardly less great was their influence on metaphysical speculation, and their theories occupy a large share of the attention of the Latin schoolmen, especially in their Aristotelian commentaries. The *Quaestiones subtilissimae* open with a discussion as to the *subjectum proprium* of metaphysic. According to the view put forward by Avicenna, being *qua* being is the subject of metaphysics, as it is written in *Metaph.* III, cap. 1 : Ἔστιν ἐπιστήμη τις ἣ θεωρεῖ τὸ ὂν ᾗ ὄν, κτλ. According to Averroes, on the other hand, God and the Intelligences are the proper subject of this science,[1] and to prove his thesis he cites various

---

[1] Averroes, *Metaph.* IV, comment. 1 ; III, comment. 14 ; XII, comment. 1.

passages also from the *Metaphysics*. For metaphysic is the science of the ' first intelligibles ' and the ultimate causes.[1] It is also called the most divine of sciences, and the most worthy of honour, for it approximates most nearly to the divine knowledge, seeing that God is the cause of the universe and therefore, in one sense, the principle of all things.[2] Again, in his division of the sciences, Aristotle distinguishes three speculative ἐπιστήμαι : physics, which is concerned with the motion of bodies ; mathematics, which treats of their figures, size, and number ; and theology, which deals with pure being and must therefore be identified with metaphysic.[3]

Scotus hesitates for a long time, in the *Quaestiones*, between these two opposing standpoints, and attempts somewhat equivocally to take a middle course. He introduces a distinction between the *subjectum* of metaphysics and the *causa subjecti*, and also between the *principales partes subjecti* and their causes. Metaphysics deals with God not as *subjectum* but as *causa subjecti*, for He is the source of all being ; and also with the intelligences as *partes principales subjecti*, though not as causes *per se*, because created beings only cause as movers, that is, in a secondary sense, by virtue of the first cause, which is uncreated.[4]   In the

[1] Aristotle, *Metaph.* 982 b : μάλιστα δὲ ἐπιστητὰ τὰ πρῶτα καὶ τὰ αἴτια. διὰ γὰρ ταῦτα καὶ ἐκ τούτων τἆλλα γνωρίζεται, ἀλλ᾽ οὐ ταῦτα διὰ τῶν ὑποκειμένων.

[2] Ibid. 983 a : ἡ γὰρ θειοτάτη καὶ τιμιωτατη· τοιαυτὴ δὲ διχῶς ἂν εἴη μόνη. ἥν τε γὰρ μάλιστ᾽ ἂν ὁ θεὸς ἔχοι, θεία τῶν ἐπιστημῶν ἐστί, κἂν εἴ τις τῶν θείων εἴη. μόνη δ᾽ αὕτη τούτων ἀμφοτέρων τετύχηκεν. ὅ τε γὰρ θεὸς δοκεῖ τὸ αἴτιον πᾶσιν εἶναι καὶ ἀρχή τις· καὶ τὴν τοιαύτην ἢ μόνος ἢ μάλιστ᾽ ἂν ἔχοι ὁ θεός.

[3] Ibid. 1026 a : ὥστε τρεῖς ἂν εἶεν φιλοσοφίαι θεωρητικαί, μαθηματική, φυσική, θεολογική. οὐ γὰρ ἄδηλον ὅτι εἴ που τὸ θεῖον ὑπάρχει, ἐν τῇ τοιαυτῇ φύσει ὑπάρχει. . . . εἰ δὲ ἐστί τις οὐσία ἀκίνητος, αὕτη προτέρα καὶ φιλοσοφία πρώτη. καὶ καθόλου οὕτως ὅτι πρώτη καὶ περὶ τοῦ ὄντος ᾗ ὂν ταύτης ἂν εἴη θεωρῆσαι, καὶ τί ἐστι καὶ τὰ ὑπάρχοντα ᾗ ὄν.   [4] *Quaest. in Metaph.* I, q. I.

Oxford Commentary, on the other hand, he displays no such hesitation, but accepts the view of Avicenna without more ado.

Both Avicenna and Averroes maintain that no science can prove the existence of its own object. It has to take the ὅτι ἐστί of its *subjectum* for granted. The latter, therefore, hands over the proof of the existence of God to physics, while the former attributes it to metaphysics. But metaphysics cannot prove the existence of its own subject-matter; therefore it cannot have God as proper object. Moreover, according to Avicenna, God does not fall under the concept of being or *ens*, for he conceives him in Neo-platonic fashion as transcending being altogether, a contention with which Scotus will not agree, for it is only on the assumption of an analogy of being, if not of a univocacy in the creator and the creature, that a rational knowledge of God is possible for man-kind.[1] Averroes was not altogether wrong, then, in attributing to metaphysic God as *subjectum*, but he erred in supposing that no science could prove the existence of its *subjectum* and so handing over the proofs of God's existence to physics. In the com-mentaries on the Sentences, however, Scotus denies that God is as such the *subjectum* of metaphysic, for of God as *subjectum* there can be only one science, namely theology.[2] But he admits, nevertheless, that both in physics and in metaphysics we find grounds for inferring the existence of the deity and reasons which point to the existence of an object which lies beyond the reach of both of these sciences and belongs as *subjectum proprium* to a third science, namely theology, which ranks above both, though their principles remain independent of it. So, too, in the first *quaestio* of the

---

[1] Cf. *Quaest. in Metaph.* IV, q. 1, n. 12 ; also *Op. Ox.* I, dist. viii, q. 3, nn. 4–12.

[2] *Op. Ox.*, Prol., q. 3 lateralis.

sixth book of the *Quaestiones subtilissimae* he sides
with Avicenna in maintaining that being *qua* being is
the proper subject of metaphysic.

The difference between the two Arabian commentators is roughly this : Avicenna wishes to place God
and his attributes wholly in the domain of theology,
while Averroes would place all Moslem theology,
except the dogmatics of the Prophet's revelation, in
the sphere of metaphysics. Thomas attempts to
reconcile these two views as follows :[1] Metaphysics
in as far as it is *scientia communissima* has three names,
Theologia, Metaphysica, and *philosophia prima.* Its
field of observation embraces the *maxime intelligibilia.*
These *maxime intelligibilia* are the *maxime universalia,*
the most general of our conceptions, the notion of
being and its *passiones,* the principle of unity and
plurality, potency and act, and so forth. As dealing
with these abstract principles of knowledge the *scientia
communissima* is called Metaphysics. But inasmuch as
the *maxime intelligibilia* also include the first causes
of things it is, in this relation, called *philosophia prima.*
Finally, in so far as the *maxime intelligibilia* are also
the *maxime a materia separata,* God and the Intelligences come within the scope of this science, which
therefore, in so far as it considers these, may rightly
be called Theology. The doctrine of Scotus on this
question, though less clearly expressed than that of
Thomas, does not differ from it in any essential respect.
Metaphysics is not concerned with God as *primum
subjectum* ; its proper subject is being as such. But
it does consider Him in so far as He falls under the
notion of *ens* in the highest manner in which He can
be considered by a purely natural science.[2]

With regard to the question of the derivation of
our knowledge of first principles Averroes maintains

---

[1] See *Comm. in Metaph.,* Proem ; III, lect. 4 ; IV, lect. 1.
[2] Vide supra, ch. iii, p. 87.

that these are innate, implanted in us by nature in every department of knowledge (*in quolibet genere entium*), and cites for the defence of his opinion a passage from the beginning of Aristotle's second book of the *Metaphysics* (A' τὸ ἔλαττον).[1] The foundation of this doctrine is his theory of the *intellectus possibilis*, which he conceived as containing the impression of the notions of all real things as matter, is impressed with form. These impressions are actualized by the active intellect, which like the passive is numerically one in all men when it comes in contact with the phantasm of our material intellect. Scotus, who like Thomas repudiates this monopsychism, refuses to concede the existence of innate ideas, and cites against the commentator the Aristotelian passage where the mind is compared to a *tabula rasa*,[2] and insists that our knowledge, even of first principles, is dependent on sense-experience.[3]

A further divergence between Scotus and Averroes arises out of the question whether in material things matter shall be taken as part of the quiddity or essence. Averroes maintains the negative answer,[4] and cites

---

[1] *Metaph.* 993 a : Ἡ περὶ τῆς ἀληθείας θεωρία τῇ μὲν χαλεπή, τῇ δὲ ῥᾳδία. Σημεῖον δὲ τὸ μήτε ἀξίως μηδένα δύνασθαι τυχεῖν αὐτῆς, μήτε πάντας ἀποτυγχάνειν, ἀλλ' ἕκαστον λέγειν τι περὶ τῆς φύσεως ... ὥστε εἴπερ ἔοικεν ἔχειν καθάπερ τυγχάνομεν παροιμιαζόμενοι, τίς ἂν θύρας ἁμάρτοι. Cf. Averroes, *Metaph.* II, comment. I.

[2] Cf. *De Anima*, III, 429 b : δυνάμει πώς ἐστι τὰ νοητὰ ὁ νοῦς· ἀλλ' ἐντελεχείᾳ οὐδέν, πρὶν ἂν νοῇ. δεῖ δ' οὕτως ὥσπερ ἐν γραμματείῳ ᾧ μηδὲν ὑπάρχει ἐντελεχείᾳ γεγραμμένον.

[3] *Quaest. in Metaph.* II, q. i, n. 2 : ' Ad Commentatorem dicendum, quod pro tanto dicuntur nobis naturaliter nota sive cognita, quia praescita compositione similicium terminorum, statim ex lumine naturali intellectus adhaeret vel acquiescit illi veritati ; tamen cognitio terminorum acquiritur ex sensibilibus, et iste intellectus dicitur habitus principiorum, quo cohaeret primis principiis. Ad aliud, cognitio principiorum, quantum ad simplicia acquiritur ex sensibilibus.'

[4] Averroes, *Metaph.* I, comment. 21 and 34.

in his defence Aristotle, *Metaph.* 1034 b : Ἐπεὶ δὲ ὁρισμὸς λόγος ἐστί, πᾶς δὲ λόγος μέρη ἔχει, ὡς δὲ ὁ λόγος πρὸς τὸ πρᾶγμα, καὶ τὸ μέρος τοῦ λόγου πρὸς τὸ μέρος τοῦ πράγματος ὁμοίως ἔχει, ἀπορεῖται ἤδη πότερον δεῖ τὸν τῶν μερῶν λόγον ἐνυπάρχειν ἐν τῷ τοῦ ὅλου λόγῳ ἢ οὔ. ἐπ᾽ ἐνίων μὲν γὰρ φαίνονται ἐνόντα, ἐπ᾽ ἐνίων δ᾽ οὔ. He remarks with reference to this passage that, while there are certain definitions in which the material element of a thing is mentioned and others in which it is omitted, in neither case does it belong to the essence of the thing. Scotus, on the other hand, agrees with Thomas in maintaining that the quiddity or *quod quid est* (τὸ τί ἐστί) is the *primo ens* which is the *compositum*, the concrete whole containing both matter and form, and decides that matter therefore *in communi considerata* forms part of the quiddity of the *species*.[1]

This controversy is directed also against Albertus Magnus, who, following Averroes, had insisted that the essence of a thing consists solely in its form.[2] Scotus deals with Albert in detail in the third book of the *Opus Oxoniense* (dist. xxii, nn. 9–17), where he reaches the same conclusion as in the passage just cited. His repudiation of Albert's theory is important because it has direct bearing on the individuation controversy, in which, as we have just seen, Scotus argues against Albert and Thomas that matter cannot be the *principium individuationis* because it is included in the

---

[1] *Quaest. in Metaph.* VII, q. xvi, nn. 5–6 : 'Ad solutionem quaestionis ... oportet distinguere de materia considerata in universali et particulari. ... Patet ergo, quod per se materia, non individualis, nec simul totius proprie sumpti, sed in communi considerata, est de quidditate speciei, non prout species dicitur forma ... sed speciei, id est, universalis infimi sive proximi individuis, cujus proprie est "quid" et primo et idem sibi.' For this distinction between *materia communis* and *materia individualis* in Thomas, *Summa Theol.* Ia pars, q. 85, art. 2.

[2] Cf. Albertus Magnus, *Comm. in Metaph.* I, text. 12.

quiddity of the *species*.   But it is also at the same time
directed against Roger Bacon in so far as he held the
Averroistic doctrine that there must be as many
matters as forms, because each form must have its
own matter.   Scotus, however, insists that matter in
its essence is not *haec materia* or individual, for were
this the case two matters could not fall under the same
notion or *ratio*,[1] and he cites in support of this contention several Aristotelian *loci*.[2]   These lead him
finally to a new argument against Albert and Averroes.
Matter and form taken *communiter* are the constituent
principles of the *compositum* taken *communiter*, for
they stand in relation one to the other as potency
and act, a relation which verifies itself in each particular *compositum*.   The *posse esse et non esse*, which
Averroes wishes to separate from the quiddity of the
compositum, is a *passio communis* which belongs univocally to the plurality of individual *composita*, and
therefore involves a common subject and a common
medium or middle term through which it can be
demonstrated.   If then, as Aristotle holds, matter be
such a *medium*, it follows that it is a *commune* and
a constitutive principle of the quiddity of the *compositum*.[3]

---

[1] *Quaest. in Metaph.* VII, q. 16, n. 3 : ' Si materia esset de se haec,
non possent duae materiae convenire in una ratione materiae . . . habet
ergo materia communitatem sibi correspondentem ad materiam sicut
forma ad formas.'

[2] *Physics* II, cap. 3 ; *Metaph.* Δ, cap. 2 ; Λ, 1071a, 18 sq. ; Z,
1035b, 27 sq. ; 1037a, 5 sq.

[3] *Quaest. in Metaph.* VII, q. xvi, n. 3 : ' Materia in universali
considerata, et forma in universali considerata, sunt constitutiva
compositi in universali considerati ; igitur ad quidditatem illius
constituti ut sic, pertinet utrumque constituens, ut sic.   Antecedens
probatur quia ratio potentiae et actus, propter quam ex materia et
forma fit unum, manet in materia et forma in universali consideratis,
nam in qualibet materia et forma particulari, est ratio potentiae
et actus ; ergo per materiam communem, cui primo inest. . . .
Contra primam rationem eorum arguitur per idem, quia posse

This argument is especially important on account of the implications it contains. By making the *posse esse et non esse* a part of the quiddity of material things as such, the *subjectum* of which is matter, Scotus links up his doctrine of *materia prima* with the Christian dogma of creation. As we have already noticed, matter in its widest and most general aspect involves the notion of creaturehood ; hence his theory of the hyle-morphic composition of the Angels. And by another line of argument creaturehood is referred ultimately to the divine free will ; for by definition the creature is that which may or may not exist. The act of creation, however, is a spontaneous act of the divine will, not necessitated even by grounds immanent in the divine nature, for the only strictly necessary being in the universe is God himself. Scotus thus attacks the Averroistic doctrine of the eternity of the world, which proved so attractive to the mind of Thomas, on two sides. On the one hand he maintains the absolute contingence of the created universe, while on the other he combats Averroes' theory of an uncreated and eternal matter.

In the same manner he will have nothing to do with the Averroist theory of the unity of the active intellect in all men, a theory to which Thomas devotes a long polemic in the *Summa contra Gentiles*. While Duns refuses to admit the strict cogency of Thomas's proofs of the immortality of the soul and insists that this fact is not logically demonstrable, he makes short work of the Arabian monopsychism and dismisses it summarily with a contemptuous reference. Not only

esse et non esse, est passio communis univoce inhaerens multis ; ergo requirit subjectum commune, de quo est demonstrabilis, et medium commune, per quod demonstretur ; si ergo materia in naturalibus est illud medium secundum illiud dictum philosophi, sequitur quod materia est communis, et ita principium constituti communis.'

is it an abomination to be detested by all theologians, but it is also philosophically untrue, for it perpetrates the vilest of errors by denying the rationality of mankind.[1] In conclusion it may be remarked that the doctrines of Scotus stand out in sharp contrast against those of Averroes, a contrast which springs from a fundamental divergence in their cosmological conceptions. That of the Arabian is strictly naturalistic in tendency, while that of Scotus is founded upon the conception of the ultimate contingence of the created world as dependent absolutely on the gratuitous exercise of the free will of God.

In his interpretation of the Philosopher Scotus is on the whole much more in sympathy with Avicenna than Averroes, and it is noticeable that in disputes between the two Arabian commentators he often takes Avicenna's side while Thomas supports Averroes. An interesting example of the different relations of the two scholastics to their Arabian predecessors is furnished by the discussion on the much ventilated passage in Aristotle's *Metaphysics*, Γ, 1003 b: εἰ δὴ

---

[1] *Op. Ox.* IV, dist. xliii, q. 2, n. 5 : ' Praeterea omnes philosophi communiter in definitione hominis posuerunt rationale tanquam ejus differentiam propriam ; per rationale intelligentes animam intellectivam esse partem essentialem ejus, nec breviter invenitur aliquis philosophus notabilis qui hoc neget, licet ille maledictus Averroes in fictione sua 3, *De anima* quae tamen non est intelligibilis nec sibi nec alii, ponat intellectum esse quamdam substantiam separatam, mediantibus phantasmatibus nobis conjungibilem ; quam conjunctionem nec ipse nec aliquis sequax ejus adhuc potuit explicare, nec per illam conjunctionem salvare hominem intelligere. Nam secundum ipsum homo formaliter non esset nisi animal quoddam irrationale excellens, per quamdam tamen animam irrationalem et sensitivam excellentiorem aliis animabus (surely *animalibus*).' Cf. also *Comm. Lit. in Metaph.* XII, summa 1, cap. 3, where in commenting on *Metaph.* 1070 a, 25 sq. εἰ δὲ καὶ ὕστερόν τι ὑπομένει, σκεπτέον· ἐπ' ἐνίων γὰρ οὐθὲν κωλύει, οἷον εἰ ἡ ψυχὴ τοιοῦτον, μὴ πᾶσα ἀλλ' ὁ νοῦς· he says : ' Ex his videtur posse colligi quod opinio Commentatoris de intellectu agente vel possibili non consonat cum opinione Aristotelis,' etc.

τὸ ὂν καὶ τὸ ἓν ταὐτὸν καὶ μία φύσις, τῷ ἀκολουθεῖν
ἀλλήλοις ὥσπερ ἀρχὴ καὶ αἴτιον, ἀλλ' οὐχ ὡς ἑνὶ λόγῳ
δηλούμενα. Thomas, following Averroes, maintains the
essential identity of *ens* and *unum*. Substance is a
unum per se; *ens* and *unum* therefore denote the same
thing in concrete fact (*realiter*), and are both predicated
of substance as such.[1] Avicenna, on the other hand,
regarded *ens* and *unum* as something superadded to
substance,[2] but this, Thomas remarks, was due to
a confusion of the *unum* which is convertible with
ens with the *unum* which is the principle of numerical
unity. This last ' oneness ' is plainly *aliquid super-
additum*. Owing, therefore, to this confusion, he was
forced to regard the former *unum* also an an addition
to substance and to make it convertible with *ens* as
an inherent accident of it, like risibility, for instance,
in man. Scotus, however, leaves on one side the
distinction between *ens* and *substantia* noted by
Thomas in Avicenna's doctrine and interprets him
as follows : *ens* and *unum* are predicated of all things,
but they are not the same things *secundum naturam*,
being only identical *secundum subjectum*, i. e. they are
always found as attributes of the same reality, the
relation between *ens* and *unum* being that of *subjectum*
and *passio subjecti*. Were they essentially identical,
then the principle of plurality could find no place in
nature, and a multiplicity of things would simply not
exist. Moreover, the two terms would be synonymous,
and to say ' one being ' would be to commit a tautology.[3] He tries to argue further that the essential

[1] Thomas, *Comm. in Metaph.* IV, lect. 2.
[2] Avicenna, III, *Metaph.*, cap. 2 ; VII, *Metaph.*, cap. 1.
[3] *Quaest. in Metaph.* IV, q. ii, n. 2 : 'Opinio Avicennae, VII°, Metaphysicae suae dicit quod ens et unum praedicantur de omnibus,
tamen non sunt idem secundum naturam, sed secundum subjectum,
sicut subjectum et passio ; quia si unum esset idem essentialiter cum
ente, sive secundum essentiam, tunc multitudo esset non ens. Item
dicendo " ens unum " esset nugatio.'

identity of *ens* and *unum* postulated by Averroes leads to awkward consequences. If we are to avoid the imputation of tautology and superfluity of definition we shall have to admit the possibility of abstracting a common term subsisting in both *ens* and *unum*, and simpler than either, which is prior to both,[1] a consequence which Avicenna might easily have admitted, for this would be just that *substantia* of which, according to the interpretation of Thomas, he made both *ens* and *unum* further conceptual determinations.

But Scotus does not take this line of defence. He proceeds to argue that we cannot predicate *unum* of *ens* by a predication *in quid*, we can only do so *denomina-tive*. *Praedicatio in quid* is not permissible, because we can say *unitas est entitas* as little as we can say *entitas est unitas*. Every *unitas* falls under the category of quantity, for when combined with another *unitas* it constitutes a number. But it may be objected that we must distinguish between the *unum transcendens*, which is one of the ' transcendent ' attributes of being, and the quantitative unit. Scotus answers, 'No!' *Numerus est multitudo mensurata uno*.[2] Wherever we have two unities side by side there must be either a generic, specific, or numerical difference between them ;[3] a generic or a specific difference without a numerical one is unthinkable, and the last, to wit

---

[1] Loc. cit. : ' Ad hoc Commentator dicit quod non est nugatio, quia non significat idem eodem modo. . . . Quaeso de istis modis, aut sunt intra conceptu mentis et unius, aut extra conceptum sub quo concipitur. Si extra, non excludit nugationem . . . si intra, tunc aut ille modus est, aut pars. Si primo modo, tunc non significant idem, quod est oppositum positi. Si secundo modo, pone definitionem pro nominibus, tunc erit aliquid bis dictum ; sequitur etiam quod ab uno et ente possit abstrahi conceptus unus communior simpliciorque utroque, et illud erit prius dictum.'

[2] Aristotle, *Metaph.* I, 1057a : ἔστι γὰρ ἀριθμὸς πλῆθος ἑνὶ μετρητόν.

[3] Scotus, loc. cit., n. 3 : ' Ubicumque est unitas et unitas, est differentia numero vel specie vel genere,' etc.

the numerical difference, involves number. But essences are classified according to specific and generic, not according to numerical, differences, as for instance Angel and man. The principle of plurality, therefore, cannot first have its beginning in the category of quantity and be applicable only to corporeal things.

Scotus' partisanship of Avicenna, and his refusal to concede the identity of *ens* and *unum*, is bound up no doubt with his extreme abhorrence of the Averroistic theory of the unity of the human intellect. It is also directed incidentally against Thomas, who interprets Aristotle in an Averroistic sense as maintaining that plurality as quantitative or numerical plurality first has its origin in the sphere of material things. This divergence of Scotus and Thomas on the nature of number is of considerable importance. It is connected with their theories on the nature of form and the principle of individuation. For Thomas numerical unity, arising as it does only in the category of quantity, draws its origin from matter ; [1] hence the Thomist doctrine of the specific difference existing between the various angels, who can only possess a specific unity because, by virtue of their substantial simplicity as pure forms, numerical unity as such must be denied them. We have also seen how easily this doctrine of the nature of number could be perverted into the Averroist heresy ; for, once separated from matter and the body, how was the soul to retain its unity and individuality? for, unlike the angelic, the soul of a human individual *A* could no longer be said to be numerically distinct from that of another individual *B* or *C*, and on Thomas' hypothesis they were always threatening to

[1] Thomas, *Comm. in Metaph.* IV, lect. 2 : ' Numerus ex divisione continui causatur. Et ideo numerus ad scientiam mathematicam pertinet, cujus subjectum extra materiam esse non potest, quamvis sine materia sensibili consideretur.'

collapse into each other, a difficulty which formed one of the most notable *cruces* of the Thomist system.

But for Scotus the case was different, and his conception of the principles of form and matter enabled him to avoid the precipice of contradiction. For him numerical difference is already given with the plurality of created substances. Every creature as such is a determined unity, a *hoc aliquid* by virtue of the principle of *haecceitas*, and is therefore already the *subjectum* of the unity which is the principle of number. The *unum* which is convertible logically with *ens* is distinct from the *unum* which forms the basis of the quantitative unit, not *realiter* but *formaliter*. Duns concedes, however, that the former, the *unum transcendens*, is the more universal because it abstracts from the property of a thing, by virtue of which it is a subject of enumeration.[1]

There was another reason too which, as Werner has suggested, may account for the preferential treatment meted out to Avicenna by Scotus. Avicenna was regarded with particular respect by Roger Bacon and other teachers of the Franciscan School. Moreover, Duns shows himself anxious to cover his interpretations of the Philosopher with the acknowledged authority of a great name, to act no doubt as a counter-weight to the redoubtable Thomas, the influence of whose

[1] Scotus, *Quaest. in Metaph.* IV, q. ii, n. 18 : ' Sequitur quod in omni creato unitas convertibilis cum ente realiter non differt ab unitate de genere quantitatis, licet semper, ut dictum est, conceptus unius transcendentis sit generalior ; quia vero nihil potest esse pars numeri, nisi in quantum limitatum, quia de ratione partis est possibilitas ad formam totius, et unum, inquantum convertibile cum ente, non dicit limitationem ; ideo ex tali, inquantum tale, non fit numerus, nec multitudo aliquo modo una, sed sola aggregatio, sicut habetur in Henrico de Gandavo, de denario praedicamentorum.' These last words may well be taken for a gloss by an editor, but they are interesting, because they form an exception to the rule of numberless citations from Henry which are made only for the purpose of combating his doctrine.

teaching was already beginning to overshadow medieval philosophy.

Scotus also raises the problem of the number of the categories, and suggests the possibility that the Aristotelian list is not exhausitve, supporting his contention by an opinion of Avicenna.

The question arises out of the exposition of a passage in Aristotle, *Metaphysics* Δ. 1017 a : Ἐπεὶ οὖν τῶν κατηγορουμένων τὰ μὲν τί ἐστι σημαίνει, τὰ δὲ ποῖον, τὰ δὲ ποσόν, τὰ δὲ πρὸς τι, τὰ δὲ ποιεῖν ἢ πάσχειν, τὰ δὲ ποῦ, τὰ δὲ πότε, ἑκάστῳ τούτων τὸ εἶναι ταὐτὸ σημαίνει, κτλ. He refers to a passage from the third book of Avicenna's *Physics* where the Arabian philosopher contends that we need not necessarily postulate only ten *genera* of being and is inclined to add several extra categories, including one of motion.[1] Scotus tentatively upholds this suggestion and asserts that any argument to the contrary can easily be disposed of, because Aristotle is only referring to the popular classification of the categories.[2] Thomas, however, takes a different view and defends the orthodox number of ten,[3] which is advocated elsewhere by Scotus in other passages of this same commentary as well as in the commentaries on the Sentences.[4]

---

[1] Avicenna, *Metaph.* III, cap. 3 : ‘Nos non cogimur observare illam divisionem famosam, qua dicitur quod decem sunt genera, quorum uniuscujusque est certissima generalitas, et quia nihil est extra ipsa ; quia aliquid invenitur, quod sub nullo genere potest collocari, sicut motus ; quia si comparatio motus ad subjectum sit praedicamentum, scilicet esse motus in subjecto, puta genus passionis, multo fortius et motus erit praedicamentum ; vel si non ponamus comparationem qualitatis ad subjectum praedicamentum, et non qualitatem, vel si tu velis ponere qualitatem genus, habes ponere motum genus. Etsi ultra ponas comparationem qualitatis ad subjectum ; ergo et sic de aliis accidentibus, et ita augebuntur praedicamenta multa augmentatione.’

[2] *Quaest. in Metaph.* V, q. vi, n. 4 : ‘Ad omnia in contrarium solvitur faciliter quia Philosophus non facit praedicamenta, sed loquitur ibi secundum famosum modum loquendi.’

[3] Cf. Thomas, *Comm. in Metaph.* V, lect. 9.

[4] e. g. *Quaest. in Metaph.* V, q. vi, n. 9 ; *Op. Ox.* II, dist. i, q. 4,

But the adherence of Scotus to the opinions put
forward by Avicenna is by no means absolute. The
two thinkers part company quite decisively on the
question of the procession of the Many from the One,
which forms the main theme of the theory of emanations taken by Arabians from Neoplatonist sources.
Avicenna had maintained that from the absolutely
simple and transcendent One only one emanation
could proceed immediately. From this First Principle,
the ineffable Godhead, proceeds a single Intelligence
(the νοῦς of Plotinus) in whose essence a difference is
posited, according to which it includes in itself
a diversity and at the same time differentiates itself
from the original One. Thus the transition from the
absolutely simple to the plurality of the created
universe is mediated. This emanating Intelligence,
inasmuch as it knows itself as possible, creates a sphere,
and, in so far as it knows itself as actual, causes this
sphere to be moved. In so far as it knows the Intelligence from which it proceeded, it causes a second
Intelligence, which moves the second sphere and in
like manner causes a third Intelligence, and the third
a fourth, and so on, till the process of emanation reaches
the world-soul and the active intellect which Avicenna,
like Averroes, conceived to be one in all human beings.
This successive process of emanation, however, must
not be regarded as taking place in time but as timelessly
coeternal with the original One. The world is thus
at once ' necessary ' and uncreated, notwithstanding its
dependence on the Deity.[1]

This half-mystical, half-naturalistic theory of the procession of the world from the one is, of course, quite
incompatible with the Scotist cosmology. Avicenna

n. 14. See also the *quaestiones* in *Librum Praedicamentorum*, where no
doubt is cast on the validity of the usual number of the categories.

[1] Avicenna, *Metaph.* VI, cap. 2 ; see also the ' Tractatus de erroribus ' in Hauréau's *Philosophie Scolastique*, vol. i, p. 368.

and the Arabians interpreted the emanations, like the Neoplatonists, in terms of intellect, and their whole cosmology emphasized the necessary character of the physical and spiritual universe.   Scotus, on the other hand, is an advocate of creationism, and regards the whole universe apart from God as the contingent creature of the divine will.   Consequently he repudiates the arguments of Aristotle for the eternity of the world[1] and reinterprets his account of the divine intelligence in such a way as to attribute to the Deity a knowledge of things outside himself.[2]   Unfortunately the two last books of the *Quaestiones subtilissimae* which are printed in Wadding's edition are undoubtedly spurious,[3] and we are left without a detailed criticism of the natural theology of Aristotle and the Arabian commentators.

Of the relation of Scotus to Avicebron we have already made mention in connexion with the doctrine of *Materia Prima* and the plurality of forms.   The writings of this Jewish philosopher became known to the Latin world through the translation of the *Fons Vitae* by Dominicus Gundisalvi.[4]   Owing to the corruption of his name, which was really Solomon ben

---

[1] *Comm. Lit. in Metaph.* XII, summa 2, cap. 1, n. 24.

[2] Ibid., cap. 6.

[3] The *quaestiones* to the eleventh book are entirely wanting, and only the first nine books were originally known to Wadding, who later discovered two copies of *quaestiones* on Books X and XII, one a manuscript and the other in an old printed edition prepared at Venice in 1505, both of which he made over to Cavell, who declared them to be genuine without formulating any sufficient reason.   The internal evidence on this point, however, is quite conclusive.   In the first place the *quaestiones* are very brief, far briefer than any of the genuine Scotist discussions.   In the second place they contain doctrines diametrically opposed to some of the chief theses of the Scotist philosophy : e. g. in q. xx of the twelfth book the author maintains that the *Intelligentiae* must differ specifically because they do not contain matter.   Again, in q. xvii of the same book, the eternity of the spheres and their movers is implied.   Numerous other instances of divergence could be cited, to say nothing of stylistic differences.

[4] This translation, which has been shown by Munk to be identical

Gebirol, into Avicebron or Avicembrol, he was
considered by some of the schoolmen to have been
a Christian. His works exercised a considerable influence on the scholastics of the thirteenth century,
which is clearly traceable in that most compendious of
thinkers Albertus Magnus. His position in the world
of Arabian and Jewish thought is somewhat singular,
and has been compared to that of Duns Scotus in
Latin thought.[1] Less faithful to Aristotle than either
Averroes or Avicenna, he combined in his doctrine
a large number of Neoplatonic elements drawn chiefly
from Plotinus and Proclus. The peculiarity of his
philosophical position lies in the fact that with the
emanationist theories of the Hellenistic thinkers, which
are predominantly intellectualistic in character, he
combined a voluntaristic conception of the development of the world-process.[2] From the supreme and
absolutely simple unity of the Godhead proceeds the
cosmic spirit, the first Intelligence which is composite,
being compounded of form and matter bound together

with the 'Mekor Chajim' of Soloman Jehuda ben Gebirol, was
discovered by Seyerlen and published by him in the *Tübinger
Theologische Jahrbücher*, nos. xv and xvi, 1856–7. See also Munk in
the *Literaturblatt des Orients* for 1845, no. 46, col. 721, and *Mélanges
de Philosophie juive et arabe* (Paris, 1857), pp. 159 sqq. A more
recent edition of this treatise is that of Cl. Bäumker (1913).

[1] Cf. W. Kahl, *Die Lehre vom Primat des Willens bei Augustinus,
Duns Scotus und Descartes*, p. 55 : ' Avicebron steht zur der arabisch-
jüdischen Scholastik in einem ähnlichen Verhältniss wie Duns Scotus
zum Thomismus. Er stellt sich dem Aristotelismus kritisch gegenüber
und nähert sich dem Neoplatonismus : aber er bricht der Philosophie
des Nous ihre intellektualistische Spitze ab und erhebt . . . den
Willen zum Prinzip der Weltschöpfung : so weist er auf Origines und
Eriugena zurück, und bereitet anderseits auf Duns Scotus vor.'

[2] Cf. Albertus Magnus, quoted by Kahl, op. cit. : ' Avicebron
autem in libro quem Fontem vitae vocari confinxit, solus inter omnes
principium primum per voluntatem agere dixit . . . quia in intellectuali natura omnium motor et determinator est voluntas ; facit
enim si vult et intelligit si vult : infinitum ergo cum sit primum
principium ad actum determinatur per voluntatem.'

by the divine will.[1] From this intelligence proceed
other intelligences in a descending hierarchy, themselves also composed of form and matter, and finally
the hylemorphic *composita* of the sublunary world.
The whole universe is thus a unity rooted in this
universal matter which is shared by all created beings
corporeal as well as spiritual, the multiplicity of
creatures being derived from the successive differentiation of this prime matter by a hierarchy of forms.[2]
The logical corollary of this cosmological doctrine is
a form of realism which posits a plurality of forms
in re, corresponding to the articulation of logical
concepts.[3] The influence of this theory on Scotus is
obvious. Though indeed he does not carry out Avicebron's conclusions to their full length, he too postulates
a grade of being in the objective world corresponding
to our generic and specific notions, a *formalitas a parte
rei*. In the same way, though he refuses to follow
Avicebron in his half-mystical cosmology, he borrows

---

[1] *Fons Vitae*, v. 31 : ' Ligans materiam et formam est *voluntas* quae
est superior illis quia unitio formae et materiae non est nisi ex im-
pressione unitatis in illis.' Bäumker reads *unitas*. But cf. v. 36.

[2] Albertus Magnus, *De Causa et Processu Univ.* I, tr. 4, cap. 8 :
' (Avicebron dixit) Prima forma intelligentia est, et prima materia
ea quae fundat et sustentat formam quae dicitur intelligentia ; et
quod forma nec ictu oculi fuerit unquam sine materia, vel materia
sine forma. . . . Secunda vero corporeitas, quae claudit materiae
primae capacitatem ; corporea enim materia est capax omnium.
Tertia vero dicit contrareitatem, quae est materia et forma elementorum, quia minoris est comprehensionis quam materia corporea,' etc.

[3] Thomas, *De Substantiis Separatis* : ' Avicebron dupliciter deceptus
esse videtur. Primo quidem quia existimat quod secundum intelligibilem compositionem, quae in rerum generibus invenitur, prout
scilicet genere et differentia constituitur species, esset in rebus compositis realis intelligenda, ut scilicet uniuscujusque rei in genere
existentis, genus sit materia differentia vero forma : secundo quia
existimavit quod esse in potentia vel esse substitutum, vel esse recipiens, secundum unam rationem in omnibus diceretur. Quibus
duabus positionibus innixus, quadam resolutoria via processit investi-
gando compositiones rerum usque ad intellectuales substantias.'

from him certain elements which he incorporates in his own teaching. The most important of these is his doctrine of *materia prima* and the hylemorphic composition of spiritual beings. Avicebron had argued that all beings which have subsistence fall under a common notion ; they must therefore possess a real subsistence common to all and each ; but this common element cannot be form, since it is by virtue of its form that an object possesses its determinate character and is differentiated from other objects. The common element must therefore be matter taken in its most general sense, *materia universalis*, of which corporeal and spiritual matter are two kinds or species. The doctrine of Scotus is very similar.[1] His *materia primo prima* corresponds to Avicebron's *materia universalis*, while the corporeal matter of the *Fons Vitae* represents Duns' *materia secundo prima*, which is the equivalent of Thomas' *materia quantitate signata*.[2] In a fashion also the voluntarism of the Jewish thinker may be said to resemble the voluntarism which was characteristic of the Franciscan School, but it is difficult to trace any real connexion between the two. Kahl indeed has tried to maintain that Scotus developed the doctrine of Avicebron in the same manner that Augustine supplemented and completed that of Origen,[3] but he is unable to bring any convincing evidence to bear on this point, and his conception of Scotus' theory of the will shows that he has failed to

---

[1] For an account of the relation of Duns Scotus to Avicebron see J. Guttmann, *Die Philosophie des Salomon ben Gebirol* (Göttingen, 1889), pp. 62 ff. ; *Die Scholastik des dreizehnten Jahrhunderts in den Beziehungen zum Judenthum und zur jüdischen Literatur* (Breslau, 1902), ch. vi.

[2] See below, vol. ii, ch. 3.

[3] Kahl, op. cit., p. 58 : ' Und wie nun Origines an Augustin einen Nachfolger fand der an die Mängel und Lücken seiner Willenslehre ergänzte, so hat Duns Scotus Avicebrons Auffassung in grossartiger Weise erweitert und zum Abschluss gebracht.'

realize the true implications of his teaching, for he ascribes to him an exaggerated form of indeterminism which is really quite foreign to him. The voluntarism of Duns and the Franciscan School generally draws its origin rather from Augustine and Anselm than from Avicebron.

Besides Avicebron, Scotus was also acquainted with the works of another Jewish thinker, Maimonides, whom he cites as the Rabbi Moyses, mentioning a treatise of his to whichhe gives the title *De Benedicto Deo*. The passage cited occurs in the second part of the *Guide of the Doubting*, and the Latin title used by Duns is derived probably from the benediction with which each of the three books opens.[1] The influence of Maimonides on the *Hochscholastik* of the thirteenth century is not unimportant. His main contribution to Christian thought was furnished by his attempt to reconcile the Aristotelian philosophy with the Jewish scriptures, and he may be regarded as the source of certain doctrines which characterize the Thomist teaching on these questions. Thus he maintains, for instance, the impossibility of giving a philosophical demonstration of a creation in time.[2] On Scotus his influence is less marked inasmuch as the Subtle Doctor adhered less closely to the doctrine of the Philosopher, but there are places in which it is yet discernible. Thus in the *De Rerum Principio*,[3] where Duns lays down the contrast between the simplicity of the divine essence and the composite nature of the creature, he cites the Rabbi Moyses as one of his authorities.

---

[1] J. Guttmann, ' Die Beziehung des Duns Scotus zum Judentum ' (*Monatsschrift für Geschichte und Wissenschaft des Judentums*, Breslau, 1894).

[2] Guttmann, *Die Verhältnis des Thomas von Aquino zum Judentum und zur jüdischen Literatur* (Göttingen, 1891), p. 63.

[3] *De Rerum Principio*, q. 7, n. 26.

In conclusion there are a few points in connexion
with Scotus's attitude towards Plato which it would
perhaps not be out of place to consider in this chapter.
In the seventh book of the *Quaestiones* on the *Metaphysics*, Duns expressly deprecates certain aspects
of the Aristotelian polemic against the Platonic ideas.[1]
The discussion is concerned with the part played by
the *formae separatae* in the generation of terrestrial
forms, and Averroes is cited as attempting to defend
Plato against his pupil. The *formae separatae* have, of
course, become identified with the *Intelligentiae* of
the Arabian cosmology, and through them with the
Angels of the Christian theology. Scotus remarks
that their influence on the terrestrial processes of
generation and decay has not been proven by the
Platonists, though he admits that the possibility of
such an influence has been demonstrated.[2] The
controversy round this point had evidently been a hot
one at Oxford, for among the doctrines censured by
Kilwardby in 1276 we find the following : ' Quod
intelligentiae creant vegetativam et sensitivam motu
caelesti mediante ', ' Quod cum intelligentia sit plena
formis imprimit illas in materia per corpora caelestia
tamquam per instrumenta.' The whole discussion
forms an excellent example of the strange perversion
of Platonism, a monstrous syncretism to which the
Middle Ages gave birth, and also of the weird and
anomalous mixture of cosmological doctrine prevalent
in the schools in the thirteenth century, in which
peripatetic, Neoplatonic, and Arabian and Jewish
theories are jumbled together in an almost incredible
confusion.

---

[1] The passage under discussion is Aristotle, *Metaph.* Z. 1033 b :
φανερὸν ἄρα ὅτι ἡ τῶν εἰδῶν αἰτία (ὡς εἰώθασί τινες λέγειν τὰ εἴδη) εἰ
ἔστιν ἄττα παρὰ τὰ καθ' ἕκαστα, πρός τε τὰς γενέσεις καὶ οὐσίας οὐδὲν
χρήσιμα, οὐδ' ἂν εἶεν διά γε ταῦτα οὐσίαι καθ' αὐτάς, κτλ.

[2] *Quaest. in Metaph.* VII, q. xi, nn. 4–5.

Scotus is not so convinced of the cogency of the Aristotelian argument as Thomas,[1] who interprets the *species separatae* differently from Averroes in a less fantastically un-Platonic fashion, while the author of the literal commentary contents himself with observing that the *formae separatae* are not necessary as agents in the generation of earthly substances, not being adapted to the explanation of generation as such.[2] But he expressly guards against any denial of the existence of the ideas in the divine mind as *universalia ante rem*. Nature, it is true, acts blindly when she reproduces things after their kind, but she acts under the direction of the divine intelligence in which exist the *rationes ideales* of all things, which are the things themselves *in esse cognito* as understood by the divine intelligence.[3] A similar insistence on the existence of ideas in the divine mind is found also in Aquinas.

---

[1] Thomas, *Comm. in Metaph.* VII, lect. 7 : ' Homo et animal non significant hanc materiam ex qua est generatio. . . . Si ergo compositum generatur, et non generatur ex hac materia per quam est aliquid, oportet quod id quod generatur non sit hoc aliquid. Et quum generatio sit simile generanti, oportet etiam quod generans sit hoc aliquid. Et ita non fit species universalis sine materia. Manifestum ergo est ex dictis quod si sunt aliquae species praeter singularia ; nihil sunt utiles ad generationes et substantias rerum ; sicut consueti sunt dicere quidam " specierum causa " ; id est ad hoc quod ponant species. Hoc enim erat una causa quare Platonici species ponebant, ut essent causa generationis in rebus. Si igitur species separatae non possunt esse causa generationis, manifestum erat, quod non erant species quaedam substantiae secundum se existentes.' But were not the Thomist angels pure forms ? If so, how do they differ from these *species separatae* ?

[2] *Comm. Lit. in Metaph.* I, summa 3, cap. 3, n. 90 sq. The text under discussion is *Metaph.* A. 991 a : πάντων δὲ μάλιστα διαπορήσειεν ἄν τις, τί ποτε συμβάλλεται τὰ εἴδη τοῖς ἀϊδίοις τῶν αἰσθητῶν, ἢ τοῖς γιγνομένοις καὶ τοῖς φθειρομένοις, οὔτε γὰρ κινήσεως οὔτε μεταβολῆς οὐδεμιᾶς ἐστιν αἴτια αὐτοῖς. . . . τὸ δὲ λέγειν παραδείγματα αὐτὰ εἶναι καὶ μετέχειν τούτων τἄλλα κενολογεῖν ἐστι καὶ μεταφορὰς λέγειν ποιητικάς.

[3] Scotus, loc. cit., n. 92 : ' Notandum quod illa ratio non destruit exemplaria sive ideas theologicas, quia in intellectu divino objective

Finally in the *Quodlibeta* Scotus sums up the controversy in almost exactly the same terms. Aristotle is justified in his polemic against Plato inasmuch as he proves that the ideas do not help to explain the processes of generation, for to explain these the concrete *compositum* is sufficient : Ἄνθρωπος ἄνθρωπον γεννᾷ. But we must not fall into the error of Averroes and deny the divine generation of the world. For the divine idea is not generative in the same sense as the Platonic was supposed to be. God working creatively on the plan of his ideas must not be equated as a cause on the same level as the forces of nature, for the supreme cause and the immediate cannot be classed in the same category.[1]

habent esse ; agens enim naturale, si intendit sibi simile generare, hoc est quia aliquod superius agens per intellectum ipsum determinat, dando sibi talem formam per quam possit, et intendit sibi simile generare. Natura enim licet agat propter finem, . . . non tamen cognoscit finem, sed dirigitur ad finem ab aliquo cognoscente : propter quod dicit Commentator . . . quod natura non agit nisi rememorata ex causis superioribus ; opus enim naturae est opus intelligentiae, qui est Deus omnia cognoscens. Sed rationes ideales sunt ipsae res positae in esse cognito et objectivo intellectui divino ; sed bene verum est quod pro univocatione generationis in istis inferioribus salvanda, non est necessarium ponere ideas Platonicas, sicut hic arguit Aristoteles.'

[1] *Quodl.*, q. vii, n. 25 : 'Aristoteles arguit contra Platonem probando quod ideae non sint necessariae ad generationem ; quia sufficit hoc aliquid ad generandum hoc aliquid ; sed nec ideae possent generare hoc aliquid, quia si generans non esset hoc aliquid, nec genitum erit hoc aliquid. Utraque consequentia satis tenet non esse genitum per ideam Platonis ; nec tamen extendenda est ad propositum nostrum, scilicet de Deo quia si idea generaret esset generans univocum, quia ejusdem speciei : non est autem aliqua causa univoca necessaria nisi compositum et materialis, sicut genitum est compositum et materiale. . . . Deus autem et potest esse causa generationis et requiritur ad generationem, non sicut causa univoca, sed aequivoca, et hoc suprema, in cujus virtute agit omnis alia causa.'

VII

FROM THOMAS TO SCOTUS

THE systematic incorporation of Arabian peripateticism with Christian speculation effected by
Albert and Thomas exercised an influence on medieval
thought as profound as it was immediate. In spite
of the vigorous opposition which it encountered both
at Paris and at Oxford, Thomism, in virtue of its
systematic coherence, reoriented, as it were, the entire
universe of scholastic thought. It became forthwith
the principal if not the unique 'system of reference'.
Not that it gave rise to a dogmatism of unimpeachable
orthodoxy which was henceforth promulgated as the
only official philosophic doctrine of the Christian
church—such a state of affairs could never have taken
place in the Middle Ages—but it developed a school
whose influence never waned and which succeeded
finally in monopolizing the attention of philosophic
Catholicism. Up to the time of the Reformation,
however, the older Augustinian tradition was able, at
least in part, to maintain itself against the newer
teaching. There were not wanting thinkers of considerable eminence who continued to propound a body
of doctrine which still contained elements characteristic
of the twelfth-century scholasticism combined with
much of the newer Aristotelianism. Foremost among
these was Duns Scotus, but he was by no means unique
in this respect, for he was preceded by a number of
independent teachers whose work must be considered
briefly in this chapter.

Among these the most profound and original was
Henry of Ghent, who taught at Paris during the last

quarter of the thirteenth century. His system in many respects resembles that of Scotus, and next to Thomas his theories occupy the largest share of Duns' polemical discussions. Hauréau,[1] indeed, has gone so far as to state that Scotus in his controversy with Thomas does little else than repeat at length Henry's arguments, a view which, as Prantl [2] recognizes, can scarcely be reconciled with the facts. Jourdain's [3] estimate in this connexion would seem to be more correct ; in spite of his undoubted ability his system was too divergent from the main current of scholastic thought to exercise any very marked influence on his successors. The main tendency of his thought, especially his theory of knowledge, shows decidedly Neoplatonic leanings [4] which, in spite of the many peripatetic elements, differentiate it from the Aristotelian tradition of the thirteenth and fourteenth centuries.

But in many respects he illustrates admirably the chief characteristics of the eclectic thinking which attempted to mediate between the older and the newer doctrines, a thinking which, as de Ruggiero has shown,[5]

[1] Hauréau, *Histoire de la Philosophie scolastique*, tom. 2, p. 276 : ' Duns Scot vint reprendre, commenter, l'une après l'autre les thèses du Docteur Solennel, et lui emprunter ses principaux arguments contre le péripatétisme ontologique de Saint Thomas.'

[2] Prantl, *Geschichte der Logik im Abendlande*, Bd. III, ch. 19, note 35, pp. 190-1.

[3] Cf. Ch. Jourdain, *La Philosophie de Saint Thomas*, tom. 2, p. 46 : ' Bien qu'il soit toujours cité avec honneur, et que son adversaire habituel Duns Scot, respect en lui, tout en combattent, une des lumières de la scolastique, il est un peu resté dans l'isolément.'

[4] M. de Wulf, in his *Histoire de la Philosophie médiévale* (Engl. trans.), p. 364, denies that Henry can rightly be called a Platonist ; but cf. Werner, 'Heinrich von Gent', etc. (*Denkschriften d. Kaiserlichen Akademie d. Wissenschaften*, Wien, vol. 28). Cf. also Huet, *Recherches historiques et critiques sur Henri de Gand*, p. 96.

[5] G. de Ruggiero, *Storia della Filosofia del Cristianesimo*, iii. 186 : ' Ma il pensatore in cui le varie contrastanti correnti dell' agostinismo

culminates in the system (and in spite of its somewhat
fragmentary nature it still remains one) of the Subtle
Doctor.

This spirit of compromise may very clearly be seen
in Henry's conception of the doctrine of form and
matter. Like Scotus, he refuses to regard matter with
Thomas and Avicenna as pure potentiality, and
endows it with a being of its own. The divine omnipotence could, if God had so willed, have brought it
into being independent of form.[1] Of itself, however,
it is in potency with respect to form, from which it
receives its actual existence.[2] On the other hand he
decides with Thomas against the hylemorphic composition of spiritual beings and maintains that the
human and angelic souls are pure forms. A similar
compromise is visible in his attitude to the question
of the plurality of forms. He maintains in agreement

scolastico, rinnovato dalla stessa antitesi col tomismo, hanno il loro
massimo potenziamento, è Duns Scoto.'

[1] *Quodl.* I, q. x: 'Est . . . in materia considerare triplex esse,
sc. esse simpliciter, et esse aliquid duplex. Unum quo est formarum
quaedam capacitas, aliud quo est compositi fulcimentum. Esse
primum quo materia habet dici ens simpliciter, habet participatione
quadam a Deo, in quantum per creationem est effectus ejus. . . . Esse
secundum, quo materia est capacitas quaedam, habet a sua natura
qua est id quod est differens a forma. . . . Esse tertium non habet
materia nisi per hoc, quod jam capit in se illud cujus de se capax
est. Unde et id quod capit dat ei tale esse. Et quia illud forma
est, quae non potest alteri dare nisi quod habet, esse igitur quod
habet forma ex natura essentiae suae per hoc, quod perficit potentiam et capacitatem communicat materiae et toti composito. Et
tale esse est illud quod materia habet in actu et per habet actualem
existentiam.'

[2] Cf. loc. cit.: '. . . materia differt a forma in composito, et
compositum non est ens nisi per formam, tunc compositum non
dicitur unum nisi quia forma sua est una. Bene verum est ergo quod
materia de se est in potentia ad actum, quem in composito nata est
recipere a forma. Tali enim esse materia de se est in pura potentia
et non est in actu nisi per formam.' Cf. also Zuccolius, *Comm. in
X Quaest. Quodl.*, Venet., 1613: 'Unde facile possemus concordare
divum Thomam cum Henrico et Scoto.'

with Thomas the unity of form in the case of inorganic bodies,[1] plants, and animals, but makes an exception of man, in whom he postulates, in common with Scotus, a plurality of forms, namely the intellectual soul, which is indeed the substantial form of the body, and also a *forma corporeitatis*, which is the *forma mixtionis*.[2] His doctrine differs from that of Scotus in that the latter posits a plurality of organic forms in the animal body [3] as well as distinguishing an *anima intellectiva* and a *forma corporeitatis*.

The logic and epistemology of Henry present several points of peculiar interest. While showing in certain respects marked similarity to Thomas and Scotus, he yet differs widely from both. His doctrine approximates far more closely to that of the earlier scholastics. While maintaining with both of the great friars the reality of the individual, he rejects the theory of cognition which both accept and alone among the thinkers of his generation denies the existence of the *species intelligibiles* and falls back on the Augustinian theory of ' innate ideas '. His doctrine has therefore

---

[1] Cf. *Quodl.* IV, q. xiii: 'Est autem positio ponentium gradus formarum in omnibus talis, sc. quod in qualibet re naturali et individuali sunt plures formae substantiales ordinem et colligantiam naturalem ad invicem habentes, et simul per suam substantiam existentes in eodem, quarum illa quae est ultima adveniens completiva est entis illius. . . . Dicimus igitur negando pluralitatem formarum re et natura differentium in rebus naturalibus a solo unico naturali productarum.'

[2] Cf. *Quodl.* III, q. xv: ' Ponendum est quod sicut materia in natura non est nata ex se subsistere omnino sine forma specifica, et nonnisi per illam in composito ; sic quantum est ordine naturae universi in dispositione divinae sapientiae, qua fines primorum connexi sunt principiis secundorum . . . nata est omnino illa forma educi de potentia materiae, nec habere esse naturae completum aut incompletum in sua essentia nec dare esse aliquod materiae, nisi simul cum anima rationali extrinsecus infusa, neque similiter ipsa anima sine illa nata est dare corpori esse, licet ipsa per se separata nata est habere esse incompletum.' Cf. also *Quodl.* IV, q. 13.

[3] Cf. Scotus, *Quaest. in Metaph.*, Lib. VII, q. xx.

been characterized by Werner as psychic sensism,[1] and is Platonic rather than Aristotelian in its general tendency. On the other hand his theory of the 'indifference' of the essence is, as Stökl points out,[2] an anticipation of the realistic aspect of the logic of Scotus, and can be traced back through Albertus Magnus to Arabian sources.[3] It forms a definite departure from the Thomistic doctrine in words rather than in fact. The essence, according to Henry's view, is of itself neither particular nor universal, but indifferent both to universality and particularity. It is only when it receives its *esse subsistentiae* in a determinate *suppositum* that it becomes particular ; and only when abstracted by the mind from this *suppositum* that it becomes in the strict sense universal.[4] The same

---

[1] See Werner's *Heinrich von Gent,* etc., *passim.*

[2] *Geschichte der Philosophie des Mittelalters,* Bd. II, p. 741 : ' Diese Auffassung des Allgemeinen weicht . . . von der thomistischen wesentlich ab. Wir werden derselben später bei Duns Scotus wieder begegnen. . . . Vorläufig genügt es davon Acht zu nehmen, dass Heinrich in der Lehre vom Allgemeinen in die Bahnen der Franziskanerschule eintritt, und als Vorläufer des Duns Scotus sich darstellt.'

[3] Cf. Albertus Magnus, *Metaph.* VI. 5 : ' Alio autem modo dicunt universale ante rem non tempore, sed substantia et ratione, et haec est forma aut causa formalis accepta constituens esse rei . . . hoc autem, cum indifferens sit in omnibus, quae sunt ejusdem speciei . . . sic indivisum habet unam ad omnia vel multa relationem,' etc. Cf. also Avicenna, *Log.,* fol. 12 r. A. : ' Animal autem in se est quoddam intellectum, quod sit animal, et secundum hoc, quod intelligitur esse animal, non est nisi animal tantum ; si autem praeter hoc intelligitur esse universale aut singulare aut aliquid aliud, jam intelligitur praeter hoc quoddam, sc. id quod est animal, quod accidit animalitati.' Scotus, as we shall see, gives this doctrine a quasi-realistic significance.

[4] *Quodl.* III, q. i : ' Sic autem essentia est indifferens ad universale et particulare, quod ex se nec est universalis nec particularis, sed solum habet rationem particularis in quantum recipit ab altero esse subsistentiae in supposito determinato. Esse vero universalis recipit in quantum per intellectum abstrahitur a suppositis, in quibus habet esse tanquam unum in multis, et iterum per praedicationem applicabile multis.'

theory in almost identical words is found in Scotus,[1] who gives it a slightly more realistic tinge by accentuating the ' real ' nature of the grade of being corresponding to the conceptual determinations of *genera, species,* &c.[2] The Thomistic view, though expressed in a more conceptualistic formula,[3] does not, as Minges has pointed out, differ from this in its essential meaning.[4] All three thinkers thus agree in maintaining the primary reality of the individual as well as the objective validity of the universal concept, and their differences are, broadly considered, of minor import, in many cases reducible to a mere terminological difference.

Henry rejects the Thomist distinction of the *esse* and the *essentia*.[5] The *esse* and the *essentia* cannot

---

[1] Cf. Scotus, *Quaest. de Anim.*, q. xvii, n. 14 : ' Universale accipitur aliquando pro intentione secunda quae consequitur operationem intellectus, qua intelligitur quidditas absolute . . . et isto modo est in intellectu tanquam aliquid factum per operationem intellectus. . . . Aliquando autem universale accipitur pro re subjecta intentioni secundae, i. e. pro quidditate rei absoluta, quae, quantum est de se nec est universalis nec singularis, sed de se est indifferens, et tale est objectum intellectus directum, non autem est in intellectu subjective sed tantum objective.'

[2] Cf. *Op. Ox.*, Lib. II, dist. 3, q. 1 : ' Aliqua est unitas in re realis absque omni operatione intellectus, minor unitate numerali sive unitate propria singularis.' Cf. also *Quaest. in Metaph.* VII, q. 13 : ' Intelligendum quod universale completum est, quod est in pluribus, non actu sed potentia propinqua ; tale nihil est nisi ex consideratione intellectus. . . . In Socrate enim non solum secundum considerationem intellectus, sed secundum ordinem naturalem perfectionum unitive contentarum, prius est animal quam homo, et homo quam hic homo . . . et homini secundum gradum proprium naturaliter priorem gradu singularitatis non repugnat in multis esse . . . sicut ergo commune est in natura et sua unitas . . . est illa. . . Cuicumque enim gradui reali entitatis correspondet realis unitas.'

[3] For this distinction, see *Summa Theol.*, Lib. I, q. 85, art. 2 ; *Comm. in Libr. Arist. de Anima*, II, lect. 12.

[4] ' Der angebliche excessive Realismus des Duns Scotus ', ch. 2 (*Beiträge z. Gesch. d. Philos. d. Mittelalt.*, 1908).

[5] *Quodl.* I, q. 9 : ' Et sic in quacumque creatura esse non est aliud re ab ipsa essentia . . . immo ipsa sua essentia, qua est id quod est, quaelibet creatura habet esse.'

differ (as Thomas had supposed) *realiter*, for we cannot maintain that a thing exists by virtue of something other than its essence.[1] Neither can we maintain that the *natura* and the *suppositum* are distinct : both are but two aspects of the same reality.[2] Yet we must distinguish between the essence, quiddity, or form, and the *suppositum* in so far as the one is the universal and the other the particular.[2] What, then, is the principle of individuation ? Henry refuses the Thomistic solution of *materia quantitate signata*, and proposes in its stead a pure negation,[3] the exact meaning of which is by no means easy to understand. He seems to be striving after something that he finds it difficult to express, and he succeeds rather in stating the problem than in solving it. But the trend of his thought is clear. He is working towards the doctrine of *haecceitas*, which forms the coping-stone of the

[1] Cf. Thomas, *Summa Theol.* I, q. 3, art. 4 ; *Summa contra Gent.* I. 22 : ' Esse actum quendam nominat ' ; ibid. II. 53 : ' Ipsum esse comparatur ad omnes substantias creatas sicut actus earum.'

[2] Cf. Henry, *Quodl.* IV, q. iv : ' Essentiae sive naturae est identitas secundum rem cum eo cujus est . . . quoniam solum modo differt secundum rationem significandi et intelligendi modo abstracto et concreto.'

[3] Op. cit. V, q. vii : ' Est igitur dicendum quod in formis specificis creatis . . . ratio individuationis ipsarum, qua determinantur in suppositis, et quae est ratio constitutiva suppositi, est negatio, qua forma ipsa, quae est ex se specifica in esse rationis, ut est terminus factionis, facta est indivisa omnino in supposito et individualis et singularis privatione omnis divisibilitatis per se et per accidens, et a quolibet alio divisa. . . . Quae quidem negatio non est simplex sed duplex, quia est removens ab intra omnem plurificabilitatem et diversitatem, et ab extra omnem identitatem, ut dicatur ita haec, quod tantum haec, non habendo sc. intra se possibilitatem ad esse aliud et aliud, sicut habet forma speciei, et iterum tantum haec, quod non sit aliqua alia suae speciei. Et haec duplex negatio omnino formaliter rationem formae determinat, qua determinatione supra essentiam formae constituitur suppositum absolutum, quod vere dicitur hoc aliquid, quasi tantum hoc et non aliud, nec intra se nec extra, et sic nullo modo aliud quid.'

Scotist logic. For in one aspect the *haecceitas* is barely more than a negation ; it adds nothing to the specific or formal determination of the individual ; it is the substrate of no accident. It is merely that which gives a thing its ultimate reality and makes it just this thing and not that, the principle of ' Besonderheit ', which distinguishes two individuals of the same natural kind.[1] Once more we find in Henry the connecting link between the Thomist and the Scotist systems.

Henry's theory of knowledge need not detain us long. His denial of the *species intelligibiles* severs his connexion with Scotus no less than with Thomas.[2] It is interesting to note, however, that his doctrine approximates more closely to the tradition of the Franciscan School, in many respects resembling that of Saint Bonaventura and Cardinal Matthew of Aquasparta.[3] Passing on to his psychological teaching, we find a marked deviation from the Thomist system.

---

[1] Cf. *Op. Ox.*, Lib. I, dist. iii, q. 6 : ' Et si quaeras : quae est ista entitas individualis, a qua sumitur differentia individualis ? Estne materia, vel forma vel compositum ? Respondeo ; omnis entitas quidditativa, sive partialis, sive totalis, alicujus generis est de se indifferens, ut entita quidditativa, ad hanc entitatem et illam, ita quod ut entitas quidditativa est naturaliter prior ista entitate ut haec, et ut prior est naturaliter, sicut non convenit sibi esse hanc, ita non repugnat sibi ex ratione sua suum oppositum. Et sicut compositum non includit suam entitatem, qua est hoc, inquantum natura, ita nec materia inquantum natura includit suam entitatem, qua est haec materia, nec forma inquantum natura includit suam ; ergo ista entitas non est materia vel forma nec compositum, inquantum quodlibet istorum, est natura, sed est ultima realitas entis, quod est materia, vel quod est forma, vel quod est compositum.' Cf. also *Rep. Par.*, Lib. II, dist. xii, q. 8. It is interesting to note that this doctrine of individuation appears later in Suarez ; cf. Suarez, *Metaph. Disput.*, tom. I, disp. v, sect. 6.

[2] For an account of Henry's theory of knowledge, see de Wulf, ' L'exemplarisme et la théorie de l'illumination spéciale dans la Philosophie de Henri de Gand ' (*Revue Néo-scolastique*, 1894).

[3] Vide supra, ch. v, pp. 194, sqq.

Henry denies Thomas's *distinctio realis* between the substance of the soul and its faculties. The essence of a thing, he tells us, is the principle of its activities ; there can therefore be no question of a real distinction. But he posits a conceptual difference, for we can distinguish different faculties in so far as we can distinguish several operations of the one substance.[1] Here again we see in an incomplete form the nucleus of the Scotist doctrine of the formal distinction. Scotus meets the problem by positing a *distinctio formalis a parte rei* ; he quotes Henry's theory with apparent approval, but criticizes it on the ground that by making the activity of the soul coincide with its substance it fails to distinguish between the mediate and immediate principles of activity, and so cannot maintain consistently the distinction between the will and the intellect, nor uphold the primacy of the former.[2] He then proceeds to formulate his own view ; the faculties are not 'essential parts' of the soul but rather, as it were, *passiones*, like the *passiones entis* (*bonum*, *verum*, and *unum*)—they are not the essence formally, but formally distinct both from this and from each other. On the other hand, like the divine attributes, they are 'unitively' contained in

---

[1] *Quodl.* III, q. xiv : 'Substantia animae, quae est una secundum rem, secundum diversa esse et secundum diversas determinationes sortitur rationes diversarum potentiarum, intellectivarum et sensitivarum ; cum in radice nihil sit potentia in eadem nisi simplex substantia, quae in se considerata, essentia sive substantia est et forma animati ; considerata vero secundum diversa esse per diversas determinationes et operationes ad diversas actiones et diversa objecta dicitur potentiae diversae, quae non ponunt supra essentiam ejus nisi solum respectum ad diversas actus speciei.' Cf. also Thomas, *Summa Theol.*, Lib. I, q. 77 : 'Respondeo dicendum, quod impossibile est dicere, quod essentia animae sit ejus potentia, licet hoc quidam posuere,' etc.

[2] *Op. Ox.* II, dist. xvi, q. unica : 'Non quaerimus hic de potentia prout dicit respectum ad actum, sed quaerimus de fundamento istius respectus,' etc.

the soul and identical with it. We must distinguish two moments : in the first we have the soul as such, in the second its operative nature or, to use an Aristotelian distinction, second entelechy, according to which it is capable of operating in this or that manner, and the faculties, which are the principles of these operations, are contained ' unitively ' in the essence.[1]

In his defence of voluntarism against the intellectualism of the Thomist school Henry appears as the immediate forerunner of Scotus.[2] Unlike Scotus, however, he emphasizes even more than Aquinas the passive nature of the intellectual processes in consequence of his Platonizing theory of intuition, and contrasts these with the active nature of volition.[3] The essence of freedom consists in the fact that the act of the will stands under no necessity of compulsion ; the will maintains itself indifferent to opposite objects and can decide freely to choose one or the other.[4] It is true that it is not free to choose the bad as such, but this in no wise derogates from its freedom,[5] for

---

[1] Loc. cit. : ' Sic ergo possumus accipere de intellectu et voluntate, quae non sunt partes essentiales animae, sed sunt unitive contenta in anima quasi passiones ejus, propter quas anima est operativa ; non quod sint essentia ejus formaliter, sed sunt formaliter distinctae, idem tamen identice et unitive, ut . . . probatum est de attributis divinis. Imaginandum est ergo, quod anima quasi in primo instanti naturae est natura talis ; in secundo instanti est operativa sive potens operari secundum hanc operationem vel illam, et potentiae, quae sunt principia istarum operationum ; continentur unitive in essentia.'

[2] Cf. Kahl, *Die Lehre vom Primat des Willens bei Augustinus, Duns Scotus, u. Descartes*, p. 65 : ' Fast gleichzeitig mit Thomas . . . erfuhr der Willens primat eine wissenschaftliche Begründung durch Heinrich von Gent. . . . Er ist der unmittelbare Vorläufer Duns Scotus, dem er in der Kritik der Thomistischen Willenslehre die Wege gewiesen hat.'   [3] Cf. *Summa Theol.*, art. xlv, q. 2.   [4] *Quodl.* III, q. xvii.

[5] Ibid. : ' Et licet voluntas . . . necessario feratur in bonum absolute, et ita non libere a determinatione, hoc non est contra rationem libertatis simpliciter, quoniam oppositum bono, sub ratione qua bonum, non est nisi malum. Quod autem voluntas non habeat se ad malum, in nullo derogat libertati, sicut patet in Deo et beatis.'

although the intellect always presents the object of
the will *sub specie boni*, the latter is free to choose the
less rather than the greater good.[1] It is thus rendered
independent of the intellect, even though the activity
of the latter is a requisite condition of its operation.[2]
As to the question of the priority of the will or the
intellect Henry, as we may expect, decides in favour
of the former. For the faculty whose *habitus* is the
higher will itself be the higher, and the *habitus* of
the intellect is wisdom, while that of the will is love,
which is the higher of the two activities.[3] Indeed love,
as it were, enters into its object and therefore the will
is united more perfectly to it than the intellect.[4]

The similarity of this doctrine to the teaching of
Scotus is most striking. It differs from it hardly more
than in verbal expression. It is only in the last citation
that we can detect the hint of a divergence. When it
comes to the conception of the nature of man's final

---

[1] *Quodl.* I, q. xvi: 'Dicendum est igitur absolute, quod bono et
meliore proposito, potest eligere minus bonum voluntas.'

[2] Cf. *Summa Theol.*, art. xlv, q. 2: 'In actu volendi . . . ipsa
voluntas se ipsa ex se ipsa elicit actum volendi, quo se quodammodo
facit in volitum et unit se volito. Etsi enim actus volendi necessario
praesupponit actum intelligendi, quia non movet se voluntas, vel—ut
magis proprie loquar, volens per voluntatem—nisi in bonum cognitum,
bonum tamen cognitum nullam impressionem aut motum facit in
voluntatem, sed voluntas in objectum ostensum se ipsa movet se ipsam,
ac si visus non perficeretur intus respiciendo, sed extra mittendo, prae-
sentato visibili ad rectam oppositionem.' Cf. also *Quodl.* I, q. xvi:
'Libertas ergo principaliter est ex parte voluntatis, ut, si velit, agat
per electionem, sequendo judicium rationis, vel contra ipsam sequendo
proprium appetitum. Ita quod advolendum nihil faciat simpliciter
ratio, nisi quod proponat volibilia. Licet ad volendum per electionem
necesse est praecedere rationis sententiam, quia aliter voluntatis
appetitus non esset electivus.'

[3] *Quodl.* I, q. xiv.

[4] *Quodl.* XIII, q. ii: 'Voluntas unitur fini per dilectionem, quia
ipsa subintrat finem, sese in ipsum quoad id quod est, quantum
possibile est, transformando. Et propterea voluntas perfectius unitur
fini et verius quam intellectus, quanto verius et perfectius est rei
uniri secundum se ipsam quam secundum speciem summa.'

beatitude Henry seems almost to abandon his activist notion of the will and to adopt a sort of mystic quietism. The state of beatitude consists not only in the act of the will and of the intellect but rather in the object itself, in the ingression of the divine essence into the beatified soul,[1] a conception quite foreign to Duns Scotus,[2] who criticizes it by remarking that such a state of beatitude would be consistent with unconsciousness. Henry's doctrine on this point bears quite plainly the trace of Neoplatonic influences, and is an example of a form of mysticism which from very early times found its expression in Christian thought. It may be noted, too, that his moral psychology is Platonist rather than Aristotelian. Thus in assigning the virtues to the various faculties he attributes faith to the intellect, hope to the irascible, and love to the concupiscible,[3] an arrangement strongly reminiscent of the ' Republic ', and widely divergent from the scheme both of Thomas and of Scotus, who are agreed in assigning both hope and love to the will.

So far we have been able to note a fundamental

---

[1] Cf. *Quodl.* XIII, q. xii : ' Dico quod vera beatitudo humana . . . consistit non solum in actu voluntatis et intellectus, in quibus non est nisi beatitudo creata ratione ipsorum actuum ; sed principalius consistit in ipso objecto quod est ipsa beatitudo increata, quae Deus est, inquantum est bonum voluntatis in qua, per actum beatitudinis voluntatis creatae ipsa anima humana mediante voluntate se transformat, ut convertatur in illud, prout possibile est secundum naturam . . . ut autem ex se exeat et incipiat esse quod amat, fieri non potest, nisi per circuminsessionem, non animae illabentis divinitati, sed potius e converso divinitatis illabentis in animam. . . . Circuminsessio autem sive illapsus talis fit potius in essentia animae . . . et deinde per derivationem etiam ipsa divinitas illabitur potentiis animae . . . cui jam illapsa est ut est substantia,' etc.

[2] Cf. Scotus, *Rep. Par.*, Lib. IV, dist. xlix, q. 1 : ' Illapsus prior est secundum naturam, quam operatio, quia illapsus est primo in essentia, et secundo in potentiis, sequitur operatio ; igitur sine contradictione primus actus . . . potest separari a secundo . . . et sic Michael beatus erit sicut dormiens, non sicut operans.'

[3] *Quodl.* VIII, q. 15.

agreement between the system of Henry and Scotus on the majority of the controversial issues raised by the Thomistic innovations. Indeed in his work on the philosophy of Christianity De Ruggiero has gone so far as to class Henry among the English School.[1] But so close an association is apt to be misleading. Great as was the influence of the Flemish Doctor on the thought of Scotus, we have only to examine and compare the natural theology of the two thinkers to see how profound the essential difference between them really is. No two lines of thought coexisting in the one general type of system, which may be called Scholasticism, could be more diverse than the speculative ontologism of the one and the almost positivistic empiricism of the other. Between them is a great gulf fixed, the gulf of a radical diversity of temperament. For, as we shall see, in spite of his voluntarism, it is in the contemplation of the eternal essences in the divine mind that Henry finds the fulfilment of his theological speculation, while to Scotus the whole basis of a speculative theology is abhorrent inasmuch as it seems to endanger his most fundamental thesis of the divine freedom, and like the old Hellenic mythology to set Necessity above Zeus himself.

The width of this divergence will be apparent when we examine the Scotist critique of the ideology of Henry and Thomas. All three doctors are agreed in maintaining the existence of the ideas as archetypes in the divine mind after which created things were formed, exemplary causes or *rationes fiendi rerum*.[2] It is only when they are regarded in addition as *rationes*

---

[1] *Storia della Filosofia del Cristianesimo*, vol. iii, p. 178, note 1 : ' Includiamo il dottore belga Enrico tra i maestri inglesi per l'affinità delle dottrine e per l' influsso da lui esercitato su Duns.'

[2] Cf. Thomas, *Summa Theol.* I, q. 15, art. 1 ; Henry, *Quodl.* VII, q. i ; Scotus, *Op. Ox.*, Lib. I, dist. xxxv, q. unica ; *Rep. Par.*, dist. xxxvi, q. 2, etc.

cognoscendi, grounds of the divine intelligence, that Scotus begins to raise objections. The obscure details of the controversy need not detain us here, but its main outline is of the highest importance to the understanding of the Scotist system. Both Henry and Thomas postulate the existence of *relationes rationis* eternally present in the divine mind, ideal relations or ' Erkenntnissgründe ' of the divine knowing,[1] as the form by means of which God knows created things. God knows himself immediately ; he only knows created things by knowing his own essence as imitable *ab extra,* and it is this knowledge which constitutes the eternal ideal relation between God and the creature.

Scotus criticizes this conception on the following grounds : In the first place these *relationes* are superfluous. They do not perform the function for which they were invented. They would need more *rationes* or ' Erkenntnisgründe ' to make them intelligible— and so *ad infinitum* [2]—the ' Third Man ' argument of the *Parmenides* of Plato.[3] In the second place the theory is not consistent with itself : for the *ratio* as the ground of knowledge must be prior to the act of knowing ; it is not the product of the knowledge, but is presupposed in it, and must therefore be regarded on this theory as a *relatio realis.*[4] Surely

---

[1] Thomas, loc. cit., art. 1 and 2 ; Henry, *Quodl.* V, q. 3 ; IX, q. 1.

[2] *Op. Ox.,* Lib. I, dist. xxxv, q. unica : ' Istae rationes sunt cognoscibiles ab intellectu divino, quaero qua ratione cognoscendi, si aliis rationibus, determinantibus essentiam ut est ratio, vel determinantibus essentiam, ut est primum objectum respectu objectorum secundorum, proceditur in infinitum, quia iterum ad istas alias rationes intelligendi praecedent aliae, et sic nunquam istae aliae rationes sunt intelligibiles a Deo, quia opportebit ipsum ante ipsas intellectas, intelligere alias infinities.'

[3] Cf. Plato, *Parmenides,* 132.

[4] *Op. Ox.,* Lib. I, dist. xxv, q. unica : ' Contra opinionem . . . videtur sequi quod istae rationes erunt reales, quia ratio intelligendi, ut est ratio, praecedit naturaliter intellectionem, et per consequens

determinism with a vengeance and heresy to boot!
(So at least Scotus would seem to imply.) But this
whole conception of the idea is a hysteron-proteron;
the ideal *rationes* or *relationes*, call them what you
will, are only the things as known, the products, not the
grounds of the divine knowing. They are not, therefore, *rationes cognoscendi* but only *fiendi*. God needs no
intermediate 'form' or *ratio*, but knows things directly
through his own essence.[1]

The same issue dominates another controversy
between Scotus and Henry. The latter had maintained
that the essences of created things existed *secundum
esse essentiae* in the divine mind from all eternity, for
the creature, in so far as it is known to God, eternally,
has indeed a real *esse essentiae*.[2] Scotus rejects this
theory on the grounds that it abolishes creation in
the true meaning of the word, and substitutes for
productio ad esse simpliciter a mere *productio ad esse
secundum quid*. The ideal being of mere thought is
not being proper, it is only a derivative and secondary
form of being, an *esse intentionale*, which is only an
esse secundum quid.[3] The controversy seems obscure and
to reduce itself to a purely verbal dispute, for Henry,
no less than Scotus, and in opposition to Thomas, had

quoad nihil, quod est ejus, ut est ratio intelligendi, causatur per
intellectionem, nec sequitur intellectionem. Si igitur sub relatione
rationis est ratio intelligendi lapidem, illa relationem producitur in
essentia per intellectionem lapidis, quia praecedit naturaliter illam
intellectionem; sed istam non praecedit nisi illa quae est essentiae,
ut essentia; hac autem non producitur, quod conceditur ab eis . . .
igitur ista relatio erit in essentia ut est ratio, et non per aliquam
actionem intellectus.'

[1] *Op. Ox.*, Lib. I, dist. xxv, q. unica: 'Etsi essentia ut cognita, sit
ratio deveniendi in notitiam lapidis, tamen videtur postea quod intellectus divinus possit cognoscere lapidem in se, et non praecise per hoc
quod comparat essentiam suam ad lapidem, quia sic sine tali comparatione alterius ad ipsum, possumus nos intelligere lapidem,' etc.

[2] *Quodl.* IX, q. i.

[3] *Op. Ox.*, Lib. I, dist. xxxvi, q. unica.

maintained the necessity of a creation in time.[1] Nevertheless it is significant because no less than the controversy over the ideal relations (and indeed it is the same problem) it represents an attempt to break away from the sterile and purely formal construction of the divine experience and to arrive at a deeper and more adequate conception of the creative activity of God.[2]

But it was within the Franciscan Order that the tradition was slowly ripening which was to bear its finest fruit in the philosophy of Duns. Already before 1290 the Augustinian opposition to the newer doctrine of Thomas was almost moribund in the Dominican schools, and the increasing rivalry between the two orders tended to sharpen the antagonism in the field of philosophical controversy. In the year 1284 the Minorite William Lamarre had written a *Correctorium fratris Thomae*,[3] in which he had attacked the whole Thomist theory of form and matter and attempted to point out its heretical consequences, foreshadowing in certain important respects the later polemic of Scotus. William maintained not only the hylemorphic composition of spiritual substances, which was characteristic also of the Scotist teaching, but also the doctrine of the plurality of forms in an extreme degree which was repudiated by the ' Subtle Doctor '.

---

[1] *Quodl.* I, q. vii.

[2] For a more detailed comparison of the ideology of Scotus with that of Henry and Thomas see below, vol. ii, ch. vi.

[3] The original manuscript of this work has not survived ; it has come down to us in the form of quotation in the *Defensorium* attributed to Aegidius Romanus, but probably the work of Johannes Parisiensis (Jean Quidort). Cf. Prantl, *Geschichte der Logik im Abendlande*, Bd. III, pp. 189 and 201, note 27. I cite, after Prantl, the Venice edition of 1516 (*Defensorium seu Correctorium fundamentarii doctoris Egidii Romani . . . in Corruptorium [sic] Angelici doctoris sancti Thomae . . . a quodam emulo depravatorum*, Venet., 1516, fol. ?).

For not only did he postulate a *forma corporeitatis* in addition to the intellectual soul; he even went so far as to break up the vital principle into three separate forms, a vegetative, a sensitive, and an intellectual, after the manner of Kilwardby,[1] a theory which Scotus rejects on the ground that it is contrary to the principle of economy.[2]   William likewise attacked the Thomist doctrine of individuation because of the difficulty it entailed with regard to the disembodied soul, a difficulty which bordered dangerously on the Averroistic heresy.[3]

It is in Richard of Middleton, the ' Doctor Solidus ', a Franciscan of the English school, who died at the close of the thirteenth century, that we shall find the immediate forerunner of Duns Scotus.   Erdmann[4]

---

[1] Cf. *Defensorium*, 1. 18 r. A: ' Haec positio de unitate formae substantialis reprobatur . . . primo, quod ex ipsa sequuntur plura contraria fidei Catholicae, secundo quia contradicit philosophiae. . . (B) . . . Si sola anima intellectiva immediate esset perfectio materiae primae, tunc in homine non esset forma animalis nec mixti. . . . Forma una et eadem numero dabit esse corporale et spirituale . . . . (18 v. A) Ponimus formam animae intellectivae prius perficere materiam suam spiritualem, et mediante hac materiam suam corporalem. . . . Sunt duae quae sunt incompletae, qui dant esse incompletum corpori humano, quod perficitur et completur adveniente anima rationali. . . . Vegetativa, sensitiva, et intellectiva sunt tres formae quae se habent secundum esse completum et incompletum, secundum potentiam et actum, convenientes quoad essentialem unitatem. . . . Pluralitas ergo formarum non est contra unitatem compositi essentialem, nisi sint tales quae non se habent secundum esse incompletum et completum.' For Kilwardby's doctrine see Denifle u. Ehrle, *Archiv für Literatur u. Kirchengeschichte*, etc., Bd. V, p. 627.

[2] Cf. Scotus, *Quaest. de Anima*, q. xi, art. 2.

[3] Cf. *Defensorium*, f. 54 r. B : ' Individuationem animae fieri per corpus, videtur esse falsum . . . quia sequitur ex hoc quod vel anima post separationem a corpore desinat esse, vel saltem quod post mortem hominum erit unus intellectus tantum vel anima . . . quod est error Averrois.' Vide supra, ch. v, p. 156.

[4] *Grundriss der Geschichte der Philosophie*, sect. 204 : ' Fast in allen Punkten, in welchen Duns Scotus dem Thomismus entgegentritt, erscheint Richard von Middelton als sein Vorgänger,' etc.

has emphasized, perhaps somewhat too strongly, the points of similarity between the two thinkers. While agreeing with him on many points Scotus rejects much that was characteristic in his doctrine, and it is almost impossible to designate any one individual as the true predecessor of the great master, so various and so diverse are the sources of his teaching. Richard studied at Oxford and Paris, and after spending many years abroad probably returned to Oxford, and died *circa* 1300, so that it may well be that he exercised a direct influence on the early training of his younger contemporary.

Like Roger Bacon, Richard places Theology among the practical sciences,[1] a classification which, as we have already noted in an earlier chapter, forms one of the principal characteristics of the Scotist philosophy. Nor is the motive for such an arrangement difficult to understand : the Franciscan School, more mystically inclined than the Dominican, laid greater emphasis on the affective aspect of theology, while its insistence on the primacy of the will, both in God and man, provided some defence for the synthesis between faith and reason which was daily becoming more imperilled, and gave to theology an autonomy which in the end proved fatal. The *credo ut intelligam* of Anselm forms the main guiding-thread of Franciscan theology, and Richard is only following out its inevitable consequences when he declares that theological belief is independent of philosophical argument.[2] There is also one other important respect in which he appears as a forerunner of the later terminist school. His rejection of the theory of *species intelligibiles* and his markedly conceptualist doctrine of universals place him rather among thinkers like Petrus Aureolus and

[1] *In Libros Sentt.*, Prol., q. 4.
[2] *In Sentent.*, Lib. III, dist. xxii, art. 5 : ' Fidei sacramentum philosophiis argumentis liberum est.'

Durandus than among the true School of Scotists. Indeed, though Scotus accepts in a modified form the theological consequences of Richard's voluntarism, his epistemology may be regarded as a reaction against the 'nominalistic' tendencies of his colleague.

Richard's theory of knowledge presents several points of great interest. His refusal to accept the intelligible *species* leads him to a position resembling Ockham on the one hand, and on the other, Locke. We do not know things immediately, but by a sort of inference from their properties proceeding from a knowledge of the accidental species, given in sense perception to the conclusion that these properties must be attributed to a subsisting being.[1] And it is from a comparison of the differences that we reach the distinction of one substance from another.[2] A knowledge of things therefore *in regulis aeternis* is impossible for man in his earthly condition, for the ideas are really identical with the divine essence, of which we can have no immediate intuition. In his account of the nature of universals Richard takes up a pronouncedly anti-realist position, criticizing the notion of the *universale in re*. The universal exists neither in nor apart from the particular ; nor can we assume a real unity, or identity of *species*, less than

[1] *In Sentent.*, Lib. II, dist. xxiv, art. 3, q. iii : 'Via naturae, et de lege communi non cognoscimus substantiam per propriam ejus speciem, sed per suas proprietates argumentando, eo quod in illis est aliqua similitudo subsistentiae ; non enim modo univoco. Per species enim accidentium, quae mediante sensu recipiuntur in intellectu, cognoscit intellectus intentionem entis dependentis. Et ex hoc argumentando concludit, quod illi enti natum est aliquod ens subsistere. Et tandem concludit illud ens esse per se subsistens.'

[2] Op. cit., ibid. : 'Postea ex illis proprietatibus ulterius venatur differentias substantiae, et tantum potest procedere, quantum potest ex illis proprietatibus elicere, et non plus naturaliter. . . . Unde et philosophicum venabantur differentias substantiarum, hoc faciebant ex comparatione substantiarum ad earum proprietates, et tantum descendebant, quantum per proprietates poterant manuduci.'

numerical unity, such as Scotus does actually postulate.[1]
Still, Richard's conceptualism is not of the thoroughgoing terminist type, and he retains vestiges of the
so-called 'moderate' realism, for he does not deny the
fundamentum in re or 'objective' basis of our universal
concepts.[2]

With regard to the question of the divine ideas
Richard takes up a position midway between that of

---

[1] Op. cit., Lib. II, dist. iii, art. 3, q. i : 'Dixerunt aliqui, quod
universale quorumcumque singularium est in reali existentia, non
separatum a singularibus in quolibet singulari, quod sub ipso continetur
existens indivisum. Unde universale hominum, cum unus homo corrumpitur, quia in aliis remanet totum . . . et cum aliquis homo generatur, universale homini non generatur, sed ille homo, universale, quod
in aliis erat salvatum, in se suscepit. Et hoc dicebant illud esse, quod
est proprium objectum intellectus et primum, et illud quo intelligitur
singulare per reflexionem (cf. Thomas, *Summa Theol.*, Lib. I, q. 86,
art. 1), quia enim est in singularibus, ideo per cognitionem ipsius
reflectitur intellectus ad singularium cognitionem. Et cum dicebatur
quod idem creatum non potest esse in pluribus suppositis indivisum,
dicebant hoc esse verum de identitate in numero, non de identitate
in specie (cf. Scotus, *Rep. Par.*, Lib. II, dist. xii, q. 8 ; *Op. Ox.*,
Lib. I, dist. ii, q. 7). Sed haec opinio falsa est, et improbabilis. . . .
Praeterea, aut ipsum universale esset de ratione cujuslibet singularis,
aut non. Si sic, tunc res creata simplex indivisa esset de ratione
plurium suppositorum ; quod est impossibile : solius enim divinae
essentiae proprium est quod sine multiplicatione sui sit tota de
ratione plurium. Si non, tunc ipsum universale realiter existere, ut
dicunt, esset inutile, quia non esset utile ad singularium existentiam,
cum esset aliquid extra essentiam eorum, nec ad eorum cognitionem,
cum non esset de ratione eorum.'

[2] Cf. ibid. : 'Dico ergo quod ipsum universale duo complectitur,
sc. id quod est universale, ut ipsum hominis vel angeli essentiam, ut
intellectam praeter unitatem et multitudinem numeralem, et ipsam
universalitatem, quae est praedicabilis de pluribus. Sed neutro modo
est in reali existentia angelus universalis, nec quaecumque res alia,
quia ipsa universalitas est res constituta ratione, et dicitur secunda
intentio.' Cf. Thomas, *De Actu et Potentia*, q. vii, art. 6 : 'Nihil est in
rebus quae sunt extra animam, cujus similitudo sit ratio generis vel
speciei. Nec tamen intellectus es falsus, quia, ea quorum sunt istae
rationes, sc. genus et species, non attribuit rebus secundum quod sunt
extra animam, sed solum secundum quod sunt in intellectu.'

Henry and that of Scotus. He concedes the dual aspect of the ideas as *exemplars* or *rationes factionis* as well as *rationes cognitionis*.[1] These exist *ab eterno* in the mind of God.[2] On the other hand, he somewhat paradoxically agrees with Scotus in maintaining that though the essences of created things are known eternally to the divine intelligence, they have not existed *ab eterno*.[3]

In dealing with the problem of creation Richard maintains, in common with Henry and Scotus as against Thomas, that creation *ab eterno* is an impossibility, and he carefully distinguishes creation from the act of conversation *in esse*. To say that God could have created the machinery of the world from all eternity is to say that he is capable of committing a contradiction, which is absurd.[4]

Richard's psychology is distinctly Augustinian in character. He holds, like Lamarre and Kilwardby, the doctrine of the plurality of substantial forms in the human being. These forms are disposed hierarchically; thus the lowest, the *forma corporeitatis*, only gives the body an incomplete and imperfect sort of

---

[1] *In Sentent.*, Lib. II, dist. xxxvi, art. ii, q. ii.

[2] Loc. cit., q. iii: 'Restat ergo quod pluralitas idearum in divino intellectu attenditur secundum diversas relationes rationis divinae essentiae, quae est forma divina intellectus ad diversas creaturas; et quia relatio rationis non consequitur rem nisi inquantum est intellecta, ideo dico quod pluralitas idearum est in Deo per hoc, quod Divinus intellectus intelligit essentiam suam ut diversarum creaturarum repraesentativam, et ut ab eis imitabilem, quamvis autem ab eterno non fuerit creatura in esse reali, neque una neque plures, tamen ab eterno fuerunt per divinam essentiam a divino intellectu intellectam repraesentatae creaturae divino intellectui et ab eterno fuerunt in divina essentia plures rationes secundum rationem ad diversas creaturas non realiter existentes, sed divino intellectui repraesentatas.'

[3] Cf. op. cit., Lib. I, dist. xix, q. iii: 'Sicut essentiae omnium naturarum ab eterno fuerunt intellectae a divino intellectu, quamvis ab eterno non fuerunt; ita veritates, quamvis ab eterno nonf uerunt tamen ab eterno non fuerunt in intellectu.'

[4] Op. cit., Lib. II, dist. I, art. 3, q. iv.

being : hence the corruption of the flesh begins at the moment of death. The body so informed stands as *materia proxima* to the soul, which is also composite, being made up of substantial parts, the vegetative, sensitive, and intellectual, and is only first perfected by it.[1] His doctrine of the will is much influenced by Anselm, like that of Scotus, which it closely resembles. For though a voluntarist, Richard does not defend a purely arbitrary and motiveless volition. The will is moved by four causes. By God, as the prime cause of all things, by the intellect inasmuch as it presents the object to the will and disposes it to the volitional act, by the object itself in so far as it evokes in the will a tendency towards it, and by sensual desire, in that it also inclines the will to a sensual good. But sensual desire does not necessitate the will, nor does the intellect determine it ; for in the last resort the will moves itself by determining itself to action and eliciting its own act. All other influences remain inoperative unless and until the will moves itself ; it may therefore be said to be an *instrumentum se movens*.[2]

Before we close this chapter there is one more thinker whose relation to Scotus remains still to be considered, namely Aegidius Romanus (Egidio della Colonna), the Augustinian hermit who taught at Paris during the last quarter of the thirteenth century. A pupil, according to William of Tocco, of Thomas Aquinas, he founded a school of numerous disciples and was proclaimed doctor of his order, which preserved the general outline of his teaching until the decaying body of scholasticism finally dissolved before the advent of the new learning. His teaching forms still another example of a ' mixed system ' in which Thomist and Augustinian doctrines are found side by side in a somewhat confusing juxtaposition. His logic and

[1] *In Sentt.*, Lib. II, dist. xvii, art. 1, qq. iii–v.
[2] Cf. *Quodl.* I, q. xvi.

metaphysic are decidedly Thomist, while his psychology inclines to Augustinianism. Though there is scarcely any trace of his influence to be found in Scotus, there are certain points in his doctrine which render a comparison between the two doctors not uninstructive.

Like Thomas, Aegidius posits a sharp distinction between essence and existence; the latter is an actuality impressed by God on all beings and must be separated from the essence, which stands to it in the relation of potency to act. Should we fail to observe this distinction we should be unable to maintain the doctrine of creation,[1] for all creatures would be as much 'necessary' beings as God, in whom alone essence and existence are identical. We have already seen the function which this distinction performs in the Thomist system,[2] where the potentiality implied in the composition of *esse* and *essentia* is the characteristic of creaturehood. The necessity for such a differentiation springs from the conception of form and matter common both to Aegidius and to Thomas and reveals itself most plainly in the doctrine of the latter that spiritual beings are *substantiae separatae*, or pure forms. This distinction between essence and existence finds a place no less prominent in the Scotist system, but it was effected in a widely different manner. For Scotus this principle of creaturehood is matter,

---

[1] *Quodl.* I, q. vii : ' Esse ergo nihil est aliud quam quaedam actualitas impressa omnibus entibus ab ipso Deo, vel a primo ente ; nulla enim essentia creaturae est tantae actualitatis, quod possit actu existere, nisi ei imprimeretur actualitas quaedam, et illa actualitas impressa vocatur esse. . . . Ex hoc etiam patere potest quomodo creatio sit rerum. Nam si essent res simplices, et non esset ibi compositio inter essentiam et esse, non video quomodo creari possent. Sicut enim non generatur per se nec materia nec forma, sed compositum ; sic nec creatur essentia per se separata ab esse, nec creatur esse separata ab essentia ; sed creatur totum compositum ex essentia et esse.'

[2] Vide supra, ch. v., p. 151.

materia primo prima, whereas that of concrete existence
is the *ultima realitas entis* or *haecceitas*, a view which
Aegidius implicitly repudiates.[1] For his theory of
the nature of form and matter agrees in its main essentials with that of Thomas. He accepts his doctrine of
individuation,[2] regards matter as pure potency,[3] and
controverts the notion of a plurality of substantial
forms.[4]

In his teaching on the nature of the universals
Aegidius, like Richard of Middleton, develops the
conceptualistic side of the Thomistic doctrine. He
rejects both the ' Platonic ' and the ' Aristotelian '
views and propounds a theory of his own which bears
a striking resemblance to the solution of Roger Bacon.
The concept which exists in the mind, the *species
abstracta*, is called a universal because it refers to
a plurality of individuals, not because it is predicated

---

[1] Cf. Werner, *Die Scholastik des späteren Mittelalters*, Bd. III :
' Der Augustinismus des späteren Mittelalters ', p. 75 : ' Wenn es
den Anschein hat als ob Aegidius durch sein Dringen auf die reale
Auseinanderhaltung von esse und Essenz sich der scotistischen Anschauung von der Zusammengesetztheit alles Geschaffenen aus
Materie und Form einigermassen nähere, so scheidet er unmittelbar
durch die Art und Weise ab, in welcher er die Seynseinheit eines
jeglichen Geschaffenen begründet.' Werner cites in support of this
statement *De Ente et Essentia*, q. x : ' Esse quantum est de se, dicit
summam actualitatem possibilem reperiri in entibus ; talia enim
non possunt in eodem plurificari, quia tunc illa haberent per se ordinem
ad invicem, et unum de se esset possibile respectu alterius, et quia
esset tale non esset esse, sed esset forma. Et ideo, sicut in eodem non reperiuntur plures albedines, quia tunc unus esse perfectio alterius, quod
non patitur ratio albi . . . sic, nec in eodem esse poterunt plura esse,
quia unum perficeretur per aliud, quod non patitur ratio ipsius esse.'

[2] *Quodl.* I, q. 11 : ' Hoc ergo modo fit individuatio ; quia materia
habet esse extensum per quantitatem, et in diversis partibus materiae
recipiuntur diversae formae ; forma dividitur, et divisa individuatur
per materiam extensam. Sed cum extensio per quantitatem fiat,
ad quantitatem est recurrendum, cum loqui volumus de individuatione
corporum.'

[3] Op. cit. II, qq. xii–xiii.

[4] Cf. *Quaestiones de Ente et Essentia*, q. x.

of this plurality, but because it is that in which the individuals are similar.[1] Moreover he refutes in advance, as it were, the ' indifference ' theory of Scotus by maintaining that the *esse essentiae* is merely an *esse rationis* existing only in the consideration of the mind. Thus both the *esse universalitatis* and the *esse essentiae* are *entia rationis,* the one being the object of the first, the other of the second ' intention '.[2] He thus undermines the whole Scotist position by denying the objective reality of the universal, which the realistic side of Duns' teaching attempted to preserve. The *universale in re* has vanished, leaving the *universale in intellectu* to maintain as best it may a precarious hold, by what means we know not, on the objectivity of the external world.

[1] *In Libr. Sentt.* I, dist. xix, q. 1, art. i : ' De universali sunt diversi modi dicendi. Nam Plato posuit universalia esse abstracta ; volebat enim de omnibus rebus esse multa per participationem et unum per essentiam. . . . Alia positio universalis erat Aristotelis, qui voluit quod universale est id quod praedicatur de rebus, nec proprie est substantia, eo quod est commune multis, nec habens proprium esse nec per se esse ; hoc autem universale nec est quid reale solum, nec quid rationis solum, sed quantum ad esse materiale, est quid reale, et est in particularibus, esse tamen formale recipit ab anima. . . . Isti autem duplici modo universalis superadditur modus tertius, sc. quod species, quae est in intellectu abstracta, dicitur universale, eo quod habet respectum ad plura, non quia de pluribus praedicatur, sed quia pluribus est similis.' For Bacon's view see above, ch. iv, pp. 127 sqq.

[2] *Quodl.* II, q. vi : ' Res considerata secundum esse essentiae, habet esse rationis, et intellectus est ille qui fertur in ipsam essentiam secundum se ; et ipsa essentia creata secundum se non habet esse, sed solum habet considerationem apud intellectum. Unde esse essentiae, prout est aliud ab esse naturae, est esse secundum intellectum, et esse essentiae non differt ab esse universalitatis, quasi unum sit esse rationis et non aliud, ut isti videntur dicere dum volunt quod res ut habet esse particulare, habeat esse naturae, ut vero habet esse essentiae, habeat esse quod nec sit esse naturae nec esse rationis. Utrumque enim, tam esse universalitatis quam esse essentiae, est esse rationis ; sed esse essentiae est esse rationis tanquam intentionis primae, esse universale est rationis tanquam intentionis secundae.'

The psychology of Aegidius, like that of Duns, contains many Augustinian elements ; he attempts, as Scotus likewise did, to recognize the older psychological classification of the faculties of the soul, *memoria, intellectus, voluntas*, with the Aristotelian theory of knowledge, an attempt which led him into many inconsistencies.[1] In his doctrine of the will he compromises between the psychological determinism of Thomas and the voluntarism of the Franciscan School, and his theory is full of ambiguities. Freedom is founded *radicaliter et primordialiter* in the immateriality of the soul, *ex proximo* in the intellect which presents the will with its object, and *formaliter* in the will, through which a man determines himself to one or the other of two alternatives.[2] Aegidius thus far follows the Thomistic doctrine fairly closely, but he agrees with Scotus in conceiving the essential feature of beatitude to lie in the satisfaction of the will rather than that of the intellect, even though he interprets it with Thomas as consisting in the *visio Dei*.[3]

[1] See Werner, op. cit., pp. 130 f.

[2] *Quodl.* IV, q. xxi.

[3] Ibid., q. xviii : 'Visio ergo potest esse beatitudo . . . non quia est aliquid intellectus, nec quia est ad intellectum pertinens, sed quia est objectum voluntatis. Unde dato quod non esset ibi actus intellectus, et esset objectum voluntatis finale, esset ibi beatitudo. Sic etiam, si ab hujusmodi visione . . . tolleretur quod esset finis voluntatis, quantumcumque esset intellectus, nullo modo esset ibi beatitudo.'

VIII

THE SIGNIFICANCE OF SCOTUS FOR MEDIEVAL THOUGHT

IT is the common fate of all distinguished philosophers to be compressed eventually into a few paragraphs in the histories of philosophy : such is the strange guerdon of their last and grandest immortality. But in this process of abbreviation a 'system', like other organic structures, is liable to suffer loss of coherence, and the greater the subtlety of the thinker the more exquisite is the torture and the more outrageous the distortion. But of all those who have been subjected to this epitome none have suffered more severely than Duns Scotus. He has been seized upon by the devouring chroniclers of thought, who have indeed condensed him, but unfortunately without that due regard for symmetry which the poet has so carefully prescribed. Nor is the reason for this inadequate treatment very far to seek. The voluminous character of his works renders a first-hand acquaintance with them almost impossible except for the specialist, while the extreme subtlety of his criticism, which is for ever balancing upon a razor-edge of distinction poised between two conflicting opinions, make anything but a detailed exposition of his doctrine liable to end in a gross misrepresentation. It is as if we were to attempt to reproduce a delicate and complicated architectural design with a camera whose picture is no larger than a postage stamp. Moreover, his own theories are dispersed over a maze of myriad syllogisms, scattered piecemeal over the thousands of his pages, and the fragments when collected have to be sorted out and fitted together like the pieces of some ingenious puzzle.

We need not, therefore, feel much surprise if we find that the most opposite extremes of doctrine have been placed to the credit of Duns by the various writers who have attempted to summarize his thought. Thus, to take what perhaps forms the most remarkable example, his logical and metaphysical teaching has been accused of the most divergent tendencies, varying from pantheism and extreme realism on the one hand to that bogy of the historian of scholastic philosophy, nominalism, on the other. Even scholars so eminent as Hauréau and Stöckl have not succeeded in avoiding a one-sided presentation of his teaching which, to say the least of it, is highly misleading. Thus while Bayle,[1] Hauréau,[2] Kleutgen,[3] and Mausbach,[4] all regard the doctrine of *materia prima* and the *universalia a parte rei* as an anticipation of the monistic doctrine of Spinoza, and Stöckl [5] also detects in him a tendency towards pantheism, Prantl,[6] Schwane,[7] and Erdmann [8] agree in perceiving in him the seeds of nominalism. Willmann,[9] moreover, would accuse him of both tendencies ; in his opinion the doctrine of the *formalitates* paves the way for the Cartesian theory of extended substance, which forms the starting-point of Spinoza's pantheism ; while the denial of the *intelligibilia* of the Thomists and the assertion of the primacy of the will in God form the two main

---

[1] *Dictionnaire historique et critique*, vide sub verbo ' Abélard '
[2] *Histoire de la Philosophie scolastique*, tom. II, 2, ch. xxii.
[3] *Philosophie der Vorzeit*, vol. i, p. 297.
[4] Wetzer und Welte, *Kirchenlexicon* (2nd ed.), vol. ix, column 1704, art. ' Thomismus und Skotismus '.
[5] *Geschichte der Philosophie des Mittelalters*, vol. ii, pp. 796 sqq.
[6] *Geschichte der Logik im Abendlande*, vol. iii, ch. xix, pp. 203–32.
[7] *Dogmengeschichte der Mittleren Zeit*, p. 80.
[8] *Grundriss der Geschichte der Philosophie*, pp. 214–16.
[9] *Geschichte des Idealismus*, vol. ii, pp. 512 ff.

pillars of the nominalism of the fourteenth century. Willmann concedes, however, that the actual teaching of Scotus himself was realistic in its tendency, but he insists that it was a realism less sheltered from attack than that of Thomas Aquinas.

So, too, with regard to the primacy of the will over the intellect, both in the human and in the divine spirit, the Scotist teaching has almost universally been misrepresented, and an extreme form of indeterminism attributed to Duns which is in fact quite foreign to his actual doctrine. How false and misleading the general conceptions of Scotus' system which these historians of scholastic thought have formed really turn out to be, on closer examination, has been admirably demonstrated by the works of Dr. Parthenius Minges,[1] who stands almost alone in his refusal to exaggerate the divergences of the Thomist and the Scotist doctrines.

Indeed it may readily be conceded that the estimation of Duns Scotus' doctrine presents peculiar difficulties. Not only is his style obscure, redundant, and verbose, and his argument complicated and involved,[2] but his doctrine is also sporadically distributed over a vast mass of commentary and polemic in such a way that it is often necessary to balance and weigh against one another small fragments often only containing a few sentences, gathered together from a large number of separate *quaestiones*, in order to arrive at a judgement as to what his own teaching is

---

[1] I refer especially to four dissertations : *Ist Duns Scotus Indeterminist?* ; *Der angebliche Excessive Realismus des Duns Scotus* ; *Das Verhältnis zwischen Glauben und Wissen, u.s.w. bei Duns Scotus* ; and *Der Gottesbegriff des Duns Scotus*, etc.

[2] Cf. the judgement of his commentator and editor, Maurice O'Fihely (Mauritius a Portu, Mauritius Hibernicus), Archbishop of Tuam : 'Sensa ipsa brevia sunt et occulta, et quibus nisi totus adsis hallucineris.' 'Pertransibis lento passu illud chaos metaphysicale Scoticum.'

on any particular topic. Moreover, his distinctions are so subtle and his terminology is so abstract that it is often nearly impossible to discover what he really means, so precariously does he balance himself between contrary opinions and so unscrupulously does he employ the sharp and brittle weapons of syllogistic combat. And, though his style of argument differs only in degree of complexity from that of his contemporaries, the abstract verbalism imposed by the syllogistic form, combined with the over-subtlety of his terminology, render him, if not the most difficult, yet without doubt the most irritating of the medieval schoolmen.[1]

Yet in spite of all these defects, which constitute so serious an obstacle to the study of his works, Duns Scotus is the most powerful and interesting thinker of his age. Less systematic than Thomas, he is perhaps for that very reason less confined in his outlook, and his capacity for criticism is far more acute and penetrating. It is in him, rather than in the Angelic Doctor, that the scholastic philosophy reaches the highest point of its development. Notwithstanding the fact that he never left behind him a finished and well-rounded system like that of Thomas, he shows a wider range of thought and a greater degree of consistency, and above all a far deeper appreciation of the philosophical needs of Catholic Christianity, than his more famous rival. Almost alone among the historians of medieval thought Prantl has realized his merits, and his judgement is worth quoting in full.

[1] Prantl, op. cit., ch. xix, p. 202 : ' Anziehende Reize als Schriftsteller besitzt er wahrlich nicht, denn seine Methode besteht bis zur Ermüdung des Lesers darin, dass er unablässig bei jeder Frage oder jeder Thesis mit *Videtur quod non* die möglichen Gegengründe (zuweilen wirklich mit haarsträubender Spitzfindigkeit) aufstöbert, sodann unter *in oppositum* die Gegengründe der Gegengründe und die positiven Gründe vorführt, und hierauf zuletzt die *solutio* darbietet, und zwar meist mit detaillirter Rückbeziehung auf die Gründe und Gegengründe.' See also Taylor, *The Medieval Mind*, vol. ii, p. 513.

After speaking of the difficulties of his style, in the passage quoted in the last foot-note, he continues : ' Aber hinter dieser struppigen Form steht ein Denken, welches, soweit diess im Mittelalter überhaupt möglich war, wenigstens weiss was es will und auf Grundlage der damaligen allgemeinen Anschauungen die Trag- weite der Begriffe durchmisst, und diess ist im Ver- gleiche mit der Bornirtheit eines Albert und eines Thomas jedenfalls für den Leser wohlthuend.'[1]

The traditional view that Scotus marks a decline from the perfect equilibrium of the Thomist system is quite unjustified by the facts. The discord between faith and reason, on which such stress has been laid, is more apparent than real, as we have already noted. There is nothing in the actual teaching of Scotus which can be regarded as the necessary prelude to the so-called scepticism of the ' Terminists '—a scepticism which has been widely misunderstood. The gap between faith and reason was from the very first implicit in the Thomist system and widened necessarily with a critical advance. And if the chasm begins to become more apparent in Scotus it is because Duns' criticism is more subtle and more penetrating than that of Thomas, and his thought, for all its abstractness, more comprehensive. His polemic against the speculative theology of Aquinas springs not so much from a fainter belief in the validity of reason as from a revolt against the over-emphasis laid by Thomas on the cosmo- logical conception of form and from a desire to grasp more deeply the infinite activity of the Divine Being.

It would be a profound mistake therefore to give too much weight to the comparison between Scotus and Kant which Ueberweg makes in his *History of Philosophy*, where he maintains that

' The relation of Duns Scotus to Thomas of Aquino was

---

[1] Prantl, op. cit., p. 202.

similar to that of Kant to Leibnitz. Thomas and Leibnitz
were both dogmatists ; Duns Scotus and Kant were critics
who disputed more or less the arguments for the theorems of
natural theology . . . but did not deny the theorems themselves ;
both founded the convictions for which the theoretical reason
no longer furnished them with proofs on the moral will, to
which they assigned priority over the theoretical reason. A
fundamental difference is indeed to be found in the circumstance
that for Duns Scotus the authority of the Catholic Church,
for Kant that of the moral reason, is the final court of
appeal ; and in the further circumstance that Kant's critique
is radical and universal, while that of Scotus is only partial.
But as Scotus to the doctrines of the Church, so Kant to
the convictions of the universal religious consciousness ever
maintains the positive relation of one who assents to them in
that particular sense in which that consciousness understands
them.' [1]

[1] *A History of Philosophy from Thales to the Present Time*, translated
by G. S. Morris, 4th ed., London, 1885, vol. i, p. 454. Cf. Willmann,
Gesch. des Idealismus, ii, pp. 516 ff.
In Baumgartner's edition of Ueberweg's *Grundriss der Geschichte
der Philosophie der patristischen und scholastischen Zeit* (Berlin, 1915),
p. 577, this judgement is considerably modified : ' Mit Recht kann
man sagen Duns Scotus verhält sich zu Thomas von Aquino ähnlich
wie Kant zu Leibniz. Thomas und Leibniz sind Dogmatisten ; Duns
Scotus und Kant sind Kritiker. Ihre Tendenz geht in erster Linie
dahin, die überkommenden Behauptungen und Beweise auf ihre
Stichhaltigkeit zu prüfen und ihre Mängel und Schwächen aufzu-
decken.
' Bis zu diesem Punkte ist die Parallele zwischen Duns Scotus und
Kant zweifellos richtig und höchst interessant. Sie würde aber schief
und direkt falsch werden, wenn man sie weiter führen und Scotus
im Sinne Kants des Skeptizismus gegenüber den Gottesbeweisen und
der Metaphysik überhaupt zeihen würde, oder wenn man bei Scotus
wie bei Kant einen Primat der praktischen Vernunft gegenüber der
theoretischen finden wollte, als ob bei ihm die metaphysischen
Ueberzeugungen, da für sie die theoretische Vernunft keine Beweise
mehr liefern könne, auf dem sittlichen Willen als Postulate der praktischen Vernunft basiert wären.
' Tatsächlich spricht Scotus zwar von einem Primat des Willens.
Derselbe hat aber nichts gemeinsam mit dem Primat der praktischen
Vernunft bei Kant. Die Bedeutung des Willensprimats bei Scotus
liegt auf dem gebiet der Psychologie, der Theologie, und der Ethik,
aber nicht auf dem der Erkenntnistheorie. Auch der Umstand dass

No account of the teaching of Scotus could be more dangerously misleading. Scotus is, philosophically speaking, a dogmatic realist no less than Thomas; [1] indeed his realism is even more pronounced, and his theory of the *universale a parte rei* forms the culminating point of the dogmatism of the Middle Ages. Nor does he found his natural theology on the postulates of the moral will—such a notion is quite foreign to the scholastic mind. Like Thomas, he recognizes a double source of truth, the data of reason, the mediation of sense cognition through the activity of the *intellectus agens*, and the supernatural revelation handed down in the sacred scriptures and the teaching of the Church. The Kantian conception of the practical reason is something wholly different, and any parallelism drawn between it and the Scotist notion of *scientia practica* is wholly illusory. The rationalism and the criticism of the critique differs radically from the rationalism

Scotus die Theologie eine praktische Wissenschaft nennt, hat mit kantischen Gedankengängen nichts zu tun. . . . Scotus ist nicht Skeptiker. Den Gottesbeweisen und der Metaphysik ist er nicht skeptisch gegenüber gestanden wie Kant.'

[1] Cf. the article (unsigned) in the *Enciclopedia universal illustrada Europeo-Americana*, s.v. 'Escoto': 'No falta quien haya querido ver una cierta semejanza entre Escoto y Kant por el carácter critico de la filosofía del primero; pero como notan algunos autores si Escoto tiene algo de Kant es solamente en cuanto sus críticas no alcanzan mas allá de los usos de la razón teórica, jamás sobre el valor del uso de esa misma razón. Además, Escoto es un verdadero dogmatista mientras Kant fué el demoleder de todo dogmatismo.' But the author of this article is surely mistaken when he goes on to attribute the method of the Hegelian Dialectic to the logical influence of Scotus: 'Lo que sí puede afirmarse que, tanto Kant como Spinoza y Hegel, deben por lo menos la mitad de su fama á lo mucho que bebieron en las obras de Escoto. El método Hegeliano por lo menos no fué concebido sin conocer la metodización lógica que Escoto señaló cinco siglos antes.' This statement is surely a most gross exaggeration, and there is not a scrap of evidence that Hegel or Kant were at all influenced by Duns. Nor is there the slightest trace of a method in Scotus even remotely resembling that of the Hegelian Dialectic.

of the thirteenth and fourteenth centuries; the psychological foundation of the two types of thinking is fundamentally diverse, and the conclusions reached are not less dissimilar.[1] The Scotist doctrine of the will, as Minges has shown, bears only the most superficial resemblance to the Kantian theory of the practical reason.[2]

There is also another important respect in which Scotism rather than Thomism represents the culmination of medieval philosophy. In Duns Scotus all the conflicting currents of scholastic[3] thought seem to flow together. The Christian mysticism of Augustine and Anselm, and the twelfth-century doctors, with its strongly marked platonizing tendencies; the mixed Platonism and Aristotelianism of Robert Grosseteste, William of Auvergne, Alexander of Hales, and Saint Bonaventura; the newer peripateticism of Albertus Magnus and Thomas Aquinas; the 'new' logic of William Shyreswood,[4] Petrus Hispanus, and Lambert of Auxerre; the Arabian and Jewish philosophy of Avicenna, Averroes, and Avicebron; all these contribute to the development of his thought and the formation of his doctrine, which is thus a unique restatement of the great problems which confronted the minds of the Christian philosophers of the Middle Ages.[5] And if his thinking is not always completely

[1] On the medieval attitude towards faith and reason see Prof. Gilson's admirable *Études de Philosophie médiévale*, Strassbourg, 1920; especially the first and third essays, ' Le sens du rationalisme chrétien' and ' La doctrine de la double vérité '.

[2] Cf. *Das Verhältnis zwischen Glauben u. Wissen*, etc., ch. 2, p. 103.

[3] I use the word ' scholastic ' in the sense laid down by M. de Wulf in §§ 29–31 of his book, *Scholasticism Old and New*, where he opposes Scholasticism to the purely naturalistic thought of the Averroists and other heretical sects.

[4] Cf. Prantl, op. cit., vol. iii, ch. xix, p. 202.

[5] Cf. G. de Ruggiero, op. cit., vol. iii, p. 180 : ' Nella filosofia di Duns, si affollano con maggior tumulto, quei diversi temi spirituali e storici che già vedemmo in atto di sovrapporsi nelle dottrine dei suoi

coherent, nevertheless it is often the richer for its lack
of consistency and the more significant for its incongruities. It is true that this eclectic spirit is confined
within the limits of the ecclesiastical authority, but
these limits are less narrow than they appear to be
at first sight, and it is combined with a freedom and
a width of range which raise Duns Scotus above the
ranks of his contemporaries and make him after Erigena
and Abelard perhaps the most interesting thinker of
the Middle Ages.

To examine in detail the influence which the writings
of Scotus exercised upon his successors is a task which
lies beyond the scope of the present volume,[1] but we
cannot complete this chapter without surveying as
briefly as possible certain developments of Duns'
teaching which can be traced in the half-sceptical empiricism of his fellow Franciscan, William of Ockham,
who died about the year 1347, and who, according to
common tradition, had attended the lectures of the
Subtle Doctor at Paris.[2]   Now Ockham, though he
cannot in any real sense be regarded as a disciple of
the Scotist School, incorporated in his teaching many
elements of what we may call the Franciscan type of
scholasticism which are also to be found in Duns, the
critical aspects of whose thinking he developed and extended, especially in the domain of natural theology.[3]
And just as many of the characteristic features of
Scotism were evolved from a critical reconstruction

precursori. L' empirismo e l' intuizionismo mistico, il volontarismo
e il razionalismo ; e, nelle fonti storiche, l' agostinismo originale
e quello del medio evo, la filosofia arabo-giudea, il tomismo, con-
fluiscano, spesso discordamente, nel suo pensiero.'

[1] For a sketch of the main characteristics of the post-Scotist
scholasticism see Werner, *Die Scholastik des späteren Mittelalters*,
vol. ii, ' Die nachscotistische Scholastik ' (Vienna, 1883).

[2] The accuracy of this tradition is, to say the least of it, very
doubtful. Cf. Little, *The Grey Friars in Oxford*, p. 224.

[3] Cf. Stöckl, op. cit., ii, pp. 986 sqq.

of the system of Thomas, so much of Ockham's teaching developed out of a criticism of the doctrines of Duns. But, in spite of his acuteness and penetration, he lacked the many-sided constructive spirit of the Subtle Doctor, and his thinking is consequently mainly negative in character.

An interesting example of the one-sided elaboration of certain elements of Duns' logical theory is furnished by the 'terminist' epistemology of Ockham, which isolates and develops the conceptualistic tendencies of his teaching. As we have already seen, Scotus rejects the theory advanced by Thomas that the adequate object of the intellect is the quiddity of the material thing, and its corollary that the individual as such is known only indirectly *per quandam reflexionem*.[1] He insists strongly on the fact that we have a direct intuitive knowledge of the individual which is intelligible *per se*,[2] and in the *De Rerum Principio* propounds a doctrine of a double *species*, one individual and one universal, which is not unlike that of Roger Bacon[3] and is strangely reminiscent of some of the conceptualist theories of the eleventh and twelfth centuries.[4] Moreover, his repudiation of *materia quantitate signata* as the principle of individuation led him to formulate his own theory of *haecceitas* in terms which are almost identical with those used by that great champion of the individual, a theory which is also markedly conceptualist in its associations,[5] while the unity which he attributes to the universals, a real unity which is less than a numerical unity though it appears at first sight to indicate a typically realist logic, turns out on closer examination to be capable also of a pronouncedly conceptualistic interpretation.[6] But it must be

---

[1] Vide supra, ch. v, p. 149.   [2] *De Rerum Principio*, q. xiii.
[3] Vide supra, ch. iv, p. 133 ; see also vol. ii, ch. i, pp. 24 sqq.
[4] See vol. ii, ch. iii, p. 116.   [5] Vide supra, ch. iv, p. 129.
[6] See vol. ii, loc. cit.

remembered that at the same time Scotus holds to the Thomist doctrine of the *species intelligibiles* and the 'abstraction' by the 'active' intellect of the universal *in re*, which as mere *natura* is only potentially universal and actually universalized by the intellect itself.

The development of these conceptualistic features in the teaching of Ockham is not difficult to trace. From the notion of the *haecceitas*, with its insistance on the ultimate reality of the individual, it was easy to pass to a wholly subjective conception of the universal. For if the individual alone is real, and possesses its reality as it were of its own right, being composed of *this* individual form united to *this* individual matter, and not of a universal form somehow diversified and particularized by an unknowable ὕλη, then the need for a universal as a metaphysical entity is gone, and all that is necessary to knowledge is a conceptual universal constructed by the mind by isolating the various characteristics common to a number of similar individuals. And with the 'real' universal disappears also the intelligible *species* 'abstracted' by the mind, and the distinction between the active and the potential intellect. We have, as Scotus rightly saw, a direct knowledge of the individual, but knowledge is no longer a matter of 'abstracting' a universal nature immanent in things from its individuating conditions, but a direct intuition of the individual reality. And once the sole reality of the individual is recognized, the question of individuation vanishes of course automatically.

Already Godfrey of Fontaines (*d.* 1303) had raised the cry against the assumption of a real universal, and had disposed of the problem of individuation with the formula *res communitur non existunt*. The singular is alone the 'first substance' and exists *per se*; the species is only the 'second substance', a complex of attributes

predicated of the various particulars.[1] A similar
position was taken up by Petrus Aureolus (*d.* 1322),
who, like Scotus and Ockham, was a member of the
Franciscan Order.   In a manner which reminds us of
Bacon he protests that the question concerning the
principle of individuation is altogether idle : for a
thing is not individualized by an individual form
added to a specific form ; it is singular just in so far

[1] Cf. *Quodl.* VII, q. v : ' Res non existunt nisi singulariter, prout
nomine proprio significantur ; communiter autem sive secundum
suam communitatem, non existunt, sed solum intelliguntur.'   So
also (ibid.) : ' Cum suppositum dicat individuum in genere substantiae,
est ens per se existens et in se subsistens.   Tale quid autem est substantia prima, quae secundum Philosophum in libro.   Praedicamentorum proprie et principaliter et maxime dicitur substantia.   Ergo
in sua ratione non includit nisi quae ad rationem substantiae pertinent.
Etenim propria substantia dicitur, ut dictum est ; et sic quamvis
non habeat esse sine quantitate, inquantum est substantia materialis,
tamen illa per se in sua ratione non includit.   Ex quo videtur quod
quidquid importata natura significata nomine communi, sive abstracto
sive concreto, sub ratione communi et indeterminata de principali
et per se significato, cum, ut visum est, hoc non sit nisi id quod ad
substantiam pertinet, hoc totum et natura importat sub ratione
propria et determinata suppositum significatum nomine individui
in genere substantiae, sive in abstracto, sive in concreto.   Unde
sicut humanitas significat talem entitatem ex carnibus et ossibus . . .
constitutum, quod non est nisi accidentibus indeterminatis, sive sine
quantitate indeterminata et qualitate . . ., licet non significat illa
naturam modo quo intelliguntur ista : ita haec humanitas, puta
Socrateitas, significat entitatem ex determinata anima et corpore
constitutam, quae non est sine accidentibus determinatis, licet non
significat talem naturam sub modo quo talia accidentia intelliguntur ;
et omnino proportionaliter dicendum est de hoc homine, puta
Socrate, comparato ad hominem, quod hujusmodi accidentia determinata non magis sunt de significato vel ratione individui, puta
Socratis, quam accidentia indeterminata de ratione speciei, puta
hominis, cum species tanquam substantia secunda de individuo
tanquam de substantia prima per se et essentialiter praedicetur.   Ex
iis patet quod Socrates est ens per se, quia contra ens per accidens
distinguitur.   Ergo non includit per se aliquid ad naturam accidentalem pertinens per se, scilicet, significato principali,' etc.   Cf.
Hauréau, *Histoire de la Philosophie scolastique,* tom. ii, 2, pp.
291 sqq.

as it exists, for the singular alone can have real existence.[1] It is manifest, therefore, that the universal is nothing but a conception fabricated by the mind.[2] He rejects too the whole theory of the *species intelligibiles*. The object of the intellect in the act of understanding is not a form or *species* ' abstracted ' from the phantasm, or ' impressed ' upon the *intellectus possibilis*; it is the thing itself, e. g. a rose *habens esse apparens*, that is, as directly perceived in a kind of intellectual intuition.[3] We may call this *esse intentionale* a *species* if we wish to do so, but the *species* is not the object of the understanding interposed as it were between the mind and the thing; it is really identical with the act of understanding itself.[4]   For, were we to assume the

[1] *In Sentt.* II, dist. ix, q. iii, art. 3 : ' Quaerere aliquid per quod res quae extra intellectum est, singularis sit, nihil est quaerere. Hoc enim quaerere est, an sit res extra intellectum universalis, et adveniat sibi aliquid, quod faciat eam particularem ; quod nihil est, quia omnis res eo ipso, quod est res, non includens conceptum, illa eo ipso est singularis.' Cf. op. cit., dist. xii, q. 2, art. 1 : ' Quoad unitatem essentiae individui demonstrati arguo sic : Ex materia et forma fit una res numero demonstrata, nec est quaerenda causa, quare unum fiat ex his.'

[2] *In Sentt.* I, dist. xxiii, art. 2 : ' Manifestum est quod ratio hominis et animalis, prout distinguitur a Socrate, est fabricata per intellectum, nec est aliud nisi conceptus. . . . Non enim facit has distinctiones natura in existentia actuali.'

[3] Op. cit., dist. ix, art. 1 : ' Nulla forma realis existens subjective in intellectu vel in phantasmate est ponenda, ad quam aspiciat intellectus, cujus productio dictio appelletur.   Forma illa, quam nos aspicere experimur, dum intelligimus rosam simpliciter aut florem, illa non est aliquid reale impressum intellectui subjective aut phantasmati, sed nec aliquid reale subsistens, sed est ipsamet res habens esse intentionale conspicuum.' Cf. ibid. : ' Omnis intellectio exigit rem positam in esse intentionali, et illa est forma specularis, de qua isti loquuntur, sed deficiunt a veritate . . . quod habeat esse reale . . ., quod sit subjective in intellectu vel phantasmate . . ., quod per illam procedat intellectus ad res, cum illa sit vera res quam intellectus speculatur. . . . Res ipsae conspiciuntur mente, et illud quod intuemur, non est forma alia specularis, sed ipsamet res habens esse apparens, et hoc est mentis conceptus, sive notitia objectiva.'

[4] *In Sentt.* II, dist. xi, q. iii, art. 1 : ' In intellectu distinguitur actus

existence of such a *forma specularis*, we should have to
maintain either that the process of knowledge ter-
minated with it, or else that by means of it knowledge
reaches out to something outside or beyond it, i.e.
the 'thing'. Both of these hypotheses are untenable ;
the first because it would confine knowledge merely
to our ideas, which is absurd ; the second because it
would make the first object of the intelligence something existing within the mind and not outside it, and
we should have a kind of perverted Platonism.[1]
Knowledge, according to Aureolus, is thus the self-
conformation of the intellect to the external object
present to it *in esse intentionali*, a self-conformation
which is brought about by the active intellect.[2]

primus, qui est species, ab actu secundo, qui est intellectio. Non
enim sunt duae realitates ut intellectus, sed eadem realitas dicitur
species quoad realitatem praecise et a causa intellectionis, et ex hoc
habet praecise quod sit actus primus ; eadem autem realitas etiam
ut connotat rem secundum esse objectivum apparens, dicitur intelligere.'

[1] Loc. cit.: 'Praeterea si sit forma aliqua specularis, realiter
inhaerens intellectui, ad quam terminetur aspectus intellectus, aut
in illam ultimate quiescit, aut per illam ad res extra procedit. Sed
nec potest dari istud, nec illud. Primum quidem non ; quia tunc
scientiae non essent de rebus, sed de talibus idolis, quod omnino
aestimandum est absurdum. Secundum etiam non. Tum quia
contra experientiam. Experimur enim nos aspicere formam rosae, et
per eam ulterius ferri in rosam. Tum quia primum objectum intellectus esset aliquid existens intra et non res extra : et eodem modo,
primum objectum habitus scientifici et actus ejus, qui est scire,
esset quaedam forma specularis actualis, et rediret quantum ad hoc
error Platonis, dicentis quod intellectus aspicit ad exemplar, non ad
ipsas res.'

[2] Werner, *Die nachscotistische Scholastik*, p. 86 : 'Die Spezies
als *actus intelligendi* ist die Selbstverähnlichung der intellectiven
Seele mit dem zu erkennenden Objecte. Diese Selbstverähnlichung
vollzieht sich in Kraft des *Intellectus agens*, welcher sonach der
Mittler des concreten Inhaltes der Erkenntnis ist, während der Intellect als solcher oder der Intellect vor aller actuellen Intellection
das Seiende in seiner indeterminierten Allgemeinheit zum Objecte
hat.'

Cf. also Aureolus, loc. cit. : 'Actus intellectus appellatur conceptio

But it remained for Ockham to complete and to systematize the conceptualist criticism of the scholasticism of the thirteenth century. Like Godfrey and Aureolus, he rejects the whole problem of individuation as nugatory. Only the singular exists, and every real thing is singular in its own right, for there is no real universal which has somehow to be particularized.[1] He subjects Duns' theory of individuation to a long and searching critique,[2] and denies the admissibility of his formal distinction between the common nature or specific essence and the *ultima realitas entis* or *haecceitas*.[3] The same thing (*res*) cannot at one and

inquantum adspicit rem formatam sub habitudine producentis et sub habitudine ejus, cui producitur in esse apparenti. Concipere enim est producere intra se. . . . Quia per actum intellectus res producitur in esse apparenti intra ipsum intelligentem, merito totum hoc appellatur conceptio, et res sic posita appellatur conceptus ; . . . actus autem intellectus, inquantum adspicit in ratione producentis rem hujusmodi apparentem, intantum appellatur formatio vel dictio vel locutio ; actus vero intellectus, inquantum est illud, cui res illa formatur et cui producitur in esse apparenti et relucenti, intantum dicitur intellectio vel intuitio.'

[1] *In Sentt.* I, dist. ii, q. 6 : 'Quaelibet res singularis se ipsa est singularis, . . . quia singularitas immediate convenit illi, cujus est. . . Sicut illud quod est singulare, se habet ad esse singulare, ita quod est universale, se habet ad esse universale ; ergo sicut illud quod est singulare, non potest per aliquid additum sibi fieri universale vel commune ; ita illud quod est commune, non potest per aliquid sibi additum fieri singulare : ergo quidquid est singulare, per nihil additum est singulare se ipso. . . . Omnis res extra animam est realiter singularis et una numero.'

[2] *Loc. cit.* : 'Dicitur quod in re extra animam est natura eadem realiter cum differentia contrahente ad determinatum individuum, distincta tamen formaliter, quae de se nec est universalis nec particularis, sed incomplete est universalis in re, et complete secundum esse in intellectu. Et ista opinio est, ut credo, opinio subtilis doctoris. . . . Et est de intentione doctoris, quod praeter unitatem numeralem est unitas realis minor unitate numerali. . . . Non est ergo ista entitas materia vel forma vel compositum, inquantum quodlibet istorum est natura, sed est ultima realitas entis, quod est materia, et entis quod est forma, et entis quod est compositum,' etc.

[3] *Loc. cit.* : 'Contra istam opinionem potest argui duplici via

the same time be a common nature shared by all individuals of the same kind, and also proper to each. Were we to assume the Scotist distinction we should have to suppose that there are as many common natures as there are individuals, which is absurd.[1] Ockham's own view approximates to that of Walter Burleigh,[2] namely that the individual *compositum* is made up out of the combination of a particular form with a particular matter.[3] This was, as we have

primo, quod impossibile est, in creaturis, aliqua differre formaliter, nisi distinguantur realiter. . . . Secunda via potest argui . . . quod non est vera, etiam posito quod esset talis distinctio.' Cf. *Expos. aur. Praedicab. de Genere*: 'Proprie et stricte loquendo, nihil distinguitur ab aliquo per aliquid nisi per se ipsum vel intrinsecum sibi, sicut homo non distinguitur ab asino nisi per se ipsum vel per aliquam partem essentialem sui.' Cf. also *In Sentt.* I, dist. ii, q. iii : 'Nihil reale potest distingui nec esse idem ratione cum aliquo reali, ita quod, sicut distinctio rationis et identitas rationis se habet ad entia rationis, ita differentia realis et identitas realis se habet ad entia realia, et hoc forte non excludendo distinctionem formalem et identitatem, ubi debet poni.'

[1] *Summa Totius Logicae*, I. xvi : 'Videtur tamen aliquibus, quod universale aliquo modo est extra animam et in individuis, non quidem distinctum ab his realiter, sed tamen formaliter . . . . Sed haec opinio videtur esse irrationabilis, quia in creaturis non potest esse aliqua distinctio qualitercumque extra animam, nisi ubi sunt res distinctae. . . . Item eadem res non est communis et propria. . . . Item si natura communis esset eadem realiter omni differentiae individuali, ergo tot essent realiter naturae communes, quot sunt differentiae individuales.'

[2] Burleigh, *Expositio, s. art. vet.*, f. 24 r. A (Venice, 1485) : 'Species de genere substantiae componitur ex genere et differentia et ex omnibus superioribus ad ipsum, et hujus ratio est, quod effectus particulares sunt causae particulares, et effectus universalis sunt causae universales, . . . sed individuum est effectus particularis et species est effectus universalis, et ideo individuum non componitur nisi ex hac materia et hac forma, quae sunt causae particulares.'

[3] Ockham, loc. cit.: 'Et ideo non est imaginandum, quod in Socrate sit humanitas vel natura humana distincta a Socrate quocunque modo, cui addatur una differentia individualis contrahens illam naturam, sed quidquid imaginabile substantiale existens in Socrate vel est materia particularis vel forma particularis vel aliquid

seen,[1] the view also of Roger Bacon, and though expressed in different words it does not differ very widely from the theory of Scotus which Ockham is trying to oppose. For if we read the passage in the two commentaries on the Sentences dealing with this point [2] more carefully we shall find that, as Minges has pointed out,[3] Duns is attempting to express the same theory as that held by Burleigh and Ockham, the chief difference between the two views being that Scotus emphasizes more strongly than his successors the metaphysical ground of the universal notions which we predicate of individuals belonging to the same kind. And it would appear that Ockham attempts to magnify for controversial purposes the divergence of the two theories, and so either misunderstands or distorts the Scotist notion of the formal distinction [4] and the reality of the universal.[5]

This fact will be the more clearly grasped when we have examined his theory of the nature of the universals. Starting out from the real order, we find that nature produces only the singular;[6] she never generates a universal. Whence then do these universals draw their origin? They are not things but concepts, concepts of a secondary order, *intentiones secundae*, posterior to the *intentiones primae*, or 'first impressions', which are always ideas of singular objects and refer directly to them.[7] But the 'second intentions' have

compositum ex his, et ideo omnis essentia et quidditas et quidquid est substantiae, seu sit realiter extra animam, vel est simpliciter et absolute materia vel forma vel compositum ex his.'

[1] Vide supra, ch. iv, p. 129.
[2] *Op. Ox.* II, dist. iii, q. 6, n. 15 ; *Rep. Par.* II, dist. xii, q. 8, n. 8.
[3] *Der angeblich exzessive Realismus des Duns Scotus*, pp. 46 sqq.
[4] See vol. ii, ch. iii, p. 114 sq.
[5] Ibid., p. 115 sq.
[6] *In Sentt.* I, dist. ii, q. iv: 'Agens naturale in agendo intendit veram rem singularem, quia illud intendit, quod per se et primo producitur ; sed res singularis per se et primo producitur.'
[7] Cf. *In Sentt.* I, dist. xxiii, q. i : 'Intentio prima vocatur res

no direct reference to real things; they are 'signs'
or 'fictions' which are predicated of a number of
(real) individuals,[1] and serve as the 'terms' of mental
propositions or judgements,[2] 'standing for' the
singular things which are grouped together by the
mind under a specific or generic notion.[3] With the
details of this terminist logic and the theory of the
'sign' we are not here concerned;[4] the important
thing for our purposes is to note the way in which
Ockham, while rejecting *in toto* the notion of a *universale in re*,[5] attempts to safeguard the validity of our
universal conceptions, and so prevent himself from
plunging into scepticism. For, though the universal
is merely an *intentio* and has no 'objective' existence,
as we should say, it is not, as those of his detractors
who call him nominalist would contend, a mere *flatus
vocis*. For, though it is not a 'thing', but merely
a concept or sign, it is by no means an arbitrary

realiter existens, intentio autem secunda vocatur aliquid in anima
rebus applicabile praedicabile de nominibus rerum, quando non
habent suppositionem personalem, sed simplicem, sicut sunt species
et genus.'
[1] *Summa Totius Logicae*, cap. xv : ' Universale est intentio animae
nata praedicari de multis.' Op. cit., cap. xiv : ' Quodlibet universale
natum est esse signum plurium et natum est praedicari de pluribus.'
' Intentio animae dicitur universalis, quia est signum praedicabile
de multis.'
[2] *In Sennt.* I, dist. 2, q. iv: ' Purus logicus non habet disputare
utrum universalia quae sunt termini propositionum, sint res extra
animam vel tantum in anima, vel in voce, vel in scripto ; et ideo non
distinguit, sed aliquando attribuit rei, quod convenit universali
termino propositionis et aliquando e converso.'
[3] For a detailed discussion of the doctrine of *suppositio* see *Summa
Totius Logicae*, I, cap. pp. 63–77.
[4] For a detailed account of Ockham's logic see Prantl, *Gesch.
d. Logik*, etc., v. 3, pp. 329–420.
[5] *In Sentt.* I, dist. ii, q. iv : ' Nulla una res numero non variata
nec multiplicata est in pluribus suppositis vel singularibus nec etiam
quibuscumque individuis creatis simul et semel,' etc.   ' Nulla res
realiter distincta a singularibus rebus et intrinseca eis est universalis
et communis eis.'

convention instituted by the human mind without reference to any external reality at the pleasure of the will.[1] It is a natural sign, the term of a mental proposition, an *intentio* which may also be called a *similitudo* inasmuch as it is a representation of a real object.[2] For the term man does not signify primarily a common nature which exists in a number of individuals—it simply signifies all individual men ; and the person who first invented the word ' man ', on seeing a particular man, invented the word to mean that particular man and also any other substance similar to him.[3] The universal is thus a sort of plan or type which refers indifferently to all singular objects of

[1] *In Sentt.* I, dist. ii, q. viii : ' Quarta posset esse opinio quod nihil est universale ex natura sua, sed tantum ex institutione, illo modo quo vox est universalis, quid nulla res habet ex natura sua supponere pro alia re, nec vere praedicari de alia re, sicut nec vox, sed tantum ex institutione voluntatis. . . . Sed haec opinio non videtur vera.'

Cf. op. cit. II, q. xxv : ' Universalia et intentiones secundae causantur naturaliter sine omni activitate intellectus et voluntatis a notitiis incomplexis terminorum, per istam viam, quia primo cognosco aliqua singularia in particulari intuitive vel abstractive, et hoc causatur ab objecto vel ab habitu derelicto ex primo actu, et habita notitia statim ad ejus praesentiam, si non sit impedimentum, sequitur naturaliter alius actus distinctus a primo terminatus ad aliquid tale esse objectivum, quale prius vidit in esse subjectivo, et ille actus secundus producit universalia et intentiones secundas.'

[2] *Summa Totius Logicae*, I, cap. xii : ' Quando aliquis profert propositionem vocalem, prius format interius propositionem unam mentalem, quae nullius idiomatis est, intantum quod multi formant frequenter interius propositiones aliquas, quas tamen propter defectum idiomatis exprimere nesciunt. Partes talium propositionum mentalium vocantur conceptus, intentiones, similitudines, intellectus.'

Cf. *In Sentt.* I, dist. ii, q. viii : ' Universale non est aliquid reale habens esse subjectivum, nec in anima nec extra animam, sed tamen habet esse objectivum in anima, et est quoddam fictum habens esse tale in esse objectivo, quale habet res extra in esse subjectivo.'

[3] *Summa Totius Logicae*, I, cap. 43 : ' Substantiae secundae significant multa. Hoc enim nomen " homo " non significat primo unam naturam communem omnibus hominibus, sicut multi errantes imaginantur, sed significat primo omnes homines particulares. Ille enim qui primo imposuit hanc vocem " homo " ad significandum,

a certain kind, and in so far as it resembles them is able to stand for the particular real objects of which it is a representation.[1] It will thus appear that Ockham, though he denies the notion of a common *natura* which exists *realiter* in all the individuals, nevertheless insists on an objective ground actually present in nature as the basis of our universal conceptions. And this objective ground is the similarity of essence of individuals of the same kind. His position is thus not really so far removed from that of Scotus as might at first sight be supposed. In fact the difference between the two scholastics is largely one of terminology, for the common *natura* postulated by Duns is not numerically but only quidditatively the same in all individuals of the same species, and resolves itself ultimately into something very like the similitude of essences maintained by Ockham.[2]

With the disappearance of the *universale in re* the basis for the distinction between the active and the potential intellect also vanishes, but the use of the two terms is still retained. The intellect is called ' active ' in so far as we regard the process of understanding as being an activity of the soul, ' possible ' in so far as we look upon knowledge as something received by or impressed upon it, but agent and recipient are identical.[3] Knowledge thus becomes for Ockham, as

---

videns aliquem hominem particularem, instituit hanc vocem " homo " ad significandum illum hominem et quamlibet talem substantiam qualis est homo ille.'

[1] *In Sentt.* I, dist. ii, q. viii: ' Ita enim sicut domus ficta, si fingens haberet virtutem productivam realem, est exemplar ipsius artificiati : ita illud fictum esset exemplar respectu singularium, et id potest vocari universale, quod est exemplar indifferenter respiciens omnia singularia extra, et propter illam similitudinem in esse objectivo, potest supponere pro rebus extra habentibus consimile esse extra intellectum. Et illo modo universale non est per generationem, sed per abstractionem, quae non est nisi fictio quaedam.'

[2] See vol. ii, ch. iii, p. 116.

[3] *In Sentt.* ii, q. xxv : ' Intellectus agens et possibilis sunt omnino

for Petrus Aureolus, a kind of intellectual vision or intuition ; the mediating *species* disappears, and in its place we get the *intentio*, which is not the ' idea ' through which an external ' thing ' is known, but is identical with the act of understanding itself.[1]

idem re ac ratione. Tamen ista nomina vel conceptus bene connotant diversa : quia intellectus agens significat animam connotando intellectionem procedentem ab anima active ; possibilis autem significat eandem animam connotando intellectionem receptam in anima : sed idem omnino est efficiens et recipiens intellectionem.'

[1] *Quodl.* IV, q. ix : 'Ideo dico quod tam intentio prima quam secunda est vere actus intelligendi, quia per actum potest salvari quidquid salvatur per fictum ; eo enim quod actus est similitudo subjecti, potest significare et supponere pro rebus extra . . . potest esse genus et species sicut fictum. Ex quo patet quod intentio prima et secunda realiter distinguuntur, quia intentio prima est actus intelligendi significans res, quae non sunt signa intentio secunda est actus significans intentiones primas.'

Cf. *Summa Totius Logicae*, I, cap. xii : 'Illud autem existens in anima . . . aliquando vocatur intentio animae, aliquando conceptus animae, aliquando passio animae, aliquando similitudo rei. . . . Sed quid est in anima id quod est tale signum ? Dicendum est quod circa istud sunt diversae opiniones. Aliqui enim dicunt quod non est nisi quoddam fictum per animam ; alii quod est quaedam qualitas subjective existens in anima distincta ab actu intelligendi ; alii dicunt quod est actus intelligendi. Et pro istis est ratio illa quod frustra fit per plura quod potest fieri per pauciora ; omnia autem quae salvantur ponendo aliquid distinctum ab actu intelligendi, possunt salvari sine tali distincto, eo quod supponere pro alio et significare aliud ita potest competere actui intelligendi sicut illi ficto ; ergo praeter actum intelligendi non oportet ponere aliquid aliud.'

Cf. also *In Sentt.* I, dist. xxvii, q. ii : 'Manifestum est, in intellectu esse actum intelligendi et etiam habitum, sed utrum species aliqua praevia actui sit ponenda in anima vel non, est dubium. Utrum etiam praeter actum intelligendi sit aliquis conceptus formatus per actum intelligendi vel etiam sit aliquis conceptus habens tantum esse objectivum, est dubium. Utrum etiam sit aliqua species in intellectu, quae non posset esse sine actu intelligendi, est dubium. De primo dubio et tertio dico quod species neutro modo dicta est ponenda in intellectu, quia nunquam ponenda est pluralitas sine necessitate, sed . . . quidquid potest salvari per talem speciem potest salvari sine ea aeque faciliter. . . . Sed de secundo dubio est mihi magis dubium, hoc tamen est mihi probabile, quamvis non affirmem, quod in intellectu

But it is in the domain of natural theology, even more than in that of logic, that Ockham's one-sided development of the Scotist doctrine becomes significant. The dividing line between natural reason and revelation which had already been drawn by Albert and Thomas, while seeming to safeguard the independence of both Philosophy and Theology, had actually introduced into medieval thought a dualism which contained implicitly within itself the seeds of disruption. Without any essential divergence from Thomist principles Scotus had developed a little further the positivistic naturalism of the Angelic Doctor. To Thomas the notion of creation in time was insusceptible of proof by natural reason ; arguments for and against were so evenly balanced that the court of metaphysic was unable to judge between them, and the case was referred to the supreme jurisdiction of a supernatural revelation. In exactly the same manner Duns refers two other important metaphysical issues to the same ultimate tribunal, the divine omnipotence and the immortality of the soul, but in the latter case he expressly states that, though

praeter ipsum actum intelligendi, quando intelligit aliquid commune ad plura, est aliquid vel subjective vel objective, quod est aliquo modo simile rei intellectae, quod a multis vocatur quasi quoddam idolum, in quo ipsa res cognoscitur, quamvis rem singularem cognosci in illo non aliud sit, quam ipsum idolum cognosci.'

This *idolum* here mentioned corresponds to the *esse apparens* of Aureolus, and must not be confused with the *species intelligibilis* of Thomas and Scotus which is criticized by Ockham in his commentary on the Sentences, Lib. II, qq. xv-xvii. For a further account of Ockham's theory of knowledge see Hauréau, *Histoire de la Philosophie scolastique*, tom. 2. 2, pp. 438 sqq.

It is also interesting to note Ockham's formulation of the principle of parsimony in the passages just quoted, which follows the Scotist model and is always methodological, not ontological. The form in which it has commonly been attributed to him, ' Entia non sunt multiplicanda praeter necessitatem ', is a later perversion and is never found in Ockham's own writings. Cf. the article by W. M. Thorburn in *Mind*, July, 1918.

the rational evidence is not absolutely in favour of it, the balance of probability lies on the affirmative side. It must be remembered also that no less than Thomas he refuses to admit that the arguments of the infidel against those mysteries which are revealed only by faith can ever be logically conclusive. They can always in the last resort be reduced to a paralogism. With Ockham the divorce between faith and reason has gone much further.[1] Not only the attributes of God, his unity, intellectuality, omnipotence, &c., but even his existence is not strictly demonstrable by natural reason. In the same way the immortality of the intellectual soul escapes our logical faculties.[2] In contrast to Duns he denies the unity of the spiritual form, and postulates beside the intellectual soul an *anima sensitiva*,[3] which alone can be shown by natural reason to be the form of the body. The influence of the Averroism which was so fashionable at the school of Padua is here quite plainly apparent. Indeed Ockham is disposed to regard the monopsychism of the

[1] Our judgement of the significance of Ockham's advance on Scotus, in the direction of theological scepticism, will of course be influenced by our views concerning the authenticity of the *Theoremata*, a question on which I do not venture to make any definite pronouncement. But even if we do regard them as genuine, we shall have to balance them against the teaching of the more authenticated and completer works like the *De Primo Principio* and the commentaries on the Sentences. And we must remember also that the *Theoremata* are a mere fragment, the original text of which was confessedly very much confused.

[2] *Quodl.* I, q. x : 'Intelligendo per animam intellectivam formam immaterialem incorruptibilem quae tota est in toto et tota in qualibet parte, non potest sciri evidenter per rationem quod talis forma sit in nobis, nec quod talis anima sit forma corporis. Quidquid de hoc senserit Aristoteles non curo, quia ubique dubitative videtur loqui. Sed tria ista sola fide tenemus.'

[3] *In Sentt.* II, q. xxii : 'In homine praeter animam intellectivam est ponere aliam formam, scilicet sensitivam, super quam potest agens naturale corrumpendo et producendo.' Cf. op. cit., Lib. IV, q. vii ; *Quodl.* II, q. x.

commentator as the correct interpretation of Aristotle's doctrine of νοῦς,[1] and therefore the normal conclusion, if we may so call it, of the unaided human intellect.

With regard to his conception of theology Ockham starts out from a basis not very unlike that of Scotus.[2] Of the truths concerning the divine nature some are necessary and others contingent. A certain number of both these classes of truths can be known supernaturally, though contingent truths cannot be known 'scientifically' either naturally or supernaturally.[3] Now knowledge falls into two kinds, intuitive and abstractive; but to the human intellect, *pro statu viae*, only an abstractive knowledge of God is possible. We may conclude, then, that God can infuse into the human mind an abstractive knowledge of himself, and that the traveller in this vale of tears can have a distinct abstractive notion of deity.[4] The further question then arises whether these theological truths can be known scientifically. To this Ockham gives a long and somewhat complicated answer. None of the intrinsic properties of the deity can be demonstrated of the divine essence in such a way that the divine

[1] Werner, *Die Nachscotistische Scholastik*, p. 66.

[2] See above, ch. iii; also vol. ii, ch. v, pp. 148 sqq.

[3] *In Sentt.*, Prol., q. i: 'Dico ergo ad quaestionem, quod praecise non intelligo quaestionem de notitia evidenti scientifica, sed de notitia evidenti in communi; quia quaedam veritates theologicae supernaturaliter cognoscibiles sunt necessariae, et quaedam contingentes, quae nec naturaliter nec supernaturaliter possunt scientifice cognosci.' Cf. ibid.: 'Circa quintum ad formam quaestionis dico quod Deus de potentia sua absoluta potest causare notitiam evidentem in intellectu viatoris aliquarum veritatum theologicarum, et forte aliquarum non.'

[4] Ibid.: 'Quarto concludo ex praedictis quod notitia Dei distincta est viatori communicabilis manente viatore; quia sola notitia intuitiva repugnat viatori ergo si abstractiva potest fieri sine intuitiva, sequitur quod notitia abstractiva deitatis distincta potest esse in viatore manente viatore.'

Cf. Scotus, *Quodl.*, q. vii, n. 10. See vol. ii, ch. v, p. 149, n. 2.

essence as such is the subject, and something which is really identical with it is predicated of it.[1] Nor can any notions common to God and the creatures, and predicated of him *in quid*, be demonstrated *a priori* of the divine essence *in se*.[2] There are, however, certain 'connotative' and 'negative' conceptions common to God and the creature which can be demonstrated of the divine essence, and that in a sense *a priori*, provided that we have a knowledge of the divine essence *in se*; e.g. we may argue, All being is good; God is a being; therefore God is good. And the knowledge acquired by such a syllogism may be called science.[3] But the connotative and negative conceptions which are proper to God and not to the creature, such as omnipotence, infinity, immortality, creativeness, and so forth, cannot be demonstrated *a priori* of the divine essence *in se*.[4] Finally, all the notions predicable of

---

[1] *In Sentt.*, Prol., q. ii: 'Prima conclusio erit ista: quod nihil intrinsecum Deo potest de divina essentia demonstrari; ita quod divina essentia in se subjiciatur et aliquid quod est realiter divina essentia praedicetur in se.'

[2] Ibid.: 'Tertia conclusio est ista, quod conceptus communes praedicabiles in quid de Deo et creaturis, non possunt de divina essentia in se demonstrari a priori; nec de conceptu proprio sibi et simplici, si talis erit possibilis.'

[3] Ibid.: 'Quarta conclusio est quod conceptus connotativi et negativi communes Deo et creaturis possunt de divina essentia demonstrari; et hoc si aliqui sint de divina essentia in se cognita dubitabiles. Hoc patet quia omne commune praedicabile adaequate de aliquo communi, potest demonstrari de quolibet contento sub illo communi per illud commune tanquam per medium: sed tales conceptus praedicantur et primo et adaequate de aliquo communi ad Deum et creaturas: ergo per illud tanquam per medium possunt demonstrari de quolibet contento. Et ideo forte hic est demonstratio et aliquo modo a priori: Omne ens est bonum; Deus est ens; Ergo,' etc.

'Quod autem tali syllogismo acquiratur scientia proprie dicta; et per consequens est demonstratio, patet: quia est habitus veridicus et non intellectus nec sapientia, etc.; ergo est scientia.'

[4] Ibid.: 'Quinta conclusio est quod conceptus connotativi et

God *in se* which are doubtful of the composite
conception which we have of God *de facto* can be
demonstrated of that conception through the divine
essence as such taken as a middle term or through
a distinct conception of deity. For example a human
mind, not yet raised to the beatific state, might doubt
the proposition ' God is '. And God could implant
in that mind an abstractive notion of Himself by
means of which he could form a demonstrative
syllogism, the conclusion of which would be ' God is '.
For he might argue thus : The divine essence is ; God
is the divine essence ; therefore God is. But his two
premises are not knowable by us *de communi lege* ; they
can only be apprehended by a mind which has either
an intuitive or an abstractive knowledge of divinity
in se, and therefore such a conclusion is only demonstrable *a priori* to a mind thus illuminated ; it cannot
be mediated by a conception common to God and to
the creature.[1] Ockham thus concludes, in a manner

negativi proprii Deo non sunt de divina essentia in se demonstrabiles
a priori. Et ideo esse creativum, esse omnipotens, esse eternum,
infinitum, immortale, et sic de aliis, non sunt de divina essentia in se
demonstrabiles.'

[1] Ibid. : ' Sexta conclusio est quod omnia praedicabilia de Deo
in se, quae sunt dubitabilia de conceptu composito proprio Deo
quales habemus nos de facto, sunt de illo conceptu demonstrabiles
per divinam essentiam in se, tanquam per medium, vel cognitionem
distinctam deitatis. . . . Verbi gratia aliquis non beatus potest dubitare
istam propositionem " Deus est " : et postea potest Deus causare
notitiam abstractivam in illo intellectu : illo posito iste poterit facere
syllogismum demonstrativum in quo erit ista conclusio, " Deus est ",
quam primum dubitavit : ita quod in majori praedicatum istius
propositionis quam de facto habemus praedicabitur de ipsa divina
essentia in se, vel de cognitione distincta essentiae divinae ; et in
secunda ipsa divina essentia praedicabitur de isto subjecto istius
conclusionis. Ac si argueretur sic : Essentia divina est ; Deus est
essentia divina ; ergo Deus est. Verumtamen illae duae praemissae
non sunt nobis possibiles ; sed tantum possunt apprehendi ab intellectu
intuitive vel abstractive intelligentem ipsam divinitatem in se. Et
ideo soli tali sunt illae conclusiones in se demonstrabiles a priori, quae

resembling that of Scotus, that for a mind endowed with an adequate conception of the divine essence theology would be a science in the proper sense of the term, but that for human minds in their earthly condition, unaided by a special revelation, it is not a science in the strict meaning of the term.[1] He agrees also with Duns in rejecting the notion which was put forward by Thomas that the revealed truths of Theology can be regarded as the principles or conclusions of a science, and adds a characteristically sceptical comment to the effect that from the philosophical standpoint of natural reason they appear to be false.[2] But he criticizes the conception of theology as a practical science ; strictly speaking, theology is not a single form of knowledge or science ; it is composed of a number of distinct propositions, some of which are speculative and some practical. Thus, for instance, the propositions ' God is the creator of the world ', ' God is Three and One ', &c., &c., are all speculative, for they have no direct bearing on action, and do not as such provide us with norms for conduct. Others, however, are practical : e. g. ' God should be loved with all the heart ', ' The Sabbath day must be kept holy ', because they are truths which are categorically regulative.[3]

non possunt demonstrari de deo per aliquod commune tanquam per medium.'

[1] *In Sentt.*, Prol., q. vii : ' Alia est opinio quae ponit quod quamvis credibilia possint evidenter sciri, non tamen a nobis pro statu isto de communi lege. Et ideo theologia secundum quod communiter addiscimus eam, non est scientia proprie dicta respectu talium credibilium ; quamvis aliquorum posset esse scientia. Et istam opinionem reputo veram.'

[2] *Summa Totius Logicae*, III, cap. 1 : ' Et sic articuli fidei non sunt principia demonstrationis nec conclusiones, nec sunt probabiles, quia omnibus vel pluribus vel sapientibus apparent falsi, et hoc accipiendo sapientes pro sapientibus mundi et praecipue innitentibus rationi naturali.'

[3] *In Sentt.*, Prol., q. xii : ' Ideo aliter dico ad quaestionem quod

Ockham is thus at one with Scotus in denying the possibility of any *a priori* deduction of the divine existence or the divine attributes on the ground that we are unable to form any notion of the divine essence as it really is.[1] The only conception of God which it is possible for us to form is a compound notion made up of attributes 'abstracted' empirically from our knowledge of the created world,[2] and so combined as to yield a definition which is proper to God alone, seeing that it is applicable solely to Him.[3] The notion

theologia non est una notitia vel scientia ; sed habet vel continet plures notitias realiter distinctas quorum aliquae sunt practicae simpliciter et aliquae speculativae. Hoc, declaratur quia omnis notitia quae non habet pro objecto ipsam praxim, nec aliquid operatum per praxim est speculativa ; et omnis notitia quae habet pro objecto totali vel partiali ipsam praxim, vel operatum per praxim, hoc est, terminum importantem praxim vel operatum per praxim, quod de novo habet esse per ipsam praxim, quae est magis directiva operis sive dictative sive ostensive solum, quod sit notitia incomplexa praxis, est practica : quia per hoc distinguitur notitia speculativa a practica, sicut declaratum est. Sed aliquae notitiae theologicae sunt tales, sicut istae sunt speculativae : Deus creat mundum ; Deus est trinus et unus ; Pater generat ; et hujusmodi, de quibus non potest esse nisi notitia speculativa. Et aliquae veritates sunt practicae, sicut : Deus est diligendus ex toto corde ; et Sabbatum est sanctificandum ; Orandum est pro loco et tempore ; et hujusmodi. Dico ergo quod aliqua pars theologiae est practica ; quia est de operibus nostris, accipiendo opera nostra pro omnibus quae sunt in potestate nostra, sive sint operationes sive operata ; et aliqua speculative ; quia non est de talibus.'

[1] *In Sentt.* I, dist. iii, q. ii : ' Nec divina essentia, nec divina quidditas, nec aliquid intrinsecum Deo, nec aliquid quod est realiter Deus, potest hic cognosci a nobis, ita quod nihil aliud a Deo concurrat in ratione objecti.' Cf. Scotus, *Quodl.*, q. vii, n. 10. See vol. ii, ch. v, pp. 150 sqq.

[2] Ockham, loc. cit. : ' Essentia divina vel quidditas divina potest cognosci a nobis in aliquo conceptu sibi proprio, composito tamen et hoc in conceptu cujus partes sunt abstrahibiles naturaliter a rebus.'

[3] Loc. cit. : ' Sed cum sunt communia multa habentia aliquod unum contentum omnia communia simul accepta faciunt unum proprium illi. Quod ex quo sunt distincta communia, oportet quod aliquid contineatur sub singulo, quod sub nullo aliorum contineatur.

thus formed, though it does not show us God as He exists in and for Himself, is yet sufficient to stand for Him and to give us some knowledge about Him.[1] But he refuses to regard the conception of an infinite being as the most adequate that we can form of the Deity, and rejects Duns' theory of infinity as an intrinsic mode of the divine being on the ground that it is essentially a negative attribute, and cannot therefore truly express the mode of the divine being.[2] Moreover, his whole attitude to the positive attributes of the divine essence is ' nominalistic '. The divine perfections are all identical with the divine essence and

Ergo omnia illa communia simul accepta nulli alii possunt convenire. Sed multi sunt conceptus simplices naturaliter abstrahibiles quorum quilibet communis est Deo et alicui alteri : ergo omnes illi simul facient unum conceptum proprium Deo, et ita cum possit cognosci quod ille conceptus de aliquo verificatur, Deus in illo conceptu cognoscetur.'

[1] Ockham, loc. cit. : ' Denominatione extrinseca potest dici aliquid cognosci ex hoc quod aliud immediate cognoscitur quid est proprium sibi, et hoc stare et supponere pro eo. Et non sequitur . . . ergo per hoc quod conceptus cognoscitur non cognoscitur Deus . . . sed sequitur quod propter hoc non cognoscitur immediate et in se, sed in alio bene potest cognosci. Et hoc non est aliud nisi quod cum non possumus Deum in se cognoscere, utimur pro eo uno conceptu proprio, attribuendo sibi quidquid potest Deo attribui, non pro se sed pro Deo, et illum conceptum praedicamus, non pro se, sed pro Deo, de omni illo de quo posset Deus ipse in se cognitus praedicari.'

[2] *In Sentt.* I, dist. iii, q. iii: 'Contra istum modum dicendi ostendo quod conceptus entis infiniti non sit formaliter in se perfectior conceptus omni conceptu possibili haberi de Deo ; quia nullus conceptus negativus est formaliter perfectior conceptu positivo. Sed conceptus entis infiniti est includens ultra conceptum entis aliquid negativum. . . . Praeterea quod dicit quod infinitum non est quasi passio nec attributum Dei, sicut bonum et verum, etc. Contra : quia omne quod demonstratur de aliquo quod non praedicatur de eo primo modo dicendi per se, est passio illius : sed infinitum est hujusmodi respectu Dei, qui nihil negativum vel includens negationem praedicatur de positivi per se primo modo. Ergo infinitum est passio illius . . . sicut esse immortale, incorruptibile et hujusmodi. Ex isto patet quod infinitum non dicit gradum intrinsecum per se et primo, sed magis ex consequenti.'

with each other.[1] The formal distinction *a parte rei*
postulated by Scotus is inadmissible, for, as we have
already seen,[2] there is no middle term between a
distinctio realis and a *distinctio rationis*. The various
perfections which we distinguish in the divine nature,
such as the divine justice, goodness, wisdom, or mercy,
are distinguished solely and simply by our thinking.
The perfection which is God Himself is single ; the
perfections which we predicate of Him are only signs
or concepts through which we think the unitary
perfection of His essence. They must not, therefore,
be called attributes, for they have no separate *esse*,
wherefore the ancients spoke of them only as the
divine names.[3]

Having thus rejected the possibility of any *a priori*
demonstration of the divine existence, and having
retrenched severely the validity of our relativistic
conceptions of the divine being, Ockham proceeds to
submit the *a posteriori* demonstrations of God's
existence and attributes to a destructive and sceptical
criticism, in the course of which he rejects the whole
line of argument upon which Thomas in the *Summa*

---

[1] Op. cit., dist. ii, q. i : ' Sapientia divina omnibus modis est
eadem essentiae divinae quibus essentia divina est eadem essentiae
divinae et sic de bonitate divina et justitia, nec est penitus aliqua
distinctio ex natura rei vel non identitas.'

[2] Vide supra, p. 279.

[3] *Quodl.* III, q. ii : ' Aliter accipitur distingui ratione improprie,
secundum quod competit uni, et hoc est improprie distingui, quia
proprie loquendo, si aliquid distinguitur, ab alio distinguitur. Et
sic distingui ratione est habere diversas rationes, sive correspondere
diversis rationibus. . . . Et sic Deus dicitur distingui ratione ; quia
correspondet diversis conceptibus sine omni distinctione a parte sui. . . .
Sed quod aliquid unum et idem realiter sit vere, et realiter illa quae
distinguuntur ratione, ita quod non correspondet eis sicut signatum
suis signis, sed sit ista distincta ratione, est impossibile. . . . Dicendum
ergo quod attributa divina distinguuntur ratione, quia attributa
non sunt nisi quaedam praedicabilia mentalia, vocalia, vel scripta,
nata significare et supponere pro Deo, quae possunt naturali ratione
investigari et concludi de Deo.'

contra Gentiles and Scotus in the *De Primo Principio*
and the two commentaries on the Sentences had laid
so much stress. Even the bare existence of a God is
not strictly speaking demonstrable ; the reasons which
we can bring forward to support it are only probable.[1]
Thus the physical proof *a motu* on which Thomas lays
so much emphasis depends upon two principles, both
open to doubt. For we can conceive of beings which
are able to move themselves, as, for instance, an Angel
or the soul, or even weight, which falls by moving
itself.[2] Nor is it impossible to imagine an infinite
regress of moving causes.[3] Already Duns himself
had raised doubts concerning the validity of the
proof from motion and had called in question the
Aristotelian principle, *Omne quod movetur ab alio*. But
Ockham goes much further and attacks the whole
via ab efficientia. We cannot argue from the world
to God, because any given event can be accounted for
by its immediate efficient cause, and the existence of
God therefore ' explains ' nothing.[4] Nor must we
postulate His existence as first cause, for the eternity
of the universe can never be disproved. Similarly,

---

[1] *Cent. Theol.*, conc. 1 : ' Verumtamen de necessitate ponendi an
scilicet demonstrabile sit vel probabile Deum esse, vel per se notum,
non videtur aeque planum. Et ideo circa istam materiam dignum
duco aliqualiter disputandum ; praemissa tamen ista protestatione,
quod si aliquid dixerim . . . quod non sit bene dictum, nunc pro tunc
revoco. . . . Deducit Aristoteles iii Physicorum primum movens
immobile medio tali : omne quod movetur ab alio movetur, etc. . . .
Sed ista ratio quamvis sit aliquibus probabilis, tamen non videtur
demonstrativa.'

[2] Ibid. : ' Possum rationabiliter dicere aliquid se ipsum movere,
sicut anima et angelus, quae producunt varios suos actus, et gravitas
ipsa, quae movendo seipsam descendit,' etc.

[3] Ibid.

[4] *Quodl.* II, q. i : ' Non potest probari naturali ratione quod Deus
sit causa efficiens immediata omnium. Tum quia non potest sufficienter probari quin aliquae causae, puta corpora caelestia, sint suffici-
entes respectu multorum effectuum, et per consequens frustra
poneretur causa immediata efficiens illorum. Tum, quia si posset

it is impossible to demonstrate that God is the final cause of all things.[1] We are thus thrown back on faith right at the outset ; the whole of natural theology has disappeared and we are left only with a theology of revelation.

The same fundamental scepticism is also apparent in Ockham's treatment of the divine attributes. Even the unity of God is not rationally demonstrable ; we could only prove it were we able to prove His existence.[2] Moreover, it is possible to think of many worlds with many prime movers, or even of one world with many prime movers acting in concert.[3] And even granting God's existence and unity, it cannot be proved that he stands in any relation of intimacy to our world. We cannot even demonstrate that he knows anything outside himself ; [4] in fact the God of natural reason, if he exists at all, is the self-mediating deity of Aristotle. Nor can the infinity of the divine power be proven even if we grant the indemonstrable hypothesis that God is the creator of the universe. For even if we suppose the universe as such to contain an infinite number of entities all of these are finite, and from an infinite sum of finite effects we are not justified in inferring an infinitely powerful cause.[5] In the same

probari naturali ratione quod Deus sit causa efficiens omnium ; et non posset naturali ratione probari quod esset causa partialis necessaria vel insufficiens omnium, aeque faciliter posset probari naturali ratione quod esset causa sufficiens omnium, et frustra ponerentur aliae causae efficientes. . . . Ex istis sequitur demonstrative quod non potest probari quod Deus sit causa mediata alicujus effectus, quia si posset probari quod Deus esset mediata causa respectu unius effectus, posset probari quod est causa immediata respectu alterius in genere causae efficientis. Sed secundum non potest probari ; ergo nec primum. Et ex hoc sequitur quod nec potest probari naturaliter quod Deus sit causa efficiens totalis respectu cujuscumque effectus, nec partialis.'

[1] *Quodl.* IV, q. iii.
[2] *Quodl.* I, q. i ; cf. *In Sentt.* II, dist. ii, q. 10.
[3] *Cent. Theol.*, concl. 2.   [4] *Quodl.* II, q. ii, ad 1.
[5] *Quodl.* III, q. i : ' Licet Deus sit efficiens omnium, tamen per

way it is impossible to demonstrate, as Scotus had already shown, the theological dogma of the divine omnipotence.[1]

Like Scotus, Ockham is a voluntarist, and accords to the will the primacy over the intellect. Freedom in the wider sense is opposed to compulsion and belongs to intellect and will together in so far as they compose one *potentia libera*. In the narrower sense, however, it belongs to the will alone and signifies the indifference of the will as regards the choice of any particular object, for the will is not at all subject in its choice to the dictates of the intellect.[2] It can choose deliberately to act against the better judgement.[3] Ockham is here following very closely the theory of the will laid down by his predecessor, and he agrees with him in regarding the fact of free will as one of the immediate data of experience ; [4] it is only when he comes to apply the

hoc non potest probari quod Deus sit infinitus in vigore, quia effectibus infinitis simul producibilibus non potest probari infinitas causae ; sed quilibet effectus producibilis a Deo est finitus : ergo omnes effectus producibiles a Deo sunt finiti ; ergo per efficientiam illorum non potest probari infinitas Dei.' Cf. *Cent. Theol.*, concl. 3.

[1] *Cent. Theol.*, concl. 4 : ' Istam conclusionem tenent Catholici tanquam ex priore sequentem, quia ex quo est virtutis infinitae intensive videtur sequi ipsum esse omnipotentem. Verumtamen imaginatur ab aliquibus aliquid posse esse infinitae virtutis intensive respectu unius actionis ; quod non respectu cujuscumque : ut si ignis poneretur infinitae virtutis respectu calefactionis ; ex hoc tamen non sequitur quod esset omnipotens,' etc.

[2] *Quodl.* I, q. xvi : ' Vocol ibertatem potestatem qua possum indifferenter et contingenter effectum ponere, ita quod possum eundem effectum causare et non causare, nulla diversitate circa illam potentiam facta.'

[3] *In Sentt.*, Prol., q. i : ' Voluntas potest libere velle oppositum illius quod est dictatum per intellectum.'

[4] *Quodl.* I, q. xvi : ' Non potest probari (*sc.* libertas voluntatis) per aliquam rationem, quia omnis ratio probans accipit aeque dubia et aeque ignotum conclusioni vel ignotius. Potest tamen evidenter cognosci per experientiam, per hoc quod homo experitur quod quantumcumque ratio dictet aliquid, potest tamen voluntas hoc velle vel nolle.'

doctrine of indeterminism with all the rigour of his
relentless logic to the divine will that he begins
seriously to diverge from the teaching of the Subtle
Doctor. Starting out from the thesis maintained also
by Scotus [1] that God can do all things which do not
entail a contradiction,[2] he proceeds to draw from it
the most extreme and exaggerated conclusions. The
assumption of the human nature by the divine in the
Incarnation was only one out of a number of possible
alternatives : God might, if he had wished, become
incarnate in an ass or even in a stone.[3] Beyond this
abstract and formal law of self-consistency there are
no bounds to the arbitrary power of the divine will,
and the whole moral law depends solely and absolutely
on the divine will. It is true that the good will is
the will which acts in conformity with right reason,
but in the case of the divine will this conformity is
not previous to the act of volition, for it is just because
the divine will has willed it that the right reason
dictates that it should be willed.[4] For the will of God

---

[1] *Op. Ox.* I, dist. xlii, n. 2.

[2] *Cent. Theol.*, concl. 5 : ' Quinta conclusio est ista quod Deus
potest facere omne quod non includit contradictionem. Ista conclusio sequitur ex proxima praecedente. Quia omne possibile omnipotens potest facere : sed omne quod non includit contradictionem
possible est fieri : ergo omne quod non includit contradictionem Deus
potest facere.'

[3] *Cent. Theol.*, concl. 6 : ' Sexta conclusio est ista ; quod Deus
potest assumere omnem creaturam sive omne aliud a Deo in unitate
suppositi. Ista conclusio sic probatur. Deus assumpsit aliquam
creaturam sive naturam in unitate suppositi ; ergo Deus potest
assumere omnem. Ista consequentia patet, non gratia formae, sed
gratia materiae ; quia non videtur major ratio quare potuit unam
assumere melius quam aliam : et omnes sunt compossibiles ; ergo
potuit assumere omnem. . . . Item non includit contradictionem Deum
assumere naturam asininam ; ergo deus potest facere. Consequentia
ista patet per conclusionem proxime praecedentem, et pari ratione
potest assumere lapidem et lignum,' etc.

[4] *In Sentt.* I, dist. xli : ' Potest dici quod omnis voluntas recta est
conformis rationi rectae, sed non est semper conformis rationi rectae

can be bound by no obligation to any act whatever, and an act is right simply because it is willed by Him.[1] Thus all the conditions which appear to limit the divine will regarded as willing *de potentia ordinata*, are transcended and superseded as it were *de potentia absoluta*, with the result that man's ethical nature and his supernatural destiny become the sport of the arbitrary fiat of an absolutely indetermined volition of God. Neither grace nor sin can exercise any compelling power over the divine dealings with mankind. For though of his ordinate power God cannot grant eternal life to any one who has not the supernatural gift of *charitas creata*, he can do so, if he wills to do it, of his absolute power, and no proof of the necessity of supernatural grace can be adduced. Nay, more, he can even deny everlasting happiness to one who is actually in possession of supernatural grace,[2] a conclusion which Scotus expressly repudiates.[3] Neither the damnation of the innocent nor the salvation of the guilty entails an absolute contradiction, and both therefore are possible to the divine omnipotence.[4]

praeviae, quae ostendat causam quare voluntas debet hoc velle. Sed eo ipso quod voluntas divina hoc vult, ratio recta dictat quod est volendum.'

[1] *In Sentt.* I, Lib. IV, q. viii : ' Deus autem ad nullum actum potest obligari ; et ideo eo ipso quod Deus vult, hoc est justum fieri.'

[2] *In Sentt.* I, dist. xvii, q. i : ' Aliquis potest esse Deo acceptus et carus sine omni forma supernaturali inhaerente.' Cf. ibid. : ' Ego autem pono quod nulla forma, nec naturalis nec supernaturalis potest Deum sic necessitare, quia non includat contradictionem quod talis forma quaecumque praevia beatitudini sit in anima, et tamen quod Deus nunquam velit sibi conferre vitam aeternam. Imo ex mera gratia sua liberaliter dabit cuicumque dabit ; quamvis de potentia ordinata aliter non posset facere propter leges voluntarie et contingenter a Deo ordinatas.'

[3] *Op. Ox.* I, dist. xvii, q. 3, n. 18 ; Cf. Minges, *Der Gottesbegriff, u.s.w.* ch. 6.

[4] Loc. cit., q. ii : ' Non includit contradictionem aliquem actum esse meritorium sine omni habitu supernaturali formaliter inhaerente. Quia nullus actus ex puris naturalibus, nec ex quacumquae causa

Ockham is here only making explicit what was already implicit in the voluntaristic teaching of Scotus. And we might go even further and maintain that he was only developing the implications which lay concealed under the dogmatic form of the doctrine of Grace as understood and interpreted by the medieval church. But his development is wholly one-sided, and he neglects the rationalistic elements which are throughout present in Duns' ethics.[1] And whereas for Scotus the commandments of the second table may under certain circumstances be dispensed from by especial divine command, in order to meet hard cases as it were, for Ockham the whole decalogue rests contingently upon the absolute indeterminism of the divine will.[2] Duns, it is true, does in the last resort seek to justify these dispensations by means of an almost Hobbist theory of the divine sovereignty, but side by side with this teaching he preserves also the main features of the rationalistic ethics of Aristotle, apparently unaware of the vast inconsistency of these two incompatible principles. In Ockham even the

creata, potest esse meritorius, sed ex gratia Dei voluntarie et libere acceptante bonum motum voluntatis tanquam meritorium. Et ideo sicut Deus voluntarie et libere acceptat bonum motum voluntatis sicut meritorium, quando elicitur ab habente charitatem ; ita de potentia sua absoluta posset acceptare eundem motum voluntatis, etiam si non infundet charitatem.' Cf. op. cit. III, q. 8 : ' Deus potest aliquem acceptare in puris naturalibus tanquam dignum vita aeterna sine omni habitu charitatis, et etiam reprobare sine omni peccato.'

[1] See vol. ii, ch. viii.

[2] Cf. Ueberweg, *Grundriss der Geschichte der Philosophie der patristischen und scholastischen Zeit,* ed. x, Baumgartner (Berlin, 1915), pp. 605–6 : ' In Der Ethik wandelt Ockham in den Bahnen des Duns Scotus, geht aber viel weiter als dieser, insofern er das gesammte Sittengesetz, alle Gebote des Dekalogs in den Willen Gottes begründet sein lässt, so dass sie jederzeit und beliebig abgeändert werden können. Das Sittengesetz gilt nicht als etwas an sich Notwendiges. Es wäre denkbar das Gott durch einem anderen Willen anderes als gerecht und gut sanktionniert hätte. Was gut ist, ist nur gut weil es Gott will und akzeptiert.'

attempt to harmonize the two doctrines disappears, and his continual emphasis on the absolute indeterminateness of the divine volition produces a kind of moral scepticism which is thoroughly characteristic of his whole system.

We have now examined briefly the principal types of doctrine which were current in the philosophical world at the time when Duns Scotus embarked upon his teaching career, and we have noted a few of the developments which his doctrine received at the hands of the greatest of his successors. Our final task in this volume will be to estimate, as shortly as possible, the significance of Scotus in the history of medieval thought. If we consider the condition of scholasticism during the closing years of the thirteenth century we shall find that outside the Thomist system all was chaos and confusion. The older 'Augustinian' doctrine had never been systematic; its growth had been one with the development of medieval life, and just as round an ancient castle a township might gradually spring up, almost haphazardly and fortuitously, yet not without vital contact with a people's needs, its winding streets conforming to no particular plan and its crooked houses exhibiting no uniformity of structure; so medieval thought had grown up amidst the ruins of the civilization of ancient Rome under the protecting shadow of the Catholic Church, each generation and each 'school' adding its characteristic contribution, often a little incongruously, to the heritage of the past, until piece by piece a more or less definite body of doctrine had developed which was bound together not so much by the articulation of its logical structure as by the more flexible bond of mystical experience. Then, with the beginning of the thirteenth century, the great change had come. The new logic found its way into the schools of western Europe, the whole field of philosophical knowledge was suddenly expanded and enlarged, and in the teaching of Albert and Aquinas scholasticism became for the first time a system. The Thomist teaching gained a success which was as brilliant as it was immediate. The rediscovery of Aristotle had brought about an intellectual revolution which may well be compared with that wrought by the advance of science in the nineteenth century, and beside his gigantic system the older attempts to explain the universe appeared crude and barbarous. Philosophy, once the mere handmaid of theology, had become mistress in her own house, emancipated once and for all from theological tutelage. But the mind of man moves slowly, especially where theological matters are concerned, and the older teaching continued for a time to hold its ground. Scattered but not subdued, the adherents of the older tradition carried on a desultory but persistent guerrilla warfare, of which the *Correctorium fratris Thomae* may be regarded as a typical manœuvre, organized principally by the Franciscan School and maintained with all the subtlety of the logician and the ingenuity of the theologian. For though in a sense the newer teaching had come to stay, it contained within itself many elements which could never be assimilated satisfactorily by Christian thought, and it introduced a dyarchy of Faith and Reason which was ultimately responsible for the downfall of scholasticism. Though it seemed for a moment that the two had met together and been reconciled in a bond of peace, each agreeing to respect the integrity of the other's province, in the long run such a division was in fact impossible; it contained from the first the seeds of its own dissolution. For knowledge is ultimately one and indivisible; its sources and its principles cannot be duplicated, and the attempt of Thomas to make theology a science standing above philosophy and independent of it was doomed to failure from the beginning. The garment

of truth is indeed seamless ; it may not be divided
without peril, and a rent spells scepticism, as subsequent
scholastics were very quickly to discover.

The main characteristic of the period between
Thomas and Scotus is its eclecticism, the attempt to
adjust the differences of the older and the newer
tradition and to achieve a unity which should include
both. The consequence of this groping is everywhere
apparent, and reveals itself in a confusion of conflicting
theories such as we have seen exemplified in the writings
of those philosophers whose thinking we have just
reviewed. There is little or no systematic coherence
of thought, and few of them seem to realize any definite
connexion between the isolated theorems they defend.
Everywhere there is a welter of controversies, unor-
ganized and unarticulated ; single issues variously
disputed and variously determined by contending
parties. Philosophy has come down from heaven and
entered the debating hall, for such indeed the lecture
room of the medieval universities might well be called,
and Thomism is the perpetual subject of the debate.
It was the task of Scotus to clear up all the confused
issues and to formulate a definite and coherent
criticism of the doctrine of his great rival, and at the
same time to lay down an opposition, a connected
system which should serve as an alternative to that of
the Angelic Doctor.

Such, then, was the work which Duns set out to
accomplish, but he left it only half finished. More
than three-quarters of his writings are in the form of
commentary, full of acute and penetrating criticism
and suggestive statements, but inevitably fragmentary
and disconnected. The systematic exposition is
wanting, but it would be a mistake to suppose that
therefore his thought was incoherent.[1] The few

---

[1] The judgement of G. de Ruggiero on this point seems to me to
be an exaggeration. Cf. *Storia della Filosofia del Cristianesimo*, vol. iii,

constructive treatises he has left behind him show an
unmistakable grasp of an essential unity of thought,
and it may well be that they were but preliminary
studies for a greater treatise which he never lived to
complete. And the foundations of this system were
well laid. Had he ever completed the superstructure
in all the minute detail of the *Summa Theologica* of
Thomas, he might have eventually become the official
doctor of the Catholic Church. But by an irony of
fate his work has lain neglected since the beginning
of the eighteenth century, and the current of modern
thought has passed it by, while the Roman Church in
more recent times has devoted herself almost exclu-
sively to the study of the Thomistic philosophy and
disregarded a system which in many ways is more
suited to serve as the speculative basis for the Catholic
faith.

For the purer Aristotelianism of Aquinas was but
indifferently adapted to the Christian tradition. The
peripatetic scheme of the universe was so radically
different from the metaphysical assumptions upon
which Christianity is grounded that the task of recon-
ciling the two standpoints was from the very beginning
impossible. How clearly Scotus realized this is shown
by the fact that he differs essentially from Thomas

p. 177: 'Ma la presenza di motivi tanti disparati—empirismo,
misticismo, voluntarismo, insieme col vecchio bagaglio dell' agostinismo
medievale e delle inconciliabili formule aristoteliche—in seno alla
stessa scuola, toglie la possibilità che essa crei un sistema abbastanza
compatto e organico come quello tomista. Anche nel maggior-
rappresentante, anzi in lui più che in altri, in Duns Scoto, invano
ci affaneremo a cercare uno stretto nesso organico tra le singole
dottrine.' Far more just is the estimate of Kahl, *Die Lehre vom
Primat des Willens*, etc., pp. 77–8: 'Seine Werke bekunden einen
Scharfsinn und eine Gedankentiefe die ihn den grössten Denkern
aller Zeiten ebenbürtig an die Seite stellen: um so mehr müssen
wir es bedauern dass sein System ein Torso geblieben ist, ein colossaler
freilich, der als das Denkmal eines riesenhaftes Geistes aus der alten
Zeit in die neue herüberragt.'

only on those points where the doctrines of the latter are manifestly difficult to reconcile with the Christian faith.[1] The clearest example of such a difference is found in the varying conceptions of the nature of form and matter held by the two scholastics. Thomas keeps strictly to the Aristotelian view; matter is pure potency, the ubiquitous correlative of form, which of itself has no existence either actual or possible. But such a cosmology is obviously inconsistent with the Christian standpoint; to Aristotle matter and form are coeternal constituents of an eternal world, and Thomas realizes that the same theory is implied in his own doctrine; hence his insistence that creation in time cannot be shown philosophically to be necessary. To save himself he has to introduce another dualism, abstract and obscure, between essence and existence, the significance of which is so definitely brought out by Aegidius Romanus in the passage we have just cited. But for Scotus such a difficulty does not exist. He follows the older Augustinian tradition, and for him matter is something positive, a world-stuff created by the divine will, out of which, by the successive imposition of forms, the diversity of creatures is differentiated. It is true that we must not interpret this concept of matter along the lines of the physical theories of the nineteenth century; the Scotist *materia primo prima* is still, as Schneid points out, a purely abstract metaphysical entity;[2] nor must we regard

---

[1] Cf. Carreras, *Ensayo sobre el voluntarismo de J. Duns Scot*, p. 65 : ' El choque de la filosofía aristotélica con la teología tradicional provocó un grupo de problemas muy tipicos, . . . Duns Scot toma de su época la peculiaridad de los problemas metafísicos planteados ; pero su crítica sagaz se complace en poner al descubierto las inconsecuencias implicadas en el intelectualismo de los peripatéticos latinos y en mostrar la incompatibilidad de las doctrinas genuinas de Aristóteles con algunos supuestos básicos de la teología tradicional.'

[2] Cf. Schneid, *Die Körperlehre des Johannes Duns Scotus*, pp. 2 sqq. It is interesting to compare with the Scotist doctrine some of the

the stages of its progressive determination as belonging to the temporal order ; but it represents nevertheless an attempt to give some philosophical basis to the doctrine of creation, and in endowing matter with a real existence of its own Scotus is pointing the way along which the subsequent progress of scientific speculation has evolved.

So, too, in his psychology he differs from Thomas in a similar manner. The attempt to interpret the Christian conception of the soul, in all the depth and fullness of its content, as we find it in Augustine, in terms of the Aristotelian notion of the ' psyche ' had been obviously inadequate. The implications of the Thomist doctrine were too clear to escape immediate observation ; Lamarre's charge of Averroism was too nearly justified to pass unheeded, and even though Thomas successfully rebutted it, it was only at the price of sacrificing his consistency and abandoning in actual fact his theory of individuation.[1] Moreover, the writings of Siger of Brabant and the Latin Averroists made it at least doubtful whether after all the Averroistic interpretation of the *De Anima* was not nearer to the original meaning of Aristotle than that of Thomas.[2] And at any rate the difficulty of the

more recent developments of modern physics, which seem to be moving away from the more concrete notions of the nineteenth century towards a more abstract conception of the nature of matter.

[1] Vide supra, cap. v, p. 156.

[2] Cf. E. Gilson, *Études de Philosophie médiévale*, pp. 52–75 : ' La doctrine de la double vérité.' Prof. Gilson on p. 64 quotes certain passages from Jean de Jandun which throw a very interesting light on this question. Jean taught at Paris at the beginning of the fourteenth century, but it is not easy to establish his identity ; there is some doubt whether he is the same John who was the joint author with Marsilio of Padua of the *Defensor Pacis* or whether he must be identified with John of Ghent, the pastor of Kieldrecht and canon of Paris (*v.* de Wulf, *History of Mediaeval Philosophy*, pp. 442 sq.). In the former case, he would hardly have been a contemporary of Scotus ; in the latter, he would have been teaching at Paris at the same time

doctrine remained in the shape of an awkward dilemma, to which we have already alluded. The attempt to reconcile Aristotle with Christianity at this point breaks down completely. But it is just here that Scotus diverges from the Peripatetic doctrine and goes back to the more profound teaching of Augustine ; soul and body, though substantially united, are yet two separate entities. Thus the existence of both after death can be upheld, and the doctrine of the life of the departed spirit entails no special difficulties. It is true that the Scotist position has its own crux in the substantial union of two beings which are virtually each of themselves substances, but it should be kept in mind that such a difficulty which would be fatal to Thomas, with his view of the purely potential existence of matter as solely the correlative of form, does not necessarily conflict with the Scotist theory, which conceives the relation of form to matter on an entirely different plan. And it is manifest that Scotus' teaching is more in harmony with the Christian faith ; not that he regards himself as having

as Duns. Whichever of these two men was the author of the works cited does not materially affect our contention : they are valuable as giving a typical standpoint of the Averroist school which throughout the latter part of the thirteenth and the beginning of the fourteenth centuries exercised an important influence on medieval thought. John accuses Thomas of vain contradictions of the Commentator : ' Et intelligendum quod sanctus Thomas qui in omnibus aut pluribus in quibus potuit conatus fuit contradicere Commentatori . . .,' *Quaest. de Phys.*, audit. VII, 2. ' Dico quod ego non credo ei in hoc, sicut nec in aliis conclusionibus philosophicis in quibus contradicit Commentatori ; et magis credendum est Commentatori in illis quae debent probari demonstrative,' ibid.; cf. also *De Anima*, iii. 23, sub fin. ' Vel dicamus expositores latinos non expressisse hunc modum necessitatis intellectus agentis ; quod non provenit ex ignorantia, nec ex eo quod illi non crediderunt illum esse unum entium ; sed hoc contingit multis ex eo quod ipsi in senectute sua magis fuerunt intenti circa theologica quam circa philosophica, et ideo multas conclusiones philosophiae naturalis praetermiserunt sine sufficienti declaratione.'

provided a strict proof of the immortality of the soul—
he expressly denies that such a proposition can be
demonstrated [1]—but he has at least made it possible
to maintain such a doctrine without involving himself
in the contradictions which beset the Thomist view,
contradictions which, however much Thomas tries to
conceal them, remain but thinly veiled.

The same tendencies may also be observed in connexion with the other great line of cleavage between
Thomas and Scotus, the controversy between intellectualism and voluntarism. Once more Thomas
stands forth as the champion of a purer Aristotelianism
as against the Augustinian tradition. He attempts to
safeguard the freedom of the will, but his interpreta-
tion of *voluntas* in terms of $\pi\rho o\alpha i\rho\epsilon\sigma\iota\varsigma$ leads him
to something very like intellectual determinism, for
such indeed the notion of *necessitas finis* virtually
becomes. [2] Consequently his theory of the will,
however stoutly he tries to maintain its freedom, is
continually haunted by the ghost of the Socratic
paradox. This comes out most plainly in his doctrine
of moral evil,[3] and furnishes another instance of the
inadequacy of the Peripatetic philosophy to serve as
a vehicle for the expression of the Christian ethics.
What greater contrast could there be in the whole
field of ethical theory than that between the Aristo-
telian doctrine of $\phi\rho\acute{o}\nu\eta\sigma\iota\varsigma$ and the overpowering sense
of sin felt by Augustine and St. Paul? Yet Thomas is
for ever attempting to translate the Pauline theology
into the philosophic terms of the Nicomachean *Ethics*.

Scotus also attempts to fit his ethics into an Aristotelian frame, but in a lesser degree. His adherence
to the tradition of Anselm and Augustine provides
him with a theory of the will which is less defective

---

[1] Cf. *Op. Ox.*, Lib. IV, dist. xliii, q. 2.
[2] Cf. *Summa Theol.* Ia 2ae, q. 9, art. 1 ; q. 10, art. 2.
[3] Cf. *Summa contra Gent.*, Lib. III, cap. vi.

and more in harmony with the teachings of the Church, while his refusal to recognize any determination by a necessary end [1] leaves room for human responsibility in a way which is ultimately impossible for Thomas, who, like Aristotle, is unable to give a satisfactory account of ἀκρασία.

The full range of the controversy between intellectualism and voluntarism is brought out in the different conceptions of the divine being held by the two scholastics. In the case of Thomas, no less than that of Aristotle, it is to his cosmological conceptions that we must look for the guiding thread of his philosophy. The notion of form is the dominating concept of his theology which gives it its characteristically intellectualistic tendency and differentiates it from that of Scotus. We see this most clearly in the controversy on the nature of the Trinitarian Process. Thomas tries to interpret the generation of the Son by the Father as an act of the divine intellect, in common with Henry of Ghent and Godfrey of Fontaines.[2] Henry and Godfrey conceived the divine essence as the *quasi-materia* from which the son is generated, while Thomas takes it to be the *principium quo*. The first of these views is crudely naturalistic (in fact Henry employs the materialistic metaphor of heat rays from a fire) and is disposed of by Scotus without much difficulty.[3] But Thomas has also illegitimately used a conception taken from natural philosophy when he bases his contention on the theory that, not the *proprietas individualis*, but the *natura* as such is the

---

[1] Cf. *Op. Ox.*, Lib. I, dist. i, q. 4 : ' Voluntas creata non necessario tendit in finem sibi ostensum, nec in universali nec in particulari,' etc.

[2] Cf. Thomas, *Summa Theol.* I, q. 41. Henry, *Summa Theol.*, art. 54, q. iii ; *Quodl.* VIII, q. ix. Godfrey, *Quodl.* IX, tom. 8. Godfrey does not employ quite the same language as Henry ; he conceives the divine essence as the *subjectum generationis,* a view which practically coincides with that of Henry.

[3] *Op. Ox.*, Lib. I, dist. v, q. 2.

principium agendi, as being that in which generator
and generated are united.[1]   According to Scotus,
however, the *forma* in which generator and generated
are assimilated can have only conceptual or meta-
phorical significance; it cannot be the *principium
elicitivum* of a real act.[2]   He refuses to regard the
Trinitarian Process in God as a formative activity, the
absolute self-information of the divine essence, just
as he rejects another conception dear to the heart of
Thomas, namely the notion of the divine ideas as
forms which though identical with the divine essence
are somehow prior and not posterior to the act of the
divine intelligence.

It is not difficult to see the motive underlying
Scotus' repudiation of this employment of the cosmological ' Formbegriff '.   Its deterministic trend is
obvious, and however much Thomas may identify the
divine will with the divine essence, no less than the
divine intellect, his tendency is to interpret the being
of God in intellectualistic terms.   But to Scotus such
an interpretation is too naturalistic.   While he agrees
with Thomas in maintaining the impossibility of any
a priori proof of God's existence, he lays great stress
on the ontological argument of Anselm,[3] and his
ground conception of the divine nature is the ontological notion of infinite being.   Hence his refusal
to admit this application of the notion of form to
God in his absolute spirituality ; for he will not have
the infinite being subjected to any limiting conditions.
It is this same conception that underlies his polemic
against the *rationes aeternae* of Henry and Aquinas
and which forms the basis of his voluntarism.   Thus

---

[1] Thomas, loc. cit., art. 5.

[2] *Op. Ox.*, Lib. I, dist. vii, q. unica.

[3] *Op. Ox.*, Lib. I, dist. ii, q. 2, n. 32.   See also Werner, ' Die
Psychologie, u.s.w., des Duns Scotus ' (*Sitzungsberichte der kaiserlichen
Akademie der Wissenschaften*, Wien, vol. xxvi, pp. 422 sqq.).

once more, in the account he gives of the Trinitarian Process, he falls back upon the older tradition of Anselm and Augustine. The procession of the Son from the Father is not an act of the divine intellect but of the *memoria fecunda* [1]; only on this supposition can the Son be something really different from the Father, and the hypostatic difference of the Holy Ghost from both be maintained. Thus by this interpretation of the eternal generation in God as the immanent act of His infinite being, the threefold distinction of Augustine of *intellectio*, *voluntas*, and *memoria* is preserved, which on the Thomistic hypothesis did not come into its rights. Scotus is seeking for something less abstract than the Thomist view, and he tries to reach a more profound conception of the divine generation than that of an intellectual act ; the *productio ad intra* must rest on something more fundamental, and here the Augustinian concept of *memoria* (which in fact he only half understood [2]) comes to his aid, as expressing more than the merely intellective aspect of the divine nature.

But it is in his critical rather than his constructive aspect that Scotus has found a place in the histories of philosophy. His refusal to concede the strict demonstrability of certain theological propositions

---

[1] Cf. *Quodl.*, q. i.

[2] The divine *memoria* for Augustine expresses something more fundamental to the divine nature than either the divine *intellectio* or the divine *voluntas* : it is the very ground of the divine being itself. Cf. *De Trinitate*, xii. 15. In Scotus, on the other hand, the two notions of *memoria* and *intellectus* are almost impossible to keep apart, and in one passage he actually identifies them. Cf. *Rep. Par.* IV, dist. xlv, q. 3. It is true that he is here speaking of the human and not of the divine *memoria* and *intellectus* and that in *Quodl.*, q. i he implies a distinction between them, but he never makes it plain exactly what that distinction is, and in his treatment of the human as opposed to the divine spirit it is scarcely possible to draw any clear line between the intellectual as opposed to the sensitive memory and the intellect itself.

by the light of pure reason, has been regarded as the beginning of the decline of scholastic thought and as pointing the way to the scepticism of the terminist school. But, as we have seen, this was in a sense the inevitable outcome of the adoption of the Aristotelian system. Christianity and Peripateticism were from the first mutually incompatible, and the former had failed to produce a satisfactory philosophy of its own. The refusal to concede to theology a strictly scientific character was but one aspect of the dualism between the natural and the supernatural which could only have been avoided by a naturalism completely out of harmony with the main tendencies of the thought of the age. The Scotist critique of the Thomist system only served to accentuate a discord already latent in it ; it was a criticism not of the propositions themselves, which Thomas had thought to establish by natural reason, but of the strict validity of the arguments which he had used in his attempt to do so. For Scotus, no less than Thomas, believed in the truth of just those doctrines which he denied to be demonstrable. And in the last resort the difference on this point between the two thinkers was not vital to the main issue. Both alike admitted the existence of truths which were indemonstrable by reason and cognizable by divine revelation ; neither, however, would concede the possibility of a real conflict or contradiction between the two orders of verity. The actual assignment, therefore, of a particular proposition to one side of the dividing line or the other was a matter of comparatively small importance, because it entailed no absolute difference of principle.

It was only when the cumulative psychological effect of the transference of one thesis after another to the region of revelation at last made itself felt that the dualism already implicit at the very beginning became intolerable and the breakdown took place.

By insisting more strongly than Thomas on the volitional aspect of theology and its practical nature Scotus hoped to secure more perfectly its independence while at the same time avoiding conflict with philosophical speculation. His criticism had laid bare the essential inadequacy of Arabian Peripateticism to be used as the basis for Christian thought; but he himself was likewise unable to make good the deficiency. And though he succeeded partially in building up a system which, through its incorporation of certain elements of the older tradition, harmonized more easily than that of Thomas with the teachings of the Church, his synthesis was too incomplete and too late in time to arrest the process of decay. For the Middle Ages were in a sense already over; the period dominated by the conception of a dyarchy of Pope and Emperor had already closed, before men knew it, with the fall of the house of Hohenstaufen. And just as Greek thought only reached its maturity when the days of the city state which had fostered it were already numbered, so the scholastic philosophy put forth its finest flowers only when the conditions which had produced the 'Ages of Faith' were already ceasing to be operative. For the owl of Minerva flies only when the day is ended.

A LIST OF
WORKS ATTRIBUTED TO DUNS SCOTUS

THE edition of Wadding (Lyon, 1639) contains the following writings :

De modis significandi, seu Grammatica speculativa.

Logicalia :

  Super universalia Porphyrii, qq. xxxvi.
  In librum Praedicamentorum, qq. xliv.
  In primum librum Perihermenias, qq. xii.
  In secundum librum Perihermenias, qq. x.
  In duos libros Perihermenias operis secundi, qq. xiii.
  In libros Elenchorum, qq. lvi.
  In librum primum Analyticorum Priorum, qq. xxxvii.
  In librum secundum Analyticorum Priorum, qq. xiii.
  In librum primum Posteriorum Analyticorum, qq. xlvii.
  In librum secundum Posteriorum Analyticorum, qq. xiii.

Quaestiones in VIII libros Physicorum Aristotelis. (Spurious.)
Quaestiones super libros Aristotelis de Anima.
Meteorologicorum libri IV. (Spurious.)
Tractatus de Rerum Principio.
Tractatus de Primo Rerum Omnium Principio.
Theoremata. (Doubtful.)
Collationes.
Tractatus imperfectus de Cognitione Dei.
Quaestiones miscellaneae de Formalitatibus. (Doubtful.)
In XII libros Metaphysicorum Aristotelis expositio. (Spurious.)
Conclusiones utilissimae Metaphysicae. (Spurious.)
Quaestiones subtilissimae super libros Metaphysicorum Aristotelis.
Quaestiones in IV libros Sententiarum, seu Opus Oxoniense.
Quaestiones in IV libros Sententiarum, seu Reportata Parisiensia.
Quaestiones Quodlibetales, qq. xxi.

The edition of Wadding was reprinted by L. Vives (Paris, 1891-5), together with a treatise *De Perfectione Statuum*, which is almost certainly spurious.

The following works which have not come down to us have also been attributed to Scotus by various writers :

Lectura in Genesim. (Attested by Leland, Pits, Jacob le Long, etc.

Commentarii in Evangelia. (Attested by Bartholemew of Pisa, Gonzaga, and the authors cited above.)

Commentarii in Epistolas S. Pauli. (Attested by Sixtus Senensis, Pits, Possevinus, and others.)

Sermones de Tempore.

Sermones de Sanctis.

A large number of other writings undoubtedly spurious have also been attributed to the Subtle Doctor, among which the following are the more important :

Tractatus Doctoris Subtilis ad Regem Angliae. (Bibl. Reg. Hisp. MS. 1718.)

Disputatio Scoti de Opera Lapidis Philosophalis. (Bibl. Nat. Paris, Fund. Lat. No. 11202.)

Opusculum Doctoris Subtilis super aliquos Canones Arzachelis. (Cambridge Univ. Library, MS. Ee 3. 61a.)

Tractatus de Trinitate. (Oxford, Bodl. Digby MS. No. 54.)

Tractatus de Arte Divina. (Lyon, Bibl. Publ. MS. No. 317.)

The following works also exist in manuscript :

Quaestio Disputata de Principio Individuationis. (Erfurt, Cod. Amplon., fol. 369.)

Quaestiones super Librum Divisionis Boethii. (Magdalen Coll. Oxford, 38.)

Collationes, not printed in Wadding's edition. (Balliol Coll. Oxford, 209 ; also Merton Coll. MSS. 65, 90.)

Tractatus de Cognitione Dei. (Merton Coll. MS. 90.) (Not in Wadding.)

[For the text of the last two of these *opuscula* see the Appendix at the end of the second volume of this work.]

Note on the ' Reportata Parisiensia '

In his essay entitled ' Le premier livre des *Reportata Parisiensia* de Jean Duns Scot ', published in the *Annales de l'institut supérieur de Philosophie,* Louvain (T. 5. 1923) Mgr. A. Pelzer discusses the problem of the text of the first book of the *Reportata.* He begins by pointing out the meaning of the term *reportatum,* which is used to denote an account of a disputation or a lecture written down not by the author but by a member of his audience. This account or *reportatum* was afterwards submitted, in certain cases, to the lecturer or disputant for his approval and certified by him to be correct. In the case of the first book of Parisian *Reportata* of Duns' lectures on the four books of Sentences we have to deal with several documents of different value. (1) The little ' reportation ' of Brother H. of High Germany. (2) The great 'reportation ' which was examined and certified by Duns himself. (3) The corrupt ' reportation ' which was printed at

Paris for Jean Mair in 1517–18. (4) The abridgement of the great 'reportation' made by William of Alnwick. (5) The texts derived from this abridgement, namely : (*a*) the *résumé* of the abridgement, made probably by William of Missali, known as the *Tabula super primo Scoti de reportatione* (Cod. Vat. lat. 890. ff. 1 r.–3 r.) ; (*b*) the *editio princeps* of the abridgement, *Joannis Scoti . . . super primo sententiarum reportationum Parisiensium* (Bologna, 1478) ; (*c*) the corrupt edition of the abridgement published as the first book of the *Reportata Parisiensia* by Wadding in his edition of 1639. The main conclusion arrived at by Mgr. Pelzer is that Wadding's text which has for so long a time been accepted as authentic is really a conflation of William of Alnwick's abridgement of the great 'reportation' certified by the Subtle Doctor himself and the corrupt 'reportation' published by Jean Mair (Grandjohn) in 1517.

The great 'reportation' exists in three manuscripts—Borghese 325, ff. 1 r.–92 v. ; Merton College, Oxford, 59, ff. 1 r.–190 v. ; Vienna Staatsbibliothek 1453, ff. 1 r.–125 v.   At the end of the Vienna MS., which like that in the Borghese library belongs to the end of the fourteenth century, the following 'explicit' is to be found :

'Explicit reportacio super primum sententiarum sub magistro johanne scoto, et examinata cum eodem venerando doctore.'

The Merton College MS. is one of those written by Johannes Reynbold, and is dated 1455.

It is evident, Mgr. Pelzer concludes, that Wadding's text can no longer be regarded as authoritative, and that a new edition taken from the MSS. of the certified 'reportation' is much to be desired.

BIBLIOGRAPHIES

§ 1. *Bibliography of Editions*

FROM 1472 onwards numerous editions of the various treatises ascribed to the Subtle Doctor were printed, chiefly at Padua, Venice, and Paris, but no complete edition of his works was made until that of Wadding in 1639. The bibliography of Scotus is still somewhat obscure and contains many problems which yet remain to be solved. The following list, which, however, makes no pretence to completeness, contains the principal editions.

Opus Oxoniense

The first printed edition of the great commentary on the Sentences was brought out in an abbreviated form by Joannes de Colonia, together with the *Quodlibeta*, the *Quaestiones* on the *Metaphysics*, and the *De Anima*, and printed in Venice by Master Vindelinus de Spira in 1472. Numerous editions followed.

1472. (Questiones super IV libris Sententiarum, etc.) Begin. (fol. 13, sig. a 2, preceded by 11 leaves containing table and a blank leaf): *Incipiunt questiones magistri Johannis Scoti abbreviate et ordinate per alphabetum* (By Johannes de Colonia) *super IV libris sententiarum, quodlibetis, qq. metaphysice et de anima. per Magistrum Vindelinum de Spira.* (Venice.)

[388 printed leaves; without title-page or catchwords; printed in double columns, 36 lines to a full page.]

1472. Book I (Questiones super libro primo Sententiarum.) Begin. (fol. 1 r.): *Utrum homini pro statu isto sit necessarium aliquam,* etc. End. (fol. 246 r.): *Expliciunt questiones Joannis Scoti theologi acutissimi sacri minorum ordinis: super primo sententiarum: Quod opus ab Antonio Trombeta: theologo: patavino . . . ingenti diligentia emendatum est,* etc. (Venetiis 1472, fol.)

[247 leaves, without title-page, pagination, or register.]

1474. Book IV (Questiones super libro quarto Sententiarum). Begin.: *Johannis scoti subtilissimi doctoris theologi in quartum sentenciarum opus anglicanum feliciter incipit,* etc. (A. Koburger, Nuremberg, 1474, fol.).

[Without title-page, pagination, signatures, or catchwords; printed in double columns, 51 lines to a full column.]

1474. Book II (Questiones super libro secundo Sententiarum.) Begin.
(fol. 2 r.), preceded by one leaf containing the table) : *Circa
creatorem*, etc. End. : *Expliciunt questiones Ioannis scoti . . .
super 2° sentenciarum ab excellentissimo sacre theologie professore
T. Penket . . . emendate per magistrum A. de Stedael.* (Venice (?),
1474, fol.)
   [158 leaves, without title-page, pagination, register, or
catchwords, printed in double columns, 40 lines to a full
column.]

1477. (Complete.) (Quaestiones super libris Sententiarum). Begin.
(sig. a 2) : *Prologus. cupientes aliquid de penuria*, etc. End.
(part 4) *Johannis Scoti in 4um sentenciarum opus . . . recognovit
Thomas Anglicus*, etc.
   *Expensis . . . Johannis de Colonia sociique ejus Johannis
Manthen de Gherretzem.* (Venetiis 1477, fol.)
   [Printed in double columns, 51 lines to a full column ;
without catchwords or pagination.]

1481. (Complete.) Begin. : *Johannis duns scoti . . . scriptum super
primo (-4°) sentenciarum incipit feliciter.* (With *Quodlibetum*.)
End. : *Finit quodlibet Johannis duns scoti . . . post scripta
ejusdem super quatuor libris sentenciarum per Thomam panchet . . .
castigata*, etc. 5 pts. (Impensis Antonii koburger : Nurnberge,
1481, fol.)
   [Without title-page, pagination, signatures, or catchwords ;
printed in double columns, 71 lines to a full column.]

1490. (Complete ?.) *Primus (-quartus) sententiarum doctoris subtilis
Scoti :* with *tabula Scoti* and the *Quodlibeta* and the *De Primo
Principio :* containing the text of the sentences of Peter Lom-
bard. Edited by Gratianus Brixianus. (Industria Bernardini
de Novara. Venetiis 1490, fol.)
   [It is doubtful whether more than the first two books were
published. See *Brit. Mus. Catalogue of Printed Books* under
'Duns'. The *tabula*, however, serves for all four. According to
Bertoni, the work was completed, but he gives the place of
publication as Padua. See A. Bertoni : *Le bienheureux J. Duns
Scot*, p. 471.]

1497. Book IV. Edited by Johannes Grillot and Antonius Capella.
Printed at Paris.

1497. (Complete.) *Scoti in IV libros Sententiarum Scriptum Oxoniense
castigatum atque emendatum, additis responsionibus ad argumenta
suis locis et annotationibus opinionum diversorum Doctorum.* At
the end of the first book are appended some *additiones*, while at
the end of the second the *Opusculum in secundum librum sententiarum* of Bartholomew Bellati is added. Printed at Venice.

1506. Book I, with the ' conclusiones ' of Master Henry Gorichem, edited by Maurice O'Fihely and printed at Venice by Simon de Luere. *Primus scripti Oxoniensis doctoris Subtilis fratris Joannis Duns Scoti . . . super sententias. (Textus Primi sentētiarum cum conclusionibus magistri Henrici Gorichem, etc.) per Simonem de Luere pro dño Andrea de Torresanis de Asula.* (Venetiis 1506, fol.)

1513. Complete edition by Maurice O'Fihely (Mauritius de portu), printed by A. Grandjohn (Jean Mair) at Paris.

1517. Book I, edited by Antonius de Fantis, printed by Jacobus de Burgofranco. (Papiae, 1517.)

1518. Complete edition with *Quodlibeta, Collationes, De Primo Principio,* and *Theoremata.*
Primus (–quartus) liber doctoris subtilis fratris Johannis Duns Scoti . . . super sententias . . . Habes . . . Quaestiones quodlibetales, Johannis Duns Scoti cum collationibus ejusdem . . . Et tractatum de primo rerum omnium principio atque Theoremata. Printed by A. Grandjohn at Paris. 5 pts.

1519. Book IV. Printed at Paris *Zimpensis adoci Badii Ascensii.*

1597. Complete edition, together with *Quodlibeta, Collationes,* and the epitome of de Fantis : edited by Melchior Flavius.
Fratris Johannis Duns Scoti . . . in quatuor libros sententiarum perutiles quaestiones . . . annotationibus exornatae . . . nuncque noviter impressae atque . . . recognitae. Resolutiones quaestionum Johannis Duns Scoti . . . in librum primum-quartum sententiarum . . . a . . . Melchiore Flavio . . . variis illuminibus illustratae . . . Quaestiones quodlibetales . . . Collationes][seu disputationes quaestionum J. D. S. . . . in libros sententiarum epitome . . . auctore A. de Fantis. Printed at Venice by J. Bapt. and J. Bern. Sessam. 9 pts., fol.

1600. *Resolutiones in IV libros Sententiarum Joannis Duns Scoti . . . per Joannem Forsanum in lucem . . . tradita.* Printed at Paris.

1603. Complete edition with commentary by F. Damianus Giner. Printed at Valentia by A. Franci.

1609. Book I, with commentary edited by Johannes ab Incarnatione. *P. P. Fr. Joannis Duns Scoti . . . Oxoniensis scriptum in librum primum Sententiarum Magistri Petri Lombardi. Nunc primo ordinatum et expurgatum per Fr. Joannem ab Incarnatione,* etc. (Coimbricae 1609, fol.)

1614. Complete edition with commentary by Johannes Yribarne y Yriburu. Printed at Saragossa by P. Casarte.

1617. Complete edition with *Quodlibeta* and *Collationes* by Paulinus Berti. Printed at Venice by J. Salis.

1620. Complete edition with life of Scotus, etc., by H. Cavell.
Fratris Johannis Duns Scoti . . . in primum (–quartum) Senten-
tiarum quaestiones subtilissimae. Nunc noviter recognitae . . . per
H. Cavellum . . . Accesserunt per eundem vita Scoti, apologia pro
ipso contra A. Bzovium. Printed at Antwerp by J. Keerbergius,
2 pts., fol.
[Incorporated by Wadding in his edition of 1639.]

1624. Book III, with commentary, edited by J. de Ovando.
Subtilissimus . . . Joannes Duns Scotus elucidatus . . . circa tertium
librum Sententiarum. Ejus littera articulata, elucubratione
exornata . . . in clarissimum redacta methodum a . . . J. de Ovando.
Printed at Valentia, fol.

1661. Complete edition with commentary by Johannes Poncius.
Commentarii theologici quibus Joannis Duns Scoti quaestiones
in librum Sententiarum elucidantur et illustrantur, authore . . .
Joanne Poncio. (With text of Scotus.) Printed at Paris.
4 pts., fol.

1702. Complete edition with commentary, by P. G. Mahler.
Theologia Duns subtilis Scoti, in quatuor libros Sententiarum . . .
elucidata per P. G. Mahler. (Tugii Helvetiorum. (Zug.))

Reportata Parisiensia

The first edition of this work was taken from William of Alnwick's
abridgement of the big ' reportation ' which was certified by Scotus
himself, and was printed in Bologna in 1478. Only the first book was
published. Several editions followed at the beginning of the sixteenth
century.

1478. Book I. Begin. : *Circa primum sententiarum. queritur primo,* etc.
End. : *Johannis Scoti . . . super sententiarum questiones reporta-*
tionum a Bartholomeo Bellato . . . emendate cum diligentia finiunt
feliciter, etc.
Impensis . . . Johannis (Schreiber) *de Annunciata de Augusta.*
(1478, fol.)
[Without title-page, pagination, or catchwords ; printed in
double columns, 48 lines to a full column.]

1481. Book I, edited by Thomas Penketh.
Begin. (fol. Q 1, sig. a 2, recto) : *Incipit scriptum super primo*
sententiarum editum a fratre Joanne duns, etc. (Fol. 263 r. :
sig. hh) : *Explicit scriptum super primo sententiarum . . . per . . .*
Thomam penketh anglicum . . . maxima cum diligentia emendatum,
etc. (Fol. 280 r.) : *Et sic est finis harum additionum,* etc.
(Johannes de Colonia, Venetiis.)
[280 printed leaves ; in double columns ; without title-
page or pagination.]

1505. Complete (?) edition by Philippus de Bagnacavallo with *Quodlibeta*, printed at Venice for Andreas Torresanus de Asula by Bernardinus Vercellensis.

1517–18. Edition by Franciscus de Bellavalle, printed by A. Grandjohn at Paris.

1522. Edition by Mauritius Hibernicus, printed at Venice.

1607. Edition with *Quodlibeta* by Petrus Tartaretus, printed at Venice.

1635. Edition by H. Cavell, printed at Cologne. Incorporated by Wadding.

Quaestiones Quodlibetales

The first edition was edited by Thomas Penketh and printed at Venice in 1474.

1474. Begin. (fol. 1 r.) : *Cuncte res difficiles ait Salon. ecc. i. et cui intelligat esse difficiles subdit*, etc. End. : *In ista tabula primus numerus notat cartam. 2º notat columpnam. littera a notat precipium columpne. b. medium. c. finem. Albertus Stedal.* (Venice, 1474.)

[Without pagination or register ; 111 ff., printed in double columns, 40 lines to a full column.]

1477. Edition by Thomas Penketh.
Begin. (sig. a 2) : *Cuncte res difficiles ait Salon*, etc. End. : *Et sic est finis horum colibetorum a Johanne Duns . . . editorum per Thomam penketh*, etc.
Impensis Johannis de Colonia sociique ejus Johannis Manthen de Gherretzem. (Venetiis 1477, fol.)

[104 printed leaves ; in double columns, 51 lines to a full column ; without catchwords or pagination.]

1490 (?) Another edition printed at Venice by Bernardinus de Novara.

1497. Edition by Bagnacavallo.
Questiones quodlibetales Scoti. End. : *Expliciunt questiones quodlibetales edite a fratre Joanne duns . . . Per . . . Philippum de bagnacavallo . . . ordinis minorum . . . emendatae.*
Impresse sumptibus Octaviani Scoti per Bonetum Locatellum. (Venetiis 1497, fol.)

[53 numbered leaves ; printed in double columns, 66 lines to a full column.]

1513. Edition together with the *Collationes* by Mauritius Hibernicus, printed at Paris by Johannes Parvus.

1520. Edition together with *Collationes* by Antonius de Fantis, printed at Lyon by Jacobus Myt.

1519. Edition by Petrus Tartaretus, printed at Paris.
1530. Another edition, printed at Lyon by J. Crespin.

Quaestiones super Libros Metaphysicorum

1497. Edition by Mauritius Hibernicus, printed at Venice by Boneto Locatelli.

[The text of this edition was incorporated by Wadding.]

1499. Edition, together with the *De Primo Principio* and the *Theoremata*. Printed at Venice. (Very rare.)

Conclusiones Utilissimae Metaphysicae

1503. Edition by Johannes de Camerino, printed at Venice.

Expositio in XII Libros Metaphysicorum

1501. Edition by Mauritius Hibernicus, printed at Venice by Boneto Locatelli.

[The text of this edition was incorporated by Wadding.]

1520. Edition by Peter Vidone, printed at Paris.

Quaestiones De Anima

1485 (?). Edition by Gomesius Ulisponensis, printed at Venice (?).

1517. Edition with the logical treatises of Franciscus de Mayronis by Hieronymus de Nuciarellis, printed at Venice.

Logicalia

The first known edition of the logical treatises was printed at Barcelona in 1475 (?). It contains the *Quaestiones* on the universals of Porphyry and the *Quaestiones* on the Categories and *De Interpretatione* of Aristotle, together with those of Antonius Andreas on the *Liber Sex Principiorum* of Gilbert de la Porrée. The title is as follows :

1475 (?). Begin. : *Clarissimi doctoris subtilis Johannis Scoti questiones incipiunt super universalia porphirii ac libris praedicamentorum periermenias Aristotelis. Quibus sui discipuli Antonij Andree questiones sex principiorum connectuntur.* End. : *Finis questionum libri sex principiorum Antonij Andree doctoris subtilis discipuli foeliciter adest.* (Barcelona 1475 (?), fol.)

[87 leaves of text, printed in double columns, 47 lines to a full column. Register, a–l.]

1483. *Quaestiones* on the universals of Porphyry and on the categories and *De Interpretatione* of Aristotle, with the *Quaestiones* of Antonius Andreas on the *Liber Sex Principiorum* of Gilbert de la Porrée and the *Expositiones* of Johannes Anglicus on the *Universalia* of Scotus. Printed at Venice, fol.

1485. Another edition of the same treatises without the *Expositiones* of Johannes Anglicus.

Begin. (sig. a ii) : *Clarissimi doctoris subtilis Joannis Scoti questiones incipiunt super universalibus porphirii ac libris predicamentorum periermenias Aristotelis. Quibus . . . Antonii Andree questiones sex principiorum connectuntur.* Printed at Venice, fol.

[59 printed leaves without title-page or pagination, printed in double columns, 56 lines to a full column. Register, a–k.]

1492. Another edition of the same treatises, by Nicolaus Iudeeus. Begin. : *Clarissimi doctoris subtilis Joannis Scoti Questiones incipiunt super universalibus porphirii ac libris predicamentorum periermenias Aristotelis. Quibus sui discipuli A. Andree questiones sex principiorum connectuntur.*

Impressum per Joannem et Gregorium de gregoris. (Venetiis 1490, fol.)

1492. Another edition with the *Expositiones* of Johannes Anglicus. *Questiones Scoti super universalibus predicamentis et periermenijs. Questiones Antonij Andree super sex principiis. Expositiones fratris Joannis Anglici super questionibus universalium Scoti.*

Mandato Octaviani Scoti per Bonetum Locatellum. (Venetiis 1492, fol.)

[Sheet A, consisting of title-page and five leaves of text, is without pagination. The numeration of leaves begins with sig. B i, which is numbered 6, and the numeration is continued to fol. 78, where the text ends. This is followed by two numbered leaves containing the table. Printed in double columns, 62 lines to a full column.]

1493. *Elenchi Johannis Scoti Duns.* Edited by O. Jontus, and printed at Venice (?).

1497. *Quaestiones super posteriorum Aristotelis.* Edited with a preface by M. Campagna, and printed at Venice by Simon de Luere, fol.

1504. Complete edition with commentary by Mauritius Hibernicus. Printed at Paris.

1512. *Quaestiones* on the *Prior* and *Posterior Analytics* by Philippus Pincio Mantuanus, at Venice.

1512. *Quaestiones* on the universals of Porphyry, the *Categories* and the *De Interpretatione* of Aristotle, together with the *Quaestiones* of Antonius Andreas on the *Liber Sex Principiorum* of Gilbert de la Porrée and the *Expositiones* of Johannes Anglicus, printed at Venice by Pincio Mantuanus.

1583. Complete edition by Constantius Torri (Sarnanus) with his treatise *De Secundis Intentionibus* and *De Formalitatibus Scoti.* Printed at Venice by F. Franciscus.

1600. Another edition of the same by Sarnanus, printed at Venice.

1610. Another edition, printed at Venice by A. Turinus.

1622. Complete edition by Sarnanus, re-edited by Antonius Rocco. *Ursellis, sumptibus Antonii Hierati.*

Quaestiones in VIII Libros Physicorum

William Cave cites an edition printed at Venice in 1504, which is the first printed edition of which we possess any record.

1513. The *Quaestiones in Libros Physicorum* attributed to Scotus printed at Paris under the name of Marsilius of Inghen, and again at Venice in 1516.

1617. Edition with annotations by F. de Pitigianis, edited by Hilarion de Sacchetti, printed at Venice.

1618. Another edition, printed at Cologne.

De Modis Significandi seu Grammatica Speculativa

1480. Edition printed at St. Albans under the name of Albert of Saxony. *Liber modorum significandi Alberti.* (Apud Villam Sancti Albani.)

1497(?). Edited under the name of Albert of Saxony. *Alberti de Saxonia de modis significandi.* (Londinii apud S. Thomam Apost.)

1499. *De Modis Significandi Seu Grammatica Speculativa.* Printed by Simon de Luere. (Venice, fol.)

1512. Edition by Mauritius Hibernicus.—*Subtilissimi Joannis Scoti tractatus de modis significandi.* Printed at Venice.

1515. Another edition. *Modi significandi Alberti de Saxonia. Liber impressus Londinii per Wynandum de Worde.*

1520. Printed in Bencovich's *Epideicticon,* at Paris.

1605. Edition by Augustinus Gothutius, printed at Paris under the title *De Grammatica Speculativa.*

The only approximately complete edition of Scotus's works was that edited by Wadding and printed at Lyon in 1639. The title is as follows :

> R. P. F. Duns Scoti O. M. Doctoris Subtilis opera omnia quae hucusque reperiri potuerunt, collecta, recognita ; notis, scholiis, et commentariis illustrata a PP. Hibernis collegii Romani S. Isidori Professoribus : (Luca Waddingo, F. Pitigiano, Mauricio a Portu, Hugone Cavello, Francisco Lycheto, Joanne Poncio, Antonio Hiquaeo) ; jussu et auspiciis R. P. F. Joannis Baptistae a Campania . . . Authoris vita a L. Waddingo descripta, G. Bartolucci solutiones contradictionum apparentium. Ediderunt L. Waddingus, H. Cavellus et J. Tyrrell. (Lugduni : sumptibus L. Durand, 1639, fol.)

This edition has been reprinted without Wadding's life of Scotus and the *Solutiones* of Bartolucci, and with the addition of the *Tractatus de*

Perfecttone Statuum, which has been ascribed to Scotus, by L. Vives, Paris, 1891–5, in twenty-six volumes.

Father M. Fernandez Garcia, O.F.M., has edited the following works :

Quaestiones Disputatae de Rerum Principio. (Quaracchi, 1910.)
Grammatica Speculativa. (Ibid., 1902.)
Opus Oxoniense. (Ibid.)
 Tom. i, 1913.
 Tom. ii, 1914.

§ 2. *Commentaries, etc.*

OLDER WORKS (15th to 19th CENTURIES)

ACETTI, H. D'ORCO : *Expositio quaestionum Scoti in Praedicamenta Aristotelis.* (Bergamo, 1600.)

ALBERGONI, F. E. : *Resolutio doctrinae Scoticae in qua quid Doctor Subtilis circa singulas, quae exagitat, quaestiones sentiat, et si oppositum alii opinantur, brevibus ostenditur.* (Padua, 1593 ; Lyon, 1643.)

AMBROSINI, J. A. : *Enchiridion philosophicum universam Aristotelis philosophiam complectens, juxta mentem Scoti.* (Naples, 1689–93.)

AMICO, B. : *In Aristotelis libros de coelo et mundo textus applicatio et disputationes in quibus . . . Scoti . . . sententiae expenduntur*, etc. (1649.)

ANDREAS, A. : *Tria principia . . . secundum doctrinam . . . Scoti*, etc. (Venice, 1490.)

ANGELETTI, C. M. : *Asserta theologia ad mentem Scoti.* (Florence, 1739.)

ASCARGORTA, J. DE : *Manuale confessariorum ad mentem Subtilis Doctoris.* (Madrid, 1724.)

AYMER, A. J. : *Exercitationes theologico-morales de actibus humanis et peccatis, juxta veriora Doctoris Subtilis principia, scholastica methodo studiosae juventuti accommodata.* (Bologna, 1762.)

BARON, B. : *Johannes Duns Scotus . . . per universam philosophiam . . . contra adversantes defensus*, etc. (Cologne, 1664.)
 Doctor Subtilis in materia de Trinitate contra adversantes defensus. (Lyon, 1666.)
 Johannes Duns Scotus . . . de Deo Trino contra adversantes quosque defensus, etc. (Cologne, 1668.)
 Doctor Subtilis de Deo Uno defensus. (Lyon, 1670.)
 Johannes Scotus de Angelis defensus. (Florence, 1676.)

BARROS, A. : *Ven. P. et Doctor Joannes Duns Scotus, O. M. theologi eminentissimi atque academiae Subtilium Antesignani quaestiones quatuor voluminum scripti Oxoniensis super sententias et quodlibeta.* (Rome, 1754.)

BASCETTI, C. : *Viridarium theologicum parvum in IV libros Sententiarum Joannis Duns Scoti theologorum subtilium principis.* (Vicenza, 1688.)

BECERRA : *Asserta theo-subtilia vel theologica systematica Doctoris Subtilis de essentia et efficientia voluntatis divinae et moralitate voluntatis humanae.* (Barcelona, 1737.)

BELLUTI, B. : *Disputationes de Incarnatione Dominica ad mentem Scoti* (Catana, 1645.)
Bartholomaei Mastrii . . . et Bonaventurae Belluti, philosophiae ad mentem Scoti cursus integer. (Venice, 1678.) See also Mastrius.

BENCOVITCH, B. : *Scoticae subtilitatis Epideicticon.*—Containing :
Logicalia Scoti adjecta notis.
Antonii Andreae de sex principiis.
Sirrecti formalitates cum expositione Antonii Trombeta, Bruliferi epithomatibus Mauritiique adnotationibus ; Johannis Anglici et Mauritii Hibernici in universalia Scoti, una cum ejusdem Scoti Grammatica Speculativa. (Paris, 1520.)

BENJUMEA, B. A. : *Commentarii in octo Physicorum Aristotelis libros . . . ad mentem . . . Joannis Duns Scoti,* etc. (Lyon, 1677.)

BERMINGHAM, F. : *Summa Scotica S. Theologiae de Deo Uno et Trino juxta methodum Angelici Doctoris et Subtilis Doctoris mentem.* (Rome, 1656.)

BERNIQUUS, J. : *Tractatus theologicus de divina scientia ad creaturas terminata juxta mentem Mariani Subtilisque Doctoris Joannis Duns Scoti.* (Alcalá, 1705.)

BERTI, P. : *Quaestiones in IV libros Sententiarum et Quodlibeta Scoti,* with *tabula generalis* of Fantis. (Venice, 1617.)

BERTRAND, E. : *Summa theologiae Scoticae ad instar Summae D. Thomae, in qua doctrina Joannis Scoti Doctoris Subtilis per easdem quaestiones et articulos, ac sub eisdem titulis quibus S. Thomas suam exposuit, distribuitur, dilucidatur, stabilatur.* (16- ?)

BERULLUS, M. DE : *Cursus theologicus ad mentem Doctoris Subtilis.* (Grenoble, 1646–70.)

BILINIUS, DE POSNANIA : *Commentaria in primum librum Sententiarum Joannis Duns Scoti.* (Strassburg, 1612 ; Venice, 1626.)

BIONDI, F. A. : *Disputationes Scoticae in quibus divinae praedestinationis et reprobationis mysterium juxta doctrinam Scoti dilucidatur.* (Bologna, 1625.)

BOLOGNI, J. : *Disquisitiones in formalitates Scoti.* (Palermo, 1652.)

BORDONI, F. : *Tractatus de formalitatibus Doctoris Subtilis ab objectis vindicatis.* (Parma, 1662.)

Bosco, J. de : *Theologia sacramentalis scholastica et moralis ad mentem Doctoris Subtilis Joannis Duns Scoti D. Augustino conformis.* (Vol. I, Louvain, 1665–78 ; vol. II, Antwerp, 1685.)

Boyvin, J. G. : *Philosophia quadripartita Scoti.* (Paris, 1668.)
Theologia Scoti a prolixitate et subtilitate ejus ab obscuritate libera et vindicata. (Paris, 1664.)
Theologia quadripartita Scoti, etc. (Paris, 1678.)
Philosophia Scoti a prolixitate et subtilitas ejus ab obscuritate libera et vindicata. (Paris, 1680.)

Brambilla, H. : *Distinctio in prologum Sententiarum Joannis Duns Scoti.* (Venice, 1674.)

Brancasius, Cl. : *Theologia Scotica.*
Tomus I. *De Deo Trino et Uno in quo agitur de absolutis, ubi germana Scoti mens aperitur atque ad ejus institutum disceptatur.* (Naples, 1638.)
Tomus II. *In quo agitur de respectivis, sive de Tribus Personis Divinis.* (Ib., 1640.)
Tomus III. *De Angelis.* (Ib., 1646.)

Brancatus, L. : *Commentarii . . . in tertium (et quartum) librum Sententiarum Joannis Duns Scoti.* 8 volumes. (Rome, 1653–82.)

Brassavola, I. : *De secundis intentionibus ad mentem Scoti.* (Venice, 1591.)
Quaestionum universalium Joannis Duns Scoti expositio eruditissima. (Venice, 1599.)

Bratkowitz, A. : *Commentaria in XII libros metaphysices ad mentem Scoti.* (Cracow, 1640.)

Brescia, L. de : *Breves, faciles ac perutiles Ysagoges in Joannis Scoti formalitates.* (Brescia, 1537.)
(Re-edited with notes by Constantius de Sarnano : Sharralea identifies this work with the treatise of Antonius Sirrectus, q. v.)

Briceno, A. : *Apologia de vita et doctrina Joannis Scoti Doctoris Subtilis. Celebriores controversiae in primum librum Sententiarum Scoti, admixtis potissimum dissertationibus metaphysicis.* (Madrid, 1638.)

Brinkmann, A. : *Fructus scotico-theologicus ex lib. II et IV Sententiarum,* etc. (Fulda, 1719.)
Manipuli ex IV lib. Sententiarum, sive theologia universalis cum corollariis. (Fulda, 1725.)

Brulifer, S. : *Magistri Stephani brulifer Formalitates in doctrinam Scoti.* (Paris, 1490.)
Venerabiliso. S. Brulifer . . . formalitatum textus una cum ipsius commento perlucido. (Basel (?), 1501.)
Excellentissimi atque perfectissimi humanarum divinarumque literarum

doctoris fratris Stephani Brulifer . . . reportata clarissima in IV S. Bonaventurae doctoris seraphici Sententiarum libros Scoti Subtilis secundi. (Basel, 1501.)
Epithomata in formalitates juxta doctrinam Scoti, etc. (Paris, 1519.)

BRUODINE, A. : *Armentarium theologicum ad mentem Doctoris Subtilis.* (Prague, 1676.)
Oeconomia minoriticae scholae Salomonis Doctoris Subtilis, quadraginta columnis sustentata. . . . Haec est universae theologiae scholasticae manualis summa, materias omnes in scholis tradi solitas stylo claro et succincta methodo complectens. (Ibid., 1663.)
Corolla oeconomiae pars altera complectens tractatus de virtute et statu religioso, etc. (Ibid., 1664.)

CABRA, J. J. DE : *Totius philosophiae tam veteris quam recentioris dogmata Subtilis Marianique Doctoris Joannis Duns Scoti doctrinae accommodata, et ad usum studentium Capuccinorum Provinciae utriusque Baeticae in brevissimum compendium redacta.* (Cordova, 1801.)

CADENA, S. : *Dicta philosophica in VIII libros physicorum ad mentem Scoti.* (Turin (?), 165– (?).)

CALDERONI, J. S. : *Tractatus theologici* :
  I. Apologetica et Scoticae doctrinae vindex.
  II. De praedicatis quidditativis Dei.
  III. De sanctitate divina et virtutibus moralibus prout ad Deum pertinent.
  IV. De libera arbitrio deque scientia media.
  V. De gratia actuali.
  VI. Quodlibet.
  VII. De altissimo Incarnationis mysterio.
  VIII. De fide divina. (Alcala, 1699.)

CANCELLARIA, B. DE : *In XII libros metaphys. Aristotelis secundum intentionem Scoti conclusiones, explicationes textus, et quaestiones utilissimae probantur.* (Naples, 1713.)

CAPORELLA, P. P. : *Quaestio de matrimonio et divortio Henrici VIII et Catherinae a quodam Fr. Joanne minorita scripta ad mentem Doctoris Subtilis.* (Naples, 1542.)

CARTAGENA, J. DE : *Selectae Disputationes in IVum librum Sententiarum ad mentem Doctoris Subtilis.* (Rome, 1607.)

CASCIA, P. V. DE : *Dilucidatio assertorum Scoti, quae ab aliquibus contradictoria reprobantur.*
Contradictionum umbrae apparentes in dictis Doctoris Subtilis Scoti, ex Quaestt. sup. Univers. ; Praedicament. ; Periherm. ; De anima ; et metaphysica ejusdem. (Perugia, 1649.)

CASIMIRI, F. A. : *Scotus dilucidatus in IIum librum Sententiarum, mirifico, brevi, ac facili ordine, in quo etiam omnes controversiae inter D. Thomam et Scotum explicantur.* (Naples, 1597, 1607.)

CASSINIS, S. : *Liber isagogicus in apices Scoti.*
Expositio triplex in octo Physicorum Aristotelis . . . de mente commentatoris et Doctoris subtilis Scoti. (After 1510.)

CASTELL, A. : *Athenaeum minoriticum novum et vetus Subtilis, Seraphici, et nominalium nonnullas exambiens quaestiones.* (Saragossa, 1697.)

CENSIO, H. : *Medulla aristotelica philosophica tripartita ex logica, physica, et metaphysica ad mentem Scoti.* (Perugia, 1618.)

CENTINI, M. : *De Incarnatione et de Sacramentis ad mentem Scoti.* (Messina, 1637.)

CIODINO, J. B. : *Pupillae philosophiae Aristotelis metheorum et parvorum naturalium cum lucidissimis quaestionibus ad sententiam Scoti.* (Venice, 1617.)
Praxis sphaerica tribus libris disposita cum quaestionibus ad sententiam Scoti libri decem. (Venice, 1617.)
Lumen doctrinae Scoti, in quo de specie intelligibili, de formalitatibus, modis intrinsecis, ideis divinis, etc. agitur. (Ibid., 1617.)

CIORLA, V. : *Disputationes logicales collectae ex doctrina Scoti.* (Rome, 1646.)

COEN, A. : *Disputationes theologicae de Deo sacramentorum institutore, sive in librum IVum Sententiarum, in qui reductive agitur de indulgentiis et censuris ad mentem Doctoris Subtilis.* (Ypres, 1686 ; Antwerp, 1700.)
Disputationes theologicae de Deo Uno et Trino . . . ad mentem Doctoris Subtilis. (Ghent, 1696.)

COLGAN, J. : *Theologia secundum principia Scoti.* (Louvain, 1639.)

COLOMBO, B. : *Novus cursus philosophicus Scotistarum complectens universam philosophiam rationalem, naturalem, moralem et trans-naturalem.* (Lyon, 1669.)

COLONIA, J. DE : *Quaestiones magistri Joannis Scoti abbreviatae et ordinatae per alphabetam super IV libros Sententiarum, Reportata, Quodlibeta, metaphysica, et de anima.* (Venice, 1475 ; Basel, 1510.)

COSTENI, M. : *Tabula naufragii, seu Tractatus Speculativus et moralis de indulgentiis, de suffragiis, et censuris ecclesiasticis, juxta doctrinam P. F. Joannis Duns Scoti Doctoris Subtilis, O.M., omnium theologorum facile principis.* (Mainz, 1636.)

CROSS, J. : *Dialectica, logica, metaphysica, physica naturalis, mathe-matica, rudimenta universa ad mentem Doctoris Mariano-subtilis.* (Douai, 1684.)

CUELLAR, J. DE : *Cursus theologicus juxta mentem Venerabilis Doctoris Subtilis.* (Madrid, 1725.)

DAVENPORT, C. : *Deus, natura, et gratia, juxta mentem Doctoris Subtilis.* (Lyon, 1634.)

DAVID, P. : *Summula tractatus de praedestinatione ad mentem Doctoris Subtilis ejusque fidelissimi interpretis Magistri Angeli a Monte Piloso, O. F. M. Conventualis,* etc. (Paris (?), 1646.)
Summula philosophica ad mentem Scoti. (Paris, 1649.)

DAXECORTESIO, D. : *Exercitia scholastica in universam theologiam, practicam et speculativam, in quibus relicta inutilium disputationum superfluitate, et demisso cavilloso opinionum examine, veritas ipsa ... clare et breviter enodatur et irrefragabili SS. Scripturarum approbatorum CC., summorumque PP. auctoritate roboratur, necnon SS. Patrum et orthodoxorum TT. praecipue Doctoris Subtilis doctrina eadem veritas ostenditur, firma, solida, et stabilis adversus haereticos tam veteres quam recentiores.* (Padua, 1677, 1690.)

DE LA TORRE, H. : *Cursus integer artium ad mentem Scoti.* (Saragossa, 1653.)
Commentaria in Ium et IIum lib. Sententiarum ad mentem Scoti. (Saragossa, 1685-9.)

DELGADILLO, C. : *Bipartitus de poenitentia tractatus, in cujus priore parte de ea quatenus est virtus, in posteriore vero de eadem quatenus est sacramentum, legitima Subtilis Doctoris mens ... aperitur,* etc. (Alcalá, 1658.)
Duo tractatus ; alter de incarnatione ; alter de adoratione, in quibus legitima Doctoris Subtilis ... Joannis Duns Scoti ... mens ... aperitur et propugnatur. (Ibid., 1653.)
Secundum principium Complutense seu tractatus de Angelis, in quo legitima Subtilis Doctoris ... mens, etc. (Ibid., 1652.)

DE RADA, J. : *Controversiae theologicae inter Sanctum Thomam et Scotum,* etc. (Part I. Salamanca, 1586; II. Venice, 1601 ; III. Rome, 1614 ; IV. Cologne, 1620.)

DIAZ, F. : *Theoremata theologiae ex primo libro Sententiarum Doctoris Subtilis.* (Madrid, 1666.)

DOMENICUS, A. S. P. DE A. : *Integer philosophiae cursus ad mentem Subtilis Marianique Doctoris.* (Madrid, 1729-34.)

DUPASQUIER, S. : *Summa theologiae Scotistae, in qua ... religionis Christianae mysteria explicantur ... ad mentem Doctoris Subtilis.* (Padua, 1719.) (Republished at Caen in 1895.)
Summa philosophiae scholasticae et Scoticae. (Lyon, 1692.)
Summa Scotisticae in qua ex fidei lumine, S. Scripturae oraculis, Ecclesiae traditionibus ac decretis, ex SS. PP. ac TT. sententia rationis ductu, religionis Christianae mysteria, dogmata, sacramenta et leges breviter ac scholastice explicantur et propugnantur ad mentem Doctoris Subtilis. (Chambéry, 1698.)

DURANDUS, B. : *Clypeus Scoticae theologiae contra novos ejus impugnatores.* (Marseilles, 1685.)

DUVALLIUS, A. : *Notae in Librum Ecclesiae Lugdunensis adversum Joannem Scotum.*
  (1) Col. 1255, vol. ii. *Auct. Bibl. Patr.* (Paris, 1610.)
  (2) Col. 1098, vol. ix. *Magn. Bibl. Patr.* (Cologne, 1618.)
  (3) p. 662, vol. xv. *Max. Bibl. vet. Patr.* (Lyon, 1677.)
  (4) p. 738, vol. i. *Vet. Auct. de Praedestinat.*, ed. G. Mangoin. (Paris, 1650.)

FABER, P. : *Philosophia naturalis Joannis Duns Scoti*, etc. (Parma, 1601 ; Venice, 1602 ; Padua, 1622.)
  Disputationes theologicae . . . secundum seriem distinctionum Magistri Sententiarum et quaestionum Scoti . . . in quibus doctrina Scoti defenditur, etc. (Venice, 1613.)
  Expositiones et disputationes in XII lib. Aristotelis metaphysicorum, quibus doctrina Scoti magna cum facilitate illustratur. (Published by Ferchius, Venice, 1637.)

FANTIS, A. DE : *Tabula generalis Scoticae subtilitatis . . . universam Doctoris Subtilis peritiam complectens*, etc. (Lyon, 1530.)
  Quaestionum Joannis Duns Scoti in libros Sententiarum epitome. (Venice, 1597.)

FERCHIUS, M. : *Epitome theologicum M. Ferchii Veglensis . . . in IV libros Sententiarum Scoti.* (1647.)

FERRARI, J. A. : *Philosophia peripatetica adversus veteres et recentiores praesertim philosophos, firmioribus propugnata rationibus Joannis Duns.* (Venice, 1746.)
  Theologia scholastico-dogmatica ad mentem Joannis Dunsii Scoti (Ibid., 1760.)
  Veteris et recentioris philosophiae dogmata Joannis Dunsii Scoti doctrinis accommodata. (Ibid., 1757.)

FERRARIS, H. DE : *Loci communes ex libris Sententiarum et Quodlibetis Joannis Scoti.* (Venice, 1597.)

FLAVIUS, M. : *Resolutiones in IV libros Sententiarum Joannis Duns Scoti . . . per Joannem Forsanum in lucem . . . tradita.* (Paris, 1600.)

FLORIANO, C. J. DE : *Joannis Duns Scoti philosophia nunc primum recentibus placitis accommodata.* (Milan, 1777.)

FIDONI, S. : *Formalitatum tractatus ad mentem Doctoris Angelici et Subtilis.* (Rome, 1655.)

FONIO, J. B. : *Disputationes et quaestiones ex universa theologia de felicissimis penetralibus Joannis Duns Scoti depromptae in Ium librum Sententiarum.* (1688.)

FRANCIS-FELIX of Madrid : *De Divina Incarnatione tractatus ad mentem Doctoris Subtilis.* (Paris, 1651.)

FRASSENIUS, C. : *Philosophia academica ex selectissimis illustrium philosophorum, praesertim vero Aristotelis et Doctoris Subtilis rationibus ac sententiis ordinata.* (Paris, 1668.)

Scotus Academicus seu universa Doctoris Subtilis theologica dogmata, quae ad nitidam et solidam academiae Parisiensis methodum concinnavit, selectissimis SS. patrum oraculis firmavit et illustravit, necnon explicatione graviorum controversiarum quae nunc temporis in scholis agitari solent ditavit Cl. Frassen. (Paris, 1672–7, 1680.) (Republished, Rome, 1900–2.)

FROLICH, C. A. : *Scotus systematizatus, seu compendium theologiae scotisticae.* (Freiburg, 1745.)

FUENTE, G. DE LA : *Quaestiones dialecticae et physicae ad mentem Scoti.* (Lyon, 1631.)

GABBIANO, M. DE : *Variae observationes in Ium et IIum libr. Sententiarum Petri Tartareti et quidlibeta Scoti, adjecto indice locorum tum S. Scripturae, tum SS. Patrum.* (Venice, 1583.)

GADIO, H. : *Lectura in Quodlibeta Scoti.* (Bologna, 1533.)

GAVAZZI, M. DE : *De venerabili Eucharistiae Sacramento et Missae Sacrificio disputationes theologicae ad mentem Scoti.* (Rome, 1656.)

GAVELLO, A. : *Breviarium universae theologiae nempe speculativae dogmaticae et moralis in IV partes distributum juxta principia scholae scotistarum.* (Bologna, 1692.)
Supplementum ad breviarium, etc. (Ibid., 1700.)

GENNARI, TH. : *Dies intelligibilis scoticus in XII horas theologicas divisus ; sive dilucidissima explicatio apostolica in XII articulos distributa juxta munera XII Apostolorum.* (Venice, 1674.)

GEYSS, W. : *Lapis offensionis et petra scandali adversariis sunt sententiae philosophicae et genuinae Joannis Duns Scoti, subtilium omnium principis.* (Augsburg, 1705.)

GINER, D. : *Commentaria in IV lib. Sententiarum vel Opus Oxoniense in faciliorem methodum redactum.* (Valentia, 1598.)

GONZALEZ, D. M. : *Theologia scotica in primum (–tertium) Sententiarum Magistri ad mentem . . . Joannis Duns Scoti explanata.* (1749.)

GORRIS, G. : *Scotus pauperum, vel abbreviatus.* (Toulouse, 1486.)

GORRIS, P. DE : *Enchiridion scholasticum contradictionum quodlibetorum Doctoris Subtilis, a Const. Sarano recognitum,* etc. (Venice, 1544, 1583.)
Insigne formalitatum opus de mente Doctoris Subtilis una cum editione Urbinatis Archiepiscopi Antonii Trombetae : adjunctusque resolutissimus Tuamensis Episcopus Mauritius, necnon Doctoris Antonii de Fantis adnotationibus. (Venice, 1514.)

GRATIANUS, B. : *Lectura . . . in secundo libro Sententiarum Scoti.* (1506.)

GUITTART, R. : *Compilatio praecipuarum disputationum et quaestionum cum suis probabilioribus opinionibus theologiae moralis Mastrii juxta mentem Doctoris Subtilis.* (Geronda, 1680–4.)

HACHOFFER, A. : *Compendium alphabeticum scotico-juridicum et juridico-canonicum.* (Linz, 1739.)
Compendium alphabeticum scotistico-tractatuum theologico-polemicorum de sacramentis in genere et in specie. (Ibid., 1739.)

HAUZEUR, M. : *Collatio totius theologiae inter majores nostros Fr. Alexandrum Alensem, Patriarcham theologorum, Doctorem Irrefragabilem, S. Bonaventuram, Doctorem Seraphicum, Fr. Joannem Duns Scotum, Doctorem subtilem ad mentem S. Augustini.* (1646–52.)

HEISS, W. : *Memorabilium theologicorum dogmatum tractatus tres de Deo, una cum parergis ex universa theologia Subtilis Doctoris Scoti.* (Passau, 1750.)

HENNO, FR. : *Theologia dogmatica et scholastica . . . opus principiis thomisticis et scotisticis, quantum licuit, accommodatum.* 8 vols. (Douai, 1706–13).

HERMANN, A. : *Sol triplex in universo, i.e. universae philosophiae cursus integer trium solemnissimorum Doctorum, nempe Magni Aurelii Augustini, lactei et melliflui Bernardi, et subtilissimi Joannis Duns Scoti.* (Sulzbach, 1676.)
Tractatus theologici in libros Sententiarum ad mentem Subtilis Doctoris. (Cologne, 1690–4.)
Ethica sacra, scholastica, speculativo-practica . . . ad mentem Joannis Duns Scoti. (Wurzburg, 1698.)

HERMANN, C. : *Theologia selecta Scotistica . . . de Deo . . . de Incarnatione Divini Verbi,* etc. (1720.)

HERRERA, F. DE : *Disputationes theologicas, et commentaria in secundum librum Sententiarum . . . Scoti.* (1595.)

HICKQUAEUS (HICKEY), A. : *Commentaria in IV° libro Sententiarum ad mentem Scoti.* (Printed in Wadding's edition of Scotus, Lyon, 1639.)

HUGOLINUS of Wurzburg : *Liber speculationum scotico-theologicarum super Prologum Sententiarum, complectens CL Theoremata.*

JADERTINUS, O. : *Prolegomenon biblicae sapientiae et scoticae disciplinae in quo cum Doctoris Subtilis theologorum principis prohemialibus contexta paraenesi S. Script. porta speciosa templi sapientiae panditur sub omine Seraphici nominis.* (Venice, 1689.)

JOHANNES ANGLICUS (JOHN FOXAL) : Commentary on Scotus' logic, beginning : *Creberrime instantiusque rogatus . . . ut aliqua per modum commenti ederem supra logicam doctoris subtilis . . . Joannis Scoti vel Duns,* etc. (1485.)
Expositio universalium Scoti. (Venice, 1508.)

JOHANNES DE BERNAL (or BARRAUD) : Commentary on the *Formalitates* of J. Vallo, published under the title of *Opus Formalitatum Scoti a Joanne Vallono.* (Paris, 1585.)

JOHANNES DE DOUET : *Formalitatum Doctoris Subtilis Scoti, Antonii Sirrecti, A. Trombetae et Stephani Bruliferi eximiorum theologorum Ordinis Minorum monotessara in philosophiam Aristotelis et theologiae studiorum gratiam coadunata ; ac in tres libros capitibus sectis ordine perfacili digesta,* etc. (Paris, 1579.)

JOHANNES LAPIS : *Aureum formalitatum speculum Scoti ac Fr. Mayronis doctrinam illustrans.* (Naples, 1505.)

JOHANNES DE MONTE : *Summulae tractatibus septem super Petrum Hispanum, ad mentem Doctoris Subtilis Joannis Scoti.* (Paris, 1490 ; Venice, 1526.)

JOHANNES A NATIVITATE : *Cursus integer philosophiae ad mentem Mariani et Subtilis Doctoris.* (Ed. by Johannes a Trinitate, Segovia, 1711–13.)

JOHANNES STOBNICENSIS : *Parvulus philosophiae naturalis cum expositione textuali . . . ad intentionem Scoti,* etc. (1507.)

JOHANNES A TRINITATE and JOHANNES A NATIVITATE : *Disputationes animasticae, in quibus de anima, seu corpore animato tribus libris ab Aristotele contexto disseritur, simulque tractatus brevis in XII libros Metaphysicae ponitur. Juxta miram . . . Mariani doctoris doctrinam.* (Segovia (?), 1713.)

KAZENBERGER, K. : *Centum assertiones ad mentem Doctoris Subtilis ac Mariani Ven. Joannis Duns Scoti, O. M. ex universa theologia selectae.* (Nuremberg, 1738 (?).)
(More modern editions : Limoges, 1882 ; Quaracchi, 1906.)

KOMOROVVO, J. : *Introductio in doctrinam Doctoris Subtilis, modos distinctionum et identitatum, alios quoque terminos obscuriores ejusdem doctrinae declarans, antiquorum scotisantium solvens rationibus quorundam recentiorum, quibus impugnatur, solutis,* etc. (1508.)

KRAZ, S. : *Controversia theologica de sufficientia attritionis cum sacramento poenitentiae ad justificationem impii, una cum parergis assertionum e tertia parte Subtilis.* (Augsburg, 1741.)

KRISPER, C. : *Philosophia scholae Scotisticae.* (Augsburg, 1735.)
Theologia scholae Scotisticae. (Augsburg, 1728–9.)
Theologia scholae scholasticae . . . seu solida expositio IV lib. Sententiarum Scoti, etc. (Vienna, 1738 ; Augsburg, 1748.)

LALEMANDET, J. : *Decisiones Philosophicae.* (Munich, 1644–5.)

LANTERI, C. : *Disputationes in secundam partem Sententiarum ex subtili Joannis Duns Scoti celebrata doctrina.* (Naples, 1665.)

LEBRETON, M.: *Lectura in IV libros Sententiarum, vel parvulus Scotus Lavallensis.* (1527–8.)

LEGRAND, A.: *Encomium sapientiae humilis, seu Scotus humilis elucidatus.* (Douai, 1650.)

LELOVE, J.: *Commentarii super formalitates Scoti.* (Paris, 1581.)

LIALI, J.: *Paediae Scoticae theologiae quibus subtilissimi Scoti mens in IV Sententiarum libros, juxta SS. Patrum et praesertim S. Augustini principia aperitur.* (Venice, 1669; Padua, 1682.)
Paediae Scoticae quibus subtilissima mens Scoti aperitur juxta Aristotelis principia. (Venice, 1668–73.)

LLAMAZARES, T.: *Cursus philosophicus, sive philosophia scholastica ad mentem Scoti, novo . . . methodo disposita.* (Lyon, 1670.)
Quaestiones sive disputationes theologiae scholasticae dogmaticae et morales ad mentem Scoti. (Lyon, 1679.)

LOCHERER, A.: *Clypeus philosophico-scotisticus, sive cursus philosophicus juxta mentem et doctrinam . . . Joannis Duns Scoti elaboratus.* (Crembsii, 1740.)

LOPEZ, J. DE AYORA: *Viridarium virtutum . . . ex Scoti Sententiis nuper decerptum atque contextum.* (1509.)

LOPEZ, J. P.: *Scotus philosophicus antiquorum sapientia exquisitus et virorum nominatorum commentariis narratus.* (Barcelona, 1647.)
Commentaria in Ium et IIIum librum Sententiarum de abscondito Scoti thesauro nova et vetera proferentia. (Ibid., 1690.)

LORTE Y ESCARTIN, H.: *Mappa subtilis seu speculum Scoticum.* (Saragossa, 1693.)
Mappa scotica et augustiniana Subtilis ac Mariani doctoris conclusiones ex scripto Oxoniensi decerptas complectens, D. Augustini primi Ecclesiae Doctoris aureis sententiis cohaerescens. (Ibid., 1694.) (Re-edited by F. M. Paolini, Rome, 1910.)

LUDOVICUS DE S. LEONE: *Dislocon super Ium Sententiarum Scoti.* (15—(?).)

LUGO, P. DE: *Principia seu introductiones in via Doctoris Subtilis.* (London, c. 1508.)

LYCHETTUS, F.: *Commentarii super Quodlibeta Scoti.* (15—(?).)
Commentarii super novem libros Metaphysicae Scoti. (15—(?).)
. . . In Joannem Duns Scotum super primo, secundo, tertio Sententiarum, Quodlibetis, clarissima Commentaria. (Milan, 1519; Venice, 1589.)

LYMPNICA, S. DE: *Arcana S. Theologiae ad mentem Scoti.* (1771.)

MACEDO, F.: *Collationes doctrinae S. Thomae et Scoti cum differentiis inter utrumque,* etc. (Padua, 1673, 1680.)

MAGISTRIS, J. DE : *Quaestiones super totum cursum logice . . . cum . . . explanatione textus secundum mentem doctoris subtilis Scoti, etc.* (Cologne, 1480.)

Questiones . . . super Porphyris et veteri arte Aristotelis ad mentem doctoris subtilis. (Cologne (?), 1488.)

Summularum Petri Hispani glosulae exactissimae ad mentem Scoti doctoris subtilis. (Venice, 1474.)

MAHLER, G. : *Theologia Doctoris Subtilis Scoti in IV Lib. Sententiarum solide ac succincte elucidata.* (Zug, 1702.)

MALAFOSSIUS, P. : *Super primum Sententiarum Doctoris Subtilis Joannis Scoti . . . expositio.* (Padua, 1560.)

MANGANELLI, L. : *Discursus praedicabiles theologici speculativi in modum meditationum et soliloquiorum, per quos habetur expositio primi et secundi Cantici Canticorum Salomonis, juxta doctrinam et ordinem quaestionum Scoti in I° libro Sententiarum, utiles admodum contemplativis et praedicatoribus qui voluerint suos sermones Scoti sententiis exornare.* (Naples, 1619 ; Madrid, 1619, with life of Duns attached.)

MASTRIUS, B. : *Disputationes in Aristotelis libros physicorum, quibus ab adversantibus tum veterum tum recentiorum jaculis Scoti philosophia vindicatur.* (Rome, 1637.)

Disputationes in organum Aristotelis quibus . . . Scoti logica vindicatur. (Ibid., 1639.)

Disputationes in libros de coelo et metheoris : in libros de generatione et corruptione et in libros de Anima. (Venice, 1640.)

These three volumes make a complete *cursus philosophiae ad mentem Scoti,* and were written in conjunction with B. Belluti.

The following volumes were written by Mastrius without collaboration :

Theologia moralis ad mentem DD. Seraphici et Subtilis. (Venice, 1671, 1731.)

Disputationes theologicae in primum (–quartum) librum Sententiarum, quibus . . . Scoti theologia vindicatur, etc. (Venice, 1655, 1731.)

Scotus et scotistae Bellutus et Mastrius expurgati a probrosis querelis Ferchianis. (Ferrara, 1650.) (Written in answer to Ferchius's *Vestigationes Peripateticae.*) (Padua, 1639.)

MAURI, A. : *Processus civilis contra Scotum, pars Ia.* (Naples, 1629.)

MAURITIUS DE PORTU (O'FIHELY) : *Expositio in quaestiones dialecticas Joannis Scoti super Porphyrium ; Castigationes in quaestiones metaphysicales Scoti ; Epitomata in formalitates Scoti.* (Venice, 1514.)

De definitionibus formalitatum doctoris ac magistri sui Scoti. (Paris, 1605.)

MAYER, A. DE VILLINGA : *Heliotropicum philosophicum in viridario Doctoris Subtilis Joannis Duns Scoti,* etc. (1719.)

MAYER, C. : *Gemini justitiae actus, restitutio et contractus . . . juxta mentem . . . Joannis Duns Scoti scholastice declarati,* etc. (1718.)

MAYER, G. : *Sacratissimum Missae Sacrificium consideratum et adjunctis parergis ex universa theologia ad mentem Doctoris Subtilis, Joannis Duns Scoti.* (Salzburg (?), 1736.)

MAYER, P. : *Theologia scholastica ad mentem Johannis Duns Scoti,* etc. (Wurzburg, 1751.)

MEARISSE, M. : *Metaphysica ad mentem Doctoris Subtilis,* etc. (Paris, 1623.)

MELGACO, A. DE S. M. : *Scotus Aristotelicus, seu philosophia peripatetica juxta mentem Duns Scoti Concinnata.* (Lisbon, 1747.)

MENGOLINO, L. : *Contradictiones Scoti, tum litterales, tum virtualiter tales, tum dictis Sanctorum et Philosophorum oppositiones in prologum, primum atque secundum librum Sententiarum Subtilis Doctoris Scoti.* (1621.)

MERINERO, J. : *Commentarii in duos libros Aristotelis de ortu et interitu rerum naturalium, juxta . . . Johannis Duns Scoti mentem,* etc. (Madrid, 1659.)
  Cursus philosophicus integer juxta Doctoris Subtilis Joannis Duns Scoti mentem. (Ibid., 1659.)
  Cursus theologicus juxta mentem Doctoris Subtilis. (Ibid., 1668.)

MERON, C. : *Philosophia Scoto-peripatetica, seu in qua genuinus Doctoris Subtilis sensus circa naturalia veritatis dogmata semper doctrinae Aristotelis conformis . . . exponitur,* etc. (Paris, 1675.)

MEURISSE, M. : *De rerum metaphysicarum libri tres ad mentem Doctoris Subtilis.* (1628.)

MICHAEL PARISIENSIS : *Questiones veteris ac nove logice cum resolutione textus Aristotelis clarissima ; ad intentionem doctoris Scoti.* (Paris (?), 1508.)

MIKSSICZEK, A. : *Vera effigies . . . Joannis Duns Scoti . . . ad vivum expressa ; dum assertione ex universa theologia ad mentem ejusdem . . . propugnaret . . . A. Mikssiczek,* etc. (1744.)

MOLLOY, F. : *De Incarnatione Verbi Divini ad mentem Doctoris Subtilis.* (Graz, 1645.)

MONEGLIA, G. DE : *Methodus et grammatica speculativa ven. Doctoris Subtilis.* (Edited by Pagliettini, Paris, 1604.)

MONTEFORTINO, H. DE : *Joannis Duns Scoti summa theologica ex universis operibus ejus concinnata*, etc. (Rome, 1728–38.) (This work has been republished, Rome, 1900–3.)

MORAL, C. : *Theologia Mariana, seu Fons illimis theologiae Scoticae Marianae, e Paradiso virgineo latices suos ubertim effundens, seu B. Virginis Mariae excellentia doctrina Joannis Duns Scoti enucleata.* (Madrid, 1730.)

MORANO, L. DE : *Gladius utraque parte acutus, seu Scotus dogmaticus, in quo agitantur omnes quaestiones contra errores haereticorum super IV libros Sententiarum*, etc. (Padua, 1700.)

MOULINS, F. DE : *Cursus philosophicus ad mentem Scoti.* (Lyon, 1687.)

NOTAN, F. : *Tractatus de Sacramento Poenitentiae ad mentem Joannis Duns Scoti Doctoris Subtilis*, etc. (Mons, 1697.)

ODDO, I. : *Integer cursus philosophicus ad mentem Scoti, in quo Subtilis Doctoris doctrina declaratur, defenditur et roboratur.* (Palermo, 1664–78.) (Five volumes, of which only four were published.)

O'DEVLIN, F. : *Philosophia Scoto-aristotelica universa*, etc. (Nuremberg, 1710.)

OLIVESE, P. DE : *Tractatus logicae juxta mentem S. Thomae ac Doctoris Subtilis.* (Genoa, 1651.)

ORBELLIS, N. DE (POPE JOHN XXI) : Begin. *Excellentissimi viri . . . N. Dorbelli . . . secundum doctrinam doctoris subtilis, logice . . . expositio.* (1482.)
Super summulas Petri Hispani ad mentem Scoti. (Parma, 1482.)
Summulae philosophiae naturalis, seu logica . . . secundum doctrinam doctoris subtilis, etc. (Basel, 1494.)
Commentaria in IV libros Sententiarum, etc. (Paris and Lyon, 1498.)
Super Sententias compendium singulare eligantiora Doctoris Subtilis dicta summatim complectens. (Lyon, 1503 ; also Hagenau, 1503 ; Paris, 1517.)
Petri Lombardi quatuor Sententiarum volumina, cum . . . N. de Orbellis . . . interpretationibus, in quibus Scoti dicta . . . obscuriora . . . faciliter enarrantur, etc. (Paris (?), 1507.)
Expositio in XII libros metaphysicos secundum viam Scoti. (Edited by A. Gotuzzo, date (?).)

OVANDO, J. DE : *Subtilissimi . . . Joannis Duns Scoti elucidatio circa tertium librum Sententiarum*, etc. (Valentia, 1597, 1624.)

PALERMO, CL. DE : *Elenchus tractatuum et quaestionum quas in nostris scholis singulis quadrenniis juxta mentem Subtilis Doctoris Joannis Duns Scoti R. P. Clemens a Panormo Minister Generalis mandat peragendas pro recta atque ordinata in Universo Ordine nostrorum studentium institutione.* (1757.)

PANGER, M. : *Theologia scholastico-morali-polemica juxta verum sensum et mentem Doctoris Subtilis.* (Augsburg, 1732.)

  Quodlibetum theologicum selectarum quaestionum ex IV libris Sententiarum ad mentem Subtilis Doctoris Scoti. (Salzburg, 1702.)

PASSERO, B. : *Pinacotheca selecta praecipuarum conclusionum ac quaestionum . . . ex doctrina Scoti discussarum.* (Rome, 1621.)

PAULUS, SCRIPTOR : *Lectura Fr. Pauli scriptoris . . . quam edidit declarando subtilissimas doctoris subtilis sententias circa Magistrum in primo libro.* (Tübingen, 1498.)

PENNA, V. G. : *Cursus philosophicus ad mentem Subtilis Doctoris.* (Salamanca, 1765.)

PEREZ, A. : *Controversiae super primum librum Sententiarum, juxta subtilissimi . . . doctoris mentem.* (Saragossa, 1700.)

PEREZ DE QUIROGA, E. : *Disputationes, theologicae in primum (–tertium) librum Sententiarum, ad mentem . . . Johannis Duns Scoti,* etc. (1704–15.)

PERIUS, J. : *Subtilissimae contradictiones in Prologum, Primum atque Secundum Sententiarum Scoti.* (Florence, 1621.)

PETRUS DE AQUILA : *Scotellus* (a commentary on the Sentences abridging the doctrine of Duns Scotus). (Spires, 1480 ; Venice, 1501.) (New edition : Levanto, 1907–9.)

PETRUS DE CRUCE : *Quaestio de ratione subjecti primi scientiae secundum Joannem Scotum, an ad entia rationis extendatur.* (Venice, 1500.)

PETRUS DE S. CATH., et THOMAS DE S. JOS. : *Cursus philosophicus ad usum studentium totius Ordinis Minorum, juxta mentem Subtilis Doctoris Scoti.* (Madrid, 1692 ; Venice, 1697.)

PEUPLUS, A. : *Breviarium universae philosophiae Scoto-Augustinianae, in IV partes distinctum, rationalem, transrationalem et moralem, cum brevi reductione lectionum ad theologiam.* (Liége, 1648.)

PICAZO, J. : *Cursus integer theologicus juxta miram mentem . . . Joannis Duns Scoti,* etc. (Alcalá, 1751.)

PITIGIANIS, F. DE : *Summa theologiae speculativae, et moralis, atque commentaria scholastica in IV libros Sententiarum Joannis Duns Scoti.* (Venice, 1619, 1622.)

POMARIUS, J. : *Brevis summularum expositio juxta germanam Ven. Servi Dei Joannis Duntii Scoti philosophorum et theologorum principis, Subtilis Scholarum Magistri Doctoris Mariani,* etc. (Saragossa, 1682.)

PONCIUS, J. : *Disputationes in organon Aristotelis quibus adversariis veteribus Scoti logica vindicatur.* (Venice, 1646.)

  Integer philosophiae cursus ad mentem Scoti. (Rome, 1643 ; Paris, 1649 ; Lyon, 1672.)

  Appendix apologetica ad praedictum cursum. (Rome, 1645.)

  Integer theologiae cursus ad mentem Scoti. (Paris, 1652.)

PONTELONGO, FR. : *Disputationes logicales ad mentem subtilissimi Scoti.* (Bologna, 1647.)

POSNANIA, P. DE : *Commentaria in librum primum Sententiarum Scoti, in quibus Doctoris textus elucidatur et adversariorum sententiae refelluntur.* (Venice, 1626.)
Decisiones toties theologiae speculativae et moralis libri sex ad mentem Scoti. (Ibid., 1629.)

POSNANIA, TH. DE : *Quaestiones in universa philosophia subtilissimae ad mentem Scoti.* (15—(?).)

RABBASSÉ, J. : *Commentarium in philosophiam Scoti.* (Paris (?), 1660.)

RABESANUS DE MONTURSIO, L. : *Cursus philosophicus ad mentem Subtilis Doctoris Joannis Duns Scoti,* etc. :
Pars prima continet logicam minorem et majorem. (Venice, 1665.)
2a—*Continet VIII libros Aristotelis de Physica.* (Ibid., 1665.)
3a—*Continet III libros Aristotelis de Anima.* (Ibid., 1665.)
4a—*Secunda secundae partis Meteorologicorum IV libros complectens ac expendens.* (Ibid., 1668.)
5a—*Prima secundae partis, complectens IV libros de Coelo et Mundo.* (Ibid., 1672.)
6a—*Prima secundae partis volumen alterum, complectens libros II de Generatione et Corruptione.* (Ibid., 1674.)

RAM, E. : *De necessitate doctrinae revelatae ex mente Doctoris Mariani et Subtilis Johannis Duns Scoti.* (Würzburg, 1754.)

RAMIREZ, L. : *De triplici agone scholastico-scotico, thomistico-academico,* etc. (17—(?).)

RAPINE, C. : *Nucleus philosophiae Scoti.* (Paris, 1625.)

RELLI, F. : *Cursus philosophicus ad mentem Doctoris Subtilis.* (Pampeluna, 1651.)

ROBERTI, H. : *De Scoti distinctionibus.* (1587.)

ROCHMANNIUS, A. : *Joannis Duns Scoti primus Sententiarum illustratus, nunc per H. Kolechi recognitus.* (Venice, 1627.)
Commentaria in logicam et metaphysicam juxta mentem Scoti. (16—(?).)

RODRIGUEZ, L. : *Dialecticae Aristotelis compendium, commentaria pluresque articuli super logicam Joannis Duns Scoti,* etc. (Salamanca, 1624.)

ROSSI, A. : *De controversiis theologicis inter Scotistas.* (Bologna, 1651.)

RICCI, J. : *Apparatus ad imaginativam Doctoris Subtilissimi suscitandam, sive opus complectens principia Catholicae scientiae, ipsam scientiam methodumque ea omnia inquirendi, praevium ad analogias methodos et loca mathematica, quae in libris Sententiarum, Quodlibeticis, et Theorematis Joannis Scoti continentur, enucleanda. Cum quadruplici synopsi et syllabo.* (Paris, 1650.)

RUERK, A. : *Cursus theologiae scholasticae in via . . . Joannis Dunsii Scoti*, etc. (Valladolid, 1746.)

RUIZ, G. : *Controversiae theologicae*, prefaced with a life of Scotus. (1613.)

SAN CRUCIUS, J. : *Dialectica ad mentem Johannis Scoti*, etc. (London, 1673.)

SANNIG, B. : *Schola philosophica Scotistarum, seu cursus philosophicus completus ad mentem . . . Joannis Duns Scoti.* (Prague, 1684–5.)
Schola theologica Scotistarum. (Ibid., 1680.)

SARMENTERO, B. : *Cursus theologiae scholasticae in via Subtilis Marianique Doctoris Joannis Duns Scoti.* (1750.)

SARNANUS, C. : (See TORRI).

SASSI, A. : *Catastrosis philosophica et theologica, sive peripateticae, scoticae atque universalis doctrinae explicatio.* (Bologna, 1642.)

SCHERIUS, G. : *Disputationum . . . de Deo Trino et Uno . . . opus . . . in quo nedum mens Scoti solidatur ; verum et aliorum contradicentium opiniones . . . confutantur,* etc. (Lecce, 1646.)

SENDIN, J. : *Opus posthumum, aliquot tractatus theologicos in via Doctoris Subtilis Scoti . . . exhibens,* etc. (1699.)

SFORZA, J. M. : *Selectiora de transnaturali philosophia Aristotelis ad mentem Doctoris Subtilis.* (Foggia, 1646.)
Meteorologicae elucubrationes ex Aristotelis Meteorum libris desumptae ad mentem Scoti. (Naples, 1655.)
Scotus jurista conflatus sex disputationibus. (Lecce, 1659.)
Scotus corroboratus et contradictionibus Scholae adversae, in quo celebriores ex IV sententiarum libris controversiae theologicae . . . inter Scotum et D. Thomam ponuntur, etc. (Lecce, 1661.)
Aphorismi Scoti. (Lecce (?), 1664.)

SGHEMMA, C. : *Scotica opuscula de Deo Uno et Trino.* (Palermo, 1635 (?).)
Scoticae digressiones, cum commentariis in libros VIII Physicorum Aristotelis. (Palermo, 1635.)
Scoticum opusculum de scientia et voluntate Dei in ordine ad ultimum finem. (Ibid., 1651.)
Encheiridion Scoticum in organum logicae. (Ibid., 16—(?).)

SILVAGGI, M. : *Lectura seu expositio brevis super VIII libros physicorum Aristotelis, cum aliquibus adnotationibus de mente Doctoris Subtilis.* (Venice, 1542.)

SIRECTUS, A. : *Formalitates moderniores de mente clarissimi doctoris subtilis Scoti.* (1490.)
Hebdomades formalitatum recentiores secundum doctorem subtilem, ad usum Parisiensem. (Ferrara, 1490.)
Formalitates de mente doctoris subtilis. (1501.)

SMISING, TH. : *Disputationum theologicarum Fr. Theodori Smising, O. F. M. obs. Prov. Germ. Infer. Lovanii S. Theologiae Lectoris Tom. I. De Deo Uno in quo de natura Dei divinisque attributis, etc., disseritur, ac Subtilis Doctoris Scoti Sententiae . . . explicantur, etc.* (Antwerp, 1624.) *Tom. II. De Deo Trino.* (Ibid., 1626.)

SOKOLNICK, B. : *Libertas conscientiae a praejudiciis vindicata, sive tractatus theologicus de conscientia recta in obscuris, menti Joannis Duns Scoti accommodata.* (Prague, 1748.)

STELLA, F. : *Celebriores Thomistarum et Scotistarum theologicae controversiae.* (Milan, 1651.)

STUEMEL, F. : *Theologia sacramentalis ad mentem Scoti.* (16—(?).)
Primum et perenne mobile theologicum. (Cologne, 1680.)
Unilabium orbis subtiliter litterati de distinctione formali ex natura rei.

SURCULA, A. R. DE : *In universam philosophiam naturalem Aristotelis paraphrasis ad mentem Joannis Duns Scoti . . . VIII physicorum libros comprehendens.* (Venice, 1623.)

TARTARETUS, P. : *Commentaria . . . in IV libros Sententiarum et Quodlibeta Joannis Duns Scoti,* etc. (Paris, 1490 (?).)
Doctissimi viri . . . Petri Tartareti . . . secundum subtilissimi doctoris Scoti doctrinam . . . Summularum Petri de Hispania explanationes utilissime, etc. (1494.)
Expositio . . . Petri tartareti super textu logices Aristotelis Quaestiones cum medulla totius materiae artium quatuor librorum sententiarum et quodlibeti doctoris subtilis Scoti suis locis quotate, etc. (Paris, 1495(?).)
Clarissima totius philosophiae nec non metaphisicae Aristotelis . . . expositio. (Quaestiones cum medulla totius materiae, etc., doctoris sublitis Scott. (1494.)
Expositio in tota philosophia naturali et metaphysica Aristotelis usque ad librum VI juxta mentem Doctoris Subtilis Scoti. (Paris, 1503.)
Commentarii in Quodlibeta Scoti. (Ibid., 1519.)
Commentarii in IV libris Sententiarum juxta mentem Doctoris Subtilis Scoti. (Paris, 1520.)

TELLARDO, B. : *Trutina metaphysica theologica ad mentem Scoti.* (Salamanca, 1744.)

THEULO, B. : *Scotus moralis pro confessoribus.* (Venice, 1652.)
Scoticum scripturale. (Velletri, 1664.)
Dechachordium Scotisticum de Immaculata. (Ibid., 1673.)

TITONI, A. : *Clypeus distinctionis Scoticae seu formalis.* (Palermo, 1712.)

TORRI, C. (SARNANUS) : *Commentarius in formalitates Scoti.* (Venice, 1595.)

In universalia Scoti expositio cum tractatu de principio individuationis et de syllogismis conficiendis. (Ibid., 1581.)

Conciliatio dilucida omnium controversiarum quae in doctrinam duorum summorum theologorum passim leguntur, S. Thomae et Scoti. (Lyon, 1577, 1590.)

Directorium in logicam, philosophiam et theologiam, ad mentem Scoti. (Venice, 1580.)

(The 1590 editions of the *Conciliatio* and the *Directorium* have been reproduced by F. M. Paolini, Rome, 1911.)

TOSELLI, B.: *Institutio theologica juxta omnia fidei dogmata et doctoris subtilis scholastico nervo instructa.* (Ferrara, 1746.)

Institutio philosophica praemittenda theologiae, nunc Aristotelis et Joannis Duns Scoti acumine instructa. (Venice, 1766.)

TROMBETA, A.: *Opus doctrinae Scoticae, Patavii in Thomistas discussum, sententiis philosophi maxime conveniens,* etc. (Padua (?), 1483.)

In tractatum formalitatum Scoti sententia. Formalitates A. Syrectide mente ejusdem Scoti, etc. (1505.)

Quaestiones quodlibetales metaphysicae. Tractatus de futuris contingentibus, de formalitatibus Scoti, etc. (Edited by J. A. de Padua.)

TROTTI, B.: *Theologiae moralis primus egressus . . . ad mentem Scoti.* (Naples, 1704.)

UNTERBERGER, B.: *Controversiae scotico-theologicae.* (17—(?).)

URBINA, U. DE: *Memorial en defensa de las doctrinas del doctor Serafico S. Buenaventura y Escoto, . . . sobre el juramento que la Universidad de Salamanca hizo de leer tan solamente la doctrina de S. Agustin y S. Tomas.* (Madrid, 1628.)

VALERA, H.: *Commentaria in logicam juxta Scoti doctrinam.* (Lima, 1610.)

Declarationes marginales in formalitates Scoti. (Naples, 1533.)

VALLO, J.: *Lectura absolutissima super formalitates Scoti.* (Venice, 1566; Florence, 1580; Paris, 1584.) (See also J. de Bernal.)

VAN SICHEM, W.: *Repertorium propositionum quae sunt contra Subtilem Doctorem.* (Antwerp, 1678.)

VARAGIUS, P.: *Flores totius theologiae, medullam Sententiarum doctoris subtilis Scoti continentes,* etc. (Milan, 1509.)

VARESIO, C. F. DE: *Selectiores hujus temporis controversiae, dogmaticae fidei symbolo quo Sancta utitur Romana Ecclesia sustentatae, Joannis Doctoris Subtilissimi hypothesibus explicatae.* (Monza, 1688.)

Promptuarium scoticum ob oculos exhibens quidquid in IV Sententiarum libris et Quodlibetis Doctoris Subtilis continetur, suos in titulos digestum atque ordine alphabetico explanatum. (Venice, 1690.)

Scotus polemicus, adversus haereses, erroresque tum veteres tum recentes, solidissima spicula aeque ac subtilissima vibrans. (Rome, 1694.)

VARESIO, S. DE : *Scoticum sanctissimae Trinitatis telescopium.* (Milan, 1657.)

VARILLO, G. : *Incipit repertorium Magistri Gulielmi Varrilonis quod alio nomine dicitur vade mecum vel collectorium . . . opinionis Scoti ; sed opinionum in Scoto nullatenus signatorum.* (1485 (?).)

VASQUEZ, J. : *Memorial por la religion de S. Francesco en defensa de las doctrinas del Serafico doctor S. Buenaventura, del sutilissimo doctor Escoto y otros doctores classicos de la misma religion.* (Madrid, 1628.)

VERONA, A. DE : *Theses theologico-scholasticae quas ad mentem Doctoris Subtilis Joannis Duns Scoti, recurrentibus totius ordinis S. Patris Francisci Generalibus Comitiis, sub gloriosissimis auspiciis Sanctae Virginis Matris Clarae, P. Er. Alexander a Verona in Alma Divi Antonii Reformata Provincia Lector Theologus, publice propugnandas exponit.* (Padua, 1762.)

VIGERIS, J. : *Lectura resolutissima super primum librum Sententiarum Oxoniensis Duns Scoti.* (Venice, 1527.)

VILLAVERDE, M. DE : *Tractatus in libros de generatione et corruptione, et de anima, ad mentem Scoti.* (1658.)
Tractatus in VIII libros Physicae, in quo Sententiae Scoti proponuntur, etc. (1658.)
Tractatus in universam logicam Aristoteles . . . in quo Sententiae Scoti proponuntur, etc. (1658.)

VIOLA, L. F. : *Arcana fere omnia tum theologiae tum philosophiae quaestiones disputatae ac ultimae voluntates Subtilissimi Doctoris Joannis Duns Scoti.* (Naples, 1618.)

VOLPINI, ST. : *De consensu D. Augusti et Scoti subtilium principis de Gratia Christi.* (Venice, 1718.)

VORRILONG, G. DE : *Compendium . . . in IV Sententiarum libros juxta doctrinam Scoti.* (1510.)

VULPES, A. : *Sacrae theologiae summa Joannis Duns Scoti, et commentaria,* etc. 12 vols. (Naples, 1622–46.)
Judicium de vera rationalis animae immortalitate. (Naples, 1623.)

WIRRCHING, C. : *Theses XC ex universa theologia ad mentem Doctoris Mariani subtilis, Joannis Duns Scoti.* (Transylvania, 1765.)

WISSINGH, A. : *Flores panegyrici collecti ex vita et doctrina Ven. Servi Dei Joannis Duns Scoti, Doctoris Subtilis.* (Cologne, 1706.)

YRIBARNE, J. : *Commentaria in quartum librum Sententiarum Joannis Duns Scoti.* Vol. I (Saragossa, 1614). Vol. II (Tarragona, 1615).

ZAMORUS, J. M. : *Disputationes theologicae de Deo Uno et Trino, in quibus . . . omnes controversiae inter D. Bonaventuram, D. Thomam et Scotum . . . componuntur,* etc. (1626.)

Anonymous :

Cursus librorum philosophie naturalis secundum viam doctoris subtilis Scoti. (1494.)

Quaestionum optimarum cursus cum textualibus expositionibus super phisicorum et ceteros naturalis philosophie libros Aristotelis sicut maximi Parisius [sic] *legentes multorum peritissimorum in philosophia opiniones recitantes finaliter se resolventes ad mentem . . . Johannis Schoti,* etc. (1495 (?).) (fol. .)

Trium librorum De anima Aristotelis expositio cum ordinarissima questionum per difficultates . . . dissolutione ad intentionem doctoris subtilis, etc. (1513.)

Dies intelligibilis Scoticus in xii horas theologicas divisus, sive . . . explicatio Symboli Apostolici in duodecim articulos distributi . . . Additae sunt cuilibet articulo quaestiones . . . cum earum resolutione juxta mentem . . . Scoti. (1674.)

Idiotas, or Duns' contemplation of divine love, written by John Duns, alias Scotus, commonly styled the Subtile Doctor and Prince of Divines. (Really by Raymondus Jordanus). [The Epistle Dedicatory to Edmund Duns, Esquire, is signed W. B. (1662).]

The following works also deal with the life of Duns Scotus :

Angelus a S. Franc. : *Certamen Seraphicum provinciae Angliae pro Sancta Dei Ecclesia.*

Arriega, R. : *Vita Scoti,* etc.

Bartholemaeus (Pisanus) : *Liber aureus, inscriptus liber conformitatum vitae Beati ac Seraphici Patris Francisci ad vitam Jesu Christi Domini nostri.*

Bzovius : *Annales Ecclesiastici.*

Carta, L. : *Vita y admirabile doctrina del venerabile . . . Juan Duns Escoto.* (Gallet, 1657.)

Cavellus, H. : *Vita Joannis Duns Scoti,* prefixed to his edition of the Sentences of Duns. (Antwerp, 1620.)
Apologia pro Joanne Duns Scoto adversus opprobria, calumnias, et injurias, etc. (Paris, 1634.)

Ciolli, A. : *Vita Joannis Duns Scoti ab imposturis quorundam historicorum vindicata.* (Parma, 16—(?).)

Colganus, J. : *Tractatus de Joannis Duns Scoti Doctoris Subtilis theologorumque principis vita, patria, elogiis, encomiasticis . . . doctrina,* etc. (Antwerp, 1665.)

Dempster, Th. : *Assertae Scotiae cives,* etc. (Bologna, 1621.)
Historia Ecclesiastica. (1627.)

ECCLESTON, TH. DE : *De adventu Minorum in provinciam Angliae—Monumenta Franciscana* (Rolls series, 1.)

FERCHIUS, M. : *Apologia pro Joanne Duns Scoto in Joannem Fredericum Matensium.* (Cologne, 1619.)
Correptio Scotica Joannis Duns Scoti Doctoris Subtilis vitam et mortem explicans. (Chambéry, 1620.)
Vita Joannis Duns Scoti Doctoris Subtilis. (Bologna, 1622.)
Oratio in Joannem Duns Scotum declamata in Universitate Patavina. (Padua, 1634.)

GARCIA, M. F. : *B. Joannis Duns Scoti vitae Compendium.* (Quaracchi, 1907.)

GUZMAN, A. DE : *Vida de Juan Duns Escoto, principe y maestro de la escuela Franciscana.* (Madrid, 1671.)

HOYERUS, M. : *Oratio encomiastica de sanctitate vitae et divina sapientia Joannis Duns Scoti, Doctoris Mariani et Subtilis.* (Douai, 1636.) (Recent edition by F. M. Paolini, Rome, 1906.)

HYQUAEUS (HICKEY), A. : *Nitela Franciscanae Religionis et abstersio sordium quibus eam conspurcare frustra tentavit Abrahamus Bzovius.* (Lyon, 1627.)

ISIDORUS DE S. MICH. : *Certamen historiale panegyricum ad honorem Beatissimae Mariae Virginis ejusque fidelissimi Doctoris Joannis Duns Scoti O. M. Magistri.* (1701.)

JANSSENIUS, N. : *Animadversiones et scholia in apologiam nuper editam de vita et morte Joannis Duns Scoti, adversus Abrahamum Bzovium.* (Cologne, 1622.)

KIERIE, B. C. : *Elenchus encomiorum utriusque Ecclesiae triumphantis et militantis de Joanne Scoto, viso Entheo et Extatico, Doctore Subtili.* (Botzen, 1680.)

LEON, R. P. : *L'auréole séraphique. Vie des Saints et des Bienheureux des trois ordres de Saint François.*

MAGNESIUS, H. : *Apologia apologiae pro Joanne Duns Scoto,* etc. (Paris, 1623.)

MARIANUS FLORENTINUS : *Vita Joannis Duns Scoti . . . circa 1480 scripta*—edited by F. M. Paolini. (Genoa, 1904.)

PEREZ LOPEZ, J. FR. : *Instantes del heroe sutil ; vida del venerabile Padre y Doctor Mariano Juan Duns Escoto.* (Saragossa, 1683.)

PESAURO, C. À. (O. F. M.) : *Nolana seu Ordinis Minorum Articuli exhibiti ad processum additionalem instituendam pro confirmatione cultus ab immemorabili tempore praestiti Ven. servo Dei Johanni Duns Scoto.* (Rome, 1905.)

PONCIUS, J. : *Scotus Hiberniae restitutus,* etc. (Paris, 1660.)

RODOLPHUS: *Historiarum Seraphicae Religionis libri tres.* (Venice, 1586.)

RYCHLEWICZ, B. : *Crisis apologetica, historica et moralis de morte et fama . . . Joannis Duns Scoti principis et Coryphaei universalis scholae Franciscanae.* (Cracow, 1706.)

SCZEPANOWSKI, S. : *Commentarium de vita et scriptis venerabilis Joannis Duns, cognomento Scoti, Doctoris Subtilis et Mariani,* etc. (*Warsaw,* 1752.)

VEGLIA, M. DE : *Vita Joannis Duns Scoti.* (Padua, 1671.)

VERNULAEUS N. : *Panegyricus aetatis . . . famae, venerabilis Patris Joannis Duns Scoti,* etc. (Cologne, 1622 ; Warsaw, 1632.)

WADDING, L. : *Scriptores Ordinis Minorum.*
Vita Duns Scoti, O. M., Doctoris Subtilis, etc. (Mons, 1644.)
(Printed in his edition of Scotus' works together with the panegyric of Vernulaeus.)

WOOD, A. : *Historia et Antiquitates Universitatis Oxoniensis.* (Oxford, 1674—(?).) (Survey of the Antiquities of the City of Oxford. Edited by A. Clarke, 1889–99.)

XIMENEZ SAMANIEGO, J. : *Vida del . . . padre Juan Dunsio Escoto.* (Madrid, 1668.)

ANONYMOUS :

De vita Beati Johannis Duns Scoti Doctoris Immaculatae Conceptionis Ordinis Minorum ab omni tempore Sancti et Beati titulo nuncupati nec non de ejus cultu immemorabili antiquissimo et extensissimo. (Rome, 1905.)

Monumenta cultus immemorabilis publici et ecclesiastici, antiquissimi et extensissimi, quibus fulcitur causa servi Dei Duns Scoti. (Rome, 1905.)

§ 3. *General Bibliography*

Among more modern works, the following are the most important :

ALBANESI, C. : *La teoria delle idee senza immagini nella psicologia di Scoto.* (*Studi Francescani,* An. I, 1915.)
Intorno alla nozione della verità ontologica. (Ibid.)
Della natura del tempo secondo il Ven. dottore sottile Mariano. (Ibid., An. II, 1916.)
Studi su Scoto—La teoria del conoscere. (Rome, 1923.) See also review by E. GILSON, *Rev. d'Histoire Franç.,* 1924.

BAUMGARTEN-CRUSIUS, F. L. : *Programma de theologia Scoti.* (Jena, 1826.)

BELMOND, S.: *L'existence de Dieu d'après Duns Scot.* (*Rev. de Phil.,* 1908.)
La perfection de Dieu d'après Duns Scot. (Ibid., 1909.)
La connaissance de Dieu d'après Duns Scot. (Ibid., 1910.)
L'essenza e l'esistenza secondo Duns Scoto. (*Riv. di Fil. Neoscol.,* 1910.)
Da Giovanni Duns Scoto a Kant. (Ibid., 1910.)
Pour l'univocité. (*Études Franciscaines,* 1911.)

Le rôle de la volonté dans la philosophie de Duns Scot. (Ibid.)

L'idée de la création d'après S. Bonaventure et Duns Scot. (Ibid., 1913.)

Actualités scotistes. (*Ét. Franc.*, 1912.)

L'univocité scotiste—ce qu'elle est et ce qu'elle vaut. (*Rev. de Phil.*, 1912.)

L'univocité scotiste—ses fondements. (Ibid., 1913.)

La lingua della teodicea nel Giovanni Duns Scoto. (*Riv. di Fil. Neoscol.*, 1913.)

Études sur la philosophie de Duns Scot. I. Dieu, existence et cognoscibilité. (Paris, Beaucherne, 1913.)

Simples remarques sur l'idéologie comparée de S. Thomas et de Duns Scot. (*Rev. de Phil.*, 1914.)

Gravi inesattezze del P. G. Mattiussi a proposito di dottrine Scotistiche. (*Studi Francescani*, 1914.)

Prétendu anti-intellectualisme du Docteur Subtil. (*Études Franciscaines*, 1914.)

Simples remarques à propos de la philosophie de Duns Scot. (*Franciscana* [Iseghem], 1923.)

BERTONI, A. : *Le bienheureux Jean Duns Scot, sa vie, sa doctrine, et ses disciples.* (Levanto, 1917.)

BIHL, M. : *Zur Disputation des Duns Scotus über die unbefleckte Empfängniss.* (*Zeitschr. für Kath. Theol.*, 1906.)

CALLEBAUT, A. (O. F. M.) : *La patrie du B. Jean Duns Scot.* (*Arch. Franç. Hist.*, 1917.)

L'Écosse, patrie du B. Jean Duns Scot. (Ibid., 1920.)

Le B. Jean Duns Scot, étudiant à Paris vers 1293–1296. (Ibid., 1924.)

CARGAGENTE, C. : *Apologia y elogio del ven. Doctor Sutil y Mariano.* (1900.)

CARRERA Y ARTAU : *Ensayo sobre el voluntarismo de J. Duns Scot.* (Gerona, 1923.)

Catholic Fortnightly Review, The : Duns Scotus on the divine will. (December 15, 1910.)

Did Duns Scotus hold the famous *Disputatio Magna*? (Dec.15, 1906.)

In defence of Duns Scotus. (Art. by Preuss, 1912.)

CIGANOTTA, L. : *Metodo e sistema scientifico del Ven. Giovanni Duns Scoto, Dottore Sottile e Mariano*, etc. (Jerusalem, 1898.)

CLAVERIE, R. P. : *L'existence de Dieu d'après Duns Scot.* (*Rev. Thomiste*, 1909.)

CRESI, A. : *La posizione di Scoto nella questione dell' immortalità dell' anima.* (La Verna, 1913.)

DANIELS, P. : *Die Unechtheit der dem Scotus zugeschriebenen Schrift : Expositio et Quaestiones in VIII libros Physicorum.* (*Beiträge zur Ph. des Mittelalters*, Band VIII, Anhang III.)

Zu den Beziehungen zwischen Wilhelm von Ware und Johannes Duns Scotus. (*Franz. Stud.*, 1917.)

DE BASLY, DÉODAT-MARIE : *Le sacré cœur—Conférences selon la doctrine du Vén. Duns Scot.* (Paris, 1900.)
  Le Vén. Duns Scot. (Paris, 1902.)
  Articles in the following journals : *La Bonne Parole* ; *Revue Duns Scot* ; *L'École Franciscaine* (1901–12), the most important of which are these :
  Un tournoi théologique.
  Dieu et le Christ.
  Les deux écoles, thomiste et scotiste.
  Duns Scot et le status catholique de la pensée à l'université de Paris.
  Capitalia opera Scoti :
  T. I. *Praeparatio philosophica.* (Le Havre, 1908.)
  T. II. *Synthesis theologica.* (Ibid., 1911.)
  Les Theoremata de Scot. (*Arch. Franç. Hist.*, 1918.)

DE CAYLUS, D. : *Merveilleux épanouissement de l'école scotiste au xviie siècle.* (*Ét. Franc.*, tt. xxiv–xxvi, 1910–11.)

DEL PRADO, N. : *Duns Scot à Saint Thomas* (*Revue Thomiste*, 1910. *Escoto y S. Tomas* (*Ciencia Tomista*, 1914.)

DE NANTES, R. (O. M. C.) : *Bonaventure et Duns Scot.* (*Études Franciscaines*, 1902.)

DESBUTS, B. : *De saint Bonaventure à Duns Scot.* (*Ann. de Phil. Chrét.*, Dec. 1910.)

DEVA MARASC, G. : *Ontologismus et venerabilis Doctor Subtilis—Disquisitio critico-philosophica.* (Jerusalem, 1903.)
  Ethica generalis ad mentem ven. Duns Scoti. (Ibid., 1905.)
  Jus naturae seu ethica specialis ad mentem ven. Johannis Duns Scoti, cum triplici appendice de quaestione sociali, feminismo et arbitratu internationali. (Ibid., 1906.)

DORNER, A. : *Jahrbücher für deutsche Theologie*, 1857, ii.

DUHEM, P. : *Sur les Meteorologicorum Libri quatuor faussement attribués à J. Duns Scot.* (*A. F. H.*, iii.)

ERDMANN, B. : *Andeutungen über die wissenschaftliche Stellung des Duns Scotus.* (*Theol. Stud. u. Krit.*, Heft 3—translated into English in the *American Presbyterian Review*, vol. xiv.)

FELTEN, TH. : *Johannes Duns Scotus über das Werk des Erlösers.* (Bonn, 1911.)

FIORAVANTI, A. : *La distinzione tra l' anima e le sue facoltà nella dottrina del ven. Giovanni Duns Scoto.* (*Stud. Franc.*, 1915.)

GARCIA, M. F. : *De vita, scriptis et doctrina B. Joannis Duns Scoti.* (Quaracchi, 1910.)

Mentis in Deum elevatio duce Doctore Subtili a Mariano B. Joanne Duns Scoto. (Ibid., 1907.)

GEMELLI, A. : *La volontà nel pensiero del ven. Giovanni Duns Scoto.* (La Verna, 1906.)

Ancora sulla volontà nel pensiero del ven. G. Duns Scoto. (Ibid., 1907.)

Le Kantisme de Duns Scot ; du rôle de la volonté dans la philosophie de Duns Scot. (La Verna, 1917.)

GUTTMANN, J. : *Die Beziehung des Duns Scotus zum Judenthum.* (*Monatsschr. f. Gesch. u. Wissensch. des Judenthums.*—Breslau, 1894.)

HARRIS, C. R. S. : *Duns Scotus and his relation to Thomas Aquinas.* (*Proc. Arist. Soc.* 1924–5.)

KAHL, W. : *Die Lehre vom Primat des Willens bei Augustinus, Duns Scotus und Descartes.* (Strassburg, 1886.)

KLEIN, J. : *Der Gottesbegriff des Duns Scotus, vor allem nach seiner ethischen Seite betrachtet.* (Paderborn, 1913.)

Intellekt u. Wille nach Duns Skotus. (*Franz. Stud.*, 1921.)

Zur Sittenlehre des Johannes Duns Skotus. (*Franz. Stud.*, 1914.)

Intellekt und Wille als die nächsten Quellen der sittlichen Akte nach Duns Skotus. (Ibid., 1916, 1919–21.)

Zum Charakterbild des Johannes Duns Skotus. (Ibid., 1917.)

KLUG, H. (O. M. C.) : *Die Lehre des Johannes Duns Scotus über Materie und Form, nach den Quellen dargestellt.* (*Philos. Jahrb.*, 1917.)

Zur Biographie der Minderbrüder Johannes Duns Skotus und Wilhelm von Ware. (*Franz. Stud.*, 1915.)

Die Immaterialität der Engel und Menschenseelen nach Duns Skotus. (Ibid., 1916.)

Die Lehre des seligen Johannes Duns Skotus über die Seele. (*Phil. Jahrb.*, 1923.)

LANDRY, B. : *Duns Scot.* (Paris, Alcan, 1922. Reviewed in *Études Franciscaines* by P. Eph. Longpré.)

LEIGH, G. : Links between Duns Scotus and Dante. (*Church Quarterly Review*, July, 1923.)

LEONISSA, JOH. A : *Scotistische Theologie.* (*Jahrb. f. Phil. u. spek. Theol.*, xix, 1905.)

LONGPRÉ, E. : *La Philosophie du Bienheureux Duns Scot.* (Paris, 1924.)

LOZANO, P. : *P. Fr. Juan Duns Escoto Doctor Mariano y Sutil.* (Buenos Ayres, 1908.)

MALO, F. E. : *Impugnación de la historia de la filosofía escrita por el Ex. Zef. Gonzalez, en defensa del buen nombre del Ven. Doctor Mariano Fr. Juan Duns Escoto.* (Madrid, 1880.)

Defensa filosofico-teologica del Ven. Doctor Subtil y Mariano Fr. Juan Duns Escoto. (Orihuela, 1889.)

MATTIUSSI, G. : *Primato della volontà.* (*Scuola Cattolica,* 1906.)

MICHALSKI, C. : *Les sources du criticisme et du scepticisme dans le philosophie du XIVe siècle.* (Cracow, 1924.)
Les courants philosophiques à Oxford et à Paris pendant le XIVe siècle. (Cracow, 1921.)

MICHEL-ANGE, R. P. (O. M. C.) : *Ossuna et Duns Scot.* (*Ét. Franc.,* 1910.)

MILOSOWEC, G. : *L' immacolata concezione difesa del ven. Giovanni Duns Scoto.* (1897.)

MINGES, P. : *Zur Theologie des Duns Scotus.* (*Theol. Quartalschr.* Tübingen, 1902.)
Die angeblich laxe Reuelehre des Duns Scotus. (*Zeitschr. f. kath. Theol.,* 1901.)
Ist Duns Scotus Indeterminist? (*Beiträge z. Gesch. d. Phil. d. Mittelalters,* 1905.)
Die Gnadenlehre des Duns Scotus auf ihren angeblichen Pelagianismus und Semi-Pelagianismus geprüft. (Münster, 1906.)
Die Bedeutung von Objekt, Umständen und Zweck für die Sittlichkeit eines Aktes, nach Duns Scotus. (*Phil. Jahrb.,* 1906.)
Der Gottesbegriff des Duns Scotus auf seinen angeblich exzessiven Indeterminismus geprüft. (*Theol. Stud. d. Leogesellsch.* Vienna, 1906.)
Der Wert der guten Werke, nach Duns Scotus. (*Theol. Quartalschr.* Tübingen, 1907.)
Beitrag zur Lehre des Duns Scotus über das Werk Christi. (Ibid.)
Beitrag zur Lehre des Duns Scotus über die Person Christi. (Ibid.)
Beitrag zur Lehre des Duns Scotus über die Univokation des Seins- begriffes. (*Phil. Jahrb.,* 1907.)
Das Verhältnis zwischen Glauben und Wissen, Theologie und Philo- sophie, nach Duns Scotus. (*Forsch. z. christl. Lit. u. Dogmengesch.,* VII, 4–5. Paderborn, 1907–8.)
Der angeblich exzessive Realismus des Duns Scotus. (*Beiträge,* etc., 1908.)
Die Distinctio formalis des Duns Scotus. (*Theol. Quartalschr.,* 1908.)
Johannis Duns Scoti doctrina philosophica et theologica quoad res praecipuas praeposita, etc. (Quaracchi, 1908–12.)
Zum Wiederaufblühen des Scotismus. (*Franziskanische Studien,* 1914.)
Scotismus und Pantheismus. (*Phil. Jahrb.,* 1918.)
Zur Erkenntnisslehre des Duns Scotus. (Ibid., 1918.)
Die skotistische Literatur des xx. Jahrhunderts. (*Franz. Stud.,* 1917.)
Suarez und Duns Skotus. (*Phil. Jahrb.,* 1919.)
Skotisches bei Richard von Mediavilla. (*Theol. Quartalschr.,* 1919.)

MORELLI, M. : *Se la teologia sia una scienza pratica?* (*Stud. Franc.,* An. I., 1915.)

In quel senso la teologia sia scienza secondo la mente del Dottore Sottile.
(Ibid., 1915.)

L'atto di fede secondo la dottrina del ven. Dottore Sottile. (Ibid.,
Ann. II, 1916.)

MUELLER, J. : *Biographisches über Duns Scotus.* (Cologne, 1881.)

OLIVIER, R. P. : *Note sur l'opinion de Scot au sujet de la grâce et de la
charité habituelle.* (*Ét. Franc.,* 1906.)

O'NEILL, A. : *La causalité sacramentelle d'après le docteur subtil.* (*Ét.
Franc.,* 1913.)

Duns Scot et la preuve scripturaire de la transsubstantiation. (Ibid.,
1914.)

PAOLINI, F. M. : *De vita Beati Joannis Duns Scoti Doctoris Immaculatae
Conceptionis,* etc. (Rome, 1905.)

*Di una illustre testimonianza sopre la divina missione del B. Giovanni
Duns Scoto per insignare a defendere la dottrina dell' immacolata
concezione a Parigi.* (Ibid., 1905.)

*Monumenta cultus immemorabilis publici et ecclesiastici antiquissimi
et extensissimi quibus fulcitur causa Servi Dei Joannis Duns Scoti.*
(Rome, 1907.)

PAULUS, N. : *Eine unechte Ablassschrift des Duns Scotus.* (*Zeitsch. f.
kath. Theol.,* 1901.)

PELSTER, F. : *Handschriftliches zu Skotus.* (*Franziskanische Studien,*
1923.)

PELZER, A. : *Le premier livre des Reportata Parisiensia de Jean Duns
Scot.* (*Annales de l'Institut Supérieur de Philosophie.* Louvain,
1923.)

Jean Duns Scot et les études scotistes. (*Rev. Néo-scolastique,* 1923.)

PETAZZI, A. : *Univocità od analogia?* (*Riv. di Fil. Neo-scol.,* 1911–12.)

PLUZANSKI, E. : *Essai sur la philosophie de Duns Scot.* (Paris, 1887.)
(Italian translation by Alfani, Florence, 1892. Reviewed by
L. Robert, *Annales de Bretagne,* etc., tom. ii, p. 571.)

PRADO, N. DEL : *Duns Scot et S. Thomas.* (*Rev. Thomiste,* 1910.)
Escoto y S. Tomás. (*Ciencia Tomista,* 1914.)

PREZZOLINI, R. P. : *Cursus philosophicus ad mentem Doctoris Subtilis.*
(Rome, 1900.)

RAMIÈRE, R. P. : *La doctrine franciscaine sur le sacrament de pénitence.
Encore un mot sur la doctrine de Scot sur l'administration du sacrament de pénitence.* (*Rev. des Scien. Ecclés.,* 1873–4.)

RAYMOND, R. P. (O. M. C.) : *La théorie de l'induction de Duns Scot
précurseur de Bacon.* (*Études Franc.,* 1909.)

Pour la diffusion et la défense des doctrines de Duns Scot. (Ibid., 1909.)

Les œuvres de Scot. (Ibid., 1907.)

La philosophie critique de Duns Scot et le criticisme de Kant. (*Études Franc.*, 1909.)

L'ontologie de Duns Scot et le principe du panthéisme. (Ibid., 1910.)

Vers Duns Scot. (Ibid., 1912.)

Synthèse des doctrines de Scot sur les preuves de l'existence de Dieu. (Ibid., 1908.)

Le motif de l'incarnation—Duns Scot et l'école scotiste. (Ibid., 1912.)

Duns Scot et le modernisme. (Ibid., 1913.)

A-propos de Duns Scot et du modernisme. (*Rev. Thomiste*, 1913.)

Docteurs franciscains et doctrines franciscaines (*Ét. Franc.*, 1914.)

La pensée de Duns Scot sur les preuves de la transsubstantiation. (Ibid., 1914.)

RIDOLFI, A.: *L'induzione scientifica nel pensiero di Scoto.* (*Stud. Franc.*, An. I., 1915.)

RITSCHL, A.: *Duns Scotus.* (*Jahrb. f. deutsche Theologie*, Bd. x, 1865; xiii, 1868.)

ROOY, P. VAN: *Tractatio practica de sacramento poenitentiae, seu systema Scoti ad praxim applicatum,* etc. (Malines, 1872.)

SARRANTÉ, P. M.: *Ossuna et Duns Scot, ou la mystique de S. François.* (*Ét. Franc.*, 1909-11.)

SCHIEFFERENS, M.: *Quellenmässige Darlegung der Lehre von der Willensfreiheit bei Thomas von Aquino, mit Berücksichtigung derselben Lehre bei Duns Scotus.* (Münster, 1904.)

SCHMID, A.: *Die thomistische und scotistische Gewissheitslehre.* (1859.)

SCHNEID, M.: *Die Körperlehre des Johannes Duns Scotus, und ihr Verhältniss zum Thomismus und Atomismus.* (1879.)

SEEBERG, R.: *Die Busslehre des Duns Scotus.* (*Abhandl. f. A. von Oetlingen,* etc.) (Munich, 1897.)

Die Theologie des Duns Scotus. (1900.)

SERESI, P. M.: *Sulla dottrina e santità del B. Giovanni Duns Scoto.* (Rome, 1903.)

SIEBECK, H.: *Der Scotismus.* (*Zeitschr. f. Phil. u. phil. Krit.*, 1888-9.) *Die Willenslehre bei Duns Scotus und seinen Nachfolgern.* (Ibid., 1898.)

SYMPHORIEN, R. P.: *La distinction formelle de Scot et les universaux.* (*Ét. Franc.*, 1909.)

VACANT, A.: *La philosophie de Duns Scot comparée à celle de S. Thomas.* (*Ann. de Phil. chrét.*, 1887-9.)

Études comparées sur la philosophie de S. Thomas et celle de Duns Scot. (Paris-Lyon, 1891.)

D'où vient que Duns Scot ne conçoit point la volonté comme S. Thomas d'Aquin? (*Rev. du Clergé Français*, 1897; *Compte rendu du Congrès Intern. des Sciences Cath., Fribourg, 1898.*)

WERNER, K.: *Die Sprachlogik des Johannes Duns Scotus.* (*Sitzungs-berichte der k. Akad. d. Wissenschaften.* Vienna, 1877.)
Die Psychologie und Erkenntnisslehre des Johannes Duns Scotus. (*Denkschrift d. k. Akad. d. Wissensch.* etc. Vienna, 1877.)
Die Scholastik des späteren Mittelalters, Vol. I.—*Johannes Duns Scotus.* (Vienna, 1881.)

ZUCCHERELLI, D.: *Il pensiero del B. Giovanni Duns Scoto sulla con-tingenza del ordine etico.* (*Studi Francescani*, 1915.)
La cognizione nel pensiero del B. Giovanni Duns Scoto. (Ibid.)
Il problema criteriologico nel pensiero del B. Giovanni Duns Scoto. (Ibid.)

The following Periodicals, Encyclopedias, Dictionaries, Histories of Philosophy, etc., may also be consulted :

Archiv für Literatur- und Kirchengeschichte, ed. by H. Denifle and F. Ehrle.

Archivium Franciscanum Historicum.

BACH, J.: *Dogmengeschichte des Mittelalters.* (Vienna, 1873.)

BAEUMKER, CL.: *Die christliche Philosophie des Mittelalters—Allge-meine Geschichte der Philosophie.* (Leipzig, 1913.)

BALDWIN, J. M.: *Dictionary of Philosophy and Psychology.*

BAUR, F. C.: *Die christliche Lehre von der Dreieinigkeit und Menschen-werdung Gottes.* (Tübingen, 1842.)

Beiträge zur Geschichte der Philosophie des Mittelalters.

BELLARMIN-LABBÉ : *Scriptores Ecclesiastici.* (1728.)

BERNHART, J.: *Die philosophische Mystik des Mittelalters.* (1922.)

BOTALLA, P.: *La composition des corps d'après les deux principaux systèmes qui divisent les écoles catholiques.*

BRUCKER : *Hist. Crit. Phil.* (1776–7.)

BUDINSKY : *Historia Universitatis Parisiensis.* (1876.)

Catholic Encyclopedia, The : Article ' Duns Scotus ' by P. Minges.

CORNOLDI, A. O.: *Come debbe concepirsi la corporeità?* (*Scienza Italiana*, 1876, vol. ii, p. 316.) See also the reply by R. P. DAMASO (Ibid., vol. iii, 1877).

COUSIN, F.: *Histoire générale de la philosophie.*

CUEVAS, P.: *Historia de la filosofia.* (Madrid, 1838.)

DEMPF, A.: *Die Hauptform mittelalterlicher Weltanschauung.* (Berlin and Munich, 1925.)

DENIFLE-CHATELAIN : *Chartularium Universitatis Parisiensis.*

DE WULF, M. : *Histoire de la philosophie médiévale.* 5th ed. (Much improved.) (English translation of 3rd edition by Coffey, 1909.)
Scholasticism Old and New. (English transl. by Coffey.)
Philosophy and Civilization in the Middle Ages. (Princeton, 1919.)
La doctrine de la pluralité des formes dans l'ancienne école scolastique du XIIIe siècle. (*Rev. d'Hist. et Lit. Rel.*, 1901.)

Diccionario enciclopédico Hispano-Americano. Article ' Escoto '.

Dictionary of National Biography. Article by J. M. Rigg.

Dictionnaire historique et critique (Bayle). Article ' Abelard '.

Dictionnaire de philosophie et de théologie scolastique. Article by F. Morin.

Dictionnaire des sciences philosophiques. Article by X. Rousselot.

Dictionnaire de théologie catholique. Article ' Duns Scot ', by P. Raymond ; A. Vacant, ' Angélologie '.

DOMET DE VORGES : *Abrégé de métaphysique—Étude historique et critique des doctrines de la métaphysique scolastique.* (Paris, 1906.)

DORNER, A. : *Grundriss der Dogmengeschichte.*

DUHEM, P. : *Systèmes du monde,* t. v.

Encic. univ. illustr. Europeo-Americano. (Barcelona, 1900.) Article ' Escoto '.

Encyclopaedia Britannica (12th ed.). Article by A. Pringle-Pattison.

Encycl. Cath. Théol. Article by Von Döllinger.

Encycl. Prot. Théol. Article by A. Dorner.

EHRLE, Card. F. : *Der Augustinismus und Aristotelismus in der Scholastik gegen Ende des 13. Jahr.* (*Archiv f. Lit.- u. Kirchen-gesch.*, Bd. v, 1889.)

ENDRES, J. A. : *Geschichte der mittelalterlichen Philosophie.* (1908.)

ERDMANN, J. E. : *Grundriss der Geschichte der Philosophie.*

FITZMAURICE and LITTLE : ' Materials for the history of the Franciscan province of Ireland.' (*Brit. Soc. Franc. Stud.*, vol. ix.)

FOUILLE : *Histoire de la philosophie.*

GARCIA, M. F. : *Lexicon scholasticum scoticum philosophico-theologicum.* (Quaracchi, 1910.)

GILSON, E. : *La philosophie au moyen âge.* (Paris, 1922.)

GONZALEZ, Card. Z. : *Historia de la filosofia.* (Madrid, 1897.)

GRABMANN, M. : *Geschichte der scholastischen Methode.* (Freiburg, 1909–11.)
Thomas von Aquin. (Kempten u. München, 1912.)
Die Kulturphilosophie des hl. Thomas von Aquin. (Augsburg, 1925.)
Mittelalterliches Geistesleben. (Munich 1926.)

Grande Encyclopédie. Article by Fonsegrive. (Paris, 1885.)

HAFFNER, P. : *Grundlinien der Geschichte der Philosophie.*

HAMPDEN, R. D. : *The Scholastic Philosophy.* (Oxford, 1832.)

HARNACK, A.: *Lehrbuch der Dogmengeschichte.* III. (Tübingen, 1910.)

HASTINGS's *Dictionary of Religion and Ethics.* Article 'Scholasticism', by S. H. Mellone.

HAURÉAU, B. : *Histoire de la philosophie scolastique.*

HEIM, K. : *Das Gewissheitsproblem in der systematischen Theologie bis zu Schleiermacher.* (Leipzig, 1911.)

HERZOG-PLITT : *Realenzyclopädie.* Article by A. Dorner.

Histoire littéraire de la France. Article by E. Renan, tom. xxv.

HOEFFER : *Nouvelle Biographie générale.* Article by B. Hauréau.

JOURDAIN, C. : *La philosophie de S. Thomas d'Aquin.*

KLEUTGEN, P. : *Die Philosophie der Vorzeit.*

KREBS, E. : *Theologie und Wissenschaft nach der Lehre der Hoch-scholastik.* (Beiträge, etc., Bd. xi.)

LAROUSSE : *Grand dictionnaire universel.*

LELAND, J. : *Comm. de script. Brit.*

LITTLE, A. G. : *The Grey Friars in Oxford.* (Ox. Hist. Soc., vol. xv.)

LORENZ : *Deutsche Geschichtsquellen.*

MALLET, C. : *A History of the University of Oxford.* (Oxford, 1924.)

MARÉCHAL, J. : *Le point de départ de la métaphysique.* (Bruges, 1923.)

MARTIGNÉ, R. P. DE : *La scolastique et les traditions franciscaines.* (Paris, 1888.)

MAURICE, J. F. D. : *Mediaeval Philosophy.* (London, 1870.)

MESSER, A. : *Geschichte der Philosophie im Altertum und Mittelalter.* (Leipzig, 1912.)

MEYER : *Grosses Konversationslexicon.*

MIRAEUS : *Scriptores Ecclesiastici.*

MORONI : *Dizionario di erudizione storico-ecclesiastica.* (1878.)

New International Encyclopedia. (New York, 1914.)

PICAVET, F. : *Esquisse d'une histoire générale et comparée des philosophies médiévales.* (2nd ed. Paris, 1907.)
   Histoire des rapports de la théologie et de la philosophie. (Paris, 1888.)

PFLEIDERER, O. : *Religionsphilosophie auf geschichtlicher Grundlage.*

PRANTL, C. : *Geschichte der Logik im Abendlande.*

RENOUVIER : *Philosophie analytique de l'histoire.*

RITTER : *Geschichte der Philosophie.*

Rougier, L. : *La scolastique et le Thomisme.* (Pansig 25).

Rousselot, F. : *Etudes sur la philosophie du Moyen-Âge.*

Ruggiero, G. de : *Storia della filosofia del Cristianesimo.* (Bari, 1921.)

Sardeman, F. : *Ursprung und Entwickelung der Lehre vom lumen rationis aeternae, lumen divinum etc., bis Descartes.* (Cassel, 1902.)

Scheeben : *Handbuch der katholischen Dogmatik.*

Schindele, St. : *Zur Geschichte der Unterscheidung von Wesenheit und Dasein in der Scholastik.* (Munich, 1900.)

Schmoeller, L. : *Die scholastische Lehre von Materie und Form.* (Passau, 1903.)

Schultz : *Theologische Studien und Kritiken.* (1894.)

Schwane, J. : *Dogmengeschichte der mittleren Zeit.*

Schwartz, H : *Der Gottesgedanke in der Geschichte der Philosophie.* (Heidelberg, 1913).

Schwarz, H. : *Der Gottesgedanke in der Geschichte der Philosophie.* (Heidelberg, 1913).

Secretan : *La philosophie de la liberté.*

Seeberg, R. : *Lehrbuch der Dogmengeschichte.*

Seipel, J.: *Die volkswirtschaftlichen Anschauungen der Scholastik.* (1913.)

Siebeck, H. : *Geschichte der Psychologie.* (Gotha, 1884.)

Stoeckl, A. : *Geschichte der Philosophie des Mittelalters.* (Mainz, 1864-6.)

Stockums, W. : *Die Unveränderlichkeit des Sittengesetzes in der scholastischen Ethik.* (Freiburg, 1911.)

Taylor, H. O. : *The Mediaeval Mind.*

Tennemann : *Geschichte der Philosophie.*

Ueberweg, F. : *A History of Philosophy from Thales to the Present Time.* (Translation by G. Morris.) (London, 1885.)
Grundriss der Geschichte der Philosophie der patristischen und scholastischen Zeiten, 10th ed. by M. Baumgartner. (Berlin, 1915.)

Verweyen, M. : *Das Problem der Willensfreiheit in der Scholastik.* (Heidelberg, 1909.)
Philosophie und Theologie im Mittelalter. (Bonn, 1911.)
Die Philosophie des Mittelalters. (Bonn, 1921.)

Werner, K. : *Geschichte der späteren Scholastik.* (Vienna, 1881.)
Bd. II. *Die nachscotistische Scholastik.*
Bd. III. *Der Augustinismus des späteren Mittelalters.*
Der heilige Thomas von Aquin. (Regensburg, 1858.)

Wetzer u. Welte : *Kirchenlexikon.* Article ' Scotus ', by J. von Döllinger ; article ' Thomismus und Scotismus ', by J. Mausbach.

Willmann, O. : *Geschichte des Idealismus.*

Windelband, W. : *Geschichte der Philosophie.*

Reference has also been made to the following works :

AVELING, F. : Essay on St. Thomas Aquinas in Hearnshaw's *Social and Political Ideas of Some Great Medieval Thinkers*. (London, 1922.)

BARTHOLOMAEUS ANGLICUS : *De proprietatibus rerum.*

BAUMGARTNER, M. : *Die Erkenntnislehre des Wilhelm von Auvergne.* (Beiträge, etc., Bd. ii.)
Die Philosophie des Alanus ab insulis. (Beiträge zur Geschichte der Philosophie des Mittelalters, 1896.)
Zum Thomistischen Wahrheitsbegriff. (Festschr. f. Cl. Bäumker : Beiträge, Supplementbd. 1913.)

BAUR, L. : *Die philosophischen Werke des Robert Grosseteste, Bischofs von Lincoln.* (Beiträge, etc., vol. ix.)
Der Einfluss des Robert Grosseteste auf die wissenschaftlichen Richtungen des Roger Bacon. (Little : R. Bacon—Commemoration Essays, Oxford, 1914.)

BENN, A. W. : *The Greek Philosophers.* (London, 1914.)

BROWN, J. W. : *An Inquiry into the Life and Legend of Michael Scot.* (1897.)

CARLYLE, A. J. and R. W. : *Mediaeval Political Theory in the West.*

CHARLES, E. : *Roger Bacon, sa vie, ses ouvrages, ses doctrines, d'après des textes inédits.* (Paris, 1861.)

COUSIN, F. : *Ouvrages inédits d'Abelard, pour servir à l'histoire de la philosophie scolastique en France.* (Paris, 1836.)

DANTE ALIGHIERI : *La Divina Commedia.*

D'ARGENTRÉ : *Collectio judiciorum de novis erroribus.* (1728.)

DE REGNON : *Études de la théologie positive sur la Sainte Trinité.*

DESCARTES, R. : *Meditations. Letters.*

DEWEY, J. : Article ' Scholasticism ' in Baldwin's *Dictionary of Psychology.*

DE WULF, M. : *Études sur Henri de Gand.* (Histoire de la philosophie scolastique dans les Pays-Bas et la principauté de Liége, 1895.)
L'exemplarisme et la théorie de l'illumination spéciale dans la philosophie de Henri de Gand.

EHRLE, Card. F. : *Johann Peckham über den Kampf des Augustinismus und Aristotelismus in der zweiten Hälfte des 13. Jahrhunderts.* (Zeitschr. f. kath. Theol., 1889.)
Der Kampf um die Lehre des hl. Thomas von Aquino in den ersten fünfzig Jahren nach seinem Tode. (Ibid., Bd. 37.)
Beiträge zur Geschichte der mittelalterlichen Scholastik. (Archiv f. Lit.- u. Kirchengesch. d. Mittelalters, Bd. v.)
Zur Vorgeschichte des Conzils von Vienne. (Ibid., Bd. ii.)

Olivi's Leben und Schriften. (*Archiv f. Lit.- u. Kirchengesch. d. Mittelalters*, Bd. iii.)

Ein Bruchstück der Akten des Konzils von Vienne. (Ibid., Bd. xviii.)

Die Ehrentitel der scholastischen Lehrer des Mittelalters. (*Sitzungsberichte der Bayrischen Akademie*, 1919.)

Statuta Universitatis Bononiensis.

ESPENBERGER, J. N. : *Die Philosophie des Petrus Lombardus.*

FOBES, F. H. : *Mediaeval Versions of Aristotle's Meteorology.* (*Classical Philology*, vol. x, 1915.)

FORDOUN : *Scotichronicon.* (Ed. Hearne, Oxford, 1722.)

FRANZELIN : *De Deo Trino.*

FREUDENTHAL, J. : *Zur Beurtheilung der Scholastik.* (*Archiv* etc. Bd. iii, 1887.)

FUNKE : *Die Satisfaktionslehre des heiligen Anselms.*

GASQUET, Card. : *Roger Bacon and the Latin Vulgate.* (Little, *R. Bacon Essays.*)

GILSON, E. : *La doctrine cartésienne et la liberté.*
La liberté chez Descartes et la Théologie.

GRABMANN, M. : *Forschungen über die lateinischen Aristoteles-Uebersetzungen des XIII. Jahrhunderts.* (*Beiträge* etc., Bd. xvii.)
Die Entwicklung der mittelalterlichen Sprachlogik. (*Phil. Jahrb.*, 1922.)

GRUENWALD, G. : *Geschichte der Gottesbeweise im Mittelalter bis zum Ausgang der Hochscholastik.* (*Beiträge* etc., Bd. vi.)

GUTTMANN, J. : *Guillaume d'Auvergne et la littérature juive.* (*Rev. des études juives*, t. xviii.)
Alexandre de Hales et le judaïsme. (Ibid., t. xix.)
Die Philosophie des Salomon ben Gabirol. (Göttingen, 1889.)
Das Verhältnis des Thomas von Aquino zum Judenthum und zur jüdischen Literatur. (Göttingen, 1891.)
Die philosophischen Lehren des Isaac ben Salomon Israeli. (*Beiträge* etc., Bd. x.)

HASKINS, C. J., and LOCKWOOD : ' Sicilian translators of the twelfth century and the first versions of Ptolemy's *Almagest.*' (*Harvard Studies in Class. Philology*, vol. xxi, 1910.)

HASKINS, C. J. : ' Further notes on Sicilian translators of the twelfth century.' (Ibid., vol. xxiii, 1912.)

HEITZ, TH. : *Essai historique sur les rapports entre la philosophie et la foi.*

HELD, G. : *Roger Baco's praktische Philosophie.* (Jena, 1881.)

HENDERSON, B. : *A History of Merton College.* (Oxford Colleges series, Robinson. London, 1899.)

HIRSCH, S. A. : *Bacon and Philology.* (Little, *R. Bacon Essays.*)

HOEVER, P. : *Roger Bacons Hylomorphismus als Grundlage seiner philosophischen Anschauung.* (Limburg, 1912.)

HUET : *Recherches historiques et critiques sur Henri de Gand.* (Paris, 1836.)

JACOB, E. F. : ' John of Salisbury and the *Policraticus.*' Essay in Hearnshaw's *Social and political ideas of some great mediaeval thinkers.* (London, 1922).
The conception of Personality in mediaeval philosophy. (*Church Quarterly Review*, Jan. 1924.)

JAMES, W. : *The Principles of Psychology.*

JANSEN, B. : *Die Definition des Konzils von Vienne.* (*Zeitschr. f. kath. Theol.*, 1908.)

JOEL : *Das Verhältnis Alberts des Grossen zu Maimonides.* (Breslau, 1863.)

KOYRE, A. : *Descartes und die Scholastik.* (Bonn, 1923.)

LITTLE, A. G. : *Roger Bacon Commemoration Essays.* (Oxford, 1914.)

LOHMEYER, E. : *Die Lehre vom Willen bei Anselm von Canterbury* (1914.)

LONGWELL, E. : *Roger Bacon's Theory of Mind.*

MABILLION : *Tractatus de studiis monasticis.* (Latin transl. by Porta.)

MANDONNET : *Siger de Brabant et l'Averroïsme latin.*

MARCHESI : *L'Etica Nicomachea nelle traduzioni latine medievali.*

MORE, P. E. : *The Religion of Plato.* (Princeton, 1921.)

MUNK : *Literaturblatt des Orients*, 1845–6. Article ' Mélanges de philosophie juive et arabe.' (Paris, 1850.)

PELSTER, F. : *Thomas von Sutton, O. P. ; ein Oxforder Verteidiger der thomistischen Lehre.* (*Zeitschr. f. kath. Theol.*, xlvi, 1922.)

PELZER, A. : *Godefroid de Fontaines.* (*Revue Néo-scolastique*, t. xx, 1913.)

PICAVET, F. : *La valeur de la scolastique.*

PICOT : *Documents relatifs aux États généraux et assemblées réunis sous Philippe le Bel.* (Paris, 1901.)

POEHL, C. : *Das Verhältnis der Philosophie zur Theologie bei Roger Bacon.* (Neu-Strelitz, 1893.)

PORTALIE, P. : Article on Abelard in *Dictionnaire de Théologie catholique.*

PROTOIS : *Pierre Lombard.*

RASHDALL, H. : *The Universities of Europe in the Middle Ages.*
Roger Bacon's Compendium studii theologici. (*Brit. Soc. Franc. Stud.*, vol. iii.)

RICKABY, J. : *God and His Creatures.*

SAENZ D'AGUIRRE : *Theologia Sancti Anselmi.*

SAUVE : *De l'union substantielle de l'âme et du corps.* (Paris, 1878.)

SBARALEA : Supplement to Wadding's *Scriptores Ordinis Minorum.*

SCHILLER, F. C. S. : 'The Practical Syllogism of Aristotle.' (*Journal of Philosophy*, 1919.)

SCHNEIDER : *Thomas von Aquino und die Scholastik.*

SEEBERG, R. : Article on Petrus Lombardus in *Herzog-Platt Realenzyclopädie.*

SPETTMANN, M. : *Die Psychologie des Johannes Pecham.* (Beiträge etc., Bd. xx, Münster, 1919.)

STEINSCHNEIDER : *Die hebräischen Uebersetzungen des Mittelalters,* etc. (1893.)
Die arabischen Uebersetzungen aus dem Griechischen, etc. (*Sitzungsberichte* etc., Vienna, 1904.)

THEVET, A. : *Histoire des plus illustres et savants hommes.* (Paris, 1584.)

THORBURN, W. : Article on *Occam's Razor-Mind,* 1918.

TOCCO, William of : *Life of S. Thomas Aquinas in the Acta Sanctorum.* (1643.)

TRENDELENBURG : *Logische Untersuchungen.*

TRIVET, N. : *Annales sex regum Angliae.* (Oxford, 1719.)

TROELTSCH, E. : Article in *Göttingische gelehrte Anzeigen,* 1903.
Die Soziallehren der christlichen Kirchen und Gruppen, (1919).

TYRRELL, J. : *The Faith of the Millions.*

VOGL, S. : *Roger Bacons Lehre von der sinnlichen Species.* (Little : Essays.)

WERNER, K. : *Die Kosmologie und allgemeine Naturlehre des Roger Baco.* (*Sitzungsberichte* etc., vol. xciv. Vienna, 1879.)
Heinrich von Gent als Repräsentant des christlichen Platonismus des 13. Jahrhunderts. (*Denkschrift d. kaiserl. Akad. d. Wissensch.,* Bd. xxviii., Vienna, 1878.)
Die Psychologie und Erkenntnis- und Wissenschaftslehre des Roger Baco. (*Sitzungsberichte* etc., Vienna, vol. xciii.)
Die Psychologie des Wilhelm von Auvergne. (*Ibid.,* vol. lxxiii.)

WITTMANN, M. : *Die Unterscheidung von Wesenheit und Dasein in der arabischen Philosophie.* (Beiträge etc., Supplementbd. 1913.)

WUESTENFELD : *Die Uebersetzungen arabischer Werke in das Lateinische.* (*Abhandl. d. Gesellsch. d. Wissensch. Göttingen,* Bd. lxxii.)

ZIGLIARA, Card. : *De mente Concilii Viennensis.* (1875.)

NOTES ON THE AUTHENTICITY OF CERTAIN WORKS ATTRIBUTED TO DUNS SCOTUS

A. The *Theoremata*.

THE authenticity of this work has frequently been questioned, chiefly owing to the sceptical character of the doctrine it contains, which seemsi nconsistent with the rest of Scotus' teaching. The problem is discussed at some length by Fr. D. M. De Basly in an article in the *Archivium Franciscanum Historicum*, vol. ix (1918), and also by Fr. Longpré in his book *La Philosophie du B. Duns Scot*, pp. 29–48, 288–91.

The *Theoremata* were first printed in 1497 in the edition of Mauritius Hibernicus (Maurice O'Fihely), who in his preface refers to the mutilated state of the text : ' Textus ... valde intricatus est ... tum ratione ordinis propositionum ... tum quaestionum perplexitate et numerorum ac remissionum ... tum diuturnitate temporis et scriptorum vitio ... atque originalium hactenus raritate ', etc. Sbaralea, in his *Supplementum* to Wadding's *Scriptores Ordinis Minorum* (Rome, 1806), draws attention, in the article on Scotus (p. 411), to the fact that the *Theoremata* are referred to in the fourth chapter of the *De Primo Principio* and that the two treatises were frequently printed together (e. g. in 1497, 1499, 1625). He also points out that Theorems xiv–xvi, which have been called by the title of *Tractatus de Creditis*, obviously do not fit in with the rest of the treatise, and remarks that they should be published separately in future editions on the ground that Scotus himself refers to them in the *De Primo Principio* under the aforesaid title as distinct from the *Theoremata*, as does also Gabriel Zerbius (who wrote at the end of the fifteenth century) in *Metaph.*, Lib. XII, qq. 11 and 20. According to Fr. De Basly, Zerbius only mentions the *Tractatus de Creditis* once, but he does cite as coming from the *Theoremata* passages which occur in Theorems xv and xvi, which seems to imply that the two titles are not those of distinct works, but merely alternatives. Compare also the following : ' Non potest probari Deum carere magnitudine, ut inquit Scotus in Theorematibus, sive in tractatu de creditis ' (Zerbius, col. 1819). The *Theoremata* are also cited in a commentary on Aristotle's Physics attributed to Johannes Canonicus, viz. *Phys.*, Lib. I, q. 3 (ed. Locatelli, fol. 12 r., col. 1.; Venice, 1492) : ' Ad secundum, praetermitto illud quod dicit Scotus in Theorematibus, quod intelligibile intellectionem praecedere necesse est.' The passage referred to occurs in Theorem 1 : ' Intellectionem intelligibile natura praecedit—quod est quoniam passio praesupponit agens et omnis actio circa aliquid est ; illud circa quod est intellectio, alterum est.' According to the commonly accepted view Johannes Canonicus was actually a contemporary of Duns himself, but Fr. Longpré brings evidence to show that the author of this commentary was not John the Canon at all, but a certain Jaen Marbres, whose date is uncertain but who wrote probably in the fifteenth century. But even if the older view were still accepted, the quotation would indeed be strong evidence in favour of the main part of the *Theoremata*, but not necessarily of Theorems xiv and xvi, round which the most important issues of the dispute have centred.

According to Fr. De Basly the citations from the *Theoremata* or *Tractatus de Creditis* in the *De Primo Principio* do not go far to establish the authenticity of the former work. The citations in question are to be found in Wadding's text, which was collated from three manuscripts, of which only two can be found in the Vatican catalogue, and neither give a direct reference to the *Theoremata*. In *Cod. Vat. Lat.* 869, fol. 7 v., col. 1 we do, however, find the following sentences at the end of the *De Primo Principio* : ' Praeter praedicta de te a philosophis praedicata saepe te Catholici laudant omnipotentem, immensum, verum, praesentem, justum et misericordem. In hoc quippe tractatu primo tentavi qualiter metaphysica de dicta ratione naturali aliqualiter concludantur ; in sequenti ponentur credibilia in quibus ratio captivatur, quae tamen eo sunt Catholicis certiora, quo non intellectu nostro caecitanti et in pluribus vacillanti sed tuae soliditati veritatis firmiter innituntur.' The words ' scilicet in Theorematibus ', which follow in Wadding's edition after ' in sequenti ', seem to have been added either by a later copyist or by Wadding himself, as also the reference to the *Tractatus de Creditis* in cap. iv, n. 28. It would appear, however, that the *De Primo Principio* was a preface to a further treatise on *credibilia* ; if this treatise is not the *Tractatus de Creditis*, what is it ? Are we to postulate another work not mentioned by any tradition which was lost at an early date ? Or must we assume that the sentence from *Cod. Vat.* 869 is itself an addition, put into the first person, by a later Scotist ?

The internal evidence against the authenticity of the *Theoremata*, especially Theorems xiv to xvi, is certainly considerable. The propositions there enunciated seem to cut the ground from under the whole argument of the *De Primo Principio* in which Duns has been laying the foundations of a natural theology, though it must be remembered that the cogency of that argument was qualified by the word *aliqualiter*. But there seems to be little trace of any scepticism in the Gottesbeweise of the two commentaries on the Sentences, with which

the Theorems are equally at variance. Thus, for instance, it is stated
in Theorem xvi that the divine infinity is not strictly demonstrable
by natural reason. Now in both the *Op. Ox.* and the *Rep. Par.* as
well as the *Quaestt. Quodlibetales* the concept of an infinite being is
the most adequate notion that the human reason can form of the
divine essence (cf. e. g., *Op. Ox.*, Lib. I, dist. iii, q. 2 ; *Quaest.
Miscell.*, q. v, etc., etc.), while much space is devoted in the two
commentaries as in the *De Primo Principio* to the proof of the infinity
of God.   Fr. Longpré also points out that Ockham was plainly of the
opinion that Scotus regarded the divine infinity as proven *sufficienter*
by natural reason. (Vide Ockham, *Quodl.* VII, qq. 17–21.)   Similarly
Theorem xiv denies that God can be proved to be either wise or
intelligent or endowed with a will. This is in direct contradiction with
the doctrine of the *Reportata* ; e. g. Lib. I, dist. xxxv, q.1, n. 14 :
' Quod ita est, Deum esse intelligentem et intelligere, ostendunt
necessario effectus in universo qui sunt ab eo mediate vel immediate.'
These and other points of difference between the teaching of the
Theoremata and the doctrine of the undoubtedly genuine works of
Scotus are dealt with at length by Fr. Longpré, who regards the
evidence against their authenticity as absolutely conclusive. He also
points out that Ockham, who devotes a considerable portion of his
writings to a criticism of the natural theology of Scotus, does not
mention them, though the Venerable Inceptor shows himself particularly well acquainted with Duns' principal writings. Had the
Theoremata been genuine, he would certainly have known them and
cited them in order to accuse the Subtle Doctor of self-contradiction.

Fr. Longpré's arguments are learned and ingenious, but they can
scarcely be regarded as conclusive in the face of the sentence quoted
above from *Cod. Vat.* 869. The argument from silence is of course
never a safe one to rely on, especially when used of a period before
the invention of printing. It might well be that an early work might
be suppressed by the author himself, or, what is even more likely,
neglected in the days of his insignificance and disregarded or even
lost by the time he had become famous. The arguments drawn from
internal evidence are considerably stronger, though it must be admitted
that it is by no means unusual for philosophers to appear to contradict themselves, especially over considerable periods of time. The
Theoremata, if they are genuine at all, must belong to an early period
of Duns' writing while he was under the influence of the Oxford
school, which was then dominated by the thought of Kilwardby and
Peckham. The battle between Thomism and the older scholasticism
was still being fought out and the formal separation of philosophy
from theology still somewhat of a novelty. The exact boundary line
between reason and revelation was never easy to draw, and the distinction between ' probable ' and ' necessary ' conclusions becomes

more and more difficult to apply as the degree of probability grows greater. Moreover, the mystical tendency of the older Augustinian tradition easily lent itself to a pious agnosticism which would emphasize the need of the fallible human mind for the supernatural illumination of the faith, after the manner of the passage from the *De Primo Principio* already quoted. It cannot, however, be denied that the style of the *Theoremata* seems to differ from that of the *De Primo Principio* and to recall rather the later criticism of the age of Ockham.

While, therefore, it is not impossible to regard the *Theoremata* as a genuine work of Scotus, it is not in the least necessary to attribute to it any great significance. As a detached fragment its authority can scarcely stand against that of the great commentaries and the *Quaestiones Quodlibetales*.

B. The *De Rerum Principio*.

The authenticity of this treatise has recently been called in question by several critics. Dr. P. Minges is inclined to regard it as doubtful, and believes it to be the work of a later Scotist. (Cf. *Die Skotistische Literatur des xx. Jahrhunderts—Franziskanische Studien*, 1917; *Ist Duns Scotus Indeterminist?* Munster, 1905.) Dr. Carreras y Artau discusses the question at length in an appendix to his treatise *El Voluntarismo de J. Duns Scot* and decides that the author of the *De Rerum Principio* cannot be identified with the writer of the commentaries on the Sentences. Fr. Longpré, op. cit., pp. 22–9, condemns the work as undoubtedly spurious and expresses his conviction that it was written a decade or so before Scotus' teaching career. His main conclusion is accepted by Fr. Klug, Fr. Belmond, and Prof. Gilson.

The *De Rerum Principio* was first printed by Wadding in his complete edition of Scotus' works. According to his *censura*, the manuscript from which the text was taken, which is the only one known to be now existing, was found by Fr. Johannes Baptista Campanius in the library of Cardinal Francis Ximenes, O. F. M. It is now in the library of the College of St. Isedore in Rome, and by the kind permission of the Franciscan Fathers I was permitted to examine it. It belongs to the end of the fourteenth century and is written in an English hand. The subscription is in a later hand not earlier than the middle of the fifteenth century, and reads as follows: 'Iste questiones fuerunt determinate Oxonie per magistrum Johannem Scotum de ordine Fratrum Minorum et sunt questiones generales super philosophiam.' The title of the first *quaestio* is, 'Utrum sit dare unum primum principium rerum omnium simpliciter et absolute ?' Wadding tells us that the inscription at the beginning of the volume, which I could not find, read as follows: 'Quaestiones universales in philosophiam Johannis Scoti'. On the last leaf there is the following note: 'Iste questiones sunt ad usum Fr. Ferdinandi de Illiescas ', Now Ferdinand was confessor to King John I of Castile about 1390. Wadding identifies the treatise with one mentioned by Possevinus and others: ' Illud ipsum est quod Scotum scripsisse monent Willotus, Possevinus et Pitsaeus, de rerum principio, titulum affigentes ex ipso operis initio.' Fr. Longpré thinks that the subscript is due to a mistake of a librarian who has confused the *De Rerum Principio* with the *De Primo Principio*, but this is not very probable, because the *De Primo Principio* is a much shorter work and is not in the form of *quaestiones* at all, and the definite statement that these *quaestiones* were disputed at Oxford seems to suggest that the writer of the note possessed some information on the subject.

That there are considerable differences between the teaching of the *De Rerum Principio* and that of the two commentaries on the Sentences and the *Quaestiones Quodlibetales* cannot be denied. The tone of the former is markedly Augustinian, and its doctrine reflects very strongly the influence of John Peckham, which was predominant at Oxford at the close of the thirteenth century. (Cf. M. Spettmann, *Die Psychologie des Johannes Peckham—Beiträge* etc., 1920.) It seems, therefore, not improbable that an early work of Duns composed during the first part of his academic career at Oxford should betray in a marked degree the current opinions prevalent in his university. The contention of Fr. Longpré that according to tradition Duns' master was William of Ware, who was a strict Aristotelian, does not carry much weight, as Fr. Pelster has shown that the tradition rests on very insufficient evidence. (Vide Pelster, *Handschriftliches zu Skotus*, etc.—*Franziskanische Studien*, 1923, p. 2.) Moreover, the older teaching was strongly entrenched in the Franciscan Order, and most of the points on which the *De Rerum Principio* differs from Duns' later works can be found either in Alexander of Hales or Bonaventura. Nor can the critical method of Fr. Longpré be admitted as a really sound one. To take a group of treatises of undoubted authenticity and refuse to admit the genuineness of any works containing doctrines not found in these or differing from them is very like arguing in a circle. It excludes *a priori* the notion of any development in the thought of the Subtle Doctor over a space of time which at the least must be reckoned at nearly twenty years and which may have been considerably longer. For if we assume that Scotus was already a student at Paris in the year 1293, as Fr. A. Callebaut would suggest (*Le B. Duns Scot, étudiant à Paris vers 1293-6—Études Franciscaines*, 1923), the beginning of his Oxford career must be considerably antedated, which is in itself by no means impossible, considering the very scant and imperfect knowledge which has come down to us concerning the facts of his early life. A development in his teaching from the Augustinianism current at Oxford during his youth to the Aristotelianism which was fashionable at Paris at the opening of the fourteenth century is therefore exactly what we should expect to find, and there is not a particle of evidence to show, as has sometimes been assumed, e. g. by Dr. Carreras y Artau, that the *De Rerum Principio* was written, if indeed it was written by Scotus at all, after the commentaries on the Sentences.

Dr. Carreras has summarized with great care and learning the chief differences between the treatise in question and the later works of Scotus. They seem at first sight to constitute a formidable list, but they can, I believe, with one important exception, be supported by similar doctrines found elsewhere in works generally attributed to Scotus, the genuineness of which there is no good reason to deny. The more important divergencies may be summarized as follows :

(1) The question of the univocacy of being in God and the creature. According to the doctrine of the *De Rerum Principio* (q. i, art. 1), the concept of being is predicated of God and the creature not univocally but analogically : the unity of the notion is not a generic unity but a unity of analogy, just as the being that is predicated of substance and the categories of accident is predicated of the latter analogically, for accidents are not *entia* except in so far as they are referred to substance. (Cf. q. 19, art. 1.) The doctrine of the *Opus Oxoniense* is almost the exact opposite. The concept of being is the ' objectum primum et adaequatum ' of the human intellect, and it is predicated therefore univocally not only of God and the creature but also of the categories of substance and accident. (Cf. *Op. Ox.* I, dist. iii, qq. 2 et 3 ; dist. xviii, q. 3 ; II, dist. xii, q. 2.) The latter doctrine is also found in the literal commentary on the *Metaphysics*. (Vide *Comm. in Metaph*. IV, Lect. 1.)

The univocacy of the concept of being as applied to God and to the creature is denied in Theorem v, a fact which has often been cited in defence of the view that the *Theoremata* are spurious. It must therefore be admitted that the corroboration afforded by the passage in question is not very strong. When we come, however, to the question of the univocacy of being in the categories, we shall find a striking change in Duns' thought. In the *Quaestiones in Praedicamenta Aristotelis*, the univocy of being in the ten categories is strongly denied, as also in the *Quaestiones* on the *Isagoge* of Porphyry. (Cf. *Quaestt. in Praedicamenta*, q. 4 ; *Quaestt. super universalia Porphyrii*, q. 23.) The doctrine of analogy is also found in the *Quaestiones* on the *Metaphysics* (*Quaestt. in Metapht*. IV, q. i ; cf. V, q. i.) In view of this change of attitude concerning the univocacy of being in the categories, a similar change with regard to being in God and the creature need not surprise us. Moreover in q. xvi of the *De Rerum Principio* we find a theory which clearly marks the transition between the logical doctrine of the analogy of being and the teaching of the *Opus Oxoniense*. Though the notion of being is not logically univocal in

God and the creature, there is a metaphysical *genus* which embraces both, namely ' ens communissime sumptum '. This metaphysical *genus* is ontologically prior to the ten ' genera generalissima ' or categories, and falls immediately into two main divisions, ' ens in se ' or ' esse purum ', and ' ens habens esse '. Only the latter is further divided into the ten categories. This somewhat obscure doctrine, which is not easy to reconcile with that of q. i, appears in a more developed form in the *Opus Oxoniense* and the *Quaestiones Quodlibetales*. The univocacy of being in God and the creature is simply asserted, and the metaphysical *genus* of the *De Rerum Principio* is divided prior to the division into the ten categories into two modes, finite and infinite, which correspond with the ' ens in se ' and the ' ens habens esse ' in the earlier treatise. (Cf. *Op Ox.* I, dist. viii, q. 3 ; *Quodl.*, q. v ; see also vol. ii, ch. ii, p. 59.)

(2) Essence and existence. The *De Rerum Principio* asserts quite plainly the real distinction between essence and existence in created things, e. g. q. iii, art. 3, n. 18 : ' Sicut igitur in creaturis non sunt essentia et esse idem, quia essentia frequenter recipit esse ' ; q. vi, art. I, n. 12 : ' In omni creato differt quo est et quid est, quae sunt partes essentiales cujuslibet creaturae existentes.' In the *Opus Oxoniense* the real distinction is denied, as is also the composition of essence and existence as ' partes essentiales '. Essence and existence are distinct, but not *realiter*, only *formaliter*. (Cf. *Op. Ox.* I, dist. viii, q. 2 ; dist. xxxvi, q. unica ; II, dist. i, q. 2 ; *Rep. Par.* IV, dist. xlviii, q. 2, n. 18.) This change of view does not really afford any grounds for denying the authenticity of the *De Rerum Principio*, for we find a real distinction between essence and existence implied in another early work of Scotus, the *Quaestiones* on the first book of the *Posterior Analytics*, q. xxx : ' Substantiae duplex est esse, scilicet esse essentiae et existentiae. Esse essentiae est de essentia, esse existere non.' The substitution of a ' distinctio formalis a parte rei ' for a ' distinctio realis ' need not surprise us. The characteristically Scotist formal distinction which is met with so frequently in the two commentaries on the Sentences may well be one of the later developments of Duns' thinking. The denial of the real distinction between essence and existence in *Op. Ox.* I, dist. xxxvi, is based on the view that the ' esse essentiae ' taken by itself, i. e. apart from any reference to actual existence, is not an ' esse reale ' but an ' esse diminutum '. Thus the merely possible creature or essence which has never existed and never will exist is not entitled by virtue of its ' esse essentiae' to be regarded as possessing being except ' secundum quid '. (Cf. vol. ii, ch. vi, p. 201 sq.)

The *De Rerum Principio* states that just as the divine ideas necessarily exist, so do the essences corresponding to them ; they share the necessary character of the divine being. (Cf. q. iv, n. 54 : ' Sicut idea habet necessario esse, sic et quidditas ei correspondens . . ., sicut necesse est quod Deus sit, sic necesse est quod essentiae rerum sint, et quantum ad tale esse sunt a Deo per necessitatem suae naturae.') The *Opus Oxoniense* and *Reportata* seem to teach a contrary doctrine, but when examined the difference between the two is largely verbal. The divine ideas and the essences corresponding to them are not strictly eternal or necessary *formaliter, ex se,* or *simpliciter,* because they are not the primary object of the divine thought, which is the divine essence itself, and so ontologically prior to them. The question is closely connected with the polemic against the conception of the divine ideas held by Thomas and Henry of Ghent. (See vol. ii, ch. vi, pp. 201–6.) What Duns is here trying to emphasize is the fact that the ideas are the product and not the condition of the divine knowing, and as such they are eternal and necessary only *secundum quid.* More-over, they are quite independent of the divine will, for the divine intellect in producing them acts as a *causa mere naturalis.* (Cf. *Op. Ox.* II, dist. i, q. 1 ; III, dist. xxxii, n. 3 ; *Rep. Par.* II, dist. i, q. 2 ; *Op. Ox.* I, dist. iii, q. 4.) The real significance of the doctrine of these two later works has been admirably expounded by Dr. Minges (*Der Gottesbegriff des Duns Scotus,* etc., ch. iii. See also vol. ii, ch. vi, pp. 204–6).

(3) The distinction between the divine essence and the divine attributes, and between the faculties of the soul and its substance. The *De Rerum Principio* asserts categorically that the divine attributes are distinguished from the divine essence and *inter se* merely by our human thinking, *sola ratione.* The diversity between them arises only 'respectu intellectus concipientis esse Dei'; in reality they are identical with the divine essence ' ut sic vel sic ab intellectu concepta ' (q. xxii, n. 9; cf. q. xi, n. 2 ; q. viii, n. 7). In the *Opus Oxoniense* and the *Reportata* the divine attributes are distinguished *formaliter* from the divine essence and also *inter se.* (Cf. *Op. Ox.* I, dist. viii, q. 4, n. 17 : ' Est igitur aliqua non-identitas formalis sapientiae et bonitatis.') At the same time each of the divine attributes is identical (*idem realiter*) with the divine essence. (Cf. *Quodl.,* q. i, n. 10.) This distinction between the divine attributes is very important, as on it Duns founds his con-ception of the Trinitarian process. (See vol. ii, ch. vi, p. 187.) That there is here a considerable divergence of doctrine is undeniable, but it is not inexplicable on the assumption that the notion of the formal distinction is a subsequent development of Duns' thought. It is interesting to note in this connexion that a theory half-way between that of the *De Rerum Principio* and that of the later works is found in the *Quaestiones Miscellaneae,* q. ii, n. 4 : ' Circa istam quaestionem brevissime sic procedam : primo quin declarabo quod intellectus et voluntas in Deo non sunt totaliter idem ; secundo probabo quod non distinguuntur aliqualiter.'

With regard to the soul and its faculties, the formal distinction does not appear in the *De Rerum Principio*. The doctrine there expressed is closely allied to that of Bonaventura. (Cf. *In I Sentt.*, dist. iii, art. 1, q. iii.) The soul and its faculties are really one, for the soul is called form in so far as it is compared with the body which it perfects, but faculty only with reference to various objects and operations. (*De Rerum Principio*, q. xi, n. 15.) In the *Opus Oxoniense* the faculties are regarded as formally distinct both from the essence of the soul and *inter se*, but great emphasis is laid on the point that they are not distinct *realiter*, as the Thomist theory would suppose. Cf. *Op. Ox.* II, dist. xvi: ' Dico igitur quod non distinguuntur realiter inter se, nec ab essentia. Sunt formaliter distinctae, idem tamen identice et unitive.' The difference between the two doctrines is thus not very vital.

(4) Prime matter. The doctrine of *materia prima* in the *De Rerum Principio* differs considerably from that of the two commentaries on the Sentences and the *Quaestiones Quodlibetales*. The triple distinction of matter into *materia primo prima, secundo prima*, and *tertio prima* is only found in the former (q. viii), and never appears elsewhere in Scotus' writings. *Materia primo prima*, which is the badge of creature-hood, is shared by all created beings, corporeal and spiritual alike; it is homogeneous in angels, men, and the physical bodies corruptible and incorruptible. Its distinguishing characteristic is its passivity, its power of becoming everything. Cf. art. 2, n. 6: 'Materia enim de ratione sua nominat substantiam quamdam actu in composito existentem, cujus actualitas est imperfecta et actualitati omnis formae opposita. . . . Potentia vero passiva materiae nominat ipsam eandem substantiam sub respectu ad formam, sub indifferentia tamen ad omnes, et hoc inquantum . . . nec ut determinata seu disposita ad receptionem alicujus illarum (*sc.* formarum); nec ad unam potius quam ad aliam, et sic potentia passiva nominat materiam sub respectu ad formas . . . et hoc est potentia pure passiva ad quam habet reduci omnis ratio potentiae passivae.' *Materia secundo prima* is that which serves as a substratum of substantial change, generation, and corruption. It is quantitatively determined and is shared by all corporeal things, but it is not ' pure ' matter, being already impregnated with a kind of substantial form. Cf. n. 20: 'Dicitur autem materia secundo prima quae est subjectum generationis et corruptionis . . . quae . . . addit ad materiam primo primam; quia esse subjectum generationis non potest sine aliqua forma substantiali, aut sine quantitate, quae sunt extra rationem primae materiae.' The doctrine of the *Opus Oxoniense* is considerably different. The distinction between *primo* and *secundo prima* has vanished, and *materia prima* is the functional equivalent of both, inasmuch as it is the lowest of all created things, being *prope nihil*. (Cf. *De Rerum Principio*, q. viii,

n. 19, and *Op Ox.* II, dist. xii, q. 1, n. 9.) It is purely passive and directly receptive of all forms, and is the subject of substantial and accidental change without the mediation of any substantial form (*Op. Ox.*, loc. cit., n. 15). Like *materia primo prima*, it is a *terminus creationis.* But there is one big difference which cannot be minimized. In the two commentaries on the Sentences and the *Quaestiones Quodlibetales, materia prima* is always referred to corporeal substances and never to the spiritual creation. Angels and human souls are immaterial; they are pure forms. (Cf., e.g., *Op. Ox.* II, dist. i, q. 6, n. 2 ; dist. iii, q. 7, n. 4 ; q. 8, n. 2, etc., etc.) This significant fact was first pointed out by Fr. H. Klug (*Die Immaterialität der Engel und Menschenseelen nach Duns Skotus—Franz. Stud.,* 1916), and has been used by Fr. Longpré and Dr. Carreras as an argument against the genuineness of the *De Rerum Principio.* The case seems *prima facie* a strong one, but unfortunately the problem is not so easily disposed of. For in the *Quaestiones de Anima,* a work whose authenticity rests on very good foundations (see Pelster, *Handschriftliches zu Skotus—Franz. Stud.,* 1923, p. 31), precisely the same doctrine as that of the *De Rerum Principio* is found concerning the hylemorphic composition of spiritual creatures. Thus in q. xv, n. 3, we read : ' Respondeo quod probabiliter potest dici quod in anima sit materia, et secundum fundamenta philosophi et eorum qui ponunt contrarium ; quorum unum, quod pluralitas individuorum in una specie requirit materiam in illis individuis ; quod patet xii Metaph. ubi dicit quod non sunt plura prima moventia caelum in eadem species, quia primum non habet materiam.' (n. 4.) ' Secunda ratio principalis est haec : sicut operatio arguit formam, ita proprietas materialis materiam ; sed proprietas materiae quantum ad suum esse et quantum ad fieri, reperitur verius in spiritualibus quam corporalibus ; proprietas enim materiae, quantum ad esse, est quod est ingenerabilis et incorruptibilis ; sed inquantum ad fieri, quod tantum producatur per creationem : haec autem magis reperiuntur in spiritualibus. . . . Tertio sic. Angelus habet materiam ; ergo anima. Probatio antecedentis ; quia in quocumque genere sunt principia communia, non tantum appropriata sed realiter differentia, oportet omnes illius generis ex eis esse composita : talia sunt principia in genere substantiae. . . . Actus autem in genere substantiae est forma, et potentia in eodem genere est materia . . . Igitur cum Angelus sit species substantiae, est ex eis composita.' Moreover, the identity of matter in both spiritual and corporeal creature, which in the *De Rerum Principio* appears as a novelty borrowed from Avicebron, is also affirmed (n. 6) : ' Ad quaestionem dico quod si ex explicatione ita debet esse quod in anima vel Angelo est materia ejusdem rationis cum materia corporalium ; quod probo sic,' etc. The very difficult problem of how two composite entities like soul and body can be united in such a way that the former is the substantial form of the latter is also discussed in the same *quaestio* (n. 10) : 'Dicendum quod secundum diversos gradus in formis plures formae possunt unam jam materiam informare, per hoc quod forma praecedens tenet se ex parte materiae, et hoc terminat potentialitatem ejus, disponendo ipsam ad formam sequentem ; sicut e converso, una forma potest plures materias informare, per hoc quod altera se tenet ex parte formae, scilicet illa quae est sibi immediatior et intimior ; et sic totum compositum ex forma et materia animae informat corpus, non ratione materiae, sed tantum ratione formae principaliter informantis materiam propriam.' . . . (n. 11) 'Dicendum quod forma animae excedit suam materiam, non tamen est divisibilis, nec habens gradus reales, sicut forma acci- dentalis, sed ipsa simplex existens informat materiam jam propriam et corpus, sicut tota essentia animae informat unam partem corporis et aliam.' A comparison of these passages with the theories of the *De Rerum Principio* expounded in vol. ii, ch. iii, will show how very closely the two resemble each other. It is interesting to note also that the doctrine of the hylemorphic composition of all created sub- stances is also found in the *Theoremata*. Cf. *Theoremata*, xi : 'Unum per se et non simplex primo (i. e. God) est ex actu et potentia sive ex materia et forma.'

Such a discrepancy of doctrines needs a considerable amount of explanation, but it is not unintelligible if we assume a development of Scotus' thought from the traditional Augustinianism which was current at Oxford in his early days to the purer Aristotelianism which was fashionable at Paris. Indeed, there is a work which seems to indicate a transitional period, the *Quaestiones in Metaphysicam*, and it may well have been that a more close study of Aristotle's *Meta- physics* led him to abandon his earlier conception of matter and to adopt the more narrow conception of the Philosopher, and confine *materia* to the corporeal world. It is to be noted also that in both doctrines the positive actuality of matter is stoutly maintained against the Thomist theory of matter as pure potentiality, and the possibility of the existence of matter apart from form *per virtutem divinam* is defended both in the *De Rerum Principio* and in the *Opus Oxoniense* by almost identical arguments. (Cf. *De Rerum Principio*, q. viii, art. 6, and *Op. Ox.* II, dist. xii, q. 2.) In the *Opus Oxoniense* angels and human souls are, it is true, regarded as 'immaterial', i. e. free from corporeal matter (the only kind mentioned in the later works) but they are not entirely simple beings, for all created things are in a sense composite. Cf. *Op. Ox.* I, dist. viii, q. 2, n. 2 : 'Nulla creatura est perfecte simplex quin aliquo modo sit composita vel componibilis . . . quia habet entitatem cum privatione alicujus gradus entitatis. Componitur igitur non ex re et re positivis, sed ex re positiva et privatione . . ., nec tameni sta compositio . . . est in essentia rei, quia privatio non est de essentia alicujus positivi.' In the

Quodlibetales and in the *De Rerum Principio, materia primo prima* is looked on as the badge of creaturehood which conveys that element of potency which distinguishes the being of the creature from that of the Creator, but it is conceived not as something negative but as something positive, an actual metaphysical constituent of all created beings.

(5) The principle of individuation. Once more we find a large divergence between the theory of individuation in the *De Rerum Principio* and that of the commentaries on the Sentences. In the former treatise a theory of individuation very like that of the Thomists is quite unequivocally maintained. Individuals of the same species differ from one another by virtue of the different matter on which the form is impressed. Matter, or, to speak more accurately, matter quantified (for without quantity this and that matter are indistinguishable), is the principle of individuation in corporeal things. (Cf. p. v, art. 2; q. vi, artt. 1 et 2; q. vii, art. 2, etc.) The doctrine of the *Opus Oxoniense* is quite different. The view that matter or quantity is the principle of individuation is expressly refuted (II, dist. iii, qq. 4 et 5), and the theory of the *haecceitas* substituted; the principle of individuation is here the *ultima realitas entis*, which belongs neither to the form as such, nor to the matter as such, nor to the *compositum* as such, but to all three. The individual concrete thing is made up of *this* form and *this* matter which form *this* thing, and the thisness of form and of matter is formally distinguished from both the specific form and the matter *in communi*. (Cf. *Op. Ox.* II, dist. iii, q. 2, n. 15; *Rep. Par.* II, dist. xii, q. 8, n. 8; for a detailed discussion of this theory see vol. ii, pp. 91–8.) We seem here to be almost far enough from the theory of the *De Rerum Principio* to be able to conclude that the two treatises could not have been written by the same hand. But a more thorough examination of the question will serve to show that there are considerable variations in Scotus' account of individuation given in some of the other treatises. In the passage just quoted from the *Quaestiones de Anima* the doctrine that matter is the principle of individuation is brought forward as the first reason for arguing that the soul contains matter. In the *Quaestiones in Metaphysicam* we have quite a different doctrine. Here individuation proceeds not from matter but from form. 'Ex his potest concludi quod natura est haec per substantiam aliquam quae est forma, et prior hic lapis et per formam individualem distinguitur ab alio individuo. . . . Ad aliud dico quod est hoc per substantiam aliquam . . . quia forma individualis superaddita naturae speciei non facit differentiam specificam sed numeralem solum. . . . Unde dico quod species non praedicat totam naturam individui integraliter, sicut nec genus speciei. . . . Ad aliam quaestionem dicendum quod materia non est principium distinguendi, cum de se sit indistincta.' This latter argument is used in the *De Rerum Principio*, q. vii, to

support the view that not matter as such but matter as determined by quantity (which is a formal determination) is the principle of individuation : ' Materia non distinguitur nisi quantitate, quam re-movendo non est distinguibilis.' In other words, it is *materia secundo prima* which underlies the processes of generation and corruption. But this is already formally determined and differentiated from *materia primo prima*. (Cf. q. viii, n. 20 : ' Dicitur autem materia secundo-prima quae est subjectum generationis et corruptionis . . . quae . . . addit ad materiam primo-primam ; quia esse subjectum generationis non potest sine aliqua forma substantiali, aut sine quantitate.') In q. viii, curiously enough, it is actually argued that prime matter is that in which creation is united, form that by which its various parts are distinguished. (Cf. n. 26 : ' Mundus est vere unus. . . . Hoc autem unum non est nisi partes ejus sint ad invicem legatae ; inter se autem sunt distinctae ; ergo oportet quod in aliquo uniantur. . . . Cum igitur per formam non uniantur sed distinguantur, oportet quod haec sit materia omnino prima.) In the case of the angels the principle of individuation is somewhat obscure ; it is not *materia quantitate determinata* because the matter contained in the spiritual substance is not quantitative, nor is it *materia primo prima* as such ; it is rather distinctness of creation. (Cf. q. vii, n. 33 : ' Distinctio primae materiae duobus modis potest intelligi, vel quia una materia praeexistente fiant duae, sicut cum divido panem ; et isto modo materia non est distinguibilis sine quantitate ; nec propter istum modum ex aliquo, sc. praeexistenti, multiplicantur Angeli ; vel ita quod haec materia, vel ista, distincte creentur, et ex creatione in duobus Angelis aut simul aut divisis creationibus distinguantur : et isto modo non est distinctio per quantitatem, et ita distinguuntur materiae in Angelis.')

It would seem that in some respects the doctrine of the *Opus Oxoniense* and the *Reportata* really resembles a conflation of the apparently contradictory theories expressed in the *De Rerum Principio* and the *Quaestiones in Metaphysicam*. In the former case it was matter, in the latter case form which provided the individuating principle. In the latest statement of Scotus' teaching it is neither, but something accruing equally to both, a *formalitas* and not a form. The conception of the *ultima realitas entis* seems also to bear a recog-nizable resemblance to the *distincta creatio* of the angels. Here, as elsewhere, Scotus seems to show his genius for making a synthesis of opposing doctrines.

A number of other differences of a less important character are recorded by Fr. Longpré and Dr. Carreras, of which three are perhaps worthy of mention. In the *De Rerum Principio* (q. xviii, art. 1) the identity of time and movement is upheld : ' Hoc firmiter existimo verum, neque numerum neque tempus dicere rem aliam absolutam ultra numerata, vel ultra motum ; sicut qualitas dicit aliam rem a quantitate ; sed eamdem rem simpliciter, sed tempus addit rationem quam format mens super motum,' etc. In *Op. Ox.* II, dist. ii, q. 2, n. 8, the opposite doctrine is upheld, and time is stated to differ from motion because in a determinate quantity of time movements of different velocities can take place ; an argument which is rejected in the earlier treatise (loc. cit., n. 34). The doctrine of the soul's self-knowledge also reveals certain differences between the *De Rerum Principio* and the *Opus Oxoniense.* In the former a kind of inner sense, *sensus interior intellectualis,* is postulated (p. xv, n. 20), by which the soul knows itself; a theory which is contradicted in the latter (*Op. Ox.* II, dist. iii, q. viii, n. 14). Finally in q. x of the *De Rerum Principio* the author seems to hesitate concerning the existence of *rationes seminales* as active principles existing in matter (n. 20), but it must be noted that here he is not stating his own opinion. (Cf. n. 19 : ' Sexti ostendunt ... (n. 20) haec positio vult,' etc. The existence of *rationes seminales* as active principles is denied in several loci in the commentaries on the Sentences, e. g. *Op. Ox.* II, dist. xviii, q. 1 ; *Rep. Par.,* loc. cit. ; see also *Quaest. in Metaph.* VII, q. xii.

The last two discrepancies need not surprise us if we assume the earlier work to have been written under the influence of the older Augustinian tradition. Indeed, it would be little short of a miracle if throughout some hundreds of thousands of syllogisms no inconsistencies could be detected in the various utterances of the Subtle Doctor. Nor will the argument of silence carry very much weight. For though it is true, as Fr. Longpré has pointed out, that neither John of Reading, who was a contemporary of Scotus, nor William of Ockham cites the *De Rerum Principio,* it is nevertheless not unnatural that they should confine themselves to the larger and better known treatises which were written during the period of his celebrity. And at a time when the writing of *quaestiones* was a regular exercise of the academic routine, it need not surprise us that some of the earlier efforts of a famous teacher should be wrapped in a temporary oblivion. The internal evidence as to the date of the treatise is abundantly clear ; it belongs to the last quarter of the thirteenth century and it emanates from Oxford. It is true that as far as is known there is only one manuscript which has survived, but that is an old one, and the existence of the treatise was widely attested by the later Scotists. Thus it is mentioned among works of Duns both by Willot in his *Athenae Orthodoxorum Sodalitii Franciscani* (ed. 1598, p. 220) and also by John Pits in his *Relationes Historicae de Rebus Anglicis* (tom. i, p. 392 in the ed. of 1619), who are careful to distinguish it from the *De Primo Principio.* There seems, therefore, no adequate reason to upset the tradition of centuries and to deny the authenticity of this most interesting work on the various grounds which have been alleged, each of which would not only invalidate the attribution of this treatise alone, but also that of several others whose claim to genuineness is really beyond dispute. Criticism of this type may be very edifying in so far as it produces an illusion of consistency by accepting only what pleases it, but it cannot be regarded as scientific. For in the last resort almost all attributions can be contested, and just as in textual criticism the harder reading is to be preferred, so it is at least the sounder method to try and make the traditional theory work—a definite negation is attractive rather because it cuts the knot far more often than it unties it.

To lay down an historical order of the composition of an author's works on purely internal evidence is indubitably a hazardous procedure, but if a guess may legitimately be attempted, I should venture to suggest the following order. The *Logicalia*, the *De Rerum Principio*, the *Quaestiones de Anima*, the *De Primo Principio*, and perhaps the *Theoremata* all belong to an early period, to which also some of the *Collationes* and *Quaestiones Miscellaneae* may also be attributed. The *Quaestiones in Metaphysicam* seem to mark the transition between the doctrine of the earlier group and that of the great commentaries, which with the *Quaestiones Quodlibetales* clearly belong to the later part of the Subtle Doctor's teaching career.

INDEX

Printed in England by John Johnson at the OXFORD UNIVERSITY PRESS